NUCLEAR POWER AND POLITICS OF SOUTH ASIA : NEW DISCLOSURES

NUCLEAR POWER AND POLITICS OF SOUTH ASIA
New Disclosures

Rajkumar Singh

Hemlata Singh

KALPAZ

ISBN : 978-93-5128-047-7

Price: ₹ 990/-

First Edition, 2014

Published by

Kalpaz Publications
C-30, Satyawati Nagar,
Delhi – 110052
E-mail: kalpaz@hotmail.com
Ph.: 9212142040

Laser Typesetting: GR Computer
Printed at: G. Print Process, Delhi

Cataloging in Publication Data--DK
Courtesy: D.K. Agencies (P) Ltd. <docinfo@dkagencies.com>

Singh, Raj Kumar, 1958-
Nuclear power and politics of South Asia : new disclosures / Rajkumar Singh, Hemlata Singh.
p. cm.
Includes bibliographical references (p.) and index.
ISBN 9789351280477

1. Nuclear energy--South Asia. 2. Nuclear weapons--South Asia. 3. South Asia--Politics and government. I. Singh, Hemlata, joint author. II. Title.

DDC 333.79240954 23

Dedicated to

HANSA DEVI

Mother of Dr. Rajkumar Singh

Mother-in-law of Dr. Hemlata Singh

CONTENTS

PREFACE

The discovery and development of nuclear energy and its first military use against a non-nuclear weapon state in 1945, to a large extent, shaped the nuclear weapon threat perception of modern nation states. From the very beginning, nuclear weapons have conferred two separate sets of benefits—political and military—upon their possessor. While both facets are interrelated and mutually reinforcing, without doubt, international influence and national confidence have always been a byproduct of nuclear weapons. At first, nuclear weapons were seen simply as much bigger bombs with enormous destructive power but with the advent of thermonuclear weapons with unprecedented destructive power they could no longer be seen as just bombs. In the highly competitive and publicised nuclear one-upmanship that the US and the USSR had conducted for forty years, the acquisition of thermonuclear weapons by the latter clearly meant that now they could not only be used in the battlefield, but could be deployed and used against the heartlands of the adversaries. In line, for a couple of decades fighting a nuclear war with battlefield nuclear weapon was considered feasible but soon it also became clear that victory in such a war was meaningless because, the total devastation would be inflicted on both sides. In this situation, total ban on its proliferation was natural as well as essential for the welfare of humanity.

In the region South Asia, as elsewhere, the estimation of the probability of war with the country concerned, and of the probability of that country using or threatening to use nuclear weapons in such a war, play important roles in the development of threat perception. For India, the needed capability is generally accepted as one that enables the country to absorb a nuclear strike by either China or Pakistan and still be able to retaliate in a manner that shall be unacceptable to the country that has attacked. When China carried out its first nuclear test in 1964, two years after humiliating India in the Himalayas, there was popular pressure to follow suit but more national than global factors contributed India to the May 1974, test in which India declined to call it for military purposes. The event motivated Pakistan to gain nuclear weapon capability keeping in view the post-partition conflicts with India. Although Islamabad achieved nuclear weapon capability around 1980s, it exploded the nuclear weapon devices in May 1998, in retaliation to even its nuclear account with India. Between 1974 and 1998, India sought to maintain the position that while it did not consider it necessary to acquire nuclear weapons for the present; it had the capability to do so at very short notice, and what was more, shall do so should the situation so demand. In the Indian context, the only issues in this area on which there is consensus are that China and Pakistan are both possible future adversaries and that they both possess nuclear weapons. However, despite that internal support for retaining the 'nuclear option' had remained strong, the external environment had made the option increasingly difficult to exercise.

In post-1998 period, the evaluation and re-evaluation of nuclear weapon state's strategy continued as earlier and likelihood of China and Pakistan using or threatening to use nuclear weapons while fighting a war remained a hotly debated issue. In comparison to China, the likelihood of Pakistan using, or threatening to use, nuclear weapons during hostilities with is high as we have witnessed in course of Kargil War in 1999. In addition, one scenario, which has many proponents is that where Pakistan strongly promotes insurgency in Kashmir using the human-rights-violations-provoking strategy and India finds it difficult to contain it by taking measures within Indian territory. At this juncture, India's need to counter the insurgency promotion, by making a punitive conventional strike into Pakistan, is deterred by a Pakistani threat to employ nuclear weapons. Many feel that such a Pakistani threat, based on the argument of self-defence, will be credible since international opinion is divided on the merits of Pakistan's position on Kashmir. This actual situation has made nuclear stability a distant dream in the region and left for India no option but to adopt "Cold Start" policy and kept other alternatives open to unfold gradually as per demand of the situation. This is all the more important because of the perceived implications of the India-US nuclear deal as well as the China-Pakistan nuclear deal, and due to the potential impact of technology on the military strategies of India and Pakistan.

However, for the facts, analysis, views and misjudgements contained in the book we alone are responsible.

5th September, 2013

Dr. Rajkumar Singh
Dr. Hemlata Singh

ACKNOWLEDGEMENTS

We wish to thank the institutions and individuals for their encouragement, co-operation and good-wishes that we received and staff of the central libraries at New Delhi and other places where we got a lot of information and analytical/critical views of different subject experts. They all deserve cordial thanks.

We are deeply grateful to several persons and colleagues. Among teachers Dr. D.N. Mallik, Dr. Kirtyanand Singh, Dr. R.N. Kumar and Dr. M.R. Kazami, retired professors of the University Department of Political Science, BRA Bihar University, Muzaffarpur have been constant source of guide and encouragement at every stage. Colleagues Dr. Dhirendra Narayan Singh, Department of Political Science, MLT College, Saharsa, Dr. Chandra Prakash Singh, Department of History, Dr. Kumar Jyotivardhan and Dr. Usha Sinha, Department of Hindi, Dr. Ram Naresh Singh, Department of Maithili, West Campus P.G. Centre, Saharsa and departmental colleagues, Dr. Bijay Kumar Verma and Dr. Pawan Kumar are thankful for their co-operation and good-wishes. Eldest brother, the late Suryanath Singh, elder brother Bhuvneshwar Prasad Singh, father-in-law Ramanand Singh, retired Professor and Head, University Department of Physics, BRA Bihar University, Muzaffarpur, and most revered Smt. Lalmani Devi deserve deep sense of gratitude for their sincere good-wishes. I am no less thankful to colleagues and staff of the B.N. Mandal University, West Campus, P.G. Centre, Saharsa.

We would be failing in our duty if we do not record our honest good-wishes and gratitude to the family members including our son, Aditya Priyadarshi and Apurv Adarsh in the completion of the book.

GLOSSARY

Accelerator	–	an apparatus for increasing the kinetic energies of charged particles
Amplifier	–	a device that increases the strength of an electrical signal by drawing energy from a separate source
Anti-Ballistic Missiles	–	ABMs are weapon systems developed in the late 1960s and early 1970s by both USA and USSR
Arms Race	–	it refers to the competition to build-up more powerful nuclear weaponry
Atom	–	the smallest part of an element that can exist
Balance of Power	–	a theory that peace is more likely where potential combatants are of equal military, political or economic power
Ballistic Missile Defence	–	a term for all defensive weapons system, systems intended to protect against attack by nuclear missile
Boiling Point	–	the temperature at which the saturated vapour pressure of a liquid equals the external pressure
Chain Reaction	–	a reaction that is self-sustaining as a result of the products of one-step initiating a subsequent step
Cold War	–	the state of extreme hostility between the superpowers
Coolant	–	a fluid used to remove heat from a system either to control the temperature or to extract energy
Containment	–	a doctrine from 1947 on how the US should react to the expansion of international communist influence

Conventional War – conventional war is a war waged only with non-nuclear weaponry

Database – a large collection of information that has been coded and stored in a computer

Detente – a foreign policy process mainly concerned with an easing of tension between the USSR and the USA

Deterrence – it refers to the capacity to protect oneself from attack by another nation

Earthquake – a sudden movement or fracturing within the earth's lithosphere

Electric Power – the rate of expending energy or doing work in an electrical system

Energy – a measure of a system's ability to do work

Enrichment – the process of increasing the abundance of a specified isotope in a mixture of isotopes

Equilibrium – a state in which a system has its energy distributed in the statistically most probable manner

Fissile material – an isotope of a radioactive element that goes under nuclear fission

First strike – the use of strategic nuclear weaponry to attack an enemy without their having launched such an attack

Fossil fuel – coal, oil and natural gas, the fuels used by man as a source of energy

Intercontinental Ballistic Missile – the huge nuclear weapons systems, almost unstoppable

Isolationism – it is a foreign policy strategy in which a nation announces that it has absolutely no interest in international affairs

Just war – the theory of when it is just to fight a war

Limited war – the war in question should not spread to involve the superpowers in an all-out nuclear confrontation

Mutual assured destruction	–	is a basic concept in nuclear strategic thought
Neutrality	–	is often thought of as a rather vague state of non-involvement in international conflict
Non-proliferation treaty	–	one of the early fruits of international attempts to limit the danger of nuclear warfare
Nuclear energy	–	energy obtained as a result of nuclear fission or nuclear fusion
Nuclear fuel	–	a substance that will sustain a fission chain reaction, so that it can be used as a source of nuclear energy
Nuclear power	–	electric power or motive power generated by a nuclear reactor
Nuclear reactor	–	a device in which a nuclear fission chain reaction is sustained and controlled in order to produce nuclear energy
Nuclear weapons	–	weapons in which an explosion is caused by energy nuclear fission, nuclear fusion or a combination of both
Nucleus	–	the central core of an atom that contains most of its mass
Nuclear waste	–	any waste material that contains radionuclides
Second strike capacity	–	it means that a country must have sufficient nuclear weapons if an enemy successfully launched a nuclear attack with total surprise
Solar energy	–	the electromagnetic energy radiated from the sun
Strategic	–	it involves longer term and farther reaching preparations and planning
Tactical nuclear weapons	–	are not easily distinguishable from other conventional munitions, except in power

Terrorist groups – political groups which use violence as a matter of policy to pressurise a government to support radical social change

Thermonuclear reactor – a reactor in which nuclear fusion takes place with the controlled release of energy

Uranium – a white radioactive metallic element belonging to the actinoids

Warsaw Pact – theoretically initiated as a response to West Germany joining NATO in 1954

Wind power – the use of winds in the earth's atmosphere to drive machinery, especially to drive an electrical generator

Year – the measure of time on which the calender is based

ABBREVIATIONS

ACRS	–	Arms Control and Regional Security
ADS	–	Accelerators Driver System
AEC	–	Atomic Energy Commission/Council
AEE	–	Atomic Energy Establish
AERB	–	Atomic Energy Regulatory Board
AHWR	–	Advanced Heavy Water Reactor
AMD	–	Atomic Mineral Directorate
ASN	–	Authority of Nuclear Safety
BARC	–	Bhabha Atomic Research Centre
BHEL	–	Bharat Heavy Electrical Limited
BRIT	–	Board of Radiation and Isotope Technology
BWRs	–	Boiling Water Reactors
CBMs	–	Confidence Building Measures
CFE	–	Conventional Forces in Europe
CHTR	–	Compact High Temperature Reactor
C_4I_2SR	–	Command, Control, Communication, Computer, Intelligence, Information, Surveillance and Reconnaissance
CNLB	–	Civil Nuclear Liability Bill
CNSC	–	Canadian Nuclear Safety Commission
CNS	–	Council of Nuclear Safety
CO_2	–	Carbondioxide
CRZ	–	Coastal Regulation Zone
CSC	–	Convention on Supplementary Compensation
CTBT	–	Comprehensive Test Ban Treaty
DAE	–	Department of Atomic Energy
ECIL	–	Electronics Corporation of India Limited
EIA	–	Environment Impact Assessment
ENR	–	Enrichment and Reprocessing
EUMA	–	End User Monitoring Agreement
FAO	–	Food and Agriculture Organisation

FBRs – Fast Breeder Reactors
FICCI – Federation of Indian Chambers of Commerce and Industry
FMCT – Fissile Material Cut-off Treaty
HEU – Highly Enriched Uranium
HFRC – House Foreign Relations Committee
IAEA – International Atomic Energy Agency
ICBM – Inter-Continental Ballistic Missile
IGCAR – Indira Gandhi Centre for Atomic Research
IPCC – Inter-governmental Panel on Climate Change
KKNPP – Kudankulam Nuclear Power Plant
LEU – Low Enriched Uranium
LoC – Line of Control
LWRs – Light Water Reactors
MAD – Mutual Assured Destruction
MoEF – Ministry of Environment and Forests
MoU – Memorandum of Understanding
MOX – Mixed Oxide
MPs – Members of Parliament
MSR – Molten Salt Reactor
NCA – National Command Authority
NDA – National Democratic Alliance
NELP – New Exploration Licensing Policy
NFU – No First Use
NNWS – Non-Nuclear Weapon State
NPCIL – Nuclear Power Corporation of India Limited
NPT – Non-Proliferation Treaty
NRC – Nuclear Regulatory Commission
NRIs – Non-Resident Indians
NSCAB – National Security Council Advisory Board
NSG – Nuclear Suppliers' Group
NSRA – Nuclear Safety Regulatory Authority
NSSP – Next Steps in Strategic Partnership

NTPC	–	National Thermal Power Corporation
PAEC	–	Pakistan Atomic Energy Commission
PHWR	–	Pressurised Heavy Water Reactors
PIL	–	Public Interest Litigation
PMANE	–	People's Movement Against Nuclear Energy
PNEs	–	Peaceful Nuclear Explosions
PRC	–	People's Republic of China
PTBT	–	Partial Test Ban Treaty
PWRs	–	Pressurised Water Reactors
RRW	–	Reliable Replacement Weapon
SEU	–	Slightly Enriched Uranium
SINP	–	Saha Institute of Nuclear Physics
SNF	–	Spent Nuclear Fuel
SO_2	–	Sulphurdioxide
TAPS	–	Tarapur Atomic Power Station
TNEB	–	Tamil Nadu Electricity Board
UCIL	–	Uranium Corporation of India Limited
UNHRC	–	United Nations Human Rights Commission
UPA	–	United Progressive Alliance
WANO	–	World Association of Nuclear Operators
WEC	–	World Energy Council
WHO	–	World Health Organisation
WMD	–	Weapons of Mass Destruction

1

Nuclear Power: Scientific Origin and Development

Despite efforts made to control the number of nuclear weapons, prevent their spread, prohibit their use and seek their elimination, little headway has been achieved to reduce the risk of nuclear annihilation. The nuclear threat is an ever-present danger which must be addressed in parallel. Indeed, nuclear weapons could still be the biggest risk of all to the peace and stability of our world at the global level and regionally. The possibility remains that still more countries will acquire them and the danger persists of their deliberate or accidental use by states or non-state terrorist actors.[1] However, nuclear expertise was co-opted and gradually moved to the civilian sector for the production of energy. It is poor judgement and a deliberate act of spreading fear to compare a nuclear bomb with nuclear plant. The bomb is designed to deliver a large amount of energy over a very short period of time, leading to explosions, firestorms and massive heat energy generated to obliterate every object in its path. On the contrary, civilian nuclear applications in the form of a power plant are designed to deliver small amounts of energy in a sustainable manner over a far-larger time frame. It is designed with systems to control and cool the nuclear reaction.[2] Every single atom in the universe carries an unimaginably powerful battery within its heart, called the nucleus. This form of energy often called Type-1 fuel, is hundreds of thousands, if not millions, of times more powerful than the conventional Type-O fules, which are basically dead plants and animals existing in the form of coal, petroleum, natural gas and other forms of fossil fuel. The greenest sources of power are definitely solar and wind but solar and wind power, despite all their advantages, are not stable and are dependent excessively on weather and sunshine conditions.[3] Nuclear power, on the other hand, provides a relatively clean, high-density source of reliable energy with an international presence. According to a latest report there are twenty-nine countries operating 441 nuclear power plants, with a total capacity of about 375 GW(e). The industry now has more than 14,000 reactor-years of experience. The study indicates that most of the prosperous nations are extracting about 30 to 40 per cent of power from nuclear power and it constitutes a significant part of their clean energy portfolio.

Development of Basics

Daily we see a great variety of things in nature–the sun, moon, and stars, mountains and seas, forests and animals but we can not answer the question who was the first person to think about atoms or later on nuclear. Men and women who have studied the nature in deep, concluded long ago that everything is made of small particles. At the same time, perhaps the first simplification was provided by the chemists who were able, by processes of destruction and analysis, to recognise certain specific substances which are the basic building materials of our world. These are called elements. An element is defined as a substance which cannot be further split-up or refined by chemical analysis. It is equally wonderful that all the many hundred thousand different kinds of matter that man has found in this world, have turned out to consist of no more than ninety substances or elements. In chemical method, all matter on the earth is divided into two main groups: chemical compounds and elements, However, before this knowledge of chemistry man had been speculating on the nature of matter for hundred of years on how the various kinds of matter are build up ? In common, they had found it quite probable that each kind of matter was built up from its own absolutely identical particles, which could be further split up. For these particles, the old Greek philosophers used the name *atoms*.[4] Further, the atomic theories assumed more closely defined forms, a distinction being made between the smallest particles, of the chemical compounds, which were given the name of molecules and the smallest particles of the elements for which the name atoms was reserved. It also showed that even the smallest parts of a chemical compound must contain all those elements that make-up the compound. Alike this the fundamental fact derived that the atoms of any given element have all exactly the same weight. This fact helped in finding the relation between the weights of the different atoms, and also of determining the precise number of atoms making up the molecules of a given compound.

Historically, ancient Greece is the birth place of the word '*atom*', made up of the Greek word *atoms*, which means 'indivisible'. Among the philosophers who took up the idea, Democritus, who belonged to ancient Greece some 2,400 years ago, said that everything was made of tiny particles, or corpuscles, so small that no one could see them. The particles themselves could never change and they could not be broken down into smaller particles. He was of the view that atoms were the smallest particles that could exist. 'Let us look at a substance like water. We may take a very small amount of it, a single drop, and with some care we may divide this drop into two tiny droplets. If it were possible to get the proper tools and equipment, we might be able to go on making tinier and tinier droplets, but could we go on forever? Democritus, like other philosophers believed that at a certain point, we would obtain a droplet that could not be cut into smaller parts. The smallest parts into which water could be cut were the atoms'.[5] After him for centuries people hardly believed that atoms really existed and more people thought it as the fruit of Democritus's imagination till the early seventeenth century when Italian scientist, Galileo and English chemist, Robert Boyle indicated some furthered scientific facts. While Galileo said that he could explain odours and tastes by supposing that some substances dissolve into small corpuscles and these corpuscles might hit sensitive spots in our tongues and nostrils, and create the familiar sensation, Robert Boyle (1627-1691), held that air, and all other gases behaved as if they were made of corpuscles. Gradually, more and more facts were being explained by admitting that atoms existed. Robert Boyle, although studied the expansion and compression of air, with him atomism entered a new phase, from mere reasoning to experimental observations.

The atomic-related facts were further developed by John Dalton who first expressed a scientific atomic theory. Before his birth, chemists had come to recognise the fact: while they could separate some substances into simpler substances, there were others they could never separate. It divided the substance into chemical elements and chemical compounds. Such substances as water, salt and sugar which are made of more than one element, were called chemical compounds, while the simple substances, such as hydrogen, oxygen, carbon, chloride, and sodium were given the name chemical elements. In chemistry, Dalton had observed that compound substances like water were made up of simple substances in proportions which remained invariable. No matter how small a quantity of a compound was considered, the components were always present in the same fixed proportion by weight. Dalton assumed that finally the fundamental components, in spite of their being imperceptible, must retain their characteristic in relative proportions. He called the basic units 'atoms' and made the further assumption that atoms of one element are all identical in mass, while different elements have atoms of different mass. The determination of the proportions of the weight of the different elements in every possible chemical compound gave the chemist a means of finding the relation between the weights of the different atoms and also of determining the precise number of atoms making up the molecules of a given compound. Dalton's atomic theory was really a hypothesis, but it proved very useful in summarising a large number of quantitative data which had been obtained as the result of chemical experiments.[6] Although Dalton's theory was correct on the whole yet like Democritus he continued to say that atoms are the smallest particles into which matter divides–that atoms are indivisible. A little later the work of several physicists proved that atoms can break down into smaller pieces.

In the sphere of atoms a breakthrough came in early 1896 in Paris when the French Physicist Henri Becquerel in course of testing a number of phosphorescent substances found by accident that when a phosphorescent uranium salt is glowing, it gives off not only light but also another radiation. A few days later he discovered that the uranium salt could give off the more penetrating radiation even if it is not exposed to sunlight. The experiment encouraged the scientist to test many other substances containing uranium. Then he concluded that uranium was the element that gave off radiation spontaneously. The further work on radiation was done by Poland-born French lady scientist–Madame Marie Curie, who discovered other elements that behaved like uranium. Madame Curie done her hard work on radiation and searched several other elements—thorium, polonium and ultimately radium that gave off spontaneous radiation. While working she found that a uranium ore called pitchblende contained even stronger radiation than thorium and uranium. She called the element radium which proved to be extremely useful both in research, for the study of the nature of atoms, and medicine and for the treatment of cancers also.

Experiments on atom-related facts were going on but the concept itself helped the world to win deeper understanding of many purely physical phenomena and especially of well-known conceptions of heat and temperature. By the time, though, the chemistry investigators were comfortable with the concept of the atom supposing that heat was in reality was nothing else than movement of the atoms and molecules of the various kinds of matter. But the observation of Physicists did not stop here and it gave birth to the heat hypothesis that it as motion all the atoms would make small oscillations around their positions of equilibrium, the oscillations becoming quicker as the temperature rises. For example, if a piece of lead is heated to a sufficiently high temperature, the result may be that the oscillations become so powerful that the atoms break away from their position of equilibrium and begin to wander around among themselves, a state of affairs revealed by the melting of a lead. Hence, it is to be assumed, however, that the atoms are holding together to a certain degree in the molten lead, since it does not remain in the crucible where it was melted. If still further heat is applied the lead atoms will attain such a speed that the swiftest of them will break through the surface of the fluid and then the molten lead evaporates.[7] It explained the fact that various kinds of matter can exist in the three several states: solid, liquid and gaseous; the change in the state being nothing else but a change of the distances separating the atoms and molecules. It is from here that modern atomic physics entered the field. Several other investigations and discoveries about the nature and contents of atoms showed that they were not indivisible as it had until then been assumed, but under certain conditions they could be split up into still smaller particles, showing quite new and surprising properties. Although the word 'atoms' originally meant 'the indivisible' the term retained the symbolic meaning for the smallest quantity of an element that is still in possession of all the physical and chemical properties of this element.

Further works on structure of atom was done by J.J. Thomson, Leonard and Ernest Rutherford. The earlier work done on radioactive encouraged them to discover more and more about the atoms. While Rutherford was in Cambridge Thomson discovered the existence of very tiny particles charged with negative electricity; he called them electron. On the basis of it, he suggested in 1898 that the atom is a positively charged solid sphere and electrons are embedded in it in sufficient number, so as to make the atom electrically neutral. His model of atom can be compared to a birthday cake in which cherries are embedded. This model was quite attractive as it could explain several observations at that time. It could explain why only negatively charged particles are emitted when a metal is heated and never the positively charged particles. Related to it was the suggestion of Leonard, who noted that cathode rays could pass through materials of small thickness almost undeviated. If the atoms were solid spheres, most of the electrons in the cathode rays would hit them and would not be able to progress in the forward direction. His suggestion that the atom must have a lot of empty spaces in it, surfaced in 1903. The nutshell of his proposal was that the atom is made of electrons and similar tiny particles carrying positive charge. The works of both these scientists had certain advantages and disadvantages.

The discoveries made so far were more or less of accidental kind but a major breakthrough in this regard was revealed by Ernest Rutherford who solved the problems by doing a series of experiments from 1906 to 1911 on alpha particles scattering. His was the first true atomic experiment, carried out deliberately, with the atomic problem kept in view. Rutherford took a few years working on radioactivity and found that this radiation is made of several kinds of rays. One is a stream of very fast particles charged with positive electricity. He called these rays alpha, and the particle alpha particles. Later, he drew this conclusion that an alpha particle is about four times as heavy as a hydrogen atom, and that it carries two positive charges. A second kind of ray, he found is a stream of very fast particles charged with negative electricity. Rutherford called these beta rays and the particles of which they are made ***beta particles.*** A French scientist found a third kind of ray gamma rays. They are similar to light rays and X-rays, but more penetrating. It further certified that alpha, beta, and gamma rays must come from atoms and if atoms could give off fast particles and gamma rays two concepts emerged. First, it was not true that atoms are indivisible and secondly, atoms must contain large amounts of energy. On the basis of this experiment, he suggested that when a radioactive atom breaks down, it gives off either an alpha particle or a beta particle, and often also gamma rays. He also said that when radioactive atoms break down, they transformed into different atoms.

The radioactive change of one element into another is often called 'decay by physicists'. Rutherford also found that, as a piece of radioactive substance decays, its activity decreases and he gave name ***half-life*** to the time in which the activity of piece of a radioactive substance is cut down to one half. In the context he mentioned that some substances decay very slowly; their activity also decreases very slowly, and their ***half-life*** is very long. For instance, the half-life of uranium is 4,500 million years while the ***half-life*** of radium is 1,560 years. Further, Rutherford along with other scientists concentrated on containing enormous amount of energy and its further activities. It was an exciting thought that a tiny particle like the atom contains an enormous amounts of energy. Atoms break down with explosive violence, and pieces of atoms, alpha and beta particles, fly off at half the speed of light or even after. This means that alpha and beta particles have very great energy. Additional energy comes out of atoms in the form of gamma rays. In coming days, scientists, began to talk of the immense 'store of energy', locked up in the atoms and of the enormous amount of work that this energy could do if men were to learn to get it out of atoms and control its flow.

In 1919, Rutherford got a brilliant idea. It was to use alpha particles as 'bullets' to bombard atoms in the hope that if he succeeded, the pieces into which the atoms broke down might help him to learn how atoms are made. With perfect planning the scientist kept some nitrogen under heavy bombardment. Some of the alpha particles hit nitrogen atoms right in their centres, broke them down and made chips fly off. These chips had the same mass as hydrogen atoms and carried out one positive charge each. Later they were called ***proton.*** In the sphere bombardment of atoms proved a very useful method of research. Following the method another physicist, James Chadwick, in 1932 bombarded beryllium – a light metal with alpha particles. He found that under alpha bombardment beryllium gave off particles with the same mass a hydrogen and no-electric charge. These articles had been called ***neutrons.***[9] In general, all nuclei are constructed with only two kinds of building bricks – the proton and neutron. The proton is a heavy particle whose mass is 1836 times more than that of an electron and which is positively charged. The magnitude of the charge on the proton is exactly equal to that of the electron, but is opposite in sign. Rutherford also said that an atom must be made of a tiny nucleus charged with positive electricity, and of electrons moving around the nucleus. He, with his friend, the Danish physicist Niels Bohr shared the view that the number of protons, electrons, and neutrons is different for different elements. In each atom, the number of protons is the nucleus is equal to the number of electrons that circle around it. Since each proton carries one positive charge and one electron one negative charge, the atom is neutral. In any one element, all the nuclei have the same number of protons called atomic number.

After Rutherford's discovery of the atomic nucleus, the view came to be accepted that the atoms, and with them all matters, were built up of small positive and negative particles, though it was not at all clear what were the natural laws governing the mutual interaction between these particles. In the discoveries it was found that electrons have practically no mass while protons and neutrons account for the entire mass of an atom. A proton and a neutron have the equal mass 1. The simplest atoms is hydrogen but the most complex atom found on the earth is uranium. All uranium atoms are made of 92 electrons circling about a nucleus in which there are 92 protons. Here, it is also to clarify that there are three slightly different varieties of uranium, each with a slightly different number of neutrons in their nuclei. The nuclei of the most common variety contain 146 neutrons in addition to the 92 protons. The atomic mass of this variety is then 92 + 146 or 238. The nuclei of the other two varieties contain 143 and 142 neutrons respectively. The atomic masses of these varieties are then 235 and 234. Other elements whose nuclei contain slightly different numbers of neutrons are called *isotopes*. In short, there are three isotopes of uranium. They are uranium 238, uranium 235 and uranium, 234.

In comparison to earlier, the discovery of neutrons completed the picture of the atom but the developments failed to satisfy the physicists, and therefore, they went on bombarding atoms. Atomic bombardments had opened new possibilities. They not only revealed the particles of which nuclei are made but also proved that some elements which are not radioactive and do not change spontaneously can be changed into other elements. The work of bombardment was done further by Madame Curie's daughter Irene and her husband Frederic Joliot. They noticed something strange when in 1933 they were bombarding aluminium with alpha particles. As they hit aluminium atoms broke down, and changed into atoms that gave off a radiation and behaved like radioactive element. Joliot found that the bombarded aluminium had changed into radioactive isotope of phosphorous that does not exist in nature. Earlier Becquerel and Madame Curie had discovered natural radioactivity that spontaneously occurs in nature. Now, Irene and Frederic Joliot had discovered artificial – man-made-radioactivity. This development raised a great interest among the scientists worldwide and young physicist Enrico Fermi of Italy decided to try to produce artificial radioactivity. He started bombarding elements in order to begin with the element of the the lowest atomic number, hydrogen, and going to those of higher atomic number. Initially Fermi did not get success but suddenly his luck favoured and when he tried fluorine, it proved strongly radioactive and so did other elements. In this way Fermi, with other young physicists produced many radioactive isotopes that do not exist in nature. For example, from natural stable sodium they obtained radioactive sodium; from stable iodine and arsenic, they obtained radioactive iodine and arsenic. But when in line they bombarded uranium, the element of the highest atomic number then known, they found that they had produced more than one radioactive element. Likewise a group of scientists found that at least one of the radioactive products of uranium was not an isotope of any known element close to uranium and they had sufficient reason to believe that perhaps they made a new element of atomic number 93 which does not exist in nature.

In the meantime, experiments on bombarding uranium continued in many countries of the world but the mysterious substance, suspected to be element 93 was not less than a surprise and created the idea that men might have created an element that did not exist before. The *New York Times,* published an article in two columns under a large heading : 'Italian Produces 93rd Element by Bombarding Uranium.' Further works in the sphere were being performed by Otto Hahn and Lise Meituer mainly in Germany but the latter had to shift in Stockholm, Sweden due to political reasons. At that time, the dictator Adolf Hitler and his Nazi party were ruling Germany. Nazi did not believe in democracy and they governed by force, imposing their will on all Germans. On the other hand, without freedom, science cannot live. Scientists are used to thinking to discussing their views with others, to choosing what they want to study or to teach, but Hitler was determined to change all this. In addition, Hitler hated Jews, who were then residing in Germany. As a result, many German scientists, especially those of Jewish background, left Germany. However, despite separate dwelling the like-minded scientists kept themselves in regular touch and shared uptodate developments on new discoveries. In the meantime, chemists Otto Hahn and Strassmann informed Lise Meitner about obtaining barium from uranium. It was initially puzzling experiment. The atomic number of uranium is 92, and its atomic mass is 238. The atomic number of barium is 56 and the atomic mass of the barium in Hahn and Strasmann finding is 139. However, it was identified shortly that it was a rare gas, Krypton of atomic number 36. This 36 plus 56, the atomic number of barium equals 92 which is the atomic number of uranium.

Lise Meitner gave the name of fission to this phenomenon, the splitting in two of uranium atoms. She thought that when uranium split into two almost equal pieces, an enormous amount of energy might be released and that the two pieces might fly apart with tremendous speed. Lise guessed that fission was to be the key that would 'unlock' the store of energy. Lise and her young nephew Otto Frisch ultimately agreed to each other and made no mistake in understanding that uranium atoms underwent fission, and that the energy released in the process was probably very great. In course of it now they both decided to inform Niels Bohr who was considered the greatest living atomic physicist. They met Bohr in Denmark and discussed fission with him but Bohr suggested an experiment by which they might measure the energy released when uranium atoms split. Perhaps due to Adolf Hitler's bad reputation and cruelty the whole story of discovery now moved away from Europe and the studies of atom had gone on in other parts of the world including the United States.

Till January 1939, the political situation in Europe deteriorated further with Hitler becoming more and more aggressive and the Second World War appeared imminent. In the circumstances, many of the reputed European scientists went to the United States. So, while science in Europe was losing ground, but it was gaining in the United States. With Bohr's arrival in the United States, the news of fission spread rapidly to many Universities. The famous scientists of the time Enrico Fermi joined the US scientists' team and confirmed, 'what at the time that we thought it might be element 93, has proved to be a mixture of decay products. We had suspected it for a long time, now we are sure of it. We thought that we had a mixture of four elements while their number was closer to fifty.'[10] Thus, the developments held so far in the field of atomic or nuclear energy paved the way further for making the nuclear energy not a dream but a reality for the humanity of the globe.

Beginning of Solid Works

Nuclear power is on any nuclear technology designed to extract usable energy from atomic nuclei is a controlled nuclear reactions. Energy in various form is available around us. Matter itself is a concentration of energy. All atoms, molecules, nuclei etc are in continuous motion and have large amount of kinetic energy. But the energy that we need for our daily tasks is required in specific forms. We require energy in the form of heat to cook our food. We require energy in the form of electric current for running our fans and electric lamps etc. Cooking gas and oxygen is air contain energy but this internal energy is not in the form required to cook our food. When the two are engaged in a chemical reaction, heat is produced which is in usable form. We are getting a large amount of energy from the sun but to use an appreciable fraction of it has been a challenging task. Several centres throughout the world are working hard to develop efficient solar cells which can convert the energy from the sun to usable forms. In last decades, a solution to the energy crisis has been presented by nuclear energy. Nuclear energy may be obtained either by breaking a heavy nucleus into two nuclei of middle weight or by combining two light nuclei to form a middle weight nucleus. The former process is called nuclear fission and the latter nuclear fusion.

At the close of 1930s the concept of fission came and it raised the hope to use the energy stored in the atoms. The new thought seemed impossible to many people of the time including Rutherford who, after having broken atoms for fourteen years said, '.....We cannot control atomic energy to an extent which would be of any value commercially and I believe we are not likely to be able to do so'. Now it looked as if fission could be the key that would unlock the store of energy in atoms and that neutrons could do the job. Very simply physicists of the time thought that when a uranium atom splits in two it gives off two neutrons. We would now have two neutrons, without having to make them. These two neutrons might hit two more uranium atoms, split them, and make them give off two neutrons each. At the end of this, second step we would have four neutrons which might split four more atoms. If these gave off two neutrons each, we would then have eight neutrons which might split eight atoms. Fission of uranium might then go on by itself in a chain reaction. At each step the number of neutrons would double and the physicists concluded, a large number of uranium atoms would split. In other words to be more clear, nuclear energy is produced by fission, or breaking down of atomic particles. The nuclei of uranium break into radioactive fragments as a result of fission and generate immense heat in the process. The breaking up of a uranium atom also creates one or two free neutrons. These neutrons, in turn, are absorbed by other uranium nuclei. These uranium nuclei then break up one after another in a chain reaction.[11] The importance of a chain reaction lies in the fact that each splitting atom gives off energy. In reality, for all practical purposes the amount of energy that a single atom gives off is very small. In a chain reaction however, many atoms would split and the total amount of energy would be very large.

With the above vision and atomic facts in view the physicists of the United States of America began their works further in 1939, who had more powerful bullets for bombardment in a greater quantity than the scientists in Europe had ever had. From the time when Rutherford had first bombarded atoms with alpha particles, physicists had wanted more and better bullets than those that come spontaneously from radioactive substances. But the team of U.S. Scientists had an additional reason to be worried. No doubt this was an important piece of news that changed the outlook on unlocking the store of energy in the atoms, but was it good or bad? And at the moment it seemed bad. At the point of time, the prospect of a Second World War seemed more and more likely and the fission had been discovered in Germany, Hitler's country. Especially, the physicists who had come from Europe were worried and afraid that Hitler might have ordered all German scientists to work on fission and its use in war. In the circumstance there was a fair chance for using the nuclear energy for bad purposes by any of the war parties. At last the scientists in the US decided that someone in the American government should know of fission and of what fission might do in war. On the issue, a successful attempt to alert the United States government to the dangers of atomic explosion was made by two Hungarian physicists, Leo Szilard and Eugene Winger. In their mission, they took direct help of Albert Einstein, by far the best-known scientist of the US. Einstein, in his letter to President Roosevelt on 2nd August 1939 wrote. Some recent work by E. Fermi and L. Szilard....."leads me to expect that the element uranium may be turned into a new and important source of energy in the immediate furture......it may become possible to set up nuclear chain reaction in large mass of uranium, by which vast amounts of power.......would be generated......This new phenomenon would also lead to the construction of bombs, and it is conceivable-though much less certain-that extremely powerful bombs of a new type may thus be constructed......." The letter also stated that the Germans were doing research on fission in one of their best laboratories and that the Nazis had stopped selling uranium to other countries in order to keep it all for themselves.

It was a serious warning to the United States government as hardly after one month, on 1st September 1939 the Second World War broke out in Europe. On the other hand, the US scientists also agreed of their own free will to keep secret all studies on fission and chain reaction with a view to defeat Hitler's anti-freedom and anti-democratic way of life.

President Roosevelt received Einstein's letter on 11th October 1939, and at once appointed an Advisory Committee on Uranium. The Committee was a link between physicists and government but even at the time, the scientists were vague and uncertain when they talked of nuclear energy. One of their main difficulties was their quality of bullets. The neutrons that uranium gave off in fission were too fast and even when they hit uranium atoms they did not make these atoms split. Ultimately, Fermi and his group decided to build a 'small pile' and they collected a sufficient amount of uranium and graphite. At least this step would give information that would later be useful in building a large pile. Although their work proceeded very slowly, the results of research on uranium and graphite and their behaviour in small pile were more and more encouraging. The American scientists also exchanged views on the issue with English scientists and their hopes increased to unlock and use the store of energy in the atoms. On the other the response of the US government was also positive and President announced an all-out effort for uranium project on 6th December 1941, the day Japanese plane bombed Pearl Harbour. The United States declared war on Japan; Germany and Italy declared war on the United States. In the situation the fear that Germany might make atomic weapons and use them against the Allied nations became more intense. The scientists of United States assembled at the University of Chicago where Arthur Compton, head of the research team was working as a professor. They all began their work on chain reaction with double speed and enthusiasm. Their work was top secret and called 'Metallurgical Laboratory' or Met. Lab. in short.

Now, large scale preparations were done in the building around the University of Chicago. From the behaviour of one of these small piles, they learnt for the first time that a chain reaction was possible in practice. First of all they ordered for a six-sided ballon from the Good Year Rubber Company to build the pile inside it. The piling work grew until it looked like a huge ball flattened at the top. They found it ready to chain reaction and for final test on 2nd December 1942. It took almost four years from the news of discovery of fission. It was possible due to years of hard work, serious study and constant effort. The men who had given their time to that work, study and effort were now ready to prove that their pile was a success that fission had unlocked the store of energy to mankind. In the able guidance and calculations of Fermi the experiment of chain reaction achieved success and kept under control. It showed that men could at will, make atoms give off their inner energy and that this energy could be kept under control. Because of its success it ushered in the atomic age but scientists were still far from making the extremely powerful bombs' that Einstein had mentioned in his letter to President Roosevelt.

Following the success of chain reaction, the United States Army began to take interest in getting atomic weapons and as a result it had taken charge of the uranium project in the summer of 1942. It had created a special unit to direct the uranium project and had given it the name 'Manhattan District'. General Leslie R. Grover of the US Corps of Engineers became the head of the project, who, even before the success of chain reaction, carrying out plans for the production of atomic bombs. He, on behalf of the government also bought three vast tracts of land in three different states of America. Within a few months a secret 'atomic' city sprang up on each of these tracts. Each city undertook one part of the work on atomic bombs. However, on the issue of uranium it also became clear that natural uranium contains two isotopes: uranium 238 and uranium 235 of which only uranium 235 is likely to split into two chunks giving off neutrons and energy. When an atom of uranium 238 is hit by neutron, it captures the neutrons but does not split. In other words, uranium 235 is fissionable but uranium 238 is not fissionable. In this case, the next problem was to separate the very small amount of uranium 235 from the much larger amount of uranium 238 in natural uranium. But soon the problem of separation was solved. It was done by General Grover's secret cities whose plants were called 'Clinton Engineering Works'. One plant was to achieve this separation by a method called Gaseous Diffusion while another plant had done this by using a huge Magnet.

However, the most secret of the secret cities was in New Mexico. General Grover was of the opinion that problems related to the design and construction of atomic bomb should be carried out in an even isolated spot than those for the production of plutonium and of uranium 235. The new place Los Alamos, was most suited place for this secret mission and from November

1942 army engineers began building homes and laboratories around it. As the engineers finished a group of buildings, the scientists asked for more, and so the most secret of the three secret cities began to grow. Scientists from all parts of the United States and from England went to live in that city and disappeared from the world. Surprisingly, for two and a half years that city was not marked on the maps, was not part of New Mexico and its residents could not vote. All buildings in Los Alamos were painted green similar to the green grass and trees on the plateau. At night there were no lights in the streets. The city had two gates the West Gate and East Gate. Both gates were heavily guarded and no one, not even a young child, could enter or leave the place without showing his pass to the guards. The day started at 7.00 a.m. when the first siren went off. An hour later, when the second siren blew, it was time to start work. At noon the sirens announced launch hour, later the return to work and finally, the end of the working day. J. Robert Oppenheimer, or Oppie, as his friends called him, was the director of research in Los Alamos and the soul of the project. It was a top secret that the most famous atomic physicist in the world was in Los Alamos.

Among the scientists at Los Alamos were the American Oppenheimer, the Italians Fermi and Segre, the Danish Bohr. The United States, Great Britain, and Canada were allies in the war and they decided to work together and to establish all their atomic projects in North America. The scientists of the British mission were not all English born. They included men from Switzerland, Germany, Austria, and Poland. In addition, each of the three secret cities did its own part of the work, Oak Ridge separated uranium 235, both in the gaseous diffusion plant and with the giant magnet. Hanford operated the three big piles and produced plutonium. Los Alamos solved the problems of making an explosion and building bombs and a day came in July 1945, when the humanity saw a power never imagined in their life. The atomic or nuclear bomb was the outcome of a prodigious programme of research carried out in secret during the years 1942-1945, following the operation of the first pile.

Ultimately, the fateful day of 16th July 1945 set off the nuclear age. Not one but three things happened on that day, giving the world its nuclear teeth. The first was a meeting, the second was a testing, and the third was a sailing. The meeting took place at Potsdam, in occupied Germany. It was attended by statesmen from three future nuclear powers-US President Harry Truman, Soviet supremo Joseph Stalin, and British Prime Minister Winston Churchill. Clement Attlee, Labour Party leader and Churchill's successor-to-be, also participated. The discussions centred on the subject of terms of punishment to be meted to Germany, which had surrendered unconditionally, and to Japan which was refusing to do so[12]. By the time the conference ended, Japan had been given an ultimatum to surrender, or meet 'prompt and utter destruction'.

The world's first testing of a nuclear device took place at Trinity. It was a code name for Alamogordo, a place in the New Mexican desert almost two hundred miles south of Los Alamos. It was done in complete secrecy and meant to show whether atomic bombs would work according to calculations. It proved more powerful than the scientists had anticipated, and produced a flash of light so brilliant that it was seen by a blind girl many miles away. The event was witnessed by J.R. Oppenheimer, the director of the project the physicist Kenneth Bainbridge, and a few carefully selected scientists and military personnel. At the moment of detonation, the ground swelled, shook, pummelled, rose and fell, sending up a plume of light so bright that every blade of grass in the vicinity stood out in the sharpest and most eerie relief. Later General Farrell described the explosion in a report to the War Department, 'The whole country was lighted by a searching light with the intensity many times that of the mid-day sun. It was golden, purple, violent, grey and blue. It lighted every peak, crevage, and ridge of the near – by mountain range with a clarity and beauty that cannot be described ..... Thirty seconds after the explosion, came first the air blast, pressing hard against the people and things; to be followed almost immediately by the strong, sustained, awesome roar which warned of doomsday......' After the successful explosion the crew of US cruiser *Indianapolis* sailed from San Francisco on a mission that was directly related to both those proceedings. Carrying in large wooden crates parts of a device the captain and crew knew was important but not how important – or how ugly the cruiser was bound for Tinian Island on the South Pacific. From there, bomber planes were to take off with the device, none other than the "powerful new weapon" for its twin destination in Japan, ending the War and starting an age, the nuclear age.

The test of Trinity was soon followed by the actual use of atomic bombs in the war. In the war, Germany had already surrendered. President Roosevelt had died in the last April and President Truman had taken his place. Truman and the American nation wanted a speedy victory. On August 6, 1945 at 8.15 a.m., Brigadier Paul Tibbetz of the US Air Force flew over in a B-29, named Enola Gay and dropped a 16-kiloton uranium fission bomb on an unsuspecting Japanese city of Hiroshima. A parachute opened, a flash of light and blasts followed, and suddenly all hell broke loose. The eyes of young girl watching the parachute melted and their faces become bloated blisters. Ferocious fires raged through the city and temperature rose to 4000 degrees, melting iron and vapourizing human bodies. Skin dangled from the fingernails of extended hands seeking help. Houses were reduced to rubble by the enormous blast and people trapped inside were burned alive. Within seconds, thousands perished. The death toll rose to 140,000 within a year.[13] Three days later another bomb, named 'Fat Man', was dropped on Nagasaki, which suffered a similar fate. Estimates say that within the first two to four months of the bombings, dangerous effects of explosion killed 90,000 to 166,000 people in Hiroshima and 60,000 to 80,000 in Nagasaki. About half of them died on the first day under the direct impact, from flash or flame burns and falling debris.[14] Potsdam showed that the tallest of statesmen can take decisions history would loathe. Los Alamos showed that the greatest of scientist can take steps humanity deplores.[15] The law of warfare was thus violated by a technically advanced democratic state that swore "In God We Trust". Indianapolis was doomed by strategic miscalculation and its men by the most unexpected retaliation from nature's autonomous dynamics.

Japan is the only country that had witnessed the nuclear holocaust. Hospitals, schools, factories, offices, nursing homes, police stations, post offices, railway stations, fire engines, ambulances, tram cars, moving and stationary vehicles, homes, temples, churches and parks–everything had obliterated. A new word "Hibakusha" meaning survivors was added to the Japanese language to describe the 1945 atom bomb victims and their yet-to-be born children. Years after the bombing, survivors continue to suffer from radiation poisoning and cancers. Traumatised by the horrific experience and emotionally shattered, they lived in constant fear of disease and death.[16] Soon after the bombing many Americans express guilt and revulsion. Robert Oppenheimer, the Scientific Director of the Manhattan Project, said in November 1945 that the bomb was used against "an essentially defeated enemy". He characterised the bombs as "Weapons of aggression of surprise and of terror", which would give nations a "sleazy sense of omnipotence". In addition, subsequent historical accounts reveal that the bombing was in fact unnecessary, as the Japanese were willing to surrender much earlier. President Dwight Eisenhower confirmed this in a 1963 interview to *Newsweek.*[17] The atomic bombing was touted as an extraordinary technological and military achievement. It was called "a great moment of history." However, the end of the Second World War did not stop research on atomic energy. In post-war period many scientist-turned their attention from atomic weapons to the peaceful uses of atomic energy but most people/ nations continued to believe that it can be used both ways-for destruction in war and for development during peace.

Management of Nuclear Energy

In the years following the dropping of nuclear bomb on Hiroshima and Nagasaki in Japan in August 1945, the scientists of the day turned their attention from atomic weapons to the peaceful uses of atomic energy. From the beginning a connection between nuclear power and nuclear weapons exists because both require fissile materials. Some of the technology that can be used to produce or purify a fissile material[18] for a nuclear power plant could also be applied to producing nuclear weapons. Hence, it is not possible to separate entirely the peaceful from the military uses of atomic energy. Even today people in general are not aware that the energy from atoms could be put to important peace-time use. It can easily be transformed into useful power: electric power to light our cities and keep our industries going; heat for our homes; power to propel our boats; and perhaps all other important uses in not too distant future. But the fact of the time was that with the end of war, the world was not at peace. With this the period known as the "Cold War" set in. The Democratic Western countries and the Communist Eastern countries formed two large blocs, each with difference in ideas, about freedom and the rights of men. The two blocs were extremely suspicious of each other's intentions. Each side was afraid that the other would turn the cold war into a true war and start an attack with atomic weapons of great destructiveness. In the circumstances, an arms race in atomic weapon sphere continued as earlier and the countries that knew how to build atomic weapons went on building them.

However, the other side of the coin was not only good but encouraging too. A few people of the time along with scientists' knowledge thought on the issue positively and in coming days decks were cleared for peaceful uses of nuclear energy. Countries of the world including the US were known about the nuclear weaponisation of the nations and in December, 1953 American President Eisenhower made a bold proposal before the UN General Assembly for 'Atoms-for-Peace' plan. The President knew that the countries with large atomic projects were using most of their uranium for fissionable materials to make atomic weapons. He proposed that each of these countries should begin to pool some of its fissionable materials and distribute them to other countries for peaceful uses. He was sure that in the hands of scientists and engineers these materials would help in scientific research, medicine and agriculture and would produce abundant electricity in the power-starved countries of the world.[19] He added further that it was not general knowledge that the radio-isotopes made in reactors have very wide and varied applications: doctors use them to treat diseases, and biologists use them to study the life processes of men, animals, and plants. With their help farmers get better fertilizers, breed species of plants more resistant to disease, produce seeds that yield more, plentiful crops, and improve the breeds and products of farm animals.[20] The concept 'Atoms for Peace' plan led the convening of the first International Conference on the Peaceful Uses of Atomic Energy in Geneva, Switzerland, in the summer of 1955. Earlier, the first atomic plant in the world to generate electricity steadily and to send it out for power lines was built in the Soviet Union and it started working in June 1954.

When we put nuclear energy in process we find that it is obtained as a result of nuclear fission or nuclear fusion. In comparison to nuclear fusion, nuclear fission releases a large amount of energy to be used for different purposes. Mass for mass, uranium yields about 2500,000 times more energy by fission than carbon does by combustion. The nuclear fusion of deuterium to form helium releases about 400 times as much energy as the fission of uranium. Nuclear fission is a nuclear reaction in which a heavy nucleus such as uranium splits into two parts, called fission products, which subsequently emit either two or three neutrons, releasing a quantity of energy equivalent to the difference between the rest mass of the neutrons and the fission products and that of the nucleus. Fission may occur spontaneously or as a result of irradiation by neutrons. Nuclear fission is the process used in nuclear reactors and atom bombs. On the other hand, nuclear fusion is also a type of nuclear reaction in which atomic nuclei of low atomic number fuse to form a heavier nucleus with the release of large amounts of energy. In nuclear fission reactions, a neutron is used to break up a large nucleus, but in nuclear fusion the two reacting nuclei themselves have to be brought into collision.[21] As both nuclei are positively charged there is a strong repulsive force between them, which can only be overcome if the reacting nuclei have very high Kinetic energies. As the Kinetic energy required increases with the nuclear charge, reactions involving low atomic number nuclei are the easiest to produce. At the elevated temperatures, however, fusion reactions are self-sustaining; the reactants at these temperatures are in the form of a plasma with the nuclei possessing sufficient energy to overcome electro-static repulsion forces. The fusion bomb and the stars generate energy in this way.

In a nuclear weapon explosion is caused by nuclear fission, nuclear fusion, or a combination of both. In the fission bomb, which is called atomic bomb or A-bomb two sub-critical masses of a fissile material, uranium 235 or plutonium 239 are brought together by a chemical explosion to produce one super-critical masses. But the nuclear fusion bomb which is also called thermonuclear weapon, hydrogen bomb, or H-bomb relies on a nuclear fusion reaction, which becomes self-sustaining at a critical temperature of about 35×10^6 K. This is achieved by means of an inner fission bomb, which is surrounded by a hydrogenous material, such as heavy hydrogen or lithium deuteride. The megaton explosion produced in such a thermonuclear reaction has not yet been used in war. Discovered in 1789, by M.H. Klaproth, uranium, symbol 'U' is a white radioactive metallic element. It occurs as uranite, from which the metal is extracted by an ion-exchange process. Three isotopes are found in nature: uranium. 238 (99.28 per cent), uranium-235 (0.71 per cent), and uranium-234 (0.006 per cent). As uranium-235 undergoes nuclear fission with slow neutrons, it is the fuel used in nuclear reactors and nuclear weapons.[22] It has therefore, assumed enormous technical and political importance since their invention.

But the main process of nuclear energy takes place in a device called nuclear reactor. There are three chief fissile materials that are used in nuclear reactions: Uranium-233 (233-U), Uranium-235 (235-U) and Plutonium-239 (239-PU). In addition, Plutonium-240 (240-PU) and Plutonium-241 (241-PU) are produced and consumed in Nuclear power production but neither can be used for Nuclear Weapons. Uranium-233 is produced by neutron capture of Thorium-232 in much the same way as Plutonium-239 is produced. But Uranium-235 is currently the most common fuel in nuclear reactors. Natural Uranium must be enriched to contain about 3-5 per cent 235-U before it can be used in most conventional reactors. To create a weapon, Uranium must be enriched above 80 per cent. Highly enriched Uranium, more than 20 per cent enrichment is also used for reactors in naval vessels and for research reactors. Various techniques can be used to enrich Uranium. Plutonium-239 is the preferred isotope for nuclear weapon design as it has a lower critical mass and is easier to produce in large quantities than 235-U. 239-PU and 240-PU are produced in nearly all nuclear reactors by neutron capture on naturally occurring 238-U, and can be easily separated from the uranium. However, for the purposes of Nuclear Weapons 240-PU is an unwanted component as it has a high rate of spontaneous fission which limits a nuclear weapon from achieving critical mass for long enough to consume a large fraction of the fissile material.

A nuclear reactor is one where a controlled self-sustaining nuclear reaction takes place in which no uranium nuclei fission or break up releasing energy, manifesting as heat. In it a chain reaction is sustained and controlled in order to produce nuclear energy, radioisotopes, or new nuclides. The fuel available for use in a fission reactor are Uranium-235, Uranium-233 and Plutonium-239; only the first occurs in nature, the others have to be produced artificially. When a uranium-235 nucleus is made to undergo fission by the impact of neutron it breaks into two roughly equal fragments, which release either two or three very high energy neutrons. These fast neutrons need to be slowed down to increase the probability that they will cause further fissions of 235-U nuclei and thus sustain the chain reaction. The slowing down process occurs naturally to a certain extent when the neutrons collide with other nuclei; unfortunately, however, the predominant uranium isotope, 238-U, absorbs fast neutrons to such an extent that in natural uranium the fission reaction is not self-sustaining. In order to create a controlled self-sustaining chain reaction it is necessary either to slow down the neutrons to greatly reduce the number absorbed by 238-U, or reduce the predominance of 238-U in natural uranium by enriching it with more 235-U than it normally contains.[23] Thus, in slow neutron reactors or thermal reactors the uranium is dispersed in a slowing down medium, called moderator which can be graphite, ordinary water of high purity called light water in nuclear parlance or heavy water present in natural water to the extent of one part in seven thousand. The thermal reactors are also of two kinds–heterogeneous and homogeneous. In a heterogeneous thermal reactor, the fuel and moderator are in a separate solid and liquid phases, while in the homogeneous thermal reactor the fuel and moderator are mixed together.

In contrast in fast reactor, the fission process takes place with high-energy neutrons, not requiring a moderator. But it is necessary to use concentrated fissile materials such as highly enriched uranium or plutonium. In these reactors, large amount of heat are produced from a small volume thus requiring special materials for taking away the heat. Removal of heat from thermal reactor is done with coolants such as carbon dioxide gas or light water or heavy water. In fast reactors, it is necessary to employ a coolant such as molten sodium.[24] Even in thermal reactors, there are two basic types, those that can use natural uranium as fuel and those that require enriched uranium as fuel. Naturally, occurring uranium has two components 235-U, present to the extent of one part in one hundred and forty parts, which is fissionable and 238-U, which is not fissionable. But 238-U gets converted to artificially created fissionable material plutonium 239, after irradiation in a reactor. Similarly thorium 232 is not fissionable but gets converted to fissile 233-U after irradiation in a reactor. To gain access to PU-239 or 233-U, it is necessary to "reprocess" the spent fuel consisting or irradiated 238-U or 232-U.

In the early days of nuclear development, enrichment of uranium was carried out primarily to produce weapon grade uranium-235. The US, USSR, Britain and China built enrichment plants as part of their weapons programmes. France and later India used reactor-produced plutonium for the initial nuclear explosions. The US, USSR, Britain and China also produced reactor-made plutonium for their weapons. The US and USSR took up development of nuclear propulsion reactors for submarines and these reactors used enriched uranium as fuel and light water as moderator and coolant. These reactor designs were scaled up to provide designs for production of electricity. Such reactors are called Light Water Reactors (LWR) in the West and VVER in the Soviet Union. Typically, these reactors use uranium enriched to between three and five per cent, while submarine reactors use a higher level of enrichment.[25] Again the Light Water Reactors as developed in the US have two variants; those that produce steam in the reactor vessel are called Boiling Water Reactors (BWRs) and those where the hot water from the reactor produces steam in external steam generators are called the Pressurised Water Reactors (PWRs). On the other hand, Britain and France which initially did not have large uranium enrichment capability developed a graphite moderated carbondioxide cooled reactor that could use natural uranium as fuel. In line, Canada worked on another reactor design that could use natural uranium as fuel with heavy water as moderator and coolant. The Canadians call it CANDU reactor and the international nuclear community calls it the Pressurised Heavy Water Reactor (PHWR). Initially, India has also used the reactors that could use natural uranium as fuel. It selected the PHWR system developed in Canada and co-operated with the latter on its second nuclear power station located in Rajasthan. India had also chosen a two-unit BWR station designed by the US for the first nuclear station located at Tarapur, based on international competitive bidding.

Thus, nuclear technology developed in the context of World War-II. This new expertise and its unimaginable horror and destructive potential were demonstrated at Hiroshima and Nagasaki. The Cold War encouraged nuclear innovation. The development and innovation related to nuclear energy were closely bound to the military context. Even today the very word "nuclear" carries with it an association of fear. In comparison to other sources of nuclear energy, the fission weapon in which a mass of plutonium or uranium in excess of critical is assembled very quickly, with a flood of neutrons from a device known as an initiator. The release of energy is extremely rapid and results in a massive explosion. The concepts of nuclear reactor and nuclear plant are different in context. In a nuclear power reactor, the reaction is far slower and more controlled – the heat produced can be harnessed to boil water to spin turbines for the generation of electricity and this has been in practice for decades. The use of nuclear reactors for power generation began on 27th June 1954, at the Obninsk power plant in the former Soviet Union and has continued in different countries to this day. Likewise a nuclear weapon is different from a nuclear plant, as in the former there is no need to control or slow down the reactions that lead to a catastrophic energy release in a short time interval which is the essence of bomb. But a nuclear plant needs moderation of the reaction to sustain a steady but controlled release of energy.[26] Gradually, it was co-opted and moved to the civilian sector for the production of energy for the development of global peoples' need, comfort and aspiration.

Different Uses of Nuclear Power

Nuclear Power is an extremely valuable energy. It allows the generation of massive amounts of clean, inexpensive electricity from reasonably common resources. The most common method today to obtain this energy is through nuclear fission, other methods include nuclear fusion and radioactive decay. All current methods involve heating a working fluid as heavy water, which is then converted into mechanical work for the purpose of generating electricity or propulsion. Presently, about more than 15 per cent of the worlds' electricity comes from nuclear power, over 150 nuclear-powered naval vassels have been built and a few radioisotope rockets have been produced. The world's energy demand is projected to grow by 50 per cent by 2030. To meet the short-term demand, the use of coal and other fossil fuels will increase. In that kind of situation, Nuclear energy is one of the most viable alternatives to oil, particularly, because, it is capable of supplying such massive amounts of energy. According to Stanford study, fast breeder reactors, that convert Uranium into other nuclear fuels while generating energy, and it has the potential to generate energy for billions of year. The massive increase in demand for electricity expected in the 21st century can only be met by an energy resource capable of supply a massive amount of electricity. Coal is an option, but it is highly destructive to pollute air quality and the global environment. Nuclear energy is really the only other massive abundant, massive productive source of electricity capable of meeting these rising demands. Thus, despite the fear attached with nuclear power a large number of scholars in the US and outside, has favoured the development of nuclear energy to make the world safe from power scarcity. Among them is famous economist Jeffrey Sachs, a distinguished professor of sustainability from Columbia University, who has endorsed nuclear energy as the pivotal clean technology. Professor David MacKay, the UK government's chief scientific adviser on climate change, has said, 'You cannot meet Britain's future energy needs and reduce carbon emissions without a big expansion of nuclear power. He believes that Britain should aim to be producing four times the amount of electricity from nuclear as now. Alternative energy sources such as wind, solar and wave power will never provide more than a fraction of the country's energy needs. Relying on gas, coal and oil, with an increasing proportion imported, does not square with Britain's international climate commitments.[27] Energy is the most fundamental requirement of every society or nation as it progresses through the latter of development.

In post-World War-II decades application of nuclear energy in peacetime or non-military use of nuclear explosives became one of the most attractive alternatives. It was clear from weapon tests that nuclear explosions release vast amount of heat and excavate huge holes in the earth. From experiments it seem that there are several possible industrial applications. For instance, electrical power might be produced by using the heat of the explosion which was trapped underground. The heat could be extracted by driving tunnels to the site of the explosion and flooding the shattered rock with a heat transfer liquid. A nuclear explosion underground might also be used to break up huge quantities of rock in low grade ore-fields too poor for conventional mining. Even in case of surface explosions, it might be possible to use nuclear explosives for civil engineering excavations in remote regions.[28] In addition when a reactor works and produces atomic energy, it also produces large amounts of radioactive substances. Many of these are today adding to man's knowledge and giving him better health and better living conditions. Powers obtained from atoms directly and through reactors in the form of radioisotopes included in nuclear energy.

At the present time most of the power we need is generated by burning coal and oil. At some future time all the coal and oil in the world will be exhausted due to over-using of these resources but on the other the demand for power is growing at an amazing speed. There are several reasons for the increase in the demand for power: the population of the world is growing very rapidly; many countries that were underdeveloped are now becoming industrialised; and standards of living are rising everywhere. As a result more and more people consume more and more power in their homes, and they also want more and more goods made with machines that need power to run. At the juncture man is fortunate that it has learned to generate power from atomic energy.

The very first and foremost use of atomic energy is in generation of electric power. It is generated in an atomic power plant that is, in principle, not very different from a regular plant generating electricity from fossil fuels. A regular plant consists essentially of a boiler, a turbine and a generator. In the boiler, coal or oil burns to develop heat which changes water into steam. The steam makes the turbine turn, and the turbine drives the generator. While running, the generator produces electricity, which is then sent into power lines and distributed where needed. In an atomic power plant, a reactor—a modern atomic pile-takes the place of boiler. When the reactor chain reacts and releases atomic energy; it becomes very hot. The heat thus produced changes water into steam. As in a regular power plant, the steam turns the turbine, and the turbine drives the generator. The generator produces electricity, In most modern power plants now being built are entirely enclosed in round domes of steel or other materials that stop the passage of all radioactivity. These domes are meant to protect the population in case a reactor should not work properly and should radioactivity leak out. In modern time even poor countries are constructing smaller plants in which their scientists and engineers can learn how to generate electricity from atoms and how to solve the difficulties that arise when reactors work to make atoms split.[29] The first atomic plant in the world to generate electricity was built in the Soviet Union and started working from June 1954; the second being England in October, 1956.

The prospects for an atomic industry developing fast the world over are very good. The atomic power will help under-developed countries where there are large areas without railways or good roads, where it would be difficult to transport coal or oil. In the sense nuclear fuels are much more compact than coal or oil; for one pound of uranium can do the work of more than one million pounds of coal.

Atomic power can also be used to drive ships and to heat buildings. For the purpose of driving ships the atomic power has the advantage of being much more compact than any other fuel. In atomic ships, much of this space can be put to other uses and the ship can make many trips without refuelling. In July 1959 at Camden, New Jersey, the merchant ship *Savannah,* of the United States was launched. Apart from this the heat produced when a reactor operates may be used directly to heat buildings. At the first conference (1955) on the peaceful uses of atomic energy, this use of reactors was along the topics discussed by scientists.

But the radioactive isotopes which are produced in nuclear reactors are of no less importance. Inside a nuclear reactor there is an immense flux of thermal neutrons which can be used to make radioactive isotopes in large quantities. In the early days of work in the field of radioactivity, natural radioactive substances were used as sources of bullets for atomic bombardment, and helped the physicists gain a deeper understanding of the atoms. In early years, when only natural radioactive substances were available, their use was limited by their scarcity and high cost. Shortly, after the discovery of slow neutrons, Ernest Lawrence made much larger amounts of radioactive substances by using particles that were speeded up in his cyclotron. In 1935 Lawrence made an amount of radiosodium comparable to available amounts of natural radioactive substances. Not perfect it was, although better than radium, for radium decays very slowly and doctors cannot leave it inside a patient. Fortunately, only a few years later, Hahn and Strassmann discovered fission, and it was fission which made reactors possible that provided a much more economical way of inducing radioactivity. Reactors can produce not only radiosodium, but also a large number of other radioisotopes in great quantities and at a low cost. The large amount of radioisotopes contain dozens of different kind. Some radioisotopes are poisonous and difficult to handle, others are safe and can be fed to plants, animals, and men.[30] Biologists, doctors, and men in industry are free to choose the radioisotopes best suited to their purposes.

Soon after the discovery of radioactive elements, it was recognised that they provided an important new method for tracing the passage of small quantities of materials through mechanical or biological systems. Radioisotopes are helping biologists to study how plants, animals, and men live, grow and die; how they take up food and use it to build tissues; how they breathe; how the sap in plants and the blood in men move around to bring nourishment wherever needed; how cells and tissues become diseased and eventually die. The whole situation changed dramatically when radioactive isotopes of common elements became readily available. The widespread use of radioactive tracers is possible because all the isotopes of one element, whether stable or unstable as far as the nucleus is concerned, have exactly the same number and configuration of planetary electrons.[31] Similarly as tracers, the substance has helped biologists to study how the nutritive elements in our food are used by our bodies. They have learned that all tissues absorb fresh substances but discard old ones, and thus they are continuously being renewed. Before the use of radioisotopes, biologists believed that bones and teeth did not change; but they have now found that even bones and teeth are continuously being renewed.

Likewise, in the study of plants and fertilizers it has proved very useful. In other studies with radioisotopes, biologists have proved that plants take their nourishment not only through the roots, but also through the foliage, fruit, twings, trunks and flowers, Fertilizers labelled with radiophosphorus, for instance, have shown how the soil absorbs phosphorus, how much of it the plants can take up from the soil, what part of the phosphorus that plants take up comes from the fertilisers and what part from the phosphorus that was already in the soil. In a similar way biologists have studied how animals make use of the food they eat. Often these studies have helped in the planning of a diet for cattle and poultry that has improved the quality or the quantity of meat, milk and eggs. Scientists all over the world have recognised that radioisotopes are the most important new tool of research.

Radioisotopes are becoming more and more important in the diagnosis and treatment of diseases. In the treatment of many forms of cancer, doctors place a small amount of radioactive substance inside the cancer tissue, or near it. The radiation given off by this substance destroys the cancer tissues. Earlier, radium was the substance for cancer treatment, but now a large variety of radioisotopes are available for use. In addition Radioiodine is used to locate brain tumours, one of the most serious and painful forms of cancer. Like biologists, doctors often use radioisotopes as tracers. Among the tracer isotopes useful to medicine is radiosodium, with which salt can be labelled. As a tracer it is also very useful in the case of thyroid glands which is situated in the neck. If this organ becomes overactive or underactive, the patient's health is seriously affected. A measurement of the efficiency of the thyroid function is of great use to the clinician. The test can readily be carried out as a tracer, since the thyroid has remarkable powers for accumulating iodine.[32]

In line nuclear power is freely used in X-rays both for taking X-rays pictures and for treating diseases, but today radioisotopes, such as radiocobalt, are often used instead of X-rays. The substance cobalt contains large amounts of radiocobalt – cobalt 60 – that is made in reactors. Radio cobalt gives of very strong gamma rays, which are similar to X-rays. Cobalt units can do the work of very powerful X-ray machines, and they are easier to handle and much less expensive. The rays from cobalt units can be directed with greater precision to the part of the patient's body that needs treatment.

Thus, in ways more than one the biologists and doctors use radioisotopes. Particularly in biology and medicine radioisotopes are very useful. But in agriculture the use of irradiated seeds, the experiments to produce better crops and livestock, and the progress being made in doing away with the pests that afflict plants and animals, are already producing great financial returns. In subjects such as, physics, chemistry, metallurgy, and in other branches of science, radioisotopes are enlarging and deepening the understanding of matter and of its behaviour. The nuclear power is now offering to mankind – more power, better health, more food, more knowledge. As a result, it has strengthened scientific and technological collaboration among countries of the world at large.

Nuclear Energy vs. Nuclear Safety

The nuclear energy, in general, contains a large amount of power and medicinal effects that have proved useful for human life. It however, at the sametime, has two main dangers emanating from it. First, nuclear power plants generate large quantities of highly radioactive material. This is due to the left over isotopes (atoms) from the splitting of the atoms, and the creation of heavier atoms, like plutonium, which the nuclear power plant does not utilise. It is called nuclear waste. The actual quantity of waste output is some 100,000 times than a fossil fuel plant but it is much more radioactive. Secondly, in the history of nuclear power there have been several major incidents of plant failure beginning with the Kyshtym accident in fuel reprocessing in 1957 in the nuclear complex of former Soviet Union. Plant accidents occurred so far are due to the underdeveloped technology and human error. But all failures and accidents propel us to think and develop better and safer technologies towards better service. And in the case of nuclear power, we do acknowledge that the effects of radiation can reach a wider impact zone. In the situation improvement, and not escapism, should be our step forward.[33] The best of technological progress, while being the biggest ally of mankind, does come at an incremental risk. The key is to learn and evolve to mitigate the risk rather than use of the first incident as an excuse to disband science. Despite generally a high security standard, accidents can still happen. It is technically impossible to build a plant with 100 per cent security. A small probability of failure will always last. The consequences of an accident would be absolutely devastating both for human being as for the nature. The more nuclear power plants are built, the higher is the probability of a disastrous failure somewhere in the world.

In the early days of radioactivity, scientists were not aware of these dangers, but todays weapons of mass destruction are far more advanced than the atom bombs dropped over Japan. In addition there are important differences between an air burst, a bomb exploded high above the ground and a ground burst. Of the two undoubtedly the air burst is more effective against extended targets. But in both cases when the sequence of events starts, first the nuclear explosive is transformed into an intensely hot "ball of fire", miniature sun-which in an air burst, expands rapidly to several hundred feet in diameter. The fire ball will emit a brilliant light, much brighter than the sun; it may be last for several seconds in the case of a hydrogen bomb. The heat radiated from the fire-ball travels with the speed of light and is one of the important results of the explosion. In the second place is the blast or shock wave which also originates in the fire-ball but which travels to the target more slowly. It has a velocity only a little greater than the speed of sound. After the initial blinding flash, the ball of fire loses brilliance rapidly and rises with its cloud of swirling gases many thousands of feet in the air. The great difference between the blast from an atomic bomb and that from a high explosive bomb is the time for which the effect lasts.[34] The blast from a high explosive bomb is a sharp blow, while that from an atomic bomb is more like a strong wind in its effect.

With nuclear weapons another danger encountered by living things is the danger due to radiation of Y-rays and other radiations, passing through living tissue, ionise some of the atoms present in the tissue. The ionised atoms form very reactive chemical agents which in turn have an adverse effect on the cells of the living tissue. In course of it, if too many cells are affected, the function of vital organs will be impaired, causing death to the person exposed to the radiation. Among the results of a large dose of radiation are loss of hair and appetite, sore throat, pallor, blood spots under the skin, vomiting, diarrhoea, nose bleeding, fever and emaciation. If a nuclear weapon is exploded over a city, the population is exposed to radiation from several sources. The immediate hazard comes from the intense flash of y-rays radiated by the explosion. The radiation is intense immediately under the point of explosion, but falls of rapidly for points some distance from the centre. However, a large dose of radiation can be tolerated if only a limited portion of the body is exposed.[35] Also the effect depends on whether the dose is received all at the one time or spread over a period.

Apart from this there is a further hazard which lasts long after the bomb has been exploded, the fall out of the radioactive fission products. The immediate area of the explosion, especially downhill, will be contaminated by the heavier particles in the radioactive debris. Lighter particles may be sucked up into the upper air and carried great distances from the point of the explosion, Likewise the radioactive material covering the ground and surfaces of buildings is hazardous. But a more insidious hazard from the fallout is that the radioactive materials can be taken into the body by ingestion and inhalation. Some pass through the body fairly, rapidly and so are relatively innocuous. Others fix in the bones causing a danger which might last for years. In nutshell, nuclear power is not a clean energy source. In fact, it produces both low and high-level of radioactive waste that remains dangerous for several hundred thousand years. Generated throughout all parts of the fuel cycle, this waste poses a serious danger to human health. Currently, over 2,000 metric tons of high-level radioactive waste and 12 million cubic feet of low-level radioactive waste are produced annually by the 103 operating reactors in the United States. No country in the world has found a solution for this waste. Building new nuclear plants would mean the production of much more of this dangerous waste with nowhere for it to go.

Even today the mad nuclear arms race is high on the political agenda of most neo-cons, super-patriots, religious fanatics and arms dealers. Notwithstanding the Nuclear non-proliferation Treaty, there are about 22,000 nuclear warheads mostly in the arsenal of the US and Russia, Eight thousand are in the operational ready mode and 2,000 are on high alert. Also there are 14,000 Plutonium cores and 5000 Canned Assemblies in the storages of Highly Enriched Uranium (HEU). Moreover, 28 countries have the capacity to build at least one bomb and 12 countries can make 20 bombs.[36] According to the Nuclear Age Peace Foundation, some 500,000 kg of plutonium are in stockpiles, which could be available to sub-nationalist "freedom fighters" of any race or religion. In a nuclear war to start today by mistake or intentionally, there will be no victor, no vanquished.[37] In the circumstances, re-designing of nuclear energy for peaceful purposes would require going back to the drawing broad, a complete reassessment of risks, research on safety concerns and strategies. It would mandate enormous money, time, effort, political and administrative will.[38] Otherwise, as David Krieger of the Nuclear Age Peace Foundation rightly said, "One bomb could destroy one city. A few bombs could destroy a country and few dozen nuclear bombs could reduce the entire civilisation to total ruins."

Apart from devastation caused by nuclear detonations and use of nuclear arms, like any large scale industrial activity, there have been numerous accidents and mistakes at nuclear power plants and reprocessing facilities. Till date several major/minor accidents have occurred in operating nuclear plants across the world and have exposed its workers and residents to dangerous levels of ionising radiations. In the history of nuclear world, first such incident took place in 1957 due to a fault in the cooling system in Kyshtym nuclear complex in Russia which led to a chemical explosion and the release of 70-80 tonnes of radioactive material into the air, exposing thousands of people and leading to the evacuation of thousands more. Besides, major accidents, which have killed, maimed and exposed large populations of workers and local residents, have been reported from various other nuclear facilities–Windscale nuclear reactor, UK (1957); Idaho National Engineering Laboratory, US (1961); Three Mile Island Power Plant, US (1979); Chernobyl Power Plant, Russia (1986); Seversk, Russia, (1993); the Tokai-Mura nuclear fuel processing facility, Japan (1989); Mihama power plant, Japan (2004); Fukushima Daiichi power plant Japan (2011) and the Marcoule nuclear site, France (2011). All these accidents and many more unreported ones including from India have obviously raised questions about the desirability of nuclear energy and any real possibility of it being "safe".[39] It is also a fact that in each of these places people have not been able to return to their homes, that their lives have never been normal again and that they constantly live under the shadow of diseases and death makes nuclear energy patently dangerous.

Among all the nuclear plant accidents took place so far there have been four major incidents of plant failure–the Kyshtym accident in fuel reprocessing in 1957, the relatively smaller Three Mile Island meltdown (United States), the much bigger Chernobyl accident (USSR 1986) and the recent Japanese incident at Fukushima. The first accident was purely due to underdeveloped technology, and much of the blame for the next two disasters is attributed to human error. Of these only one–Chernobyl qualifies as "horrific". In Idaho (1961) and Mihama 2004) there were fatalities but no radiation leakage. In Windscale (1957) and Three Mile Island (1979) there was significant radiation leakage but no immediate fatalities, and the epidemiology of radiation-induced cancers is not very clear. In Seversk (1993) there were no fatalities and only a mild leakage of radiation. In Tokaimura (1989) there were two fatalities and radiation leakage but no known after effects. In both Seversk and Tokaimura, the level of exposure for nearby people was a few tens of millisieverts at most; about three-four times more than what one would receive in a CAT scan.[40] And Marcoule (2011) was not a nuclear accident at all. Even in Fukushima nobody died from radiation exposure. But the Chernobyl disaster is perhaps one of the worst in human history. It resulted from a lack of "safety culture" at the plant, design flaws in the RBMK reactor and a violation of procedure. Under it, serious radioactive contamination spread over 150,000 square kilometers in Byelorussia, Ukraine and Russia. Radioactive clouds deposited radiation thousands of kilometers away. Hundreds of thousands people had to be evacuated, and millions more were left to live in areas that were dangerous to their health and lives. Moreover, scientific studies have shown that the full consequences of the Chernobyl disaster could top a quarter of a million cancer cases and nearly, 100,000 fatal cancers. After the events on 11th September 2001, many people were reasonably concerned about the safety of nuclear power plants from terrorist activities.

In the history of nuclear plant accidents, an unparallel incident took place at 3.41 pm on 11th March 2011 in the Fukushima Daiichi nuclear power plant of Japan. In this mishappening there were extraordinary natural forces in action and no one imagined that the unlikely combination of natural and man-made disasters would occur together–a massive earthquake, a towering tsunami and the failure of the so-called fool-proof safety and containment strategies.[41] It was a 13-metre wave triggered by the 9.0 magnitude earthquake had toppled the six-metre protective sea wall, flooding the plant's six reactors and disabling all 13 of the site's back-up diesel generators, which had been switched on when the earthquake first struck. Without power, water could not be pumped into the reactors to cool them and soon they began to overheat and over pressurise. Twenty-four hours later, an explosion caused by a build up of hydrogen at reactor one ripped off the walls and roof. It was estimated after the incident that Fukushima released about a tenth of the radiation expelled into the atmosphere at Chernobyl.[42] Before the disaster Japan was the world's third biggest user of nuclear power and had been planning to increase nuclear's share of the energy mixed to 50 per cent by 2030. The incident had severely weakened Japan's attachment to nuclear power after the

Fukushima accident which sent radioactive materials into the ocean and atmosphere, contaminated the food and water supply, and forced the evacuation of 160,000 residents.

In fact, in this type of reactors water is used to cool the reactor core and produce steam to turn the turbines that make electricity. The water contains two of the least dangerous radioactive materials – radioactive nitrogen and tritium. Normal plant operations produce both of them in the cooling water and they are even released routinely in small amounts into the environment, usually through tall chimneys. Nitrogen is the most common gas in the earth's atmosphere, and at a nuclear plant the main radioactive form is known as nitrogen-16. It is made when speeding neutrons from the reactor's core hit oxygen in the surrounding cooling water. This radioactive form of nitrogen does not occur in nature. The danger of nitrogen-16 is an issue only for plant workers and operators because its half-life is only seven seconds. A half life is the time it takes half the atoms of a radioactive substance to disintegrate. The other form of radioactive materials often in the cooling water of a nuclear reactor is tritium. It is a naturally occurring radioactive form of hydrogen, sometimes known as heavy hydrogen. It is found in a trace amount in ground water throughout the world. Tritium emits a weak form of radiation that does not travel very far in the air and cannot penetrate the skin. After Fukushima, the big worries were on the reported release of radioactive materials – radioactive iodine and cesium, iodine-131 and potassium iodine.[43] The central problem in assessing the degree of danger is that the amounts of various radioactive releases into the environment are now unknown, but the properties of the materials and their typical interaction with the human body give some indication of the threat.

On the whole, Fukushima forces us to question our beliefs about nuclear energy. While nuclear power is born out of science, the nuclear industry is subject to a variety of non-scientific forces. Political, economic, military, nationalist and social factors modulate its efficacy. The crisis at Fukushima forced Japan into a fundamental rethink of its policy on nuclear power. As part of the policy in post-accident phase, dozens of nuclear reactors not directly affected by the tsunami have gone offline to undergo regular maintenance and safety checks and utilities have turned to coal, and gas-fired power plants to keep industry and households supplied with electricity imports. In line none of Japans idle reactors will be permitted to go back online until they pass stringent "stress tests" simulations designed to test their ability to withstand catastrophic events. Japan was briefly without nuclear power after Fukushima accident as all 50 working reactors were closed for safety checks. It was only in June 2012 Yoshihiko Noda, the Prime Minister of Japan, approved the restart of two reactors in Western Japan amid fears that the country would experience power cuts during the summer. It also prepared the country for a historic policy shift on nuclear power.

Based on facing the reality of the grave accident and by learning lessons from the incident, the government has decided to review the national energy strategy. On March 11, 2011, it has gone down in history as a dark day for Japan, the government's September 14, 2012 decision to end its reliance on nuclear power. By 2040 to closing down all 50 reactors will forever be remembered as a defining moment.[44] A policy document, released by the Japanese government on 14th September 2012 read, 'One of the key pillars of the new strategy is to achieve a society that does not depend on nuclear energy as soon as possible. The plan calls for renewable energy to comprise 30 per cent of Japan's future energy mix-an eightfold rise from 2010 levels and the development of sustainable ways to use fossil fuel. This is a strategy to create a new future. Japan should aim to reduce greenhouse gas emissions by about 20 per cent from 1990 levels and to reduce energy consumption through greater efficiency by about 10 per cent from 2010 levels.[45] In addition, the Fukushima mishap has had its reverberations in several other countries including France, Germany, India, China, Italy, Israel and Indonesia. By 2025, France will cut its reliance on nuclear energy by 25 per cent from the current level of 75 per cent by shutting down 24 reactors. After Fukushima, Germany, by 2020, intends to derive 35 per cent of its energy needs from renewable source. India and China, who are both pushing ahead with their own nuclear plans, have also taken pause to look at their safety aspect. Although limited but there have also been negative reactions in Italy, Israel and Indonesia. Some countries who were thinking about nuclear power have now restrained. Now perhaps, the focus will be on developing technologies for generating alternative sources of energy.

References

1. Greth Evans and Yoriki Kawaguchi, 'Nuclear Disarmament : Building the Momentum,' *The Hindu*, 29th September 2009.
2. A.P.J. Abdul Kalam and Srijan Pal Singh, 'Nuclear Power is Our Gateway to a Prosperous Future', *Ibid*,. 6th November 2011.
3. *Ibid.*
4. C. Moller and Ebbe Rasmussen, *The World and the Atom* (London: George Allen and Unwin, 1940), pp. 15-16.
5. Laura Fermi, *All About Atomic Energy* (London : W.H. Allen, 1962), pp. 1-2.
6. J.M. Valentine, *Atomic Physics* (London : The English Universities Press, 1960), pp. 13-14.
7. C. Moller and Ebbe Rasmussen, *The World and the Atom*, pp. 17-20.
8. Laura Fermi, *All About Atomic Energy*, pp. 12-14.
9. *Ibid.*, pp 17-18.
10. *Ibid.*, pp. 34-41.
11. S.H. Venkatramani, 'Nuclear Energy is Toxic', *The Times of India*, November, 2007.
12. Gopalkrishna Gandhi, 'The Lessons of July 16, 1945', *The Hindu*, 16th July 2011.
13. N.S. Sisodia, 'Lessons from an Atomic Catastrophe', *Ibid.*, 6th August 2009.
14. Gopalkrishna Gandhi, 'The Lessons of July 16, 1945'.
15. *Ibid.*
16. N.S. Sisodia, 'Lessons from an Atomic Catastrophe.'
17. As quoted in *Ibid.*
18. Fissile material is an isotope of a radioactive element that undergoes nuclear fission, either spontaneously or when irradiated by neutrons. Fissile nuclides, such as uranium-235 and plutonium-239 are used in nuclear reactors and nuclear weapons.
19. Laura Fermi, *All About Atomic Energy*, pp. 98-99.
20. *Ibid.*, p. 100.
21. A.M. Goldstein, *A Dictionary of Physics* (Delhi: CBS Publishers and Distributors, 1986), p. 179.
22. *Ibid.*, pp. 279-80.
23. *Ibid.*, pp. 180-81.
24. M.R. Srinivasan, 'A Lesson in Nuclear Reactors', *The Hindu*, 11th September 2007.

25. M.R. Srinivasan, 'A Lesson in Nuclear Reactors', *The Hindu,* 11th September 2007.
26. A.P.J. Abdul Kalam and Srijan Pal Singh, 'Nuclear Power is Our Gateway to a Prosperous Future'.
27. David Mackay, 'The Future is Green, the Future is Nuclear', *Times Online*, 4th October, 2009.
28. J.M. Valentine, *Atomic Physics,* pp. 160-61.
29. Laura Fermi, *All About Atomic Energy*, pp. 105-7.
30. *Ibid.,* pp. 115-18.
31. J.M. Valentine, *Atomic Physics*, p. 165.
32. *Ibid.,* p. 175.
33. A.P.J. Abdul Kalam and Srijan Pal Singh, 'Nuclear Power is Our Gateway to a Prosperous Future'.
34. J.M. Valentine, *Atomic Physics*, pp. 150-51.
35. *Ibid.*, pp. 151-54.
36. Dhirendra Sharma, 'Do Nations Need Nuclear Weapons?' *The Hindu* 9th August, 2010.
37. *Ibid.*
38. K.S. Jacob, 'Old Configuration, New Context', *Ibid.,* 11th April, 2011.
39. Madhumita Dutta, 'Desirability of Nuclear Power is the Real Question', *Ibid.,* 27th September 2012.
40. Rahul Siddharthan's Views in response to the above in *Ibid.*
41. K.S. Jacob, 'Old Configuration, New Context'.
42. Leo Hickman, 'Fukushima Slows Down But Does Not Halt the Nuclear March', *Ibid.*, 28th December 2011.
43. William J. Broad, 'Radioactive Releases in Japan Worrying', *Ibid.,* 14th March 2011.
44. *Ibid., editorial*, 22nd September 2012.
45. Justin McCurry, 'Japan's 30 Year Plan to be Nuclear Free', *Ibid.,* 15th September 2012.

2

India's Nuclear Power : Position with Present Status

In the years following India's independence its founding Prime Minister Jawaharlal Nehru worked energetically to defuse global tensions during the Cold War and campaigned tirelessly to eliminate what he termed these "frightful engines of destructions."[1] Having failed in endeavours over decades for global nuclear disarmament, India reluctantly weaponised its capability. In the absence of global nuclear disarmament, India's strategic interests required effective, credible nuclear deterrence and adequate retaliatory capability. In the situations, Dr. Homi Jehangir Bhabha, the founding chairman of its Atomic Energy Commission and the architect of its three-stage (thorium) programme, presented his plan for national development in November 1954 at the Conference on Development of Atomic Energy for Peaceful Purposes. Four years later in 1958, the Indian government formally adopted the three-stage plan and recognised that thorium was main source that could provide power to the Indian people for the long term. It adhered for long on the use of atomic energy for peaceful purposes but over the years the traditional concept of deterrence which aims to retain balance between mutual vulnerabilities and a capability to wreak unacceptable punishment on an aggressor has also undergone to symbolise a potential shift in focus from offence to defence.[2] Earlier, due to its unique nuclear policy India has been denied access to trade in nuclear materials, equipment and various kinds of technologies. In the Post Cold War era, perspective for civil nuclear cooperation between India and the United States arose in the context of India's requirement for adequate and affordable energy supplies to sustain its accelerating economic growth rate. It led the declaration of 18 July 2005, made by the Heads of the Government of India and the US. It also followed a safeguards agreement with International Atomic Energy Agency (IAEA) which became operational in October 2009. These understandings ended India's nuclear isolation from world trade by the Nuclear Suppliers' Group. It has paved the way for India's three-stage thorium-based nuclear power development progamme as cherished by the country long ago. In today's context, development of nuclear power with safety measures has become a precondition for countries like India who wished to be an influential regional/global power in world politics.

Analysis of India's Nuclear Policy

The closing year of 1930s as well as the opening years of 1940s were crucial for giving the nuclear power a weaponary shape finally. The problem of 1942-43 was to find means of separating U-235 from U-238 in sufficient quantities to make a nuclear bomb. It also became clear that whereas plutonium can be separated from uranium by chemical means, U-235 cannot be. The problem was finally solved and by 1943 the United States had built up the atomic laboratory at Los Alamos in New Mexico where professor J.R. Oppenheimer led a staff of more than 500 specialists of whom 300 were scientists.[3] At the same time, when scientists in the West were working solely on military application of nuclear energy, Homi Jehangir Bhabha, the architect of India' nuclear programme visualised the possibility of nuclear energy being used for civilian industrial use. More than a year before Hiroshima and Nagasaki in 1944 Bhabha declared, 'when nuclear energy has been successfully applied for power production in, say, a couple of decades from now, India will not have to look abroad for its experts, but will find them ready at home.[4] He was conscious enough about the future development of nuclear energy for the common good of mankind, He, in a letter to Sir Dorabji Tata Trust on 12th March, 1944 prophetically proposed for the setting up of an institute for fundamental research and a year later it was firmly laid as the Tata Institute of Fundamental Research with Dr. Bhabha as its Director. Indian nuclear programme, at least during its initial period clearly showed the ideas like tolerance and non-violence which were the features of Gandhi's techniques of *Satyagraha* and the peaceful transition of power that characterised the birth of Indian Republic. Accordingly, despite two atomic bombs being dropped on Japan, India's founding father demonstrated immense faith in the peaceful use of atomic energy.[5] Apart from Krishna Menon and Dr. Bhabha who talked of sharing nuclear knowledge in common interest, Nehru himself asserted: "We will not make these bombs even if we have the capacity to do so and in no event we will use atomic energy for those most destructive purposes'.[6] Thus, Indian nuclear research and programmes were purposeful, confined only to civilian research.

In fact, after the explosion of nuclear bombs on Hiroshima and Nagasaki in August 1945, peace among nations has been a necessary condition for mankind's survival. It is true that there has been no World War since 1945; it is also true that nuclear weapons have been developed and deployed in part to deter such a conflict. Nuclear revolution, in post World War II phase, has forced great powers to behave in a careful and restrained manner and to accept a compromise, which in pre-nuclear times would surely have been unacceptable.[7] It has even changed the modes of thinking, and thus we drift towards unparalleled catastrophe. Although the catastrophe Einstein envisaged has not occurred, the experience of Hiroshima and Nagasaki was more than sufficient to prevent all the nations possessing this new technology from any actual use of it under any circumstances. The Father of the Nation was at pains, following the incident and in July 1946 he observed, "The atom bomb has deadened the finest feelings which have sustained mankind for ages....It has resulted for the time being in the soul of Japan being destroyed. What has happened to the soul, the destroying nation is yet too early to see"[8] Hence, India since independence, has consistently pursued the goal of global disarmament-based on the principles of universality, non-discrimination and effective compliance. "There is only one way to end this threat and that is to abolish these weapons. Either nuclear weapons must be eliminated or human beings face the threat of extinction by weapons of their own creation".[9] Coming of nuclear age ushered the humanity in a quite new phase not known earlier.

With the end of Second World War people from all over the world have felt the need to halt the spread of nuclear weapons since the early days of the nuclear age. In January 1946, the United Nations General Assembly resolution envisaged the elimination to such weapons from the national arsenals. Surprisingly, the United State had not only been the first country to apply nuclear energy to the production of weapons but it also proposed firstly in the United Nations for the establishment of an international authority to control all atomic energy activities potentially. Its proposal was known as "Barruch Plan" but it failed miserably as shortly thereafter the USSR exploded its nuclear device in 1949, United Kingdom in 1952, France in 1960 followed by China in 1964.[10] In context, many analysts including Lewis A. Dunn and Herman Kahan and Meyor have listed various reasons or pressures encouraging a country to go nuclear. Dunn and Kahan have listed as many as fourteen factors which have been classified under several heads such as security, status or influence, bureaucratic and domestic. They have also indentified eight types of events as "trigger" activating consideration on the pressure or reasons for a country going nuclear. These are :

(i) Involvement in foreign crisis;

(ii) Reduction in alliance credibility;

(iii) Nuclearisation of the other countries;

(iv) Weakening or breakdown of international constraints;

(v) Domestic crisis; and

(vi) Changed perception and utility of nuclear weapons.[11]

Another analyst Meyor, notes three basic types of incentives. First, incentives of international political prestige and image-building. These can affect the country's appearance and posture, Second, incentives to advance national military and security objectives, to minimise external threats to the country and to strengthen its relative power position and strength. Third, incentives to support and promote domestic policies and to prevail in domestic political struggles.[12] In general, four sets of arguments are frequently advanced by threshold states aiming to retain the nuclear options–military security; political prestige and influence; economic gains; and domestic pressures and compulsions.

In 1947, when India emerged as a free country to take its rightful place in the comity of nations, the nuclear age had already dawned. In the circumstances, India stressed on the creation of a broad-based science and technology infrastructure because it believed that technological backwardness made a country politically and economically vulnerable. It decided to produce all the basic materials because of nuclear power's strategic nature and hence made the nuclear programme a major area of scientific research and development. The prevailing situation also compelled Nehru to announce before assuming office. "As long as the world was constituted on nuclear might, every country will have to develop and use the latest scientific devices for its protection." However the formal annoucement of India's nuclear policy was made by Nehru on 10th May 1954, when he said in Lok Sabha, 'I should like the House to remember that the use of atomic energy for peaceful purposes is far more important for a country like India whose power resources are limited, than for a country like, say, France, an industrially advanced counry".[13] Nehru's statement identified the basic components of India's nuclear policy. They are :

(i) Not to make nuclear weapons;

(ii) To work for and support nuclear disarmament and nuclear arms control measures;

(iii) To develop and use nuclear energy for peaceful purposes, and

(iv) Not to accept discriminatory international inspection and safeguard in respect of national nuclear facilities.

India's commitment to the peaceful use of nuclear energy during the stewardship of Jawaharlal Nehru remained firm. No doubts were cast on his bona fides in his lifetime. Not only that but Nehru assured the world on behalf of any future Government of India that his country would not go in for nuclear weapons. Inaugurating the first reactor on Asian soil on 20th January 1957, he said, "......No man can prophesy the future. But I should like to say on behalf of my Government-and I think I can say with some assurance on behalf of any future Government of India-that whatever might happen, whatever the circumstances, we shall never use this atomic energy for evil purposes. There is no condition attached to this assurance, because once a condition is attached, the value of such an assurance does not go very far."[14] But when by the year 1960 Britain and France had become nuclear powers, India, felt that a ban on proliferation was both essential and urgent and it clearly stated that the heavier responsibilities lay with the nuclear powers.

Since the early 1960s environment stands nuclearised. Both China and Pakistan possess nuclear weapons and delivery systems to pose a nuclear threat across the length and breadth of India. Substantive amount of nuclear technology moved from US to Pakistan. In situation, the basic adverse nuclear asymmetry was not likely to be resolved through disarmament in the predictable future and the only option left for India was to "exercise" the option towards a nuclear deterrent. In addition, the humiliating defeat at the hands of China in 1962 awakened India to the new realities of military power as a major factor in international politics and inter-state relations. Even at the moment Nehru, who inherited the traditions of Gandhian non-violence relied on the principle of a minimum of military power to maintain internal law and order and safeguard the country's security against any external threat.[15] However, the prevailing developments held in nuclear sphere necessitated the shift in India's defence policy. Especially, in context of 1962 India-China war Nehru admitted that it had stalled the pace of development. In fact he felt that the Chinese attack was primarily meant to derail India in its journery towards economic growth. The set-back had opened the eyes of the powers that be, leading the modernisation of the armed forces and induction of advanced weaponry in all the three wings. But as earlier Nehru, despite pressures, was firm in his stand for peaceful uses of atomic energy and in the event of Chinese nuclear threat or blackmail he hoped that the United States would provide a "nuclear umbrella"[16] to India.

After the death of Nehru in May 1963, Lal Bahadur Shastri succeeded him as the Prime Minister of India. As a result of India-China war of 1962 but particularly after 16th October 1964 when China exploded its first nuclear device, the people of India began to agitate over the likely nuclear threat that China could pose to this country. The Chinese tests showed considerable sophistication but the more worrying fact was that they have all the basic facilities viz., man-power requirements and raw-material requirements for a sustained weapon programme. The Chinese explosion provided the greatest incentive for self-reliance in defence production and hardly a week after it Mrs. Indira Gandhi, then Minister for Information and Broadcasting had said in an interview with the French Television in Paris on 22nd October 1964, "India is in a position to produce the bomb within eighteen month. But we should not deviate from our stand and should use atomic energy for peaceful purposes only."[17] Further during Lok Sabha debate on foreign affairs, in November 1964, members of different parties, including some Congressmen demanded a change in the Government's "no bomb policy". The indication was given on 27th November 1964 by the Prime Minister Lal Bahadur Shastri. Sharing the concern of members over the Chinese blast Shastri said that Government's present stand should not be regarded as permanent one. No Government can afford a static approach. He said, "I cannot say that the present policy is deep-rooted, that it cannot be set a side, that it can never be changed.......and an individual may have certain static policy..... But in the political field we can not do so. Here situations alter, changes, take place and I have to move our policy accordingly. If there is need to amend what we have said even we will say all right, let us go ahead and do so.[18] It was in that kind of situation that India, under Shastri's premiership, initiated the nuclear explosives programme in 1965 and later carried out by Mrs. Gandhi's Government. But unfortunately, given the strength of India's general anti-bomb orientation, the untimely deaths of both Lal Bahadur Shastri and Bhabha during 1966, followed by the economic difficulties and Vikram Sarabhai's opposition to pursue this scheme; India's nuclear programme got delayed by many more years.

On the other hand, earlier, by the end of the 1950s when the prospects of successful negotiations on disarmament were once again getting dark, many non-aligned nations like India, Yugoslavia, Egypt, Ghana and Indonesia mounted the pressure of their demand on activising the UN General Assembly in respect of disarmament. Also in the wake of the Chinese explosion the world powers became aware of the implications of nuclear device. A treaty banning all nuclear tests except those held underground was signed in Moscow on 5th August 1963, by the United States, the Soviet Union and Great Britain. India also signed the treaty on 5th August 1963. But this treaty did not bring about a breakthrough in relations to the problem of disarmament. It had only a limited value for it failed to secure ban on all nuclear tests by not covering the underground tests and limiting itself only to the tests on the ground, in water and in atmosphere. There was certainly a lot of use despite the ban on these.[19] India too, despite signature, had opposed it as an unequal and discriminatory instrument conferring unequal privileges on the powers then possessing equal weapons, and imposing one-sided restrictions on the non-nuclear weapon powers. In this regard, India favoured "genuine disarmament... and not just those arms control measure which suit the convenience of the major military powers. In its capacity as a responsible member of the world body, India's representative while participating in the initial debates in the UN General Assembly on Nuclear Non-Proliferation Treaty in November, 1965, stressed the need to establish "an acceptable balance of mutual responsibilities and obligations of the nuclear and non-nuclear powers.[20] Earlier India had hoped that the Test Ban Treaty of 1963 would encourage steps towards a complete and comprehensive disarmament.

Thus, the regional and global environment prevailing in 1960s compelled India to be ready for nuclearisation. In addition, China's first atomic test had indeed unleashed a national uproar which was to kick-start India's first serious debate in favour of building nuclear weapons. The sixty-ninth annual session of the Indian National Congress which followed Chinese test in January 1965, witnessed a heated debate on the issue.[21] Again, during September 1965, over one hundred Members of Parliament (MPs) from various political parties submitted to the government a joint memorandum demanding a prompt and immediate decision to develop nuclear weapons. The annual session of the Indian Science Congress in 1966 passed a resolution making the same demand.[22] At last Homi Bhabha, the founder architect of India's nuclear establishment, had to reassure the nation, that, given the political green signal, India's scientific community could explode a nuclear bomb in eighteen months. And it is in this context that the then Prime Minister Lal Bahadur Shastri was to sanction the proposal put forward by Bhabha on investigating a Subterranean Nuclear Explosion Project. This can be seen as the earliest signal of a pro-bomb tilt in India's nuclear policy.[23] By the end of 1966, there was unanimous support for a nuclear weapons programme. Further developments on the discriminatory aspects of the Non-Proliferation Treaty of 1968 which India rejected, New Delhi had decided to sustain its independence on international security by allowing her for the development of the peaceful nuclear explosion technology.

The minor shift in policy and emphasis that we visualise in India's nuclear policy is mostly due to change in regional and global perspectives. The new regional atmosphere on the subject was indicated when India's Ambassador to the UNO said on 14th May 1968. "It is a matter of concern to India that across its borders a major power, the Peoples Republic of China, continues to conduct nuclear weapon tests in the atmosphere in flagrant violation of the will of the international community and in total disregard of the grave dangers posed by such testings'. At the same time it was also considered in some quarters that it is in India's interest to balance Chinese nuclear capabilities by developing an 'Asian Balance of Power' by acquiring similar nuclear capabilities. On the other, at the close of 1960s international milieu on the nuclear issue was also deteriorating and discriminatory treaties were signed one after another.[24] In 1967, in a strategic move, the United States and Soviet Union presented to the Eighteen Nations Committee on Disarmament at Geneva on 20th August 1967, two separate identical draft of a treaty banning the spread of nuclear weapons. These were subsequently revised in January 1968 and in March 1968, making some amendments. Later, the UN General Assembly adopted and commended the treaty but in India, Mrs. Indira Gandhi, the Prime Minister of the country, criticised several articles of the treaty under which it was improper that each nuclear weapon state party to the treaty undertook not to transfer to any recipient whatsoever nuclear weapons or other nuclear explosive devices or control over such weapons or explosive device directly or indirectly, and not in any way to assist, encourage or induce any non-nuclear weapon state to manufacture or otherwise acquire nuclear weapons or nuclear explosive devices, or control over such weapons of explosive devices.[25] India refused to sign it on these very grounds, though it reiterated its pledge not to produce nuclear weapons.

India since independence had entirely contributed to the Disarmament Conference aimed to make the world nuclear-weapon free but on the other continued to review the emphasis on self-reliance. Earlier the research and development work which the Atomic Energy Commission was carrying on had been in pursuance of the national objective of harnessing atomic energy for peaceful purposes only. In opposite, the prevailing situation necessitated the development of Indian nuclear devices and the progress made so far had been informed to the Lok Sabha by Mrs. Indira Gandhi on 15th November 1972. 'The Atomic Energy Commission is studying conditions under which peaceful nuclear explosions carried out underground could be of economic benefit to India without environmental hazards." Exactly after one year on 15th November 1973 she informed the honourable members of the Rajya Sabha of the continuing interest of the Atomic Energy Commission in this field and also stated that after satisfactory answers to the problems of the possible effects on environmental and ecological conditions are available, the question of actual underground test for peaceful purposes could be considered.

On 18th May 1974, at 8.5 am, hours India had detonated its first atomic device at Pokharan (Rajasthan). The Nehru-Bhabha combination provided India's nuclear programme a chain of nuclear research and development facilities, some of them matching the most advanced in the West. Now India, had acquired capability in nuclear sphere which also means scientific, technological and industrial acquisitions right from the stage of uranium mining to developing fuels for various reactor types-designing, building and operating reactors, and atomic power stations. The nuclear device tested at Pokharan was the cheapest nuclear device build and tested by any nation in the world. Taking into account its nuclear capability, India's standing was distinct in two respects. First, the country ranked among top five nations in technology attainments along the entire nuclear fuel cycle – ahead of China except in the limited domain of weaponising – India had been pushed into the wilderness of nuclear have nots. Secondly, barring the leading industrial nations, no country has assimilated and developed plutonium-based technology, both for India's second generation atomic power programme and weapon-grade plutonium capability, as India had done.[26] However, the whole issue of explosion was clarified by Prime Minister Indira Gandhi. She said that India does not intend to make nuclear weapons of destruction. But nuclear technology and nuclear explosions, whether for peaceful or destructive purposes, cost the same. The main threat comes from China which has not been a friendly neighbour and has opted for development of nuclear weapons of destruction. The problem of nuclear deterrence by India is mainly a problem of developing a weapon system which will be adequate to deter the Chinese weapons system. In this situation India should not close her option of making nuclear weapons for defensive purposes.

'Nuclear deterrence' as a theory means–the threatened use of nuclear weapons, to keep someone else from actually doing what they may be contemplating of doing. The possibility of an adversary possessing such weapons influence the perception of nuclear weapon threat by a country. The estimation of the probability of war with the country concerned and of the probability of that country using or threatening to use nuclear weapons in such a war, play important roles in the development of threat perception.[27] It happened for the first time in the history of international relations that the very existence of a weapons system devised to enhance the security of great powers had become sufficiently threatening to those powers to provide them with a persistent and strong incentive to settle their differences, rather than to risk getting into situations where they might be forced to use the means of warfare they themselves had devised. This was, then, a new kind of international order, imposed not by design or by principle, but by fear.

Nuclear strategy, as a whole, can be regarded as a complex of pseudo-problem of which deterrence is a part. Since the aim of deterrence is to instill of caution without raising tensions, there is always a very fine balancing act between making the opponent fear the negative consequences of his own aggression and reassuring him that there is nothing to fear as long as he stays on a peaceful course. However, in military perspective, this balancing act becomes more delicate than ever because of their tremendous destructiveness and closely related advantage of striking first, if all out war appears imminent. Advocates of nuclear deterrence argue that offensive measures are necessary to make the deterrence credible in a period of rough strategic parity. The basic idea is that military capability will enhance stability only to the extent that you are able to convince your opponent that you are better prepared than him to fight, even if you are less inclined to start the fighting. The problem, of course, is that the things you do to deter the other side may also make him suspicious about your intentions.[28] Obviously, continuation of the regime of deterrence depends largely on how the contending powers calculate their gains and losses but with equal rationality and efficiency, which is rarely found in today's international politics.

Closely related to it is the aspect that whether the deterrence has worked in the past or not. Looking ahead begins by looking back. If the deterrence has not worked in the past it cannot work in future. Its past working can be known in two ways—by knowing facts from archives and files which were planned but not implemented due to deterrence; and second, by explaining conflict behaviour of the powers which, in fact vary from power to power and is totally unpredictable. The core of the deterrence theory seems eminently reasonable, and even self-evident. If the expected punishment exceeds the gain, the opponent will be deterred. The claim of nuclear deterrence is inherent in the claim itself, for it is seeking to explain something that did not happen–a non-event in the literal sense.[29] Because, the deterrence is a pseudo-problem and it cannot be solved, may be the reason for continuing to discuss and research. At most it should be respected as necessary category of intellectual discourse. Its discussion does not end but merely punctuate. It often demands sweeping arguments and wide-ranging perspective, while conclusions are highly circumscribed.

In practice, immediately after the Second World War, the USA was not in a position to challenge Soviet Union on political or strategic issue and it considered the bomb as a counter-weight to the massive Soviet military establishment. Being aware of bomb's destructive capabilities and its unique potential as an influence towards world peace. US president Harry S. Truman linked it directly to the political characteristics of the states possessing it, and equally important, of the international system to which they belonged. Besides deterring military aggression, this new kind of superiority was also thought to be essential for resisting Soviet attempts at intimidating the vulnerable West European democracies, keeping conventional military spending within reasonable bounds and maintaining US leadership in the emerging Western alliance. But the US monopoly over this new technology did not last long. The former Soviet Union was the most concerned, who put all its resources available to break US monopoly, as told by Stalin that technology has shaken the world and destroyed the balance as well. It feared attack on Soviet camp and expected the Americans to use their exclusive possession of atomic bombs to impose their political and economic schemes in Europe. The first Soviet explosion witnessed in August 1949 and it gained retaliatory capability in mid-fifties. Thus, in the first decade of the Cold War, both the US and Soviet leadership developed what we might call a defensive nuclear ideology. They felt that nuclear weapons were essential to prevent both political blackmail and large-scale military attack by other side. Despite repeated call for disarmament, both cling to their nuclear deterrent as their best hope of maintaining peace. As a result, there have been many disputes since the war, neither power has had grievance so essential as to make a world war whether nuclear or not. They did not deter each other, they were jointly, deterred by a force external to both. This force is best called common deterrence. It served as a functional equivalent to a monopoly of violence at global level. The rivals were like Siamese twin that die when they are separated.[30] Consequently, beginning with the limited test ban and the hot-line agreement, they became entangled in security cooperation with arms control.

However, in the period of nuclear deterrence there has been a multiple divergence of expectation–all out nuclear war, non-atomic wars fought with conventional weapons, "limited nuclear war of graduated deterrence," of mere tactical use of nuclear weapons and the "counter-force strategy." Military policy can no longer be mono-emphatic as it used to be in the preatomic age. Years back George F. Kennan said that he could see no grounds whatsoever for confidence in such "frantic schemes" and did not trust the calculations on which they were based.[31] War, Kennan puts it so well, as always been an uncertain exercise and the best-laid plans thereabout are frequently confounded. Variables and unknowns in calculations are greater today than ever in the past. It is pitiable that mankind may have to resign itself entirely to the negative dynamics of the weapons race. In general for both USA and USSR but particularly for the US proliferation of nuclear weapons technology to other great powers and later on to the Third World countries was a cause of concern. In its view, to ensure its usefulness and to hinder that it should instead become a destroyer of mankind, it was first of all necessary to prevent the secrets of new weapon from falling into the wrong hands. In response to India's first nuclear test of May 1974 an ad hoc body called "London Club" with a view to tighten export controls to ensure that nuclear facilities and materials sold exclusively for peaceful use were not diverted to military purposes.[32] The London Club had seven founding members, the United States, Russia, France, Britain, Germany, Japan and Canada. Under the new guideline they made them applicable to all 'non-nuclear weapon states', that is, the whole world other than the five countries that had nuclear weapon state status under the Non-Proliferation Treaty (NTP).

Changed Milieu and Moderated Nuclear Doctrine

India's explosion of May 1974, marked a watershed in Indo-American nuclear relations and in anger the US had halted temporarily the nuclear fuel shipment to Tarapur nuclear power plant until India had reassured the United State that no American-sold nuclear material or equipment would be used to make explosives.[33] Although no evidence was produced that the blast involved a breach of contract with any foreign country with which India had nuclear collaboration, yet India was isolated in the Western nuclear community. 'India's post-1974 position on the nuclear question has become unsustainable. No one regards India's objections to the NPT absolutely valid and substantial – as the real reason why it refuses to sign the treaty.'[34] This caused serious setbacks to India's nuclear programme. No one contended that any material or equipment supplied to India by America had been used in manufacturing nuclear device. It was more to do with India emerging as a nuclear capable Third World country. On the other, as earlier, India believed that the West's pre-occupation with forcing some countries to foil their attempt to enter the nuclear club is bound to be ineffective unless non-proliferation is linked to universal disarmament.

India's decision to develop nuclear energy or to go nuclear in the future is mainly caused by its protest against the discriminatory non-proliferation treaty, but it may be a response to Pakistan and Chinese nuclear power development and lastly it may even have been a deliberate attempt to join the nuclear club. It all started with Chinese aggression against India in 1962 with China becoming a nuclear power in October 1964. In a debate in the Indian Parliament as to whether India should become a nuclear weapon country or not. While speaking on the capital outlay of the Department of Atomic Energy in the Lok Sabha on 23rd March 1963, a member of the Jana Sangh Party strongly pleaded, "India should manufacture atomic weapons in view of the threats posed by the Chinese on the borders. He contended that China possessed atomic weapons and it would be impossible for India to defend its sovereignty and territorial integrity without the nuclear power".[35] But there were other members in the Parliament who were of the opinion that India should not manufacture atomic or nuclear weapons. However, the people of India, on the contrary felt that India needed to manufacture nuclear weapons as it would not violate the Test Ban Treaty of 1963, and underground explosions were allowed nor would it be going against the spirit of non-alignment.

Further the threat to India had increased with the maturing of Sino-American relationship. Pakistan connections with China was already well-established. It was furthering renewing its connections with America. All this was a grave threat to South Asia, "Islamabad's willingness to recognise China but not India as the predominant power in South Asia aggravates India's fear of China as a hegemonistic power that is in occupation of its territory".[36] In the context of strategic, political and military implications of Pakistani nuclear capability suggested that India should also formulate a response to safeguard its security and national interests. India will have to follow such a policy that would serve it best without being sentimental or pseudo-moralistic in approach. India has to be more concerned about the explicit of the ominous United States-Pakistan strategic consensus than the mere fact of United States arms supply to that country.[37] Pakistan's keen desire for a nuclear bomb was there much before India tested her nuclear device. In Z.A. Bhutto's calculations:

(i) Pak bomb will be status symbol not only for Pakistan but for the entire Islamic world;

(ii) That it would fetch aid and oil supply from the sympathetic Muslim states; and

(iii) It would give Pakistan enough leverage to put India into the defensive.[38]

It is also to mention here that the danger of a nuclear war exists more amongst the smaller nations than amongst the super powers. The smaller nations can be provoked into using the nuclear weapons as the last alternative to national demise. In a war between India and Pakistan, it is more likely that Pakistan would be the first user of nuclear weapons. The Indian armed forces feel that when the Pakistanis are outnumbered they may use nuclear weapons to prevent the defeat of Pakistan.

In the meantime, Indira Gandhi returned to power in 1980 and her government asserted that it would be vigilant in protecting the national interests. It was necessary for India to be in touch with the latest technology. India would be committed to the peaceful use of atomic energy but would keep its nuclear option open. Despite India's problems with the United States over fuel and spare parts supplies to Tarapur, India did not accept the international safeguards. During this period the development of missile technology in India grew. After Indira Gandhi's sudden demise, Rajiv Gandhi, her eldest son became the next Prime Minister of India, who too adhered to the peaceful uses of atomic energy for the development of the country. India's first medium-range missile Agni was developed during this period. It was the most impressive achievement in self-reliance in the field of the indigenous production of ballistic missile. The development of ballistic missile capability put a long chain of missiles in future, such as Prithvi, Agni, Trishul, Nag and Akash etc. But Agni is one hundred per cent indigenous whereas Prithvi is 90 per cent indigenous. Missile Agni has even the potential of being developed into an inter-continental ballistic missle (ICBM).[39] In nutshell, India has been periodically testing nuclear-capable missiles and has made known its determination to secure its assets in space.

On policy front both Indira Gandhi and Rajiv Gandhi expressed India's views in clear terms. India has always believed in the peaceful uses of nuclear energy. Indira Gandhi addressed the 38th Sesson of the UN General Assembly in New York on 28th September 1983, and exposed the dangers of Nuclear war 'Scientists', scholars and some notable soldiers have vividly described the outcome of a future nuclear war. Imagine a hundred or thousand Hiroshimas at one time .... We can all live only if we all combine in the struggle for peace.[40] In June 1988, the then Prime Minister Rajiv Gandhi made a seminal speech at the UN General Assembly and proposed a world free of nuclear weapons, an end to be achieved through an 'Action Plan for Ushering in a Nuclear-Weapon Free and Non-Violent World Order.[41] He proposed a three-stage process of total disarmament with the account on a regime that was global, universal and non-discriminatory. Rajiv Gandhi's Plan was ranked among the bolder initiatives to rid the world of nuclear weapons along with Mikhail Gorbachev's call made two years earlier for the abolition of nuclear weapons.[42] Although USSR welcomed the proposal, the US immediately rejected the Rajiv Gandhi Plan. India, however, must continue to push for the acceptance of its ideas.

Especially, in regional context, growing relations between China and Pakistan in nuclear technology and India's tense relations with Beijing and Islamabad, New Delhi continued its policy to keep nuclear option open. But as a side effect, India's retention of the option has encouraged Pakistan to continue its weapon programme. Even if India has its own nuclear weapons, Pakistan armed with nuclear weapons could do much damage to India. By March 1987, it became clear that Pakistan possesses nuclear weapon capability. Dr. Abdul Qadir Khan, doyen of the Pakistani Nuclear establishment in a interview with a British newspaper, *The Observer*, admitted that his country already has an atomic bomb and would be prepared to use it, if its existence was threatened.[43] A short while later in a *Time Magazine* interview President Zia-Ul-Haq confirmed more or less that Dr. Khan had said and revealed, "you can virtually write today that Pakistan can build a nuclear bomb whenever it wishes......Once you have acquired the technology, which Pakistan has, you can do whatever you like".[44] At the time, it was clear that Pakistani nuclear programme was based on two main pillars. Firstly, nuclear espionage and smuggling, and secondly, nuclear collaboration with its strategic ally, China. In the development of Pakistan's nuclear programme, China has played the central role. Probably China feels that nuclear armed Pakistan would be a crucial counter-weight to India. The development of Pakistan's nuclear weapon capability reminded the declaration of Z.A. Bhutto in 1966 as foreign minister, If India built a nuclear bomb, Pakistan would follow suit even if Pakistani had to eat grass to succeed in that venture.'[45] Pakistan had also refused to sign the Non-proliferation Treaty of 1968, simply because its arch-rival, India, had pledged not to accede to it.

The region of which India is a part, is the only region in the world in which three rival nations, sharing disputed frontiers, deeply hostile to each other and facing each other with nuclear capability. In South Asia, there is hostility between India and Pakistan on the one hand and between India and China on the other. The situation has reached the post proliferation stage with India and Pakistan both possessing weapons-grade fissile material and the means of delivering nuclear arms. The situation further aggravated as in the nineties the Chinese continued to provide technical assistance to Pakistan. Apart from statements on the part of Pakistan's government about its nuclear explosive devices, the Reagan administration had convincing evidence that China was helping Pakistan to operate its Kahuta uranium-enrichment plant and had given Pakistan a nuclear bomb design. China had given Pakistan enough weapons-grade uranium to fuel two nuclear weapons. In the circumstances, it is most unlikely that India would use nuclear weapons against a non-nuclear Pakistan. This would be because of India's conventional superiority. But Pakistan too gained nuclear capability around mid-1980s. An American estimated the Pakistan had established the manufacturing capacity to produce five to six bomb quantities of enriched uranium in 1985. As per the estimates of SIPRI, by 1992 Pakistan had enriched uranium sufficient for six to ten bombs.[46] Again by the time the Indian nuclear option had come under increasing siege with the five declared nuclear powers joining hands for the first time to enforce non-proliferation as a global norm. These nuclear powers had begun targeting India through the Comprehensive Test Ban Treaty (CTBT) and the proposed Fissile Materials Cut-Off Treaty (FMCT). It was this pressure that prompted two previous governments—Narasimha Rao in late 1995 and, Atal Bihari Vajpayee in May 1996, to order a nuclear test, although they retreated from their plan at the eleventh hour. H.D. Devegowda and I.K. Gujral governments also seriously considered nuclear testing. Earlier, with the assumption of BJP-led government in New Delhi the induction of nuclear weapons came on top of highly emotional domestic debate. Atal Bihari Vajpayee, the leader of the new coalition, pledged to exercise all options, including the nuclear option.

The Party in its election manifesto believed that the time has come to re-evaluate the country's nuclear policy and induct nuclear weapons.

Again on 19th March 1998, Atal Bihari Vajpayee became the Prime Minister of India as a head of the BJP-led coalition government and fulfilled the promise of nuclear test made in the election manifesto. After 24 years India had conducted successfully on 11th and 13th May 1998 five nuclear tests, three and two respectively. Going by numbers, most experts have projected the Indian capability to build nuclear weapons to be somewhere between 15 to 60 Hiroshima-type warheads. One recent estimate has put India's weapons-grade plutonium stocks by the end of 1995 at about 330 kg approximately. This study suggests that this stockpile may be translated into 60 warheads at 6 kg per weapon.[47] In another study made earlier India's stocks put at 200 to 250 kg until 1988, which translated into a little over a dozen weapons.[48] The Indian Prime Minister in an announcement said, "today at 3.45 pm conducted three underground nuclear tests in the Pokharan range. The tests conducted were with the fission device, a low-yield device and a thermonuclear device. The measured yields are in line with expected values." The opposition leaders, the former Prime Ministers : V.P. Singh, P.V. Narasimha Rao, Inder Kumar Gujral and other prominent leaders were stunned by Vajpayee's daring gamble but at the same-time unwilling to differ with him.[49] Vajpayee's government had perhaps tested India's nuclear weapons in order to enhance the country's security in the face of mounting evidence of Sino-Pak collaboration in the development of nuclear weapons and missile. This time Pakistan not only criticised bitterly India for explosions, but as expected, evened its nuclear test account with India by exploding five nuclear test on 28th May 1998. Islamabad exploded one more test on 30th May 1998, and became ahead of India in this regard. Shamshad Ahmed, Pakistan's Foreign Secretary in a statement said that Pakistan was willing to enter into talks to resolve all issues, including prevention of nuclear proliferation in the region. Pakistan's decision to exercise nuclear options is only for self-defence and to deter aggression.[50] In general, Pakistan had two basic compulsions for this nuclear tit-for-tat. First, Islamabad had to prove to India in particular and the world at large that its nuclear capability was not a fib but very real. Second and by far more vital to the survival of Nawaz Sharif government, was the dire need to reply to India's test with an exactly identical display of nuclear prowess.

As a follow up of the election manifesto, Vajpayee government re-evaluated India's nuclear in present national/ global context and issued a draft nuclear doctrine on 17th August 1999. According to military dictionary, a nuclear doctrine is a set of published or unpublished principles concerning the physical or psychological employment of nuclear weapons. Apart from reflecting a country's threat perceptions and assets, these doctrines are too often infused with ideology and national ethos. They remain only the guiding force and are not necessarily binding in practice. These principles may be found in governmental documents, official statements, or strategic debates amongst top officials and strategists.[51] In the long run, there are various other factors like a nation's political commitment and resolve as also its financial and technical capabilities that determine the nature and potential of its nuclear profile. But at the end, the exact nature of the nuclear assets as also their operational nuclear doctrine are shaped by a country's perceived security threat which in turn dictate a country's nuclear doctrine.[52] However, any analysis of a nation's nuclear posture has to be understood in the context of its threat perceptions first and only later in relation to other available assets, even if these assets, like nuclear weapons, may be directly responsible for determining threat perceptions. Traditionally, nuclear forces have been known as political weapon and not weapons of war. In the situation any such comparison of numbers, range-yield, dates, etc., can serve only a very limited purpose of outlining each country's nuclear profile.

The need for re-evaluation of India's nuclear policy was felt at large about the kind of system that we have evolved for ourselves. While the world all round us is in rapid transition, our national security system is marked by a complete absence of flexibility, innovation or imagination. It seems to be stubbornly committed to outmoded structures and systems, and shows a strange devotion to archaic thought processes. The reason is simple; we have failed to put in place the systems, structures, procedures and organisations that will enable efficient defence planning as well as effective operational employment of all the forces that we acquire.[53] Of late, the strategic environment has changed a great deal since 1998 and it is time for our Nuclear Doctrine to be urgently reviewed and revised. Not all the nuclear submarines, air craft carriers, in-flight refuellers or strike corps can provide us security unless we reform the defence system.

The Indian nuclear doctrine aims at providing India a credible minimum deterrent at an affordable pace of expenditure to create uncertainty in the minds of would-be nuclear intimidators, aggressors, and interventionists that those actions against this country would not be rational options.[54] The released document reflected the collective wisdom of India's strategic community as it represented the consensus view of the National Security Council Advisory Board (NSCAB). Like the Chinese official statement of 16th October 1964. India's doctrine asserted its commitment to disarmament, no first use, and self-defence as its major pillars. But more than the Chinese statement, Indian doctrine talks of developing a 'credible minimum nuclear deterrence with high-degree of priority being laid on ensuring the safety and survivability of India's nuclear forces.[55] Broadly, commitment to disarmament, no more physical tests, no-first use, self-defence and minimum credible nuclear deterrence can be described to be the five major elements of India's nuclear doctrine. From the basic principles of India's nuclear doctrine other components may also be derived-as-strategic triad, punitive retaliation in rapid response and shift from peacetime deployment to fully employable forces in the shortest possible time. In addition, Indian doctrines are not a copy of western doctrines because they do not subscribe to war fighting as the West did, they do not involve delegation of powers and they rule out first use. If these basic differences are understood, then one would know that the Indian nuclear doctrine is as different from the western doctrine as 'chalk is from cheese'. In general, the nuclear doctrine of India is considered as eminently sensible, extremely logical and moderate having no risk and no possibility of arms race in the region.

The core of deterrence, especially for a country which commits itself to no-first use is its ability to carry out punitive unacceptable retaliation. This is not cold war language but the appropriate language to communicate to the nuclear warriors who believe in the use of nuclear weapons first. Unless one opts to allow its society and nation to be destroyed in a cold-blooded first strike by the adversary and not do anything to deter him, it is logical to make it clear to such nuclear adversaries the consequences of his restorting to a first strike. The word unacceptable damage does not carry today the connotations of the Mutual Assured Destruction (WMD) age of Robert MacNamara and Zbigniew Brezinski. It is now recognised that one bomb on one city is unacceptable. Therefore, those who believe in wielding nuclear weapons to intimidate other nations and in the first use of nuclear weapons have to be deterred by spelling out the consequences of their actions.[56] In fact, over the years the role of nuclear weapons has undergone a subtle but important changes in deterrence strategy. The principles of nuclear deterrence are beginning to alter in a way that could profoundly impact on the still evolving post-Cold War security order. The ongoing change in affecting the face of deterrence, but not its primary purpose. Deterrence will still centre on achieving strategic objectives not through military victory in a nuclear conflict, but with the threat of war. Since, the threat has to realistically-based on ready, deliverable nuclear weapons, the symbiosis of deterrence and use will remain the key reality of the nuclear world.[57] For India, the changing face of deterrence and the emerging triangular strategic offence/defence relationship among the US, China and Russia carry important implications. In a complex world marked by conflicting trends, it is apparent that each deterrent relationship will be different from the other, premised on principles at variance with classical deterrence theory. The concept of mutually assured destruction is losing relevance. Hence, deterrence has to be constructed on principles radically different from notions of qualitative or quantitative.

Although the concept of minimal deterrence is admittedly imprecise in quantitative terms, its foundations are as much psychological as logical since it hinges on how much damage would be "unacceptable" to your adversary. Nevertheless, certain basic aspects of minimal deterrence are clear. Firstly, it does not call for a boundless open-ended arsenal. It does not even require that your offensive weapons match in number or strength those of your adversaries. It only demands that you have enough capability, in second strike to inflict "unacceptable damage" to the other side, should they be so foolish as to initiate a nuclear attack on us. In context of damage that the simplest fission weapon can do has been explicitly demonstrated in the holocaust of Hiroshima and Nagasaki. Today major cities are densely populated and if a fission weapon equal to that dropped in Japan, can kill at least double strength or over a 150,000 people.[58] Surely, this should be "unacceptable damage" to even a remotely responsible leadership in any modern country. Some people's argument of Jihadi militants taking over in Pakistan and such a fanatical leadership willing to accept such a damage are in the category of rare possibility. But any leadership that finds such a huge civilian fatalities "acceptable" is in any case beyond pale of rationality. It cannot be relied upon to feel deterred by the prospect of even a much larger attack. Deterrence has no meaning in that situation and building a larger, thermonuclear weapon is not the answer to such an irrational, suicidal adversary.[59] In short, a thermonuclear hydrogen bomb is not crucial for minimal deterrence. Standard 20kT fission weapons will be more than suffice. Pokharan I and II have exploded those successfully. The first and foremost aim of our nuclear arsenal is only to deter others from attacking us and not to wage nuclear wars or to maximise casualties on the other side as an end in itself.

In India's policy of no-first use and retaliation only the survivability of our arsenal is crucial. This is a dynamic concept related to the strategic environment, technological imperatives and needs of national security. The doctrine aims at clearly stating in unambiguous terms that any threat of use of nuclear weapons against India shall invoke measures to counter that threat and that any nuclear attack on India and its forces shall result in punitive retaliation with nuclear weapons to inflict damage unacceptable to the aggressor. With this aim in view, several experts consider that there are good reasons for creating a nuclear triad, which simply refers to the three legs that comprise most nuclear forces, the land-based international ballistic missiles (ICBMs), strategic bombers, and submarine-based long-range missiles. All nuclear powers have had, or aspire to create such nuclear triads. Despite their individual advantages and disadvantages taking together they tend to cancel out the various disadvantages to create a robust, safe, and relatively invulnerable deterrent force.[60] For example, land-based strategic bombers are large and soft targets. Land-based missiles are similarly vulnerable, because their locations cannot be kept secret from energy spy-satellites. But land-based missiles, usually deployed in underground soils, can be hardened to a certain degree so that they can survive anything but a direct hit. Likewise, a submarine-based nuclear deterrent force has also advantages and disadvantages: Submarines, especially nuclear missile submarines which rarely come to the surface, are notoriously difficult to detect and track, which makes them the most invulnerable leg of the nuclear triad. Thus, a nuclear triad, which includes all the legs of the triad, reduces the dangers, vulnerabilities and insecurity associated with any single leg. Because India will never see any merit in using nuclear weapons to strike first, it is fundamentally crucial for us with our defensive doctrine and a no-first use philosophy to ensure survivability of the nuclear arsenal to enable retaliation.[61] It is this capability which will deter the aggressor from taking recourse to war and hence provide deterrence and peace and tranquillity so essential to the development of the nation.

The draft of India's nuclear doctrine issued in August 1999 was subsequently formalised with some modifications in 2003. It explicitly stated that the country is pursuing nuclear deterrence though this was qualified as a minimal one. It also warns that "nuclear retaliation to a first strike will be massive and designed to inflict unacceptable damage."[62] Unacceptable damage, in plain English, means that these nuclear weapons would be dropped on cities, each killing lakhs or millions of innocent people. But India, unlike the cold warriors of the fifties, embarked on making nuclear weapons not as a war fighting arsenal or for use in a massive first strike, but only as an instrument of minimal nuclear deterrence. This deterrence was to be achieved with "......sufficient nuclear weapons to inflict destruction and punishment that the aggressor will find unacceptable...."[63] This policy has been repeatedly underlined and reiterated several times by the government of the day, despite efforts by hawks bent on adopting a more aggressive nuclear posture. Even very recently S.M. Krishna, India's Minister for External Affairs asserted that there would be no revision of India's no first use nuclear doctrine and said minimum credible deterrence would be maintained in view of threats and challenges. "On the nuclear doctrine, I would only like to say that there is no change in our policy. We are committed to universal, non-discriminatory nuclear disarmament and we remain firm on the commitment", he said.

In fact, since the time India became a declared nuclear power state in May 1998, there has been a concerted campaign, particularly by non-proliferation lobbies in western countries, echoed by analysts in China and Pakistan, to spread the notion that India's strategic programme has been driven by considerations of prestige and propaganda, rather than by any real security threats. Even some Indian commentators also consider that India's dominant objective is political and technological prestige, while for every other nuclear weapon state it is deterrence.[64] Only as a followup of the policy of nuclear doctrine India adopted in January 2003 formally at a meeting of the Cabinet Committee on Security, it has taken a series of graduated steps to put in place a triad of land-based, air delivered and submarine-based nuclear forces to confirm to its doctrine of no-first use and retaliation only. Currently, at least two legs of the triad are fully operational. These include a modest arsenal, nuclear capable aircraft and missiles, both in fixed underground silos and those mounted on mobile, rail and road-based platforms. Land-based missiles include both Agni-II (1500 km) as well as Agni-III (2500 km). The range and accuracy of further versions for example Agni-V (5000 km) has been tested successfully only recently and will improve with the further acquisition of technological capability and experience.[65] Further work for the third leg of the triad is in progress. We need a minimum of three Arihant class nuclear submarines so that at least one will always be at sea. The submarine-based Sagarika missiles have been developed and tested but are still relatively short in range. It is expected that a modest sea-based deterrent will be in place by 2015 or 2016.

Organisations and Nuclear Plant Materials

The most significant fact relating to India's place in the nuclear realm is that this is the area of advanced technology and credit for this will solely go the Nehru-Bhabha. As a result of their vision, India has been able to lay a sound foundation; build an extensive infrastructure backed by research and development and achieve capability along the entire nuclear fuel cycle. Capability along the entire nuclear fuel cycle also means scientific, technological and industrial acquisitions right from the stage of uranium mining to developing fuels for various reactor types, designing, building and operating reactors, and atomic power stations.[66] However, the root of India's nuclear history may be traced back to 1944 when Dr. Homi J. Bhabha wrote a letter to Sir Dorabji Tata Trust narrating the need of a nuclear power plant in India. One year later it led to the establishment of a nuclear research centre and Dr. Bhabha became its Director. At the time Jawaharlal Nehru compared the "Atomic Revolution" to the "Industrial Revolution" arguing that "either you go ahead with it or....others go ahead, and you.....gradually drag yourself".[67] With this aim in view, India from the beginning, took keen interest in the development of nuclear power capability that resulted in a chain of nuclear research and development facilities, some of them matching the most advanced in the West.

After independence in 1948, the Atomic Energy Commission (AEC) was established on the basis of Atomic Energy Act passed by the Government of India. It was policy body which provides for the development and control of atomic energy and purposes connected herewith. The Act allowed for the control of atomic energy by the Central Government. Then in 1954, the Department of Atomic Energy (DAE) was set up to encompass research, technology development and commercial reactor operation. Later the Act of 1948 was replaced by another Act of 1962. This act too provided for the development and control of atomic energy for the welfare of the country. This act sought to keep in view India's security concerns. By this time Britain and France had also become nuclear powers. The current Atomic Energy Act is of 1962, and it permits only government-owned enterprises to be involved in nuclear power. However, in regard to nuclear liability India's 1962 Atomic Energy Act says nothing about liability or compensation in the event of an accident. Also, India is not a party to the relevant international nuclear liability conventions held in Vienna, in 1997, on Supplementary Compensation for Nuclear Damage. But since all civil nuclear facilities are owned and must be majority-owned by the Central Government, the liability issues arising from these installations are its responsibility. On 10th September 2008, the Government assured the USA that India "shall take all steps necessary to adhere to the Convention on Supplementary Compensation (CSC)". The Civil Liability for Nuclear Damage Act related to third party liability was passed by both the Houses of Parliament in August 2010.

The Department of Atomic Energy (DAE) has a long list of associated institutions/organisations. It includes the Nuclear Power Co-operation of India Limited (NPCIL), Uranium Corporation of India Limited (UCIL mining and processing), Atomic Mineral Directorate for Exploration and Research (AMD, exploration), Electronics Corporation of India Limited (ECIL reactor control and instrumentation), and Bharatiya Nabhikiya Vidyut Nigam (BHAVINI) for setting up fast reactors. The DAE also controls the Heavy Water Board for production of heavy water and the Nuclear Fuel Complex for fuel and component manufacture. In sphere of research and development, the Atomic Energy Commission took the decision to set up the Bhabha Atomic Research Centre (BARC) at Trombay near Mumbai. A series of research reactors and critical facilities was built here. India had built Asia's first atomic research reactor, Apsara, and set in motion a broad-based nuclear programme. Cirus was built in 1960 under the Colombo Plan, followed by Dhruva in 1985 with fuel cycle facilities. Cirus uses natural uranium fuel, is moderated by heavy water and cooled by light water. It was supplied with heavy water from the USA and India's weapons material initially came from this Canadian-designed research reactor. Probably, it was only after the 1962 war that it was employed largely to make weapon-grade plutonium. Development of nuclear weapons apparently began in 1967. It is estimated that India may have built up enough weapon-grade plutonium for one hundred nuclear warheads. In response to India's 1974 nuclear test explosion using Plutonium from Cirus, demonstrating that nuclear technology transferred to non-nuclear weapons state for peaceful purposes could be misused the Nuclear Suppliers' Group (NSG) was formed and began regulating nuclear trade, particularly with India. This is one reason why the closure of Cirus is a condition of the NSG waiver in 2008, and the government undertook to shut down Cirus at the end of 2010. On the other Dhruva was fully designed and built indigenously, and uses metallic uranium fuel with heavy water as moderator and coolant. Dhruva is extensively used in neutron beam research studies involving material science and nuclear fission processes. It is India's high flux research reactor, capable of producing 25 kilograms of weapons-grade plutonium annually.[68] Both Cirus and Dhruva units are assumed to be largely for military purposes.

In line two other organisations were set up. The Indira Gandhi Centre for Atomic Research (IGCAR) at Kalpakkam was set up in 1971 while further in 1989 the Board of Radiation and Isotope Technology (BRIT) was separated from the BARC. At Kalpakkam two civil research reactors are preparing for stage two of the thorium cycle. Bhavini is located here and draws upon the centre's expertise and that of NPCIL in establishing the fast reactor programme. The separated BRIT is responsible for radio isotopes production. The research reactor Apsara, Cirus and Dhruva are used, along with RAPS for cabalt-60. A regular supply of isotopes for various uses commenced in early 1960s after Cirus became operational.

In 1984, a body called Atomic Energy Regulatory Board (AERB) was formed which comes under the Atomic Energy Commission but was independent of Department of Atomic Energy. Since inception it has evolved into a strong professional organisation. It reviews the design, construction, and operation of all nuclear installations and certifies the acceptability of operations and maintenance personnel. In addition to the safety of nuclear power stations, it is concerned with the safety of nuclear fuel activities and heavy water plants, and the safe management of industrial and medical radiographic equipment. Related to this is the disposal of the radioactive waste products that result from the nuclear fission process. In the context India's policy is to use what is called a 'closed fuel cycle'. The fuel after irradiation in a reactor is reprocessed to remove the plutonium and unburnt uranium. These two are fuel materials which can be used in a fast breeder reactor.[68] The fast breeder reactors reduce the amount of waste that needs ultimate storage under surveillance, a further reduction is possible when using Accelerators Driver Systems (ADS). Ultimately, India has plans to develop such systems in the third phase of the programme. However, following the two important initial accidents at nuclear power installations, at Three Mile Island in the US in 1979, and at Chernobyl in the former Soviet Union in 1986, nuclear industry leaders from all over the world got together for serious introspection. In a rare gesture of solidarity, unknown in the Cold War era, industry leaders from all over the world including the US, Europe, Japan, the USSR and Eastern Europe, gathered in Moscow in the summer of 1989 to launch the World Association of Nuclear Operators (WANO). Its objective was to spread the culture of safe operation of nuclear power plants through the sharing of operating experience, emulation of best practices and peer reviewing of operating plants to indentify improvements to enhance performance.[69] After the incidents Indian Prime Minister Rajiv Gandhi said that he would sanction new nuclear power projects only after he was satisfied with the emergency preparedness plans.

But after the nuclear plant accident at Fukushima, Japan, in March 2011 many countries of the world including India initiated a reconsideration of the role of nuclear power in their current and future energy portfolios and check of their safety features at operating plants. In India the Atomic Energy Regulatory Board is the main organisation concerned with nuclear safety in India. Although legally it is independent of the Department of Energy, in practice, it has long been criticised for being subservient to DAE, the promoting organisation for nuclear power. Historically, nuclear policy in India was not transparent and involved only a handful of people in the government. The Department of Atomic Energy has exploited this arrangement. Unfortunately, the political leadership left the operational aspects of nuclear affairs entirely to DAE without creating any institutional mechanism for independent technical and policy advice on civilian as well as military aspects. The AERB, in particular, had failed to prepare an overall nuclear radiation safety planning policy as required in 1983, and had failed to set up radiation safety directorates in 35 administrative areas to ensure the safe use of radiation in medical and industrial facilities as required by a 2001 Supreme Court order. It had undertaken only 15 per cent of the recommended level of inspections at industrial radiography and radiotherapy units, relative to International Atomic Energy Agency (IAEA) norms, and had not achieved cost recovery from licenses. These present a very poor picture of AERB's performance in nuclear related affairs.

Once again in post – Fukushima period the existence of AERB has been questioned from various quarters. The issue of nuclear plant safety was raised and S.S. Bajaj, the Chairman of AERB, assured, "We do not allow any of the reactors to operate unless all emergency plans are in place. The operators, NPCIL have to conduct an actual exercise before getting clearance for operation of the plant and also the exercises are repeated every two years". He added further, "of course, after this incident, new lessons are there for all the nuclear community to improve and fine-tune the existing emergency preparedness. We will review it in the light of the recent Japanese incident."[70] However, the overall performance of the AERB was not satisfactory and it was severely criticised by the Comptroller and Auditor General (CAG) in August 2012. A parliamentary report from the CAG on the AERB pointed out serious organisational flaws and numerous failings relating to international norms. The most fundamental issue highlighted by the report was the unsatisfactory legal status and authority of the AERB. Despite India's international commitments, awareness of best practice and internal expert recommendations, the report said, ' the legal status of AERB continued to be that of an authority subordinate to the Central Government, with powers delegated to it by the latter. According to the CAG report the organisation had failed to develop a mechanism to ensure regulatory compliance or oversee the procedures for radiological emergencies.

Although the themes of the CAG report were largely anticipated, after its coming out and in response to events of Fukushima the need for an independent, new regulatory body became imminent. A Gopalakrishnan, former AERB Chairman, in an article in December 2011, argued forcefully for an independent regulatory mechanism along the lines of the Nuclear Safety Authority (ASN) in France, the Nuclear Regulatory Commission (NRC) in the US and the Canadian Nuclear Safety Commission (CNSC). All these organisations, are independent, free of political and corporate influence, transparent, and communicate regularly with the public.[71] Earlier, after Fukushima sixteen nuclear scientists including Anil Kakodkar, former head of the Department of Atomic Energy said in their letter, "We are confident that only nuclear power that avoids being a threat to the health and safety of the population and to the environment is acceptable to society". They also added, "It is necessary to ensure that national nuclear safety regulators in all countries are fully independent in their decision-making on nuclear safety and to assure their competence, resources and enforcement authorities".[72]

As a result on 7th September 2011, the Government tabled in the Lok Sabha the much-awaited Nuclear Safety Regulation Authority Bill, 2011. It is being created ostensibly to bring about much-needed independence and transparency in administering the safety oversight of nuclear operations in India. If passed properly the Bill would create two bodies – Council of Nuclear Safety (CNS) and the Nuclear Safety Regulatory Authority (NSRA). Established as per Clause 5 of the Bill, the CNS will oversee and review nuclear and radiation safety policies and connected matters (Clause 7). One of its first tasks will be to constitute two search committees, one to select the chairperson and the other to select the members of the NSRA. Based on such selection, the Central Government will constitute the NSRA. The Clauses in the Bill are strong enough reason to insist that the final appointment of the chairperson and members of the regulatory authority should be made by Parliament, and not by the Government. In addition, the Bill authorises the Central Government to give formal directions and orders, some by means of notification to the NSRA, which the Authority has to mandatory obey. The CNS will be chaired of by the Prime Minister and will have as its members five or more Cabinet Ministers, the Cabinet Secretary, the Chairman of the Atomic Energy Commission and an assortment of "eminent experts" nominated by the Central Government.[73] The Nuclear Safety Regulatory Authority (NSRA) will be responsible for ensuring radiation safety in all civilian sector activities and will take over the functions of the existing AERB. Because of its various provisions which make the NSRA weak and subordinate to CNS, the proposed Bill has been severely criticised by many and it is said generally that this new body, NSRA will have fewer powers, and less independence than the present authority, the Atomic Energy Regulatory Board (AERB).

From the beginning of its nuclear development policy India has been working to design and develop a prototype atomic reactor by using thorium and low-enriched uranium. India's domestic uranium reserves are small and the country is dependent on imports to fuel its nuclear power industry. According to a report issued by the International Atomic Energy Agency, India has limited uranium reserves, consisting of approximately 54,636 tonnes of "reasonably assured resources," 25,245 tonnes of estimated additional resources", 15,488 tonnes of "undiscovered conventional resources," and 17,000 tonnes of "speculative resources". As per NPCIL estimates, these reserves are only sufficient to generate about 10 GWe for about 40 years.

It comprises only around 1-2 per cent of the global uranium reserves. In contrast to this figure as per official estimates shared in the country's Parliament in August 2011, the country can obtain 846,477 tonnes of thorium from 963,000 tonnes of Th02, which in turn can be obtained from 10.7 million tonnes of monazite occurring in beaches and river sands in association with other heavy metals. Indian monazite contains about 9-10 per cent Th02. Further, it was clarified in Parliament on 21st, March 2012, that "out of nearly 100 deposits of the heavy minerals, at present only 17 deposits containing about four million tonnes of monazite have been identified as exploitable. Mineable reserves are 70 per cent of identified exploitable resources. Therefore, about 225,000 tonnes of thorium metal is available for nuclear power programme. In comparison to uranium, India's thorium reserves are bigger, around 12-33 per cent of global reserves according to IAEA and US Geological Survey. Thorium is perhaps the best solution possible in the future and would be technologically and commercially the best option in another two decades. It is slightly lighter than uranium and its reserves are far more abundant by about four times than the traditional nuclear fuel.[74] It is believed that the amount of energy contained in the Thorium reserves on earth is more than the combined total energy that is left in petroleum, coal, other fossil fuels, and uranium all put together. The IAEA Report of 2005 on Thorium fuels indicated that India might have the largest reserves of Thorium in the world.

In order to develop nuclear energy two important raw materials are needed : uranium, and, to a lesser extent, thorium. In the circumstances, Indian scientists from the start began to conduct significant research in the use of thorium for energy generation and they designed a full-fledged thorium-based nuclear reactor. Dr. Homi J. Bhabha, the chief architect of India's nuclear programme conceived the idea of the three-stage nuclear programme as a way to develop nuclear energy by working around country's limited uranium resources. It was a thorium-based programme in which thorium will be most exploited in the third stage, because it is itself not a fissile material and thus, cannot undergo fission to produce energy. Therefore, for us, a closed fuel cycle involving reprocessing of uranium and thorium has been an integral part of our policy from the beginning of our nuclear energy programme. While our interest in thorium arises primarily due to the huge energy potential that thorium provides for us, it is now becoming increasingly clear that the thorium fuel cycle also offers several advantages with respect to proliferation resistance.[75] Since thorium by itself does not have a fissile component, it needs initial fissile inputs. Enriched uranium with thorium makes for an efficient fuel that could produce as much energy from mined uranium and leads to used fuel that can be recycled with a much-reduced proliferation risk. Uranium enrichment has thus a special significance in the context of the thorium-based proliferation resistant fuel cycle as well.

Contextually, being the largest owner of thorium and also being amongst the nations which will see the highest surge in power demand with its growth, the opportunity is for India to pursue its existing nuclear programme with a special focus on research and development on the thorium route as the long-term sustainable option. Apart from this thorium has many other advantages. It is estimated that thorium may be able to generate eight times, the amount of energy per unit mass compared to natural uranium. Thorium produces waste that is relatively less toxic due to the absence of minor actinides. At the same time, it is acknowledged that the long-lived high-level waste from uranium especially in light of the Indian strategy of adopting the close fuel cycle involving reprocessing for the recovery of plutonium and uranium, can be effectively managed using technologies available today.

However, despite relative goodness of thorium, uranium became the popular choice for nuclear energy programmes for two reasons: One is technological and the other is historical. The technological reason stems from the simple fact that at first one needs to produce Uranium-233 from thorium, and for this, reactors based on the naturally available nuclear fuel material, Uranium-235, are required. In addition, the recovery of Uranium-233 by large scale reprocessing of irradiated thorium, as well as the likely presence of hard gamma emitting uranium-232, pose certain practical hardles. But according to experts, all these can be overcome technologically. The second reason comes from uranium's advantage of being able to provide thorium-based fuel and due to unstable geo-political conditions thorium cannot be weaponised.[76] Unlike thorium, uranium is a source of power in world politics having destructive applications in times of emergency. Thorium bombs just cannot be made. Even today much of the current civil nuclear applications are direct offshoots of the military nuclear technologies of the Cold War period. But keeping in view the benefits of thorium, various technologies are already being developed and deployed on a test basis across the world including India.

India's Nuclear Power Uptodate

Nuclear power is the fourth largest source of electricity in India after thermal, hydro-electric and renewable sources of electricity. At present India has 20 nuclear reactors in operation in six nuclear power plants generating 4,780 MW, while seven other reactors are under construction which are expected to generate an additional 5,300 MW with many more about 39 reactors, are firmly proposed. In general uranium, plutonium and thorium are the fuel substances used in various types of nuclear reactors. There is no dearth of thorium in India, but in contrast, it has a very limited availability of uranium and country's necessity is mainly dependent on import from other countries. Plutonium is a by-product of uranium and obtained largely when uranium is in use in nuclear reactors. For nuclear fuels exploration is carried out by the Atomic Minerals Directorate for Exploration and Research (AMD). Mining and processing of uranium is carried out by Uranium Corporation of India Limited (UCIL), also a subsidiary of the Department of Atomic Energy. The exploration and mining works/discoveries are done across the country particularly in states like Jharkhand, Andhra Pradesh, Meghalaya, Karnataka, Chattisgarh, Himachal Pradesh, Maharashtra, Uttar Pradesh etc. The AMD and UCIL, with the help and advice of the Department of Atomic Energy are carrying out the fuel-related plans for the development of nuclear power in India.

India's Uranium Mines and Mills Existing and Planned

State, district	Mine	Mill	Year of Operation
Jharkhand	Jaduguda	Jaduguda	1967 (mine) 1968 (mill)
	Bhatin	Jaduguda	1967
	Narwapahar	Jaduguda	1995
	Bagjata	Jaduguda	2008
Jharkhand, East Sighbum district	Turamdih	Turamdih	2003 (mine) 2008 (mill)
	Banduhurang	Turamdih	2007
	Mohuldih	Turamdih	2012
Andhra Pradesh, Kadapa District	Tummalapalle	Tummalapalle	2012
Andhra Pradesh, Nalgonda District	Lambapur-Peddagattu	Seripally Mallapuram	2016
Karnataka, Gulbarga District	Gogi	Diggi/Saidpur	2014
Meghalaya	Kylling-Pyndeng Sohiong-Mawthabah (KMP), (Domiasiat) Wakhyn	Mawthabah	2017

In the early years of independence Dr. Homi J. Bhabha conceived of the three-stage nuclear programme as a way to develop nuclear energy by working around India's limited uranium resources. At the time, the Indian government also recognised that thorium was a source that could provide power to the Indian people for the long term. Since then India has been making advances in the field of thorium-based fuels, working to design and develop a prototype for an atomic reactor using thorium and low-enriched uranium. As the known reserves of uranium are less, the aim of long range atomic power programme in India must therefore to be the base of nuclear power generation as soon as possible on thorium rather than uranium. However, the generation of atomic power stations based on natural uranium can only be used to start off an atomic power programme......The plutonium produced by the first generation power stations can be used in second generation of power stations designed to produce electric power and convert thorium into U-233, or depleted uranium into more plutonium with breeding gain......... The second generation of power stations may be regarded as an intermediate step for the breeder power stations of the third generation all of which would produce more U-233 than they burn in the course of producing power. Uranium used for the weapons programme has been separated from the programme, using uranium from indigenous reserves. The domestic reserve of 80,000 to 112,000 tonnes of uranium is large enough to supply all of India's commercial and military reactors as well as supply all the needs of India's nuclear weapons arsenal. Currently, India's nuclear power reactors consume at most, 478 tonnes of uranium per year. Even if India were quadruple its nuclear power output to 20 GW by 2020, nuclear power generation would only consume 2000 tonnes of uranium per annum. Furthermore, the uranium requirements of India's nuclear arsenal are only fifteenth (1/15) of that required for power generation, meaning that India's domestic fissile material supply is more than enough to meet its strategic and power requirements for the foreseeable future. Indian President A.P.J. Abdul Kalam also stated while in office, "energy independence is India's first and highest priority. India has to go for nuclear power generation in a big way using thorium-based reactors. Thorium a non-fissile material is available in abundance in our country".

Around mid-1950s Dr. Bhabha presented his three-stage plan for national development and four years later (1958), the Indian government adopted the same. On the basis of the three-stage plan assuming optimistic development times many predictions were made over the years. Bhabha himself announced that there would be 8,000 MW of nuclear power in the country by 1980. The Atomic Energy Commission predicted that by 2000 there would be 43,500 MW of nuclear generating capacity. All of this was before a single unit of nuclear electricity was produced in the country. Reality was quite different. Installed capacity in 1979-80 was about 600 MW, about 950 MW in 1987, and 2720 MW in 2000. In 2007, after five decades of sustained and generous government financial support, nuclear power, capacity was just 3,310 MW, less than three per cent of India's total power generation capacity. Going a further step in a prospective way the Integrated Energy Policy of India estimated the share of nuclear power in the total primary energy mix to be between 4 per cent to 6 per cent in various scenarios by the year 2031-32. A study by the DAE, estimated that the nuclear energy share will be about 8.6 per cent by the year 2032 and 16.6 per cent by the year 2052. The 63 GW expected by 2032 will be achieved by setting up 16-indigenous Pressurised Heavy Water Reactors (PHWRs), of which ten is to be based on reprocessed uranium. Till date India believes that the development of future nuclear power is totally depend on Bhabha's three-stage programme. In the year 2009 Dr. Manmohan Singh, India's Prime Minister also stated that the nation could generate up to 470 GW power is 2050 if it managed the three-stage programme well. "This will sharply reduce our dependence on fossil fuels and will be a major contribution to global efforts to combat climate change." According to plan, 30 per cent of the Indian electricity by 2050 will be generated from thorium-based reactors.

In the first stage of the programme, natural uranium fuelled pressurised heavy water reactors (PHWRs) produce electricity while generating plutonium-239 as by product. PHWRs was a natural choice for implementing the first stage because it had the most efficient reactor design in terms of uranium utilisation, and the existing Indian infrastructure in the 1960s allowed for quick adoption of the PHWR technology. At the time India correctly calculated that it would be easier to create heavy water production facilities than uranium enrichment facilities required for LWRs. Natural uranium contains only 0.7 per cent of the fissile isotope uranium-235. Most of the remaining 99.3 per cent is uranium-238 which is not a fissile but can be converted in a reactor to the fissile isotope plutonium-239. Heavy water is used as moderator and coolant. Almost the entire existing base of Indian nuclear power, 4780 MW, is composed of the first stage PHWRs, with the exception of the two Boiling Water Reactor (BWRs) units at Tarapur. The installed capacity of Kaiga station is now 880 MW, making it the third largest after Tarapur, 1400 MW and Rawatbhata, 1180 MW. The remaining three power stations at Kakrapar, Kalpakkam and Narora all have two units of 220 MW, thus contributing 440 MW each to the grid. The two units of 700 MW each that are under construction at both Kakrapar and Rawatbhata and one planned for Banswara would also come under the first stage of the programme totalling a further addition of 4,200 MW. It is also to note here that India's uranium reserves are capable of generating a total power capacity of 420 GWe years, but in order to ensure that existing plant get a life-time supply of uranium, it becomes necessary to limit the number of PHWRs fuelled exclusively by indigenous uranium reserves. Capital costs of PHWRs is in the range of Rs six to seven crores, coupled with a designed plant life of 40 years. Time required for construction has improved over time and is now at about five years.

The second stage is of Fast Breeder Reactors (FBRs) and would use a mixed oxide (MOX) fuel made from plutonium-239 recovered by reprocessing spent fuel from the first stage, and natural uranium. In FBRs, plutonium-239 undergoes fission to produce energy, while the uranium-238 present in the mixed oxide fuel transmutes to additional plutonium-239. The stage-two FBRs are designed to breed more fuel than they consume. Once the inventory of plutonium-239, is built up thorium can be introduced as a blanket material in the reactor and transmuted to uranium-233 for use in the third-stage. The surplus plutonium breed in each fast reactor can be used to set up more such reactors, and thus grow the India's civil nuclear power capacity till the point where the third-stage reactors using thorium as fuel can be brought online, which is forecasted as being possible once 50-GW of nuclear power capacity has been achieved. The design of the country's first fast breeder called Prototype Fast Breeder Reactor (PFBR), was done by Indira Gandhi Centre for Atomic Research (IGCAR). Bharatiya Nabhikiya Vidyut Nigam (Bhavini), a public sector company under the Department of Atomic Energy (DAE), has been given the responsibility to build the fast reactors in India. From the construction of PFBR at Kalpakkam commercial generation of electricity is expected by 2015. In addition, the country proposes to undertake the construction of four FBRs as part of the 12th Five Year Plan spanning 2012-17, thus targeting 2500 MW from the five reactors. One of these five reactors is planned to be operated with metallic fuel instead of oxide fuel, since the design will have the flexibility to accept metallic fuel, although the reference design is for oxide fuel. India's fast breeder reactor is based upon the liquid metal fast breeder reactor. To sustain a chain reaction using fast neutrons, the reactor fuel must be relatively rich in fissile material. The superior neutron economy of a fast neutron reactor makes it possible to build a reactor that, after a relatively large initial fuel charge of plutonium requires only natural uranium feedstock as input to its fuel cycle. In the context doubling time refers to the time required to extract as output, double the amount of fissile fuel, which was fed as input into the breeder reactors.

In the third or final stage of nuclear power development an advanced nuclear power system involves a self-sustaining series of thorium-232, uranium-233 fuelled reactors. This would be a thermal breeder reactor, which in principle can be refuelled after its initial fuel charge using only naturally occurring thorium. According to the three-stage programme, India's nuclear energy could grow to about 10 GW through PHWRs fuelled by domestic uranium and the growth above that would have to come from FBRs till about 50 GW. Third-stage is to be deployed only after this capacity has been achieved. According to replies given in Indian Parliament on two separate occasions, 19th August 2010 and 21st March 2012, large-scale thorium deployment is only to be expected by three-four decades after the commercial operation of fast breeder reactors with short doubling time. Full exploitation of India's domestic thorium reserves will likely not occur until after the year 2050.

Apart from this, as there is a long delay before direct thorium utilisation in the three-stage programme, the country is now looking at reactor designs that allow more direct use of thorium in parallel with the sequential three-stage programme. Three options under consideration are the Accelerator Driven System (ADS), Advanced Heavy Water Reactor (AHWR), and Compact High Temperature Reactor (CHTR). In addition, Molten Salt Reactor (MSR) may also be under consideration as reported recently. Of all, the design for AHWR is ready for deployment. AHWR is a 300 MWe vertical pressure tube type, boiling light water cooled and heavy water moderated reactor, using uranium-233, thorium MOX and plutonium-thorium MOX. It is expected to generate 65 per cent of its power from thorium and can also be configured to accept other fuel types in full core including enriched uranium and uranium-plutonium MOX. There was a plan for constructing such an AHWR with a plutonium-thorium core combination in 2007. AHWR would offer very little growth for the fuel built up that is essential for wide deployment of the third-stage, and perhaps the impact on the accumulated fissile material could even be negative. The AHWR design that will be taken up for construction is to be fuelled with 20 per cent low enriched uranium (LEU) and 80 per cent thorium. The LEU for this AHWR design is readily available on the world market. If everything goes according to plan, AHWR could be operational in India by the end of 2020.

From the beginning, the nuclear power for civil use is well-established in India. As a part of larger planning the Atomic Energy Establish (AEE) was set up at Trombay, near Mumbai in 1957, and renamed as Bhabha Atomic Research Centre (BARC) ten years later. In line plans for building the first Pressurised Heavy Water Reactor (PHWR) were finalised in

1964. Its civil nuclear strategy has been directed towards complete independence in the nuclear fuel cycle, necessary because it is excluded from the 1970 Nuclear Non-proliferation Treaty (NPT) due to its acquiring nuclear weapons capability after 1970. As a result, India's nuclear power programme has preceeded largely without fuel or technological assistance from other countries. Meanwhile, India achieved a crushing success in nuclear field when on 18th May 1974, demonstrated its ability to conduct a nuclear explosion. Following this test, the US, Canada, and some other countries embargoed supply of materials or equipment required for India's nuclear programme. This was a major challenge and resulted in delays in building nuclear power stations, heavy water plants and fuel fabricating facilities, and in research and development projects. The forced isolation led to creation of wide ranging capabilities by Indian industries which geared up to supply all the materials and equipment from within the country. The Pokharan-II nuclear weapon tests of 1998 conferred on India the status of a defacto nuclear weapon power, outside the original five–the US, the , China, UK, France, and Russia.

At present, India has 20 operating nuclear power units, but the total nuclear power capacity is small because most of the units had a capacity of 220 MW. The Tarapur III and IV units, built to our own designs, were the largest at present, at 540 MW. In the couple of months the nuclear plant at Kudankulam will start which has a capacity of 1000 MW. Apart from this recently construction work is in progress of four reactors of 700 MW capacity of our own design, two at Kakrapar (III-IV), and two at Rajasthan (VII-VIII). Currently, twenty nuclear power reactors produce 4,780.00 MW, while seven under construction power reactors are expected to give 5,300 MW in near future. However, these all are far below the energy requirement of the country, and there is a need of fast breeder reactors having a large capacity. Dr. M.R. Srinivasan, former Atomic Chief, in a discussion said that we need large capacity fast breeder reactors which produce 1000 to 1650 MW in Light Water Reactors (LWRs) used in US, France, Japan, Russia, and Korea. These reactors need to be loaded with fresh fuel only once in twelve or eighteen months and the fuel is low enriched uranium. Some 80 per cent of all nuclear power plant in the world are LWRs.[77] According to Dr. Srinivasan, India is negotiating with France to build six 1650 MW reactors, in a phased manner, at Jaitapur, near Ratnagiri in Maharashtra. The country is also in discussion with the American reactor builders, Westinghouse and General Electric, regarding constructing reactors of their design at two coastal sites, one in Gujarat and another in Andhra Pradesh. But the discussions with Russia, France, and the US are in advance stage from where India intends to import some 20,000 to 30,000 MW of Light Water reactors, in the time from now to 2030.[78] India would like to have total nuclear capacity of 50,000 to 60,000 MW by 2030.

The total number of operating and under construction nuclear power plants in India is 20 and seven respectively. The first Pressurised Heavy Water Reactor was Rajasthan-I, which had Canada's Douglas Point reactor as a reference unit, was built as a collaborative venture between Atomic Energy of Canada Limited and Indian NPCIL. It started up in 1972. It was duplicated in subsequent years in several stages of evolution which can be identified as PHWRs with dousing and single containment at Rajasthan 1-2, PHWRs with suppression pool and partial double containment at Madras, and later standardised PHWRs from Narora onwards having double containment, suppression pool, and calandria filled with heavy water, housed in a water-filled calandria vault. In line Rajasthan-II was started in 1980 and these both are under safeguards. Rajasthan-I was down rated early in its life and has operated very little since 2002 due to ongoing problems and has been shut down since 2004. Rajasthan-II was restarted in September 2009 after major refurbishment, and running on imported uranium at full-rated power. Rajasthan III-IV and Kakrapar I-II are expected to be on line by 2017 after 60 months construction from first concrete to criticality. The estimated cost of these reactors are about Rs. 12,000 crore and the fuel they use will be slightly enriched uranium. Initially, this fuel will be imported.

Likewise initially Tarapur I-II, 150 MW Boiling Water Reactors established before the advent of the nuclear Non-

Proliferation Treaty. They have been using imported enriched uranium and are under the safeguards of International Atomic Energy Agency (IAEA). Late in 2004, Russia deferred to the Nuclear Suppliers' Group and declined to supply further uranium for them but in March 2006 Russia agreed to resume fuel supply. In December 2008, a $ 700 million contract with Rosatom was announced for continued uranium supply to them. The Tarapur III-IV reactors of 540 MW gross were developed indigenously from the 220 MWe model PHWR and were built by the National Power Corporation of India Limited (NPCIL). The first Tarapur-IV was connected to the grid in June 2005 and started commercial operation in September. Tarapur-IV's criticality came five years after pouring first concrete and seven months ahead of schedule. Its twin-unit III was about a year behind it and was connected to the grid in June 2006 with commercial operation in August, five months ahead of schedule. The 220 MWe PHWRs were indigenously designed and constructed by NPCIL, based on a Canadian design, while the Madras MAPS reactors were refurbished in 2002-2003 and 2004-2005 and their capacity restored to 220 MWs gross from 170. Much of the core of each reactor was replaced, and the lifespans extended to 2033/36. Kakrapar unit-I was fully refurbished and upgraded in 2009-10, after 16 years operation, as was Narora-II, with cooling channel replacement. Kaiga-III started up in February, was connected to the grid in April and went into the commercial operation in May 2007. Unit-IV started up in November 2010 and was grid connected in January 2011, but is about 30 months behind original schedule due to shortage of uranium. The Kaiga units are not under UN safeguards, so cannot use imported uranium. Rajasthan-V started up in November 2009, using imported Russian fuel, and in December it was connected to the northern grid. RAPP-VI started up in January 2010, and was grid connected at the end of March. Both are now in commercial operation. However, under civil military separation plan, eight further reactors were to be safeguarded: Rajasthan III and IV from 2010, Rajasthan-V and VI from 2008, Kakrapar I and II by 2012 and Narora I and II by 2014.

India's Operating Nuclear Power Reactors

Power Station	Operator	State	Type	Units	Total Capacity (MW)
Kaiga	NPCIL	Karnataka	PHWR	220 × 4	880
Kakrapar	NPCIL	Gujarat	PHWR	220 × 2	440
Narora	NPCIL	Uttar Pradesh	PHWR	220 × 2	440
Kalpakkam	NPCIL	Tamil Nadu	PHWR	220 × 2	440
Rawatbhata	NPCIL	Rajasthan	PHWR	100 × 1 200 × 1 220 × 4	1180
Tarapur	NPCIL	Maharashtra	BWR (PHWR)	160 × 2 540 × 2	1400
			Total	**20**	**4780**

Apart from 20 operating nuclear power reactors seven are under construction whose expected capacity is 53,00 MWe. The first four are being built at Kakrapar and Rajasthan. They are due on line by 2017 after sixty months construction from first concrete to criticality. Cost is quoted at about Rs. 12,000 crore each. Up to 40 per cent of the fuel they use will be slightly enriched uranium (SEU) about 1.1 per cent U-235, to achieve higher fuel burn-up about 21,000 MW d/t instead of one-third of this. Kudankulam-I and II are country's first large nuclear power plant comprising two VVER-1000 reactors, under a Russian financed US$ 3 billion contract. It is located in Tamil Nadu state being built by NPCIL and will be commissioned and operated by NPCIL under IAEA safeguards. Unit-I is now expected to start in April 2013 with unit-II in October. The second unit is about eight months behind unit 1. Another 500 MWe prototype fast breeder reactor is under construction at Kalpakkam near Madras by BHAVINI, a government enterprise set-up under Department of Atomic Energy. It was expected to start up about the end of 2010 and produce power in 2011, but this schedule is delayed and 94 per cent construction was reported in February 2013. Four further oxide fuel fast reactors are envisaged but slightly redesigned by the Indira Gandhi Centre to reduce capital cost. In contrast to the situation in 1990s, most reactors under construction more recently have been on schedule.

India's Under Construction Nuclear Power Reactors

Power Station	Operator	State	Type	Units	Total Capacity (MW)
Kudankulam	NPCIL	Tamil Nadu	V VER-1000	1000 × 2	2000
Kalpakkam	Bhavini	Tamil Nadu	PFBR	500 × 1	500
Kakrapar	NPCIL	Gujarat	PHWR	700 × 2	1400
Rawatbhata	NPCIL	Rajasthan	PHWR	700 × 2	1400
			Total	7	**5300 (MW)**

However, among the nuclear plant reactors, the Kudankulam (Tamil Nadu) and Jaitapur in Maharashtra drove into controversy on account of various reasons. Originally, an inter-governmental agreement on the subject was signed on 20th November 1988, by Prime Minister Rajiv Gandhi and Soviet President Mikhail Gorbachev for the construction of two reactors. The project remained in limbo for a decade due to the political and economic upheaval in Russia after the post-1991 Soviet breakup. There were also objections from the United States, on the grounds that the agreement does not meet the 1992 terms of the Nuclear Suppliers Group. Since the plant was conceived in the mid-1980s, an anti-nuclear group People Movement Against Nuclear Energy was opposing the plant for about 25 years due to the environmental impact of nuclear power and its threat to the people and environment. Consequently construction on the site began in 1997, and the estimated cost of the plan was Rs. 13,615 crore in 2001. The small port became operational in Kudankulam on 14th January 2004. This port was established to receive barges carrying over-sized light water reactor equipment from ships anchored at a distance of 1.5 kilometers. Until 2004 materials had to be brought in via road from the port of Tuticorin, risking damage during transportation.

Earlier between 1989 and 1997, the Coastal Regulation Zone (CRZ) and Environment Impact Assessment (EIA) Notifications were issued in 1991 and 1994 mandating compulsory clearances by environmental regulators before any new plant could be set up.[79] On the other the NPCIL, the Atomic Energy Regulatory Board (AERB) and the Ministry of Environment and Forests (MoEF) all claim that the EIA notification is not applicable to Kudankulam Nuclear Power Plant (KKNPP) as it had obtained clearance in 1989. Meanwhile, two significant changes were also made to the project. The first was that, contrary to the original proposal to ship out the Spent Nuclear Fuel (SNF) to Russia, the highly radioactive SNF from the nuclear power plant was to be stored, transported and reprocessed within India. The second change was equally major: the fresh water requirement was now to be met by the construction of six desalination plants instead of sending piped water from Pechiparai dam. The environmental impact of the desalination plant on coastal ecology and marine life are serious concerns with implications for the livelihoods of the fishing community.[80] Further in 2008, negotiation on building four additional reactors at the site began. Though the capacity of these reactors has not been declared, it is expected that the capacity of each reactor will be 1000 MW or I-GW. The new reactors would bring the total capacity of the power plant to 9200 MW or 9.2 GW. When completed they will become the largest nuclear power generation complex in India producing accumulative 2-GW of electric power. Both units are water cooled, water moderated power reactors. Under an inter-government agreement signed Russia is to supply to India four-third generation VVER-1200 reactors of 1170 MW. The reactors have some advanced safety features like passive heat removal system, double containment, core catcher, and hydrogen re-combiner instead of conventional systems.

The environmental and safety related issues of Kudankulam nuclear power plant got a renewed urgency for remedy in post-Fukushima accident which took place in March 2011. As a result, in October 2011 thousands of protesters and villagers living around the Russian-built Kudankulam nuclear plant in the southern Tamil Nadu state, blocked highways and staging hunger strikes, preventing further construction work, and demanding its closure as they fear of the disasters like the environmental impact of nuclear power, radioactive waste, nuclear accident similar to the radiation leak at Japan's Fukushima nuclear disaster. As against the claims made by the local people, protesters, and the voluntary organisation-People's Movement Against Nuclear Energy (PMANE), who declared that the nuclear plant is unsafe, the Government of India, constituted a panel which did a survey of the safety features in the plant, said that the Kudankulam reactors are the safest and fears of people are not based on scientific principles. A.P.J. Abdul Kalam, the former President of India in a lecture delivered at the Indian Institute of Management, Calcutta, praised the Kudankulam nuclear power plant and said, "As an individual I went to the plant. Really, it is a modern plant, and there is 2,000 MW ready to be pumped into the grid! Later after visiting the plant amid protests by villagers Kalam said he was completely satisfied and happy with the sophisticated safety features of the reactors. For protests at large scale, Indian Prime Minister Dr. Manmohan Singh including other ministers of the cabinet have separately said that the protests at the Kudankulam nuclear plant were funded by foreign NGOs. Several of India's nuclear experts have claimed that the protest movement has been created to scuttle India's indigenous three-stage closed fuel programme, which was put in place by India's desire to provide power for its future generations and to make India independent of all fossil fuels. Even a Public Interest Litigation (PIL) was also filed against the government's civil nuclear progamme in the Supreme Court. The PIL specifically asks for the staying of all proposed nuclear power plant-till satisfactory safety measures and cost-benefit analyses are completed by independent agencies. The Supreme Court in a judgement in May 2013, maintained that the Kudankulam nuclear power plant is totally safe. There is also some site related controversy about the French-aided plans, agreement signed in December 2010. It is for the first two EPR reactors, along with 25 years supply of fuel. While there have been mass protests against the units at Jaitapur, the Government of West Bengal refused permission to a proposed 6000 MW facility near the town of Haripur that intended to host six Russian reactors.

In addition to operating and under construction nuclear power reactors there are about 39 firmly proposed nuclear power plants in India. Although following the Nuclear Suppliers' Group agreement in September 2008, the scope for supply of both reactors and fuel from suppliers in other countries opened up, yet even earlier in 2005 and 2007 several Memorandum of Understandings (MoUs) were signed with foreign firms and countries for the development of nuclear power generation in India. In 2005, four sites were approved for eight new reactors. Two of the sites-Kakrapar and Rajasthan would have 700 MWe indigenous PHWR units. Kudankulam would have imported 1000 or 1200 MWe light water reactors alongside the two being built there by Russia, and the fourth site was green-field for two 1000 MWe LWR units-Jaitapur in the Ratnagiri district of Maharashtra state, on the west coast. The plan has since expanded to six 1600 MWe EPR units here. In April 2007, the government gave approval for the first four of these eight units Kakrapar III and IV and Rajasthan VII and VIII, using indigenous technology. In mid-2009, construction approval was confirmed, and late in 2009 the finance for them was approved. Site works at Kakrapar were completed by August 2010. First concrete for Kakrapar III and IV was in November 2010, and March 2011 respectively, after Atomic Energy Regulatory Board approval. The AERB approved Rajasthan VII and VIII in August 2010, and site works then began. First concrete was in July 2011, and then construction is expected to take 66 months to commercial operation. To increase generating capacity more rapidly there are also plans for eight 1000 MWe units at the Kudankulam site and in January 2007, a memorandum of understanding was signed by Russia to build four more plants, as well as others elsewhere in India. A further such agreement was signed in December 2010, and Rosatom announced that it expected to built no less than 18 reactors in India. In late 2008, NPCIL announced that as part of the Eleventh Five Year Plan (2007-12), it would start site work for 12 reactors including the rest of the eight PHWRs of 700 MWe each, three or four fast breeder reactors and one 300 MWe advanced heavy water reactor in 2009. The NPCIL said that "India is now focussing on capacity addition through indigenisation, with progressively higher local content for imported designs, up to 80 per cent. Likewise in June 2012, NPCIL announced four new sites for twin PHWR units : at Gorakhpur, Kumbariya near Fatehabad district in Haryana, at Banswada in Rajasthan, at Chutka in Mandla district and at Bheempur in Madhya Pradesh.

Between 2010 and 2020, further construction is expected to take total gross capacity to 21,180 MWe. The nuclear capacity target is part of national energy policy. Especially, after September 2008 when NSG's consent was obtained, civil nuclear cooperation agreements have been signed with the USA, Russia, France, UK, South Korea and Canada as well as Argentina, Kazakhstan, Mongolia and Namibia. On the basis of the 2010 cooperation agreement with Canada, in April 2013 a bilateral safeguards agreement was signed between the Department of Atomic Energy (DAE) and the Canadian Nuclear Safety Commission, allowing trade in nuclear materials and technology for facilities which are under IAEA safeguards.

Global Expansion of India's Nuclear Power

India's nuclear power is expected to undergo a significant expansion in the coming years in part to the passing of the Indo-US Civil Nuclear Agreement. This agreement will allow India to carry out trade of nuclear fuel and technologies with other countries and significantly enhance its power generation capacity. The international trade in nuclear material, equipment and technology is largely determined by the Nuclear Suppliers'

Group (NSG), an informal group of 45 countries. Members include the United States, Russia, France and the United Kingdom. India has been kept out of this informal arrangement and therefore denied access to trade in nuclear materials equipment and various kinds of technologies. Nuclear technology provides a plentiful and non-polluting source of power to meet our energy needs. To increase the share of nuclear power in our energy mix, we need to break out of the confines imposed by inadequate reserves of natural uranium, and by international embargoes that have constrained our nuclear programme for over three decades.[81] In the circumstances, India agreed a Civil Nuclear Agreement with the United State of America on 18th July 2005 to overcome the growing energy deficit. The essence of what was agreed in Washington was a shared understanding of India's growing energy needs. As a result of the understanding reached between the two countries, the US had committed itself to a series of steps to enable bilateral and international cooperation in nuclear energy. These include adjusting domestic policies, and working with allies to adjust relevant international regimes. There was also a positive mention of possible fuel supply to the first two nuclear power reactors at Tarapur. US support was also indicated for India's inclusion as a fuel partner in the International Thermonuclear Experimental Research Project and the Generation-IV International Forum.[82] Surely, the nuclear understanding with the US has created a greater opportunities for international cooperation in the area.

In favour and against there was a large amount of opinions and analysis of nuclear experts about the Civil Nuclear Energy Cooperation with the US. Ashley J. Tellis, a US analyst argued that the Indo-US nuclear is attractive to India because it gives it access to far more options on its civil nuclear programme than would otherwise be the case, primarily by ending its isolation from the international nuclear community. These options include access to latest technologies, excess to higher unit output reactors which are more economical, access to global finance for building reactors, ability to export its indigenous smaller reactor size PHWRs, better information flow for its research community, etc. Finally, the deal also gives India two options that are relatively independent from the three-stage programme, at least in terms of their dependencies on success or failure. The first option is that, India can opt to stay with the first stage reactors as long as the global supply of uranium lasts. The plus side of this is that it covers any risk from short-term delays or failures in implementing the three-stage programme. On the negative side, this is an option that is antithetical to the underlying objective of energy independence through the exploitation of thorium. Also according to one foreign analyst, the deal could overtime.......result in India being weaned away from its.......three-phase nuclear programme involving FBRs and advanced PHWRs. This would occur if India becomes confident that it would assure supplies of relatively cheap natural uranium, including from Australia. In any case, this distant possibility cannot be ruled out.

The Indian commentators including Anil Kakodkar, the then chairman of the Atomic Energy Commission, Indian government's official position and Indian defence establishment, have consciously welcomed the nuclear deal. Most of the Indian commentators have found in it an opportunity for India that would enable the country to end its international isolation on the nuclear front and obtain a *de facto* acknowledgement of it as a nuclear state to some degree. In addition to it being able to obtain the uranium that would increase the success potential of its three-stage programme as well as its efforts to build a "minimum credible nuclear deterrent. Anil Kakodkar made the comment publicly in a milder and conscious way keeping the country's indigenous fast breeder programme out of the ambit of international safeguards, saying, 'in the long run' the energy that will come out from the nuclear fuel resources available in India should always come from the larger share of the nuclear energy programme.....and, our strategy should be such that the integrity and autonomy of our being able to develop the three-stage nuclear power programme, be maintained, we cannot compromise that. The Indian government, on various occasions, reiterated its position clearly that India's indigenous three-stage programme is unaffected by the Indo-US Nuclear Deal and its full autonomy has been preserved. However, one view within the Indian defence establishment considered that the deal "has for all practical purposes capped Indian ability to field test and proof high yield nuclear weapons till sometime in future when Indian three-stage nuclear fuel cycle-based on thorium fuel matures into mainstream power production, thus eliminating

Indian dependence on imported nuclear fuel from NSG countries. Likewise, both right and left-wing political parties opposed the deal in the Parliament. The left feared the deal would make the country subservient to US interests, while the right felt it would limit further nuclear testing.

As a result of the nuclear understanding between India and the US on 18th July 2005, further in September 2008, the Nuclear Suppliers' Group countries waived out the restrictions imposed in relation to nuclear transaction with nations of the world. It was a diplomatic success when the NGS exempted India from the cartel's ban on atomic sales to countries that have not signed the Non-Proliferation Treaty (NPT). In the comity of nations it was evident that the seven founding members and all member with a significant nuclear export industry were in favour of recognising the reality of India's status. But those members most opposed to waiving the NSG's rules for India were those who either have a theological position against nuclear energy or who are not major players in the international nuclear industry.[83] Since early 1990s Russia has been a major supplier of nuclear fuel to India. Due to dwindling domestic uranium reserves electricity generation from nuclear power in India declined 12.83 per cent from 2006 to 2008. Following a waiver from the NSGs which allowed it to commence international nuclear trade India has signed bilateral deals on civilian nuclear energy technology cooperation with several other countries, including France, the United States, the United Kingdom, Canada and South Korea etc. India has also uranium supply agreements with Russia, Mongolia, Kazakhstan, Argentina and Namibia. Among all France was the first country to sign a civil nuclear agreement with India on 30th September 2008 after the complete waiver provided by the NSG. During the December 2010, visit of the French President Nicholas Sarkozy to India, framework agreements were signed for the setting up two-third generation EPR reactors of 1650 MW, each of Jaitapur, Maharashtra by the French Company Areva. The deal caters for the first set of two of six planned reactors and the supply of nuclear fuel for 25 years. Construction is likely to start before 2014, because of regulatory issues and difficulty in sourcing major components from Japan due to India not being a signatory of Nuclear Non-Proliferation Treaty.

In addition to the agreement of 1988, a 2008 agreement with Russia caters for provision of an additional four-third generation VVER-1200 reactors of capacity 1170 MW each. Russia has assisted in India's efforts to design a nuclear plant for its nuclear submarine. In 2009, the Russians stated that Russia would not agree to curb on export of sensitive technology to India. A new accord signed in December 2009 with Russia gives India freedom to proceed with the close fuel cycle which includes mining, preparation of the fuel for use in reactors, and reprocessing of spent fuel. The nuclear agreement with USA led India issuing a Letter of Intent for purchasing 10,000 MW from the US. However, it is said that India's nuclear liability law discourages foreign nuclear companies as this law gives accident victims the right to seek damage from plant suppliers in the event of a mishap. It has "deterred-foreign players like General Electric and Westinghouse Electric, a US-based unit of Toshiba, with companies asking for further clarification on compensation liability for private operators.

After exempting from NSGs restrictions, India had also signed nuclear agreements with Mongolia, Namibia, Argentina, Kazakhstan and South Korea. With Mongolia India signed a crucial civil nuclear agreement on 15th June 2009 for supply of uranium to India, during Prime Minister Manmohan Singh's visit to Mongolia making it the fifth nation in the world to seal a civil nuclear pact with India. The Memorandum of Understanding on development of cooperation in the field of peaceful uses of radioactive minerals and nuclear energy was signed by senior officials in the department of atomic energy of the two countries. The five agreements signed on 2nd September 2009 including one on civil nuclear energy which allows for supply of uranium from the African country Namibia is the fifth largest producer of uranium in the world. The Indo-Namibian agreement in peaceful uses of nuclear energy allows for supply of uranium and setting up of reactors. India signed two agreements with Argentina and Canada, on civil nuclear cooperation, on 14th October 2009, and 28th June 2010 respectively. On 6th November 2012, India and Canada finalised their 2010 nuclear export agreement, opening the way for Canada to begin uranium exports to India. On 16th April 2011 and 25th July 2011, India signed nuclear cooperation agreements with Kazakhastan and South Korea respectively for peaceful uses of atomic energy and participation in India's nuclear expansion programme.

As a result of the waiver from the Nuclear Suppliers' Group, India has progressed much in import of nuclear fuels-uranium and thorium. By December 2008, Russia's Rosatom and Areva from France had contracted to supply uranium for power generation. The Russian agreement was to provide fuel for PHWRs as well as the two small Tarapur reactors. Further in February 2009, the actual Russian contract was signed with TVEL to supply 2000 tonnes of natural uranium fuel pellets for PHWRs over ten years costing $780 million, and 58 tonnes of low-enriched fuel pellets for the Tarapur reactors. The Areva shipment arrived in June 2009. RAPS-2, became the first PHWR to be fuelled with imported uranium, followed by units five and six there. A Memorandum of Understanding was also signed between NPCIL and Kazatomprom for supply of 2100 tonnes of uranium concentrate over six years and a feasibility study on building Indian PHWR reactors in Kazakhstan. Under this agreement, 300 tonnes of natural uranium was to come from Kazakhstan in the 2010-11 year. Another 210 tonnes would come from Russia. A further agreement in April 2011 covered 2100 tonnes by 2014. In March 2013 both countries agreed to extend the civil nuclear cooperation agreement up to 2014. Now, India has become an important player in international nuclear business and in August 2010, the Department of Atomic Energy said that seven reactors were using imported fuel and working at full scale, while nine reactors used domestic uranium.

Since inception of India's nuclear power programme maximum exploitation of thorium, which is in abundance in the country, remained top priority and ultimate goal as well. In line the long-term goal of India's nuclear programme has been to develop an advanced heavy water thorium cycle. The first stage of this employs the PHWRs fuelled by natural uranium, and light water reactors to produce plutonium. Stage-two uses fast neutron reactors burning the plutonium to breed U-233 from thorium. The blanket around the core will have uranium as well as thorium, so that further plutonium is produced as well as the U-233 and it may be recycled there, Then in stage-three, Advanced Heavy Water Reactors (AHWRs) burn the U-233 from stage two and originally some of this plutonium with thorium, getting about two-thirds of their power from the thorium. Under a plan in 2002 the regulatory authority issued approval to start construction of a 500 MWe prototype fast breeder reactor at Kalpakkam and this is now under construction. It is expected to be operating in 2012, fuelled with uranium plutonium oxide. This will take India's ambitious thorium programme to stage-two, and set the scene for eventual full utilisation of the country's abundant thorium fuel reactors. Six more such 500 MWe fast reactors have been announced for construction, four of them by 2020. As a step further in April 2009 an AHWR critical facility was commissioned at BARC "to conduct a wide range experiments, to help validate the reactor physics of the AHWR through computer codes and in generating nuclear data about materials, such as thorium-uranium-233-based fuel, which have not been extensively used in the past.

The work on maximum use of thorium is advancing day by day and in 2009 the Atomic Energy Commission announced some features of the 300 MWe AHWR; it is mainly a thorium fuelled reactor with several advanced passive safety features to enable meeting next generation safety requirements such as 72 hours grace period for operator response, elimination of the need for exclusion zone beyond the plant boundary, 100-year design life, and high-level of fault tolerance. The advanced safety characteristics have been verified in a series of experiments carried out in full-scale test facilities. Also per unit of energy produced, the amount of long-lived minor actinides generated is nearly half of that produced in current generation Light Water Reactors. By mid-2010 a pre-licensing safety appraisal had been completed by the AERB and site selection was in progress. At the same time, the Atomic Energy Commission announced a LEU version of the AHWR. This will use low-enriched uranium plus thorium as a fuel, dispensing with plutonium input. In latest NPCIL presentation early in 2012 had LEU AHWRs being fuelled with LEU-thorium, while U-233 and thorium from fast reactors along with used fuel from those AHWRs fuelled accelerator-driven molten salt reactors. Evidently, thorium is the main element used for both these types.

In comparison to earlier, over the years India has become more conscious and focussed about the generation of nuclear power, it however, remained weak in the sphere despite the increase of both ranking and number of reactors. In past, lack of cooperation with other countries and limited uranium reserves of low quality are the main reasons behind the poor output. All of these reasons have compelled the present government to invest lot of energy in ensuring the successful conclusion of the civil nuclear cooperation agreement with the United States and it should be looked broadly in terms of India's growing energy deficit. Now, the Nuclear Suppliers Group (NSG) waiver allows India to buy uranium for its existing reactors as well as technologies to reprocess spent fuel and help reduce radioactive waste from nuclear supplier countries. With successful implementation of the civil nuclear initiative, the Indian nuclear power capacity is projected to generate 10,000 MWs, 20,000 MWs and 150,000 MWs by 2010, 2020 and 2050 respectively. India is planning to increase the present share of three per cent to 10 per cent by 2022 and 26 per cent by 2052. The more India cooperates with nuclear energy and fuel supplying countries, the easier will be for India to produce more nuclear power to meet its growing energy security challenges.

References

1. Gareth Evans and Yoriko Kawaguchi, 'Nuclear Disarmament: Building the Momentum,' *The Hindu,* 29th September 2009.
2. Brahma Chellaney, 'Atoms for Might', *The Hindustan Times,* 18th October 2000.
3. Deva Narayan Mallik, *Post-war International Politics–A Quadripartite Survery* (Muzaffarpur: Veena Mandir Publishers, 1973), pp. 45-46.
4. Brahma Chellaney, *Nuclear Proliferation The US–Indian Conflict* (New Delhi : Orient Longman, 1993), p. 1.
5. Jawaharlal Nehru, 'Atomic Energy for Peace and Progress of Mankind', in Balvant A. Desai (ed.), *Atoms for Peace* (Delhi: Radiant Publishers, 1975), p. 8.
6. J.P. Jain, *Nuclear India,* Vol. 1 (Delhi: Radiant Publishers, 1974), p. 63.
7. Dr. Rajkumar Singh, 'Nuclear Deterrence: More Real Than Myth', *Third Concept*, Vol. 19, No. 217, March 2005 (New Delhi, 2005), p.17.
8. As quoted in M.V. Ramana, 'Deeper into the Morass–Ten Years After Pokharan', *The Hindu*, 11th May 2008.
9. N.S. Sisodia, 'Lessons from an Atomic Catastrophe', *Ibid.,* 6th August 2009.
10. Tarun C. Bose, 'Whither NPT? 1995 and Beyond,' *Journal of International Relations* (1994), p. 21, as quoted in Dr. Poonam Singh, *Indo-American Relations* (Delhi: Vista International Publishing House, 2006), p. 92.

11. S.M. Meyer, *Dynamics of Nuclear Proliferation* (Chicago: University of Chicago Press, 1984), as quoted in Dr. Aftab Alam, 'Nuclearisation in South Asia-Incentives and Motivations,' *Third Concept*, Vol. 11, No. 127, September 1997 (New Delhi : 1997), pp. 16-18.
12. *Ibid.*
13. *The Times of India,* 19th May, 1974.
14. Government of India, Ministry of Information and Broadcasting, *Jawaharlal Nehru's Speeches, 1953-57* (Delhi: Publication Division, 1958), p. 507.
15. Rajkumar Singh, *Indo-Pak Nuclear Tension-1974-1998* (New Delhi: Samiksha Prakashan, 2001), p. 4.
16. For detail see Emeka Ohajunwa, *India-US Security Relations 1947-1990* (Delhi: Chanakya Publications, 1992), p. 124.
17. G.P. Ojha, *India's Foreign Policy* (Meerut: Mrinal Books, 1982), p. 135.
18. *Ibid.*
19. Deva Narayan Mallik, *Post-war International Politics–A Quadripartite Survey*, p. 463.
20. Swaran Singh, 'China Factor in India's Nuclear Policy', *Journal of Peace Studies*, Vol. 5, No. 3, May-June 1998, pp. 23-38.
21. J.K. Roy, *Security in the Missile Age* (Delhi: Allied Publishers, 1967), p. 118.
22. P.K.S. Namboodiri, 'Perceptions and Policies of India and Pakistan', in K, Subrahmanyam (ed.), *India and the Nuclear Challenge* (New Delhi: Lancers International, 1985), p. 133.
23. K. Subrahmanyam, 'Indian Nuclear Policy: 1964-98', in Jasjit Singh (ed.) *Nuclear India* (New Delhi: Knowledge World, 1998), p. 27.
24. Dr. Rajkumar Singh, *Indo-Pak Nuclear Tension*-1974-1998, p. 6.
25. *Ibid.*, pp. 6-7
26. O.P. Sabherwal, 'India's Nuclear Policy Under Siege', *One India One People*, August 1997 (Mumbai: 1997), pp. 16-17.
27. Verghese Koithara, *Society, State and Security, The Indian Experience* (New Delhi : Sage Publications, 1999), pp. 259-60.
28. Dr. Rajkumar Singh, 'Nuclear Deterrence : More Real than Myth', pp. 17-18.
29. Smith Dan, 'Uselessness and the Role of Nuclear Weapons: An Exercise in Pseudo-problems and Disconnection', in Gjelstad Jorn and Olav Njolstad (eds.), *Nuclear Rivalry and International Order* (London: 1996), pp. 86-87.
30. Van den Bergh, Godfried Van Benthem, 'Nuclear Revolution into its Second Phase', in *Ibid.*, p. 27.
31. G.F. Kennan, *Russia, the Atom and the West* (London : 1958), p. 54.
32. Siddharth Vardarajan, 'Eleventh Hour for the Nuclear Suppliers Group,' *The Hindu*, 9th August 2008.
33. Brahma Chellaney, *Nuclear Proliferation—The US Indian Conflict*, p. 32.

34. Praful Bidwai, 'Nuclear Policy in a Mess-NWFZ the Realistic Way Out', *The Times of India*, 28th November 1991.
35. B. Rahamathulla, *Indo-American Politics* 1970-78 (Delhi : Stanford University Press, 1980), p. 53.
36. R.R. Subramanian, 'The Nuclear Factor in South Asian Strategy', *Strategic Analysis*, Vol. VIII, No. 9 (1984), p. 829.
37. Dr. Poonam Singh, *Indo-American Relations*, pp. 108-9.
38. K.S. Nagar and Gautam Sharma (eds.), *India's Security and Super Power Threat* (New Delhi: Reliance Publishing House, 1990), p. 24.
39. Rajkumar Singh, *'Indo-Pak Nuclear Tension-1974-1998'*, pp. 39-40.
40. S.R. Bhansali (ed.), *Peace and Disarmament* (Jodhpur : Faculty of Law, University of Jodhpur, 1987), p. 431.
41. Sandeep Dikshit, 'Rajiv Gandhi Plan : A Valuable Solution', *The Hindu*, 9th August 2010.
42. *Ibid.*
43. S.P. Seth, 'The Indo-Pak Nuclear Duet and the US', *Asian Survey,* Vol. XXIII, No. 7 (1988), p. 711.
44. *Ibid.*
45. Brahma Chellaney, 'The Challenge of Nuclear Arms Control in South Asia', *Survival,* Vol. XXXV, No. 3 (1993), p. 122.
46. Dr. Aftab Alam, 'Pakistan's Nuclear Development and Capability', *Third Concept*, April-May 1998 (New Delhi: 1998), pp. 16-17.
47. Pervez Hoodboy, 'Pakistan and the Deep Cut Regime', in Harold A. Feiveson (ed.), *The Nuclear Turning Point: A Blueprint for Deep Cuts and Dealerting of Nuclear Weapons* (Washington : Brookings Institution, 1999), p. 227.
48. David Albright and Tom Zamora, 'India's and Pakistan's Nuclear Weapons', *Bulletin of the Atomic Scientists*, June 1989, p. 25.
49. Shastri Ramachandaran, 'Test of Liberalism – Trapped between Bomb and Bombast', *The Times of India* (Patna), 21st May 1998.
50. Rajkumar Singh, *'Indo-Pak Nuclear Tension*-1974-1998', p. 48.
51. Swaran Singh, 'Evolution of Nuclear Postures', in G.P. Deshpande, Alka Acharya (eds.), *50 Years of India China-Crossing a Bridge of Dreams* (New Delhi : Tulika, 2001), p. 371.
52. *Ibid.*, p. 370.
53. Arun Prakash, 'India's Deterrent Capabilities', *South Asia, Politics,* Vol. 8 No. 11, March 2010 (New Delhi: 2010), pp. 3-4.
54. K. Subrahmanyam, *'A Credible Deterrent – Logic of Nuclear Doctrine'*, *The Times of India*, 4th October 1999.
55. *Indian Nuclear Doctrine*, National Security Advisory Board August 1999 (New Delhi : 1999), as quoted in Swaran Singh, 'Evolution of Nuclear Postures', pp. 372-73.
56. K. Subrahmanyam, 'A Credible Deterrent – Logic of the Nuclear Doctrine'.

57. Brahma Chellaney, 'Atoms for Might'.
58. R. Rajaraman, 'The Fizzle Doesn't Really Matter', *The Hindu*, 16th September 2009.
59. *Ibid.*
60. *The Times of India* (New Delhi), 8th February 2003.
61. *Ibid.*
62. M.V. Ramana, 'Deeper into the Morass, Ten Years After Pokharan'.
63. R. Rajaraman, 'The Fizzle Doesn't Really Matter'.
64. Shyam Saran, 'Weapon That has more than Symbolic Value', *Ibid.*, 4th May 2013.
65. *Ibid.*
66. Sadanand A. Shetty (ed.), *One India One People*, August 1997 (Mumbai: One India One People Foundation, 1997), p. 16.
67. Surat Raju and M.V. Ramana, 'Why Kudankulam is Untenable', *The Hindu*, 12th November, 2011.
68. M.R. Srinivasan, 'Is the Nuclear Power Option Safe for India', *Ibid.*, 9th October 2007.
69. *Ibid.*
70. *Ibid.*, 14th March 2011.
71. Rahul Siddharthan, 'The Real Questions from Kudankulam', *Ibid.*, 14th September 2012.
72. Siddharth Vardarajan, 'Rush in Now, Repent later', *Ibid.*, 25th April 2011.
73. A. Gopalakrishnan, 'A Nuclear Regulator Without Teeth', *Ibid.*, 16th September 2011.
74. A.P.J. Abdul Kalam and Srijan Pal Singh: Our Gateway to a Prosperous Future, *Ibid.*, 6th November 2011.
75. Anil Kakodkar, 'Reversing the Logic of the Nuclear Deal', *Ibid.*, 4th July 2011.
76. A.P.J. Abdul Kalam and Srijan Pal Singh, 'Our Gateway to a Prosperous Future'.
77. *Asian Scientist*, 29th August 2011.
78. *Ibid.*
79. D. Nagasaila and V. Suresh, 'Kudankulam on Shaky Legal Ground', *The Hindu*, 5th November 2012.
80. *Ibid.*
81. *The text of statement made in Parliament* on 27th February 2006, by Prime Minister Manmohan Singh on Civil Nuclear Energy Cooperation with United States, *Ibid.*, 28th February 2006.
82. *Ibid.*
83. Siddharth Vardarajan, 'Eleventh Hour for the Nuclear Suppliers Group', *Ibid.*, 9th August 2008.

❑

3

Pakistan's Nuclear Power and Politics in South Asia

The foundation stone of Pakistan's nuclear power came into being in 1953 with the establishment of Atomic Energy Council (AEC) which was upgraded in 1956 as the Pakistani Atomic Energy Commission (PAEC). Initially, for long the nature of Pakistan's nuclear programme was peaceful use of atomic energy and it was carried out during the regime of Ayub Khan and Yahya Khan. In Pakistan decisions about nuclear requirements are made by a few individual and with military backgrounds who view these weapons as having both political and military value.[1] After the Indo-Pak war of 1965 an arranged meeting of Z.A. Bhutto, Ayub Khan and Munir Ahmed Khan, a nuclear scientist, was held at the elegant Dorchester Hotel in London but due to Pakistan's poor economic condition they did not agree to move forward in using nuclear power for military purposes. Islamabad's policy of peaceful use of nuclear policy underwent a substantial change in the period of Z.A. Bhutto, it however, expanded rapidly when President Mohammed Zia-ul-Haq became the ruler of Pakistan. In his regime Pakistan's weapons programme became operative and its first nuclear plant is at Kahuta, operating since 1984 with an annual capacity of 5-6 weapons as per Western estimates. Almost at the same time the People's Republic of China (PRC) began to cooperate Pakistan in nuclear energy following an Agreement on Peaceful Uses of Nuclear energy signed in 1986. Pakistan set up two nuclear reactors. Chasma-I and Chasma-II with the Chinese assistance and both have a capacity of 300 MW each.[2] Gradually, the nuclear atmosphere of the region was charged with the nuclear explosions of India and Paskistan in May 1998, and in latter's case most people perceived nuclear weapons as the nation's Crown Jewel. In the aftermath of Indo-US Civil Nuclear Agreement Paskitan is pursuing its nuclear expansion programmes more vigorously and its top level Executive Committee of the National Economic Council has in July 2013, approved funds to purchase two reactors from China.[3] In addition to security threat Pakistan's nuclear weapons have been imbued with great powers, including the power to keep India at bay and to lift Pakistan into the world's stage.

Initial Efforts of Pakistan for Nuclear Power

Pakistan's nuclear programme has an independent origin and first step in this direction was taken in 1953. The year witnessed the setting up of an Atomic Energy Council (AEC), under the chairmanship of Dr. Nazir Ahmed. The Council was entrusted with the following tasks :

(i) Survey of radioactive minerals,

(ii) Working out a plan for the establishment of an institute of Atomic Energy in Pakistan, and

(iii) Making recommendations on all matters connected with the utilisation of atomic energy.

The Atomic Energy Council was upgraded to the Pakistani Atomic Energy Commission (PAEC), in 1956. The new PAEC had a realistic mandate. Pakistan was to plan and develop 'peaceful' use of atomic energy with special reference to survey, procurement and disposal of radioactive materials, planning and establishment of Atomic Energy and Nuclear Research Institute, installation of Research and Power Reactors, negotiations with International Atomic Energy bodies, selection and training of personnel, application of radioisotopes to agriculture, health, industry, etc. The nature of Pakistani nuclear development activities carried out during the regime of Ayub Khan and Yahya Khan clearly pointed to the direction of peaceful use of nuclear energy.[4] The CANDU type nuclear power plant Pakistan had acquired was no doubt meant for civil purposes of electricity generation, but a military by-product had been built into it so that the fuel used in the plant could be reprocessed to obtain plutonium.

Zulfikar Ali Bhutto was in fact, the chief architect of Pakistan's nuclear policy and its nuclear programme. Under him, Islamabad's nuclear thinking underwent a significant change related to the non-peaceful uses of atomic energy. Earlier, when Pakistan's Atomic Energy Commission was established he was confident that it would vigorously pursue its objective of paving the way for Pakistan sooner than later, to join the nuclear club. The Pakistan Atomic Energy Commission should not be afraid of the USA as Bhutto had already told some Americans, including Dr. Kissinger, that they should not insult the sovereignty and self-respect of Pakistan by discussing the pros and cons of the reprocessing plant.[5] American pressure on Pakistan to refrain from buying nuclear reactors from France was part of their desire to try to contain Bhutto's over-ambitious plans. With a nuclear bomb and the ability to share it with the Arab States, Bhutto saw himself catapulted into an international role far greater than his poor country permitted him.[6]

For Bhutto, the building of a nuclear bomb was more than a reaction to India. It represented a trump card in his foreign policy. Pakistan would become the first Muslim country with the bomb. Among the rich and security anxious Arab States with whom he planned to share the secrets the success would enhance Pakistan's stature and importance incalculably. There is some evidence that heavy funds were injected by the Libyans to promote his plan which, if realised would tip the balance of power in the Middle East. 'Pakistan will develop atom bomb', Bhutto once remarked wayback in 1966 'even if we have to eat grass'. Although he categorically denied or disguised his plans in order to side step international pressures, he consistently planned and worked towards building a nuclear bomb. Earlier, when he was Minister of Fuel, Power and Natural Resources in Ayub Khan's Cabinet he began reorganising the Atomic Energy Commission, increasing their budget and lobbying in their interest. He also justified a heavy investment on nuclear research, principally on prospecting for uranium and on training scientists in nuclear research, both by sending abroad and by getting them trained within Pakistan by foreign trained scientists.

Under Bhutto's leadership Pakistan's first nuclear power plant, the Karachi Nuclear Project (KANUPP) having capacity of 137-MW and located 15 miles west of Karachi at Paradise point on the Buleji Coast, was completed in 1972. This IAEA safeguard plant was purchased from Canada and it received enriched uranium fuel from Canada and heavy water from the USA. Canada also granted a soft loan of $23 million and a credit of another $24 million to cover the foreign exchange costs of this plant. Japan provided a credit of $3.6 million for turb-generator. Canada abrogated its nuclear cooperation agreement with Pakistan in December 1976, because of Pakistan's refusal to agree to full scope safeguards.

The American non-proliferation policy, from its very beginning has been to restrict not only the development of nuclear weapon technology but also the spread of civilian nuclear technology as such to maintain its nuclear monopoly and to prevent the monolithic from attaining nuclear weapon capability. It was, in fact, determined to achieve the twin objectives of disarming America's nuclear adversaries and discouraging its potential nuclear enemies from acquiring such capabilities. In South Asia, the US policy has been discriminatory. One example, its permissive approach towards Pakistan's nuclear programme is sufficient to substantiate this assertion. While it would be an unreasonable proposition to make that the United States favoured the emergence of nuclear Pakistan but it can also not be denied that Pakistan's nuclear programme has gone ahead under the overall patronage of the United States and its turning of blind eye to Pakistan's clandestine weapons programme. Many analysts, even Americans, too, agree, that the US government did not take the desired steps to halt Pakistan's nuclear weapons Programme in time in spite of adequate information in that regard. On the other hand, the legislative measures that could have been taken were postponed several times through narrow interpretations of the legal provisions.

From a strategic view point, Islamabad's nuclear programme is driven mainly by its threat perception and security concern with respect to India. In contrast, India's nuclear calculations are centered on China which has an expanding nuclear arsenal. Pakistan sees its potential nuclear forces as a deterrent to India's conventional military advantages and strategic ambitions. India, whose military build-up was spurred by its humiliating defeat in the 1962 war with China, views its nuclear programme as the vital component of a strategic plan to deter against a more powerful China. The China factor, in the light of the Chinese aggression against India in 1962 and its claim to Arunachal Pradesh, can hardly be ignored. India is the only Asian nation that has the potential to challenge China. And naturally for China, Pakistan has become a useful pawn to undermine India. If Pakistan has allowed itself to be used by the US in the Cold War Era, today it has offered itself to China.

On May 18, 1974 at 08.05 hours India had detonated its first atomic device on a test-site at Pokharan (Rajasthan). With it, India entered the nuclear club; for the experimental plutonium device was India-made and triggered by using an implosion-burst inwards-technique. The most significant fact relating to India's place in the nuclear realm is that the area of advanced technology were due thanks to the Nehru-Bhabha combination. India has been able to lay a sound foundation and forge ahead; build an extensive infrastructure backed by research and development, and achieve capability along the entire nuclear fuel cycle. The combination (Nehru-Bhabha) provided India's nuclear progamme a chain of nuclear research and development facilities, some of them matching the most advanced in the West. Capability along the entire nuclear fuel cycle also means, scientific, technological and industrial acquisitions right from the stage of uranium mining to developing fuels for various reactor types, designing, building and operating reactors, and atomic power stations. Apart from this, certain unique features that have brought glory to the trail of nuclear technological development need to the focussed with respect to this country's plutonium-based weapon capability.

By overcoming the enormously costly uranium enrichment route, Indian scientists created weapon capability as a by-product of India's power generation programme as early as 1965-66. And so, the first Indian nuclear device—tested at Pokharan was the cheapest nuclear device build and tested by any nation in the world. Taking into account its nuclear capability, India's standing was distinct in two respects. Although this country ranks, among top five nations in technology attainments along the entire nuclear fuel cycle–ahead of China except in the limited domain of weaponising–India has been pushed into the wilderness of nuclear have-nots. Barring the leading industrial nations, no country has assimilated and developed plutonium-based technology, both for India's second generation atomic power programme and weapon-grade plutonium capability, as India has done.[7]

Ever since the partition of the sub-continent, Pakistan has viewed India with suspicion. Particularly, after the Bangladesh liberation and India's emergence as an accepted regional power, it became clear that Pakistan is no serious security threat to India. But the danger lurks in two forms. Firstly, Pakistan could act in collusion with a nuclear power to threaten India's interest or security. Secondly, she could, because of her policy of alignment, obtain at least obsolescent tactical nuclear weapons from a major nuclear power. An obsolescent weapon has only scrap value unless it is sold again as a weapon. Since the costs incurred in their manufacture are very high, there is a strong temptation on the part of the countries concerned to re-sell them. The probability of Pakistan getting such weapons from the USA and, in due course, from China cannot be ruled out. According to some observers Pakistan continued to be hostile to India and has been harbouring thoughts of revenge and watching for a suitable opportunity to restart hostilities.

The nuclear explosion by India on May 18, 1974, added a nuclear dimension to the always vexed and often tragic story of Indo-Pak relations. Although Indira Gandhi, on her part, explained in a letter to Prime Minister Bhutto the peaceful nature and the economic purposes of this experiment, and stated that India is willing to share her nuclear technology with Pakistan in the same way as she is willing to share it with other countries, provided proper conditions for understanding and trust are created. She once again repeated this assurance and hoped that the Government of Pakistan will accept India's position in this regard. Referring to Bhutto's recent statement in Lahore that India somehow poses a threat to Pakistan's security, she denied that there were any "political or foreign policy implications" of this test and re-affirmed her willingness to "settle all our differences with Pakistan peacefully through bilateral negotiations in accordance with the Shimla agreement.

The then Prime Minister of Pakistan Z.A. Bhutto, in reply on 5th June 1974, thanked Mrs. Gandhi for her letter but stressed that nuclear questions raised matters "not only of intentions but of capabilities" for government change as do national attitudes. He insisted that India's nuclear explosion had introduced an "unbalancing factor" at a time when progress was being made towards "normalising" of relations between the two countries. He added that India's rapidly developing programme for acquiring medium range missles and for placing a satellite in orbit–thus obtaining a delivery system for nuclear weapons–and its proposals to build a nuclear navy were almost "pertinent". Bhutto, while winding up the debate on India's nuclear blast in the Pakistan Assembly in June 1974, ranted against India and claimed that the country had never faced a more serious and grave situation than the one created by India's nuclear blast.[8] Pakistan also tried to raise nuclear boggy in the UN and at a UN Committee charging that India which exploded nuclear device was working on a nuclear weapons delivery system.[9]

To meet the challenge, arising out of India's nuclear blast, shortly thereafter the chairman of the Pakistan Atomic Commission said that "he will do his duty," implying that Pakistan would soon explode a nuclear device too and build up a nuclear arsenal.[10] Bhutto also took the opportunity to write to the Chinese Premier Chou-En-Lai seeking nuclear technological aid. In response, Chou agreed to sharing Chinese nuclear know/how with Pakistan on condition that Pakistan would exert to develop its own independent technology side by side. On being influenced, Bhutto prompted to set up a special committee to develop nuclear science and to appeal to all Pakistani scientists to come to the aid of their motherland. In December 1974, a Chinese delegation of scientists visited Pakistan when the committee was set up and the Chinese assured "all possible help" to enable Rawalpindi to go nuclear. At the point, the views of both China and Pakistan taken together, it would be in the Indian interest to go in for a nuclear programme and defence system. The only way left for India if it wanted to live in Peace with Pakistan was by acquiring such a distinct military superiority that Pakistan would find it futile to wage any war with India in the hope of settling any dispute by force.[11] The Indian leaders despite their military superiority to Pakistan continue to harbour fears that a Pakistan assisted actively by China could pose severe threats to India's security and integrity–although the nightmare of serious Sino-Pakistani military cooperation failed to be realised during either the 1965 or 1971 war between India and Pakistan.

Development of Nuclear Power in Post-1974 Era

In the post-Pokharan phase from 1975 onwards Bhutto pursued his quest for Pakistan's nuclear status. He held that only nations with nuclear weapons had sovereignty. It is now known that from the early 1980s, China has been assisting Pakistan in nuclear technology which was later extended to missile technology as well. All this was within the knowledge of the US and Pakistan's nuclear capability is now traced to as early as 1987. Relations between India and Pakistan are exacerbated by deep mistrust, a quick tendency to blame the other side for any misfortune, belief that the other side is dedicated to gaining the upperhand and, in Pakistan, the idea that India directly threatens the survival of the country. There is an almost paranoid tendency to see evil intent in each other's action, and conspiracy theories are endemic and readily articulated by a vast cross-section of the two populations. Although Pakistan in terms of population, land area, infrastructure and Armed forces is way behind India which makes one come to the conclusion that it can afford to carry out a proxy war because of the backing of China to develop its nuclear and missile capability, the availability of Arab petro dollars and to some extent by the support of the strong pro-Pakistan lobby in the USA. It is said that China helped Pakistan substantively in setting up the nuclear reactors. We now learn that China had decided to carry out more nuclear tests to meet the nuclear challenge by India in South Asia. Surely, the upgrading of her nuclear arsenal could only be against India.

Following the explosion Pakistan acquired its nuclear teeth during Bhutto's visit to Peking in May 1976, when a secret pact was made between the two countries and China agreed to help Islamabad produce nuclear arms. A part of Bhutto's diary revealed:

Fifteen per cent to twenty per cent of the work had been shelved for further talks with French and Chinese leaders; the major portion of the project had been completed, and we had thoroughly prepared ourselves to show the world that we also knew how to explode a nuclear bomb....My countrymen wanted me and my government to produce a nuclear bomb. They talked, more often than not, about India's possession of nuclear devices and nuclear arms. Indian leaders should not shout; they should know that Pakistan would, sooner than later; explode a nuclear device.[12]

China according to Bhutto, had agreed to share technology with Pakistan for setting up a big factory on the outskirts of Karachi to manufacture powerful tanks and anti-tank missiles. Peking had also agreed to build two industrial units in Pakistan's northern territory, he added.

The year 1976 also witnessed the signing of a Pak agreement with French firm SGN for Chasma plant after three years of negotiations. The Chasma project, however, ran into rough weather. The Indian test and other developments had meanwhile set in motion new thinking on matters of proliferation. The London meeting of the nuclear supplier countries took a new look at the export of nuclear technology and materials. The United States brought pressure on both France and Pakistan to abandon the Chasma project. France refused to do so and Pakistan could not be influenced by the offer of conventional arms. It was only after the US presented the evidence to France of Pakistani intention of using the plant for weapon purpose that the latter heeded the US pressure. By mid 1977 France had slowed down on the contract and in 1978 abandoned it completely. This incident left Pakistan to pursue the matter of nuclear power more or less alone. Bhutto viewed Pakistan's nuclear capability as the symbol of a particular civilization as he once said that Christian, Jewish and Hindu civilization have this capability. The communist powers also possess it. Only Islamic civilization was without it, but that position was about to change. He intended to share with the Arab countries Pakistan's nuclear capability. Saudi Arabia was also reported to have indicated to Pakistan that it would be willing to finance a reprocessing plant for the manufacture of Plutonium in return for the use of this facility for itself.[13]

Despite the fact that Americans did not like the development of Pak's nuclear capability, Bhutto claimed that the reprocessing facility was required to keep Pakistan's atomic power stations going. He was told by Dr. Henry Kissinger that he was insulting US intelligence. But a page Bhutto's diary indicated that Islamabad had other alternatives too. It revealed:

You know I have friends not only helpful in China but also in Saudi Arabia. As Prime Minister I built strong bridges with Saudi Arabia. Pakistan and Saudi Arabia reached an agreement on a plan to assist each other in building the defence strength. The agreement was designed to enable the two countries to come closer to each other in the light of growing need to establish a united Muslim bloc. The agreement was intended to enable Pakistan to obtain financial assistance from Saudi Arabia for purchasing effective equipment for our armed forces.

The army coup of July 1977, removed Bhutto from the seat of power and after having been overthrown he had disclosed that he had brought Pakistan to the verge of full nuclear capability. The disclosure led to an inquiry by the British Department of Energy and Trade in 1978 pertaining to Pakistani deal with a British firm for the supply of $ 1.25 million worth of electrical control equipment which goes into a nuclear bomb. According to a section of the British press, the Pakistan government had placed an order with a British electrical machinery manufacturing company for equipment which it said; it needed for a textile plant but which could be used for a nuclear project. The inquiry was made in the light of a question asked in the British House of Commons by a Labour Member, Frank, Allaun, whether the supply of equipment essential to the manufacture of nuclear weapons had the government's approval. But what was good for Islamabad was that its relations with China had been improving for several years, and its President 'is a faithful follower' of Bhutto's policy. China had secured an access to the Arabian sea and the Indian Ocean by the grace of Pakistan; if Pakistan accelerated a process of collection of arms which can have only one target, namely, India, then India would be forced to equip itself to meet this challenge.

The change of guard in Islamabad did not make any difference to the nuclear programme of the country. General Zia, who replaced Bhutto, pursued predecessor's nuclear plans and referred to US efforts "to prevent us from making bomb even though we have no such intention–if we wanted to, nobody can stop us anyway". He was determined to acquire nuclear technology for Pakistan and that he had "alternative" for this, if the French failed. The Pak Minister of Science and Technology, Ahmed Choudhary, echoed the same confidence in October 1978 when he said that he would not be helpless in case the reprocessing plant was denied to it. "Pakistan possesses scientific knowledge, expertise and formula about atomic power and nuclear reprocessing plant". Thus, despite the denial of nuclear technology by its chief nuclear collaborators, Pakistan decided to follow an alternative route of constructing its own gas centrifuge uranium enrichment plant at Kahuta. 'The Pakistani plant at Dera Ghazi Khan, which manufactured the Uranium hexafluoride feed for Kahuta, was also shipped between 1977-80 by a German firm, CES Kalthoff. The Kahuta uranium enrichment plant was entirely under supervision of Abdul Qadir Khan, a German trained Pakistani metallurgist, who had worked with FDO in Netherland and returned Pakistan in 1975. About Khan, a report prepared by the Dutch Government confirmed that he was able to procure all relevant information and documents, including blueprints of the URENCO gas centrifuge enrichment plant and list of hundred odd sub-contractors in Europe who could provide the requisite assemblies. It was Dr. Khan's innovative approach to acquire nuclear technology that Pakistan succeeded in establishing the centrifuge plants at Kahuta and Sihala.[14]

Under General Zia-Ul-Haq, Pakistan constructed a reprocessing plant capable of extracting 10 to 20 kg of Plutonium per year in accordance with the design of the French plant. Both the firms, French SGN and Belgian Belgo-Nuclear, rendered technical assistance in replication. The plant underwent cold test in 1982. Pakistan had also established a heavy water plant at Multan with a production capacity of 13 metric tons. It became operational in 1980. Belgo Nuclear was reported to have rendered technical assistance. In addition, a hexafluoridation plant was designed to convert yellow cake (natural uranium) into Hexafluoride. This plant was set up at Dera Ghazi Khan in 1980 with a production capacity of about 200 metric tons of hexafluoride per year. In setting up this plant, Pakistan sought the assistance of West German firm CFS Kalth. In 1987, Pakistan also acquired a gasification and solidification plant from Cora Engineering (Switzerland) for feeding uranium hexafluoride gas into the centrifuges and for transforming it into solid state after the enrichment process. As reported in the press, Pakistan was erecting another enrichment plant at Golra, about 10-km from Islamabad. Even the Western authors, who had been trying to chase Pakistan's nuclear weapons programme, admit that tracking Pakistan purchase was difficult in detective work. The purchaser's expert handling of secret purchases and their daring and expert actions always placed them one step ahead of the foreign detective and secret agencies deployed to stop supply of nuclear materials to Pakistan.

Pakistan Gaining Nuclear Capability Substantially

Since 1987, Pakistan had developed and deployed nuclear weapons. For instance, Dr. A.Q. Khan, in early 1987, informed an Indian journalist at the height of the Brasstack crisis, that Pakistan had enriched uranium to 90 per cent for weapons purpose. He further suggested that the USA and CIA were right in assuming that Pakistan possess, nuclear weapons. Benazir Bhutto also once stated in an interview that 'Pakistan has acquired the requisite capability for making an atom bomb– Pakistan cannot abandon its programme unilaterally'. It was in April 1988 that former Pakistan Army Chief General Mirza Aslam Beg announced the indigenous missile development programme with short range Hatf-I and Hatf-II missiles. In an article he declared that : 'Pakistan had acquired that requisite nuclear capability by achieving credible deterrence'. He revealed that two US Presidents certified falsely for three years that Pakistan did not possess a nuclear device. On the reports that Pakistan has acquired nuclear capability, US sent the Robert Gates mission to warn Pakistan that India's retaliation would be devastating. While there was no mobilisation of ground forces as alleged in the inspired US accounts, the Indian Air Force was put on alert. It was during that time Dr. Raja Ramanna, as Minister of State for Defence, announced in Rajya Sabha that while India would never be the first to use its nuclear capability against a neighbour, if one of our neighbours were to do so India would rise to the occasion. This apparently was a signal to Pakistan that India too had nuclear weapons.

Pakistan's nuclear capability is basically based on missile uranium enriched at its Kahuta facility, although it has displayed some interest in using plutonium after establishing a reprocessing plant at 'New Lab' in Rawalpindi. Kahuta began manufacturing weapons usable enriched uranium in 1986. According to one estimate, the plant could produce enough highly enriched uranium for two to three bombs annually. As stated by Senator Alan, Pakistan's Kahuta enrichment had the capacity to produce about 45 kgs. of highly enriched uranium and was being expanded to an annual capacity of between 90 to 120 kgs. Around 15 to 25 kgs. of highly enriched uranium are needed to manufacture a nuclear fission device of 15-20 kilo tonnes Hiroshima type lethality. An American estimated that Pakistan had established the manufacturing capacity to produce five to six bomb quantities of enriched uranium in 1985. As per the estimates of SIPRI by 1992, Pakistan had enriched uranium sufficient for six to 10 bombs.[15] On account of the developments, the US President has been unable to certify since 1990 that Pakistan does not possess nuclear weapons, and hence US military aid had to be cut off. The foreign secretary during a visit to the US had told the press in February 1992 that Pakistan possessed the components of a bomb. After having held the post of Prime Minister, both Benazir Bhutto and Nawaz Sharif had publicly claimed years ago that Pakistan possessed nuclear weapons.

The proliferation of missile technology in the Middle East and South Asia became evident as early as 1987-88 when oil rich Saudi Arabia acquired 60DF-3 (CSS-2) 2500 km range ballistic missile from China. In the nineties, Pakistan became a missile-capable country with overt and covert Chinese assitance. Keeping its geo-political strategy for the region in mind, China sold the M-11 series missiles to Pakistan and helped them on guidance and control systems, solid fuel and work on various M-11 missile variants. The United States, for its own geo-political reasons, obviously turned a blind eye to the strategic missile capability of Pakistan. Thus, Pakistan first acquired the missile capability through outside assistance and then gave legitimacy to its indigenous missile programme by re-tooling the missile and presenting it as one from the Hatf series. The growing arms race in South Asia–continued with outside assistance to Pakistan in both nuclear and missile fields that allow Pakistan to achieve strategic missile capability at a faster pace-adversely affected political stability. While Pakistan through dubious means and powerful allies, has managed to become a missile power, the Indian stance on the Nuclear-Proliferation Treaty (NPT) and the Comprehensive Test Ban Treaty (CTBT), in real terms, has kept it away from multifarious gains. There is, however, a vital difference between the nuclear capabilities of the two countries. In the case of Pakistan it is entirely procured from external sources. India has painstakingly built up its capability, thus, making itself more suspect in the eyes of the executive nuclear club. Both Pakistan and India had been living in a state of mutual deterrence even as the covert war in Kashmir was being waged. It was in these conditions, the Indian Foreign Secretary J.N. Dixit offered to Pakistan in January 1994 a non-paper proposing a mutual no-first use agreement. If these facts are publicised by the Indian government it would go a long way towards countering the Goebbelsian propaganda on Kashmir being a flash-point and there being very high risks of a nuclear war.

During the period 1992-94, China had exported 50 M-11 missiles to Pakistan. Pakistan successfully raised nuclear industry with the guiding support of China, who distributed the nuclear technology. One explanation for why Islamabad acquired nuclear capability with the active assistance and advice of China and others is that it is part of a calculated projection of a "threat" from India. The other explanation which is a part of the first that Pakistan seeks again to move forward in its posture. Pakistan's strategy has been to rely on generating and highlighting a "crisis" in the relations with India to move towards a more explicit nuclear posture. The linkage of nuclear issue with that of Kashmir was created in this context. The aim is to reduce the international costs of progressing its weapon status. There has been increasing evidence of China having supplied nuclear weapon technology and nuclear capable ballistic missiles and related technology to Pakistan even after China signed the NPT in 1992 and gave assurance to the US in 1995 that it had stopped transfer of technology to Pakistan. Reports of such transfer have emerged even after China provided written assurance (in October 1997) of stopping supplies.

Nuclear Explosions of 1998

After 24 years, India had conducted successfully on 11th and 13th May 1998, five nuclear tests (three and two respectively). The dramatic announcement was made by Prime Minister Atal Bihari Vajpayee which said, "Today at 3.45 pm India conducted three underground nuclear tests in the Pokharan range. The tests conducted were with the fissile device, a low yield device and a thermonuclear device. The measured yields are in line with expected values. Measurements have confirmed that there was no release of radioactivity into the atmosphere. These were contained explosions like in the experiment conducted in May 1974. I warmly congratulate the scientists and engineers who have carried out the successful tests." A momentous event like this brings in its wake of great many challenges, opportunities and responsibilities. The formidable task which the India's foreign policy now faces is to meet these challenges, seize these opportunities and discharge these responsibilities. The spectrum of instant reactions in India ranged from thrills of joy to the jingoistic "junoon". In this politically unstable, economically backward and socially restless country, where the manifestation of national strength had become a rare experience, this new found sense of achievement threw them off balance. People were delighted that at last the world took notice of India. Non-Resident Indian (NRIs) hailed the nuclear tests, viewing the nuclear tests as an expression of India's courage. It was not only the BJP but allied and opposition formations too were seeking to make political capital out of the nuclear tests carried out in Pokharan. The position taken by the Congress party, by former Prime Minister V.P. Singh, P.V. Narasimha Rao and Inder Kumar Gujral and prominent United Front figures clearly show that they were stunned by Vajpayee's daring gamble but unwilling to differ with him. Even the Left had commended the achievement of the scientific establishment while making the proforma cautionary noises against any deviation from the declared policy or commitment to disarmament.[16] Dr. A.P.J. Abdul Kalam, scientific adviser to the defence minister admitted in an announcement that in a country with such diversity of views as in India there will always be a minority opposed to nuclear weapons. But the large majority appeared to have decided to support the country's nuclear status. At the same time, they are bound to be concerned with the issue of how the new-born is to be nurtured, brought up and made to serve the national and international interests in a responsible way.[17]

Vajpayee's government had perhaps tested India's nuclear weapons in order to enhance the country's security in the face of mounting evidence to Sino-Pak collaboration in the development of nuclear weapons and missiles. However, the Presidential system and the nuclear bomb have been on the BJP's agenda. From its Jana Sangh days, this Right wing outfit has been insistent on these two points, its belief being that these would help to project India as a strong country under a strong leader. The Party's and the Sangh Parivar's disdain for the non-nationalists, also described as pseudo-secular is based in the conviction that they lack martial valour and are, therefore, responsible for all of India's ills, going back to the invasions of the past and the inability to stand up to the world at present. After 1947, while the pacifist turned to the socialist model of development and founded the anti-American non-aligned bloc, the Jana Sangh-BJP had pro-American and pro-capitalist image. There might not be anything wrong in opting for the bomb if it is genuinely required for the sake of national security. But the step must carry conviction, and not be seen as a jingoistic measure for partisan purposes. Even patriotism cannot be the last refuge of a government which refuges to think through the logic of its actions. Neither Vajpayee nor his elected or unelected advisors had convincingly argued why the doctrine governing India's nuclear policy has been changed suddenly. Nor have they told the nation what has replaced it.[18]

As the BJP led-coalition took over the reigns of administration in New Delhi, Islamabad was apprehensive of its motives and designs. The amity between India and Pakistan had become a distant dream with the test-firing of Ghauri missile by the later and former's reaction thereof. In a changed and charged atmosphere Islamabad had warned New Delhi through its Urdu daily, *Jung*, in April 1998 that "Pakistan has decided that if India goes ahead with a fresh nuclear test, it would also conduct a nuclear test without any delay for its defence needs. The retaliatory action would done within few days of any future Indian nuclear tests. When India exploded its nuclear device on 11th and 13th May 1998 respectively, Pakistan criticised it in the possible strongest terms. Responding to the tests, Prime Minister Nawaz Sharif said that Pakistan has the right to take any step which are essential for its security. This is our job and we alone have to decide it. Islamabad too, was ready for the explosion as indicated by Dr. Abdul Qadeer Khan, Pakistan's top nuclear scientist, a fortnight ago that his country was capable of carrying out a nuclear explosion and he needed only Government's permission to do so. The 15-month-old Nawaz Sharif Government was faced with its most difficult situation amid mounting domestic pressure to go for nuclear and global pressure side by side. According to some dailies there was no other option but to go for nuclear test to match India's five nuclear explosions. They stressed that Pakistan must make it absolutely clear to the US that we are totally within our rights to do whatever necessary for our defence and national security.

In the meantime, US President Bill Clinton sensed the possibility of nuclear arms race between the two countries and had urged Pakistan to "reconcile" with Indian tests and promised to guarantee its security without nuclear tests and nuclear weapons. But Pakistan's nuclear programme had gone ahead under the overall patronage of the United States. The reason behind the US soft line towards Pakistan's nuclear programme was its pressing need during the Afghan crisis. The United States had been unwilling to exert strong pressure on Pakistan to honour its non-proliferation commitments for fear that Pakistan would retaliate by restricting the assistance pipe line to Afghan Mujahideen. It was only after the withdrawal of Soviet troops from Afghanistan in February 1989, the Bush Administration invoked the Pressler Amendment, suspending military and economic assistance to Pakistan since October 1990. Hence, the war in Afghnistan, at least, led to inaction on the part of the US Policy-makers which in turn allowed Pakistan to receive a large amount of US military and economic assistance and simultaneously engage in a clandestine nuclear weapons programme. In the South-Asian context, non-proliferation is not merely a nuclear question. The larger forces and interests at work both within the region and outside have to be understood. Regional security cannot be considered in isolation from global or extra-regional conditions. At the global level, the states in the region have to participate in the process to bring about a truly legitimate and non-discriminatory non-proliferation regime. At the regional level, efforts to build bridges of understanding among the countries in the region through confidence-building measures has to be sustained. Hence, in South Asia, non-proliferation can best be achieved through a proper mix of global and regional approaches.

President Clinton's efforts to dissuade Prime Minister Nawaz Sharif from testing nuclear device were on. The offers included blandishments as the repeal of the Pressler amendment–a piece of legislation that the Pakistanis hated with visceral intensity as well as offers of military and economic aid and presumably, security guarantees as well. Clinton even climbed down from his Presidential heights and telephoned Nawaz Sharif several times, at all parts of night and day. Apart from this, as revealed by Pakistani officials, the US team led by Deputy Secretary of State Strobe Talbott that came to Islamabad on an emergency basis had offered several arguments why Pakistan should not test? They indicated, for example, that a Pakistani test would take the heat off India. Besides, the economic sanctions that the US and other countries would have to impose have a much more disastrous effect on Pakistan than on India. The US team also suggested that Pakistan would stand to gain, economically and militarily as well as in world approbation, if it refrained from testing. However, the hard-liners in Islamabad were raising the pressure for nuclear test and viewed it the only alternative left for Pakistan. Gohar Ayub Khan, Pakistan's Foreign Minister, even claimed that the ruling BJP leadership in India was suffering from a false sense of pride and indulging in brinkmanship and asserted that Pakistan's nuclear and missile programme was better than that of India. Dubbing India as a habitual aggressor he added, "hundred per cent of Indian defence preparedness is directed towards Pakistan. Every weapons system–even training and battle plans of Indian Army is Pakistan-specific".[19] Politician of all hues in Pakistan had demanded that India be declared a rougue state. Benazir Bhutto had openly urged the US to bomb India's nuclear facilities straightway. The Nawaz Sharif government had also sent high-level missions to every nuclear country, and several important non-nuclear ones, to demand that India be punished, and to ask for protection against the Indian nuclear threat. One such team went to Beijing to ask for a nuclear guarantee. Beijing had not overtly acceded to Pakistan's request, but had also not hesitated to remind Indians precisely where it could bring pressure to bear on India. Most ominous of all was Chinese declaration that it would never allow India into the nuclear club and that the US and China must work jointly to prevent this from happening.

As expected by many Pakistan evened its nuclear test account with India by exploding five nuclear tests on 28 May 1998. Making the announcement in a nation-wide broadcast, Nawaz Sharif said by carrying out the tests we have evened the account with India which had conducted similar number of nuclear explosions on May 11th and 13th in Pokharan. Islamabad exploded one more test on 30th May 1998, and became ahead of India in this regard. Shamshad Ahmed, Pakistan's Foreign Secretary, in an announcement said that Pakistan was willing to enter into talks to resolve all issues, including prevention of nuclear proliferation in the region. "Pakistan's decision to exercise nuclear option is only for self-defence and to deter aggression. About the capacity of the tests, Dr. Abdul Qadeer Khan, father of Pakistan's nuclear programme, disclosed after the first round of the blasts that the five devices detonated were boosted fission bombs using Uranium-235. One of them was a big bomb, twice as big as the one dropped on Hiroshima. According to him, the devices tested by Pakistan were very compact and can quite easily be converted into weapons. However, as a responsible country, Pakistan assured the international community, particularly India of Islamabad's willingness to enter into immediate discussions to address all matters, including urgent matters to prevent nuclear proliferation. Earlier, Nawaz Sharif too had affirmed his country's determination to engage in constructive dialogue with other countries especially with major powers in order to promote nuclear disarmament and non-proliferation. In general, Pakistan had two basic compulsions for this nuclear-tit-for-tat. First, Islamabad had to prove to India in particular and the world at large that its nuclear capability was not a 'fib' but very real. Second, and by far more vital to the survival of Nawaz Sharif government, was the dire need to reply to India's test with an exactly identical display of nuclear prowess. With economic sanctions having receded as threat to either India or Pakistan, the latter's compulsion was solely on how to generate the kind of jingoistic euphoria within Pakistan as would match that of India.

Islamabad ignored President Clinton's repeated pleadings and offers not to conduct nuclear 'tit-for-tat' tests but it did not get diluted the tilt initiated by Henry Kissinger in early 1970s which gradually became the preferred mind set in the State Department, the Pentagon and the National Security Council. Referring to the President's persistent bid to battle for "sanity on the sub-continent", White House spokesman Mike McCurry's comment was more appropriate, made on May 28, 1998, the day Pakistan evened its nuclear test account with India. "I think it would be accurate to say that the Prime Minister clearly struggled with what was apparently, for him a very difficult decision. He knew the costs, he understood exactly the President's argument–but I think he clearly felt the pressure and the burden of both domestic political opinion and also the reality of pressure he faced in the regions because of the decision by the Government of India. He sounded, in short, like someone who is very pained by a very difficult decision and, the administration, on its part, sounded as if it were about to burst into tears at Pakistan's sorry plight. Despite the fact, he conceded, although with quite sad, that the sanctions mandated by the Glenn amendment would apply equally to India and Pakistan, felt that there was a qualitative difference in the way the two had handled their nuclear compulsions. "Prime Minister Sharif was honest and straight forward in the description of the decision that he was wrestling with and in his own internal deliberations, and the Government of India was manifestly not". However, the spokesman seemed missing that Pakistan has been less than "straight forward" over the past several years when it clandestinely acquired from China nuclear material, missiles and relevant technology–the transfer of which was specifically banned by the US law and global treaties and understandings and went about constructing its bomb in the basement. Not that the US was unaware of the fact: intelligence agencies had been warning for years that Pakistan was acquiring nuclear weapon capability through Chinese assistance.[20]

Pakistan's Nuclear Power Uptodate

Even today India focusses on China's strategic modernisation programmes, Pakistan competes with India. This triangular nuclear interaction is too complex for traditional arms control and too dynamic for *Laissez-fair* politics. Pakistan's need for nuclear assets, it could be persuasively argued, was one that initially necessitated by India's experiments with nuclear devices, and, as such, primarily concerned itself with the survival of the young nation of Pakistan. Especially, in the light of the fact that India's conventional forces were mightier than Pakistan could even aspire to become given the lack of human resources, the latter was compelled to devise an effective way to counter a possible Indian offensive. Nuclear weapons, thus, proved to be a tool for survival not because it was expected to assail India in an actual military confrontation, but also because it kept the sub-continent at bay for fear of Mutual Assured Destruction (MAD). Pakistan's initial need for survival today seems to have escalated to an arms race with India.[21] Initially, Pakistani authorities embraced a doctrine of minimal, credible deterrence but later its posture began to emphasise credibility rather than minimalism. Current and prospective production rates in Pakistan are sized to support ambitious nuclear targetting objectives that are set with minimal civilian oversight. In addition, Pakistani nuclear power is not checked by any significant nuclear weapons regulation treaty because she has not ratified such treaties and that Pakistan does not abide by the no-first-strike doctrine.[22] Pakistan is the only nuclear power where the military has its finger on the nuclear button.

The enduring grudge between India and Pakistan that dates back to the days of the Indian partition, coupled with South Asia's characteristic tendency of resorting to violence as a first opinion, make nuclear ownership of these two countries an imminent peril to the region. In general, since their independence, they have remained in a constant state of hostility. Periods of peace have at best remained uneasy and have been characterised by what analyst Ashley Tellis terms, "ugly stability".[23] There witnessed a relative peace after 1971 Bangladesh War and Shimla peace accord in 1972, but on the other the nuclearisation of the region had already commenced, with India conducting a nuclear test Pokharan in 1974 and Pakistan proceeding apace in acquiring a nuclear capability. Earlier, the arms transfer from China to Pakistan began with the conclusion of the first military agreement between the two in 1966. Cooperation between them grew rapidly and by 1970 the tanks supplied by China constituted 25 per cent of the entire tank of Pakistan's disposal. The year 1966 is also a memorable time for Sino-Pakistani nuclear cooperation as on 30th June, two agreements to this effect were concluded with Beijing for scientific and military cooperation in the nuclear sector.[24] From all indications, cooperation between the two countries had developed in plutonium reprocessing and uranium enrichment through the centrifuge method by 1978. By 1984, Pakistan had received the technical information for the actual designing of nuclear weapons.[25] Beijing has not only helped Islamabad with its nuclear weapons programmes at Kahuta, Khushab and Chasma nuclear plants, but also its delivery systems-ready-to-launch M-9 (Ghaznavi/Hatf), M-11 (Shaheen), and a number of Dong Feng-21s (Ghauri) ballistic missiles.[26] This cooperation has continued despite Beijing's growing concerns over the Talibanisation of the Pakistani state and society.

After the nuclear explosion in 1998 by India and Pakistan, the South Asia region has come under nuclear threats. China had acquired this status in mid-1960s. The China's acquisition insisted India to develop its own nuclear weapons. India took its first nuclear test in 1974 with a view that Pakistan would get or had been preparing under the leadership of China. This apprehension proved true when Pakistan took nuclear tests in May 1998.[27] *The New York Times* of June 1998, pointed out that China provided blueprints for bombs, as well as highly-enriched uranium and tritium, scientists and key components for a nuclear weapon production complex, among other crucial tools.[28] Following the overt demonstration of their nuclear capability and the acknowledgement of a "force in being", there was a rational hope that both sides would grasp the futility of attempting nuclear blackmail or coercion, and eschew dangerous practices. On the basis of this premise both India and Pakistan commenced bilateral negotiations at 1998-1999, culminating in the Lahore Agreement of February 1999. The aftermath of the tests saw India adumbrate a 'no-first-use' policy, emphasising a 'second-strike' capability to achieve a minimum credible deterrent. Pakistan articulated its nuclear stance *vis-a-vis* India, its primary concern being a 'first-use' policy to deter conventional aggression. While India was purported to have taken the nuclear turn in order to ascend higher in the echelons of world politics and balance an apparent nuclear threat from China, for Pakistan it was the only deterrent to India's overwhelming conventional threat.[29] With the tests, the half-century old conflict between India and Pakistan acquired a nuclear edge.

Hardly a year after the explosions and contrary to the claims of nuclear weapons advocates, who promised peace and a cessation of war, India and Pakistan fought over Kargil bitterly and India and Pakistani officials delivered indirect and direct nuclear threats to one another at least 13 times. Kargil was the first major confrontation between two nuclear powers. At the time, it appeared that the 1998 tests convinced Pakistan's political and military leaders that the operation might be feasible with nuclear weapons to restrict any possible Indian riposte.[30] Perhaps the introduction of overt, offsetting nuclear capabilities and ballistic missiles has clearly increased tensions and risks in the sub-continent, at least in the short run, as was most evident in the intense, limited war fought in the heights above Kargil in 1999. Serious nuclear risk reduction is not possible in the absence of meaningful officials dialogue.[31] Given the dismaying history of Indo-Pakistani interactions, it is understandable why New Delhi would believe that a policy to isolate Pakistani perpetrators of Kargil and supporters of militancy in Kashmir would yield more benefits than a dialogue on risk reduction. As Pakistani officials repeatedly declare, nuclear risk reduction is inextricably linked to tensions in Kashmir. But those tensions are also inextricably linked to the transit by militant groups based in Pakistan across the LoC.[32] Thus, under structurally asymmetrical conditions and with emerging force posture and evolving command systems, India and Pakistan have both mobilised conventional forces in formal deployments and also engage in other dangerous military practices. While it remains unclear whether their nuclear forces have been shifted from peacetime conditions to formal deployments or even placed on crisis alert status, there is no guarantee that crisis-management systems in either country are secure or reliable enough to prevent miscalculation in the future. The foremost factor that must be acknowledged is that any limited or low-level conflict now carries with it the threat of escalation and nuclear inadvertence.[33] Nuclear systems are in a dangerous state of constant transition from varying levels of deployment.

Again Kargil showed levels of military activity which went beyond anything seen anywhere else in respect of two nuclear-equipped rivals engaged in a "hot conventional war" and the post-nuclear scenario of armed conventional conflict in South Asia has proved markedly different and much more serious than anywhere else.[34] Indeed, a combination of Pakistani boldness and Indian restraint since 1998 has surprised proponents of the stability/instability paradox. A small probability of lower-level conflict escalating to the nuclear threshold would not encourage such behaviour, yet Pakistani forces have repeatedly launched conventional attacks on Indian territory.[35] India has been a reluctant nuclear power.[36] and the development of the "Cold Start" dectorine[37] shows that the Indian military establishment has also warmed up the idea of limited wars under the nuclear umbrella. Kargil and other skirmishes along the Indo-Pak border and the massive face-off in 2002 bear the testimony to the fact that violence in various forms remains a legitimate means to achieve Pakistan's political objectives in Kashmir.[38] Even today the official position of Islamabad is that it will not be the first to openly employ. However, in view of those who want Pakistan nuclear weapons to 'compensate for the conventional military imbalance is now more influential than ever and is one major reason why Pakistan will not adopt a 'no first use' posture.[39] Here, nuclear deterrence works in a minimalistic way, while conventional wars between nuclear rivals are unviable and remain contained to a rational limit.[40] Nuclear weapons may have limited the risks of war, but they do not inhibit either side from engaging in low-level conflicts.

In the circumstances not clear and stable, in nuclear sphere, Pakistan continued its efforts to expand its nuclear capability particularly with the help of China as earlier. Pakistanis are emotional about their country's relations with China. This is one bilateral relationship that has no parallel in the world, many Pakistanis say. For Pakistan, the US has been off-again and on-again partner, seen as using Islamabad to achieve its strategic goals in the region and ditching it when those goals are met. On the other hand, Pakistan and China refer to each other as 'all weather friends. China has provided Pakistan the security of constant backing by a big power, while Islamabad has been an accommodating ally in the geo-strategic middle of South, Central and West Asia. It has been a willing market for Chinese goods, and an unconditional supporter of Beijing in international fora. Pakistan has also acted as Beijing's bridge to other Islamic countries.[41] The role of China in South Asian security issues as well as in future conflict scenarios is crucial when considering two realities:

(i) The historical animosity between India and China, and

(ii) The long standing 'all weather' political and military alliance between Pakistan and China.

Indian analysts often cite transfer of nuclear and missile technology from Beijing to Islamabad as evidence of an encircled threat to India.[42] For both India and Pakistan, key components of their attitudes in nuclear defence demonstrate the incompatibility between their mutual nuclear postures. In that kind of situation both strive for a secure second-strike capability as an integral element of their credible minimum deterrent doctrines. Since neither side has constructed systems that are deemed completely satisfactory and reliable, nuclear modernisation continues. From the crisis of 2001-2002 Islamabad and New Delhi have conducted several rounds of peace talks aimed at bringing a lasting settlement to the Kashmir issue. Although India and Pakistan also signed a crucial agreement on reducing the risk of nuclear accidents in February 2007,[43] yet despite the sustained peace talks and CBMs, the two sides continue a hedging strategy to guard against future uncertainty. This is done by developing more reliable nuclear delivery systems, perfecting and increasing fissile material stock, and acquiring conventional weaponry in line with contemporary war-fighting doctrines.

It is widely accepted that since its inception, Pakistan's nuclear policy has been constant response to the perceived threat from India.[44] Therefore, in order to maintain the strategic balance or to at least prevent from the present imbalance from widening, Pakistan further expands its own nuclear capabilities. After 1998, on 2nd February 2000, Pakistan formed the National Command Authority (NCA), a nuclear command and control structure. It is the apex body for handling its nukes and headed by General Musharraf. He was made responsible for both development and deployment of Pakistan's nuclear weapons.[45] In pre and post-explosion periods Pakistan deployed the missile system that can reach most parts of India. These deployed missiles include the Ghaznavi (Hatf-3, range 290-km), Shaheen-1 (Hatf-4, range, 600-800 km), and the Ghauri-1 (hatf-5, range 1,500 km).[46] Substantial development took place on the Shaheen-II (Hatf-6, range 2000-3000 km) which was tested in February 2007. These missile developments illustrate Pakistan's desire for a more secured deterrent, once the range issue had been dealt with. In addition, Pakistan is also seeking a more secured second-strike capability through the acquisition of the Agosta 90 B class submarine which can carry the nuclear capable Harpoon cruise missiles.[47] In response to India's manufacturing another delivery system cruise missile-the Brahmos, Pakistan has developed the Babur. These missiles are meant to have land, sea and air versions. Pakistan has successfully tested the nuclear capable Babur (Hatf-VII) cruise missile (range 700-km) in March 2007.[48] In order to strengthen the nuclear delivery, Pakistan is seeking to perfect its missile arsenals, both ballistic and cruise. However, in the post, 9/11 era-the nuclear concerns of Pakistan was solidified and particularly the West argued, as believed by Brigadier Muhammad, 'a nuclear Pakistan has to be kept in control, lest it leads Islamic world towards the formation of a new and powerful economic and military bloc in competition with or antagonistic to the western alliance'.[49] Brigadier Khalid Mahmud Akhtar, also writing in the 2002-*Green Book*, saw an 'American strategy of economic warfare to force Pakistan to abandon her nuclear programme.

Recently, Pakistan's nuclear programme has received a further boost since July 2005 when the US and Indian governments unveiled their nuclear cooperation agreement. A basic feature of this agreement is that by acquiring uranium from foreign sources and by placing a set of nuclear facilities on the military list India can increase its fissile material production for weaponisation purposes. This perspective also views that rather than increasing nuclear warhead production, New Delhi would use the expansion of its uranium supplies and enrichment capability to fuel its nuclear submarine project[50], a key element of India's desire to achieve a secure second strike capability under its credible minimum deterrence doctrine. In line, there are two separate perspectives of criticism; the first focusses on the non-proliferation objective, and the second on India's strategic needs. It was largely felt that the agreement will weaken the global non-proliferation regime by condoning India's nuclear weapons programme. A further objection is that even with fourteen reactors under safeguards, eight others will remain on the military list, free to manufacture plutonium for several nuclear weapons annually.[51] India has since designated some of its reactors as civilian, and open to inspection, but others still churn out spent fuel richly laden with weapons-usable plutonium. India can potentially make even more of the stuff. Now, that it can import uranium fuel for its civilian reactors, it can devote more of its scarce domestic supplies to bomb-making. In the whole issue, the US argued simply that India had a spotless non-proliferation record and that bringing it into the non-proliferation "mainstream" could only bolster global anti-proliferation efforts.. Even in Barack Obama's administration Pakistan hoped that it would eventually get a deal like India. Some in the Obama administration have also supported this on the ground that America needs Pakistan's support in the fight against al-Qaeda and the Taliban.

However, signing of the deal brought Pakistan and China closer than earlier and having been rebuffed by the United States in its attempts to secure a nuclear energy deal for Pakistan similar to the Indo-US one. Islamabad has been actively seeking Beijing's assistance instead. The issue of nuclear energy was raised in 2006 during Pakistan President Pervez Musharraf's visit to China and Chinese President Hu Jinato's return visit to Islamabad. On both occasions, Beijing reassured its "all weather always" on all strategic matters including energy cooperation, Pakistan reportedly asked for assistance with the building of a number of reactors. Even for China the deal was not considered good and the main Chinese Communist Party newspaper, *The People's Daily* accused the deal of "double standards" and added that it was likely to damage the existing non-proliferation system.[52] To China, the 123-Agreement has from its inception, represented a potent strategic alliance between the United States and India aimed at counter-balancing China's rise in the region. The daily newspaper also accused of "hegemonic ideas" and being unconcerned about "others' opinion". It went on to assert that the US clearly intended to draw "India in a tool for its global strategic pattern".[53] Although indirectly, the paper described India as "wanting to seize the opportunity to rise as big power," out of "practical political considerations". In fact, both India and the United States are concerned about the future direction of Chinese foreign policy and security policy.[54] For the United States, aiding India through nuclear cooperation as well as a strategic partnership, Washington would be able to balance China more effectively in the region. In the process, it would divert China from its main security issue Taiwan. For India, the agreement is a significant diplomatic and strategic addition to its capabilities *vis-a-vis* China, with both the possible increase in fissile material production and a strengthened strategic partnership with the United States.

In past, China has built up Pakistan as a counter to India for several decades, a policy that involved transfers of nuclear and missile technology.[55] Even before the announcement of Indo-US civil nuclear deal in July 2005, there were reports in March-2004 that China was planning to provide Islamabad with a nuclear reactor. The implication is that the Beijing-Islamabad nuclear partnership might have continued in any case. But the current pattern of nuclear cooperation between China and Pakistan is used by Beijing to lay the grounds for legitimising continued nuclear collaboration with Pakistan.[56] Further in December 2005, China began construction of the 300-MW second phase of the Chasma Nuclear Power Plant, contracted in May 2004, subsequent to the commissioning of the first phase in September 2000, parallel to the Indo-US deal, China and Pakistan also reportedly agreed to a nuclear cooperation arrangement under which as many as six nuclear reactors of at least 600 MW capacity would be provided to Islamabad. Although the Vienna-based Nuclear Supplier Group has opposed the supply of nuclear power plants to Pakistan by its member China, the latter has maintained that its agreement with Pakistan for cooperation in civil nuclear technology was signed in the 1980s before China joined the NSG. Some Pakistani Commentators, in fact felt, and argued that their country needs nuclear cooperation with the United States more than India because the gap between existing energy supplies and future energy requirement is far more serious for Pakistan than it is for India.[57] A senior Pakistani official reminded the US its nuclear policy statement of October 2006 that Washington's nuclear policy should be guided by criteria-based "approach rather than one geared toward a single country".[58] However, US government officials have stated that they have no intention of considering a similar agreement with Pakistan.

As a result of Indo-US cooperation in nuclear sphere, Pakistan increased its motivation for self-reliance on nuclear energy through indigenous fuel manufacturing capabilities.[59] In the context government officials in Pakistan stated in April 2007 that the country would set up an installation for fuel testing for use in nuclear plants in a quest for complete technological capability.[60] Pakistan's overall agenda is to redress the perceived widening of the nuclear imbalance with India. Nevertheless, Pakistani experts have admitted that Islamabad's quest for increased nuclear capability is a result of the tacit rivalry between Beijing and New Delhi and the latter's desire to catch up with China.[61] As a further step in Musharraf's regime, Pakistan had commenced construction of 1,000 MW heavy water reactor that will potentially produce adequate plutonium for as many as 50 warheads per year.[62] In addition, Islamabad set up a commercial scale nuclear reprocessing plant to allow production of weapons grade plutonium. Such activities will enable Pakistan to stockpile as much fissile material as possible before a future FMCT comes into force.[63] These developments suggest that Islamabad is attempting to diversify its nuclear weapons programme through plutonium, as opposed to its traditional reliance on uranium as fissile material.[64] Plutonium allows for more compact weapons and provides increased flexibility for the arsenal. For Islamabad, this is critical for developing a second strike capability against India.[65] However, Chinese support remained key to Pakistan's quest for some strategic benefits *vis-a-vis* India.

After signing the Indo-US civil nuclear deal finally in October 2008, once again, Pakistan's nuclear energy programme revitalised, and in quest, Pakistani President Asif Ali Zardari paid a visit to Beijing in July 2010. Among other things, Zardari urged the Chinese leadership to continue supply of civilian nuclear technology to Pakistan, despite growing international concern over China's nuclear engagement with the country. In his meeting with Chinese President Hu Jintao and Premier Wen Jaibao, Zardari said that his country needed Chinese assistance in developing "an energy mix" which included nuclear power reactors, as well as hydro-power, wind and solar energy.[66] The US Congressional Research Service report on Pakistan's Nuclear Weapons: Proliferation and Security Issue released in October 2011, noted that in addition to the growing Arsenal of warheads: Islamabad is producing fissile material, adding to related production facilities, and deploying additional delivery, vehicles'. It noted a 'radical takeover of Pakistan, which possesses approximately 90-110 nuclear warheads, or a proliferation by radical sympathisers within Pakistan's nuclear complex in case of a breakdown of control could have impact on the country's nuclear safeguards.[67] At the same time, the report cautioned that Pakistan could undertake both quantitative and qualitative improvements to its nuclear arsenal. It also noted that such development might have a link to the 2008 US-India nuclear cooperation agreement. However, in the context, a non-official bilateral discussion was held in December 2011 which recommended that India and Pakistan sign a CBM to the effect that their land-based nuclear arsenals will remain "demated" and de-alerted" in peacetime and initiate a high-level official dialogue on how new and emerging technologies will impact strategic stability.[68] In early 2012, two countries held expert level talks on nuclear CBMs and although failed to move the two countries away from their precarious nuclear balance, it achieved two things. One, Indian and Pakistani officials agreed to recommend to their Foreign Secretaries, the extension of the validity of the "Agreement on Reducing the Risk from Accidents Relating to Nuclear Weapons (2007) for another five years. Two, both sides reviewed the implementation and strengthening of existing CBMs in the framework of Lahore MoU, and agreed to explore possibilities for mutually acceptable additional CBMs.[69] Thus, till date nothing substantial has been achieved by them to bring about nuclear stability in the sub-continent. This despite the fact that a nuclear war between India and Pakistan is arguably more likely than it had been between the US and USSR during the Cold War.

Pakistan, as a further step, to have nuclear parity with India and enhance its influence in the region, in July 2013 approved funds to purchase two new nuclear power reactors from China. The 1100 MWe ACP 1000 units were together priced at 959 billion ($9.6 billion). They will be supplied by China National Nuclear Corp and built at the coastal Karachi site near Paradise Point in Sindh province about 25 kilometres west of the capital.[70] At present Pakistan has a 40-year old 125 MWe pressurised heavy water reactor at Karachi and another nuclear power plant at Chasma in northern Punjab province. This has two 300 MWe Chinese-built reactor operating with two more under construction. Before supplying this in April 2013 the Chinese authorities said they had full intellectual property rights over the design. It had completed the phase of research and design review and would move their focus to construction and market development[71]. Internally too the Pakistan Atomic Energy Commission has received the green light to start work on a second nuclear power plant in Karachi with Chinese assistance. While reports have been cropping up in the international media about KANUPP-2, which is expected to cost $9.6 billion and produce around 1000-MW. It is the first time that government documents and officials have revealed Chinese involvement in the project. It is also to note here that the Pakistan Atomic Energy Commission has chalked out a plan to install 8,000 MW of nuclear energy by 2025 from the present capacity of approximately 700-MW supplied by the plants in Karachi and Chasma.

To conclude, in a rough parity between India and Pakistan in nuclear weapon-related capabilities India is ahead, while in others Pakistan leads. The arsenals of both appeared to have doubled in size over the past decade. India has significantly larger industrial capacity and economy, by some indications Pakistan's nuclear weapons greenhouse has now the fastest-growing arsenal in the world, with 90-110 warheads, up from 65-80 in 2008 and ahead of India's 60-100. The production of warheads in the nuclear greenhouse is suggestive of the existence of a strategic paranoia at the heart of the Pakistan military's thinking–a pathology that will, if unaddressed, have consequences, for India. Pakistan's relationship with India and with the world will be shaped by the struggle now under way to shape the country's relationship with itself–a contestation that has pitted democrats against an alliance of ultra-nationalists and Islamists with an intensity never seen before. The safest route to reduce nuclear dangers on the sub-continent is through concerted, persistent, top down efforts to improve relations between India and Pakistan and the new leaders of the two can be capable of surprising shifts in long-standing nuclear and national security policies.

References

1. Michael Krepon, 'Getting Ahead of the Sum of All Fears,' *The Hindu*, 21st February 2013.
2. Nirupama Subramanian, 'Pakistan and China: Great Expectations', *Ibid.*, 23th November 2006.
3. *Kyodo News International*, 12th June 2013.
4. Dr. Aftab Alam, 'Pakistan's Nuclear Development and Capability', *Third Concept*, April-May 1998, (New Delhi: 1998), pp. 13-14.
5. B.L. Kak, Z.A. Bhutto: *Notes From the Death Cell* (New Delhi: Radha Krishna Prakashan, 1979), p 42.
6. Salmaan Taseer, *Bhutto a Political Biography* (New Delhi: Vikas Publishing House, 1980), pp. 154.
7. O.P. Sabherwal, 'India's Nuclear Policy Under Siege', *One India One People*, August 1997 (Mumbai : 1997), pp. 16-17.
8. *Navhind Times*, 8th June 1974.
9. *The Times of India*, 8th June 1974.
10. *Opinion* (Weekly), 9th July 1974.
11. Adi H. Doctor, *Essays on India's Foreign Policy* (New Delhi: National Publishing House, 1977), p. 114.

12. B.L. Kak, *Z.A. Bhutto: Notes From the Death Cell*, pp. 51-53.
13. *Ibid.*, p. 52.
14. Dr. Aftab Alam, 'Pakistan's Nuclear Development and Capability', pp. 15-16.
15. *Ibid.*, pp. 16-17.
16. Shastri Ramachandaran, 'Test of Liberalism – Trapped Between Bomb and Bombast', *The Times of India* (Patna), 21st May 1998.
17. *Ibid.*, 20th May 1998.
18. *The Hindustan Times*, 23rd May 1998.
19. *Ibid.*, 25th May 1998.
20. N.C. Menon, 'Return of the Tilt', *Ibid.*, 8th June 1998.
21. Williams D., *Pakistan to Overtake Britain as World's Fifth Largest Nuclear Power* (2011). Available : http://www.dailymail.co.uk/new/article
22. *Ibid.*
23. Ashley J. Tellis, *Stability in South Asia* (1997), as quoted in Feroz Hassan Khan, 'Challenges to Nuclear Stability in South Asia', *The Non-Proliferation Review*, Spring 2003, p. 60.
24. Harish Kapur, *India's Foreign Policy 1947-92, Shadow and Substance.* (New Delhi: Sage Publications, 1994), pp. 112-13.
25. Albright, David and Tom Zamora, 'India, Pakistan's Nuclear Weapons: All the Pieces in Place', *Bulletin of the Atomic Scientists*, as quoted in *Ibid.*, p. 113.
26. J. Mohan Malik, 'China and the Nuclear Non-Proliferation Regime', *Contemporary South-East Asia,* Vol. 22, No. 3, December 2000, pp. 445-78.
27. Vivek M. Diwan, 'Perspectives on India-China Relations', *Third Concept*, Vol. 24, No. 288, February 2011 (New Delhi: 2011), p. 9.
28. *The New York Times,* 4th June, 1998.
29. Cirincione, *J. Bomb Scare: The History and Future of Nuclear Weapons* (New York: Columbia University Press, 2007), pp. 53 and 61.
30. M.V. Ramana, 'Deeper into the Morass –Ten Years After Pokharan', *The Hindu*, 11th May 2008.
31. Michael Krepon, 'Nuclear Risk Reduction in South Asia', in P.R. Kumaraswamy (ed.), *Security Beyond Survival* (New Delhi: Sage Publications, 2004), p. 231.
32. *Ibid.*
33. Feroz Hassan Khan, 'Challenges to Nuclear Stability in South Asia', p. 60.

34. Achin Vanaik, 'The Idea That Bombed', *The Hindustan Times*, 23rd February 2000.
35. S.P. Kapur, 'India and Pakistan's Unstable Peace: Why Nuclear South Asia is not Like Cold War Europe', *International Security* (2005), 30 (2), pp. 127-52.
36. S.P. Cohen and Dasgupta, *Arming Without Aiming: India's Military Modernisation* (Washington, DC: Brookings Institution Press, 2010), as quoted in Anurag Sinha, 'Nuclear Myths and Political Realities in South Asia', p. 2.
37. W.C. Ladwig III, 'A Cold Start for Hot Wars? The Indian Army's New Limited War Doctrine', *International Security* (2007), 32 (3), pp. 158-90.
38. A.J. Tellis, C.C. Fair and J.J. Medby, 'Limited Conflicts under the Nuclear Umbrella: Indian and Pakistani Lessons from the Kargil Crisis', as quoted in Anurag Sinha, 'Nuclear Myths and Political Realities in South Asia', p. 2.
39. Achin Vaniak 'The Idea That Bombed'.
40. R.M. Basrur, *South Asia's Cold War: Nuclear Weapons and Conflict in Comparative Perspective* (New York: Routledge, 2008), pp. 103-4.
41. Nirupama Subramaniam, 'Pakistan and China: Great Expectations'.
42. Raja Menon, 'China's Proliferation and India Security', *Seminar*, June 2006.
43. India, Pakistan Sign Nuke Deal in Defiance of Train Attacks', 21st February 2007, also visit www.turkishpress. com.
44. Naeem Ahmad Salik, 'Pakistan and the Future of Non-Proliferation', *International Peace Research Institute* Journal, Vol. VI, No. 1, Winter 2006, pp. 21-45.
45. *The Hindustan Times,* 26th April 2002.
46. *Bulletin of the Atomic Scientists*, 'Pakistan's Nuclear Forces, 2007' Vol. 63, No. 3, pp. 71-73.
47. S.M. Hali, 'Second Strike Capability', *The Nation* (Pakistan), 15th August 2006.
48. 'Pakistan Military Test Fires Missile', *USA Today*, 22nd March 2007.
49. Praveen Swami, 'Pakistan's Hot Nuclear Greenhouse', *The Hindu,* 5th November 2012.
50. Scott Woods, 'Analysis of the US-India Nuclear Deal', *Defence and Security Analysis*, Vol. 22, No. 3, September 2006, pp. 325-28.
51. Gary Milhollin, 'The US-India Nuclear Pact: Bad for Security', *Current History*, November 2006, p. 373.
52. *The Hindu*, 21st August 2007.
53. *Ibid.*

54. Thomas Donnelly and Melissa Wisner, 'A Global Partnership Between the US and India', *Asian Outlook* (American Enterprise Institute), August-September 2005.
55. Mohan Malik, 'China Responds to the US-India Nuclear Deal', *China Brief*, Vol. 6, No. 7, 29th March 2006 (James Town Foundation: 2006).
56. C. Raja Mohan, 'Musharraf to Press China for two Reactors', *The Indian Express*, 12th June 2006.
57. Shameem Akhtar, 'US Nuclear Policy and South Asia', *The Dawn* 31st March 2006.
58. Nirupama Subramanian, 'Pakistan Presses US for Civil Nuclear Energy Pact', *The Hindu*, 26th October 2006.
59. Ihtashamul Haq, 'Move for Indigenous N-fuel Capability', *The Dawn*, 21st February 2007.
60. *Ibid.*, 4th April 2007.
61. Dean Nelson, 'Pakistan Upgrades Nuclear Arsenal', The *Sunday Times*, 30th July 2006.
62. Randeep Ramesh and Julian Borger, 'Pakistan Launches Huge Nuclear Arms Drive', *The Guardian*, 25th July 2006.
63. Shahid-Ur-Rehman Khan, 'Pakistan Nuclear Reprocessing Plant May Yield Weapons–Grade Plutonium', *Kyodo World Service*, 7th May 2007.
64. Joby Warwick, 'Pakistan Expanding Nuclear Programme', *The Washington Post*, 24th July 2006.
65. Dean Nelson, 'Pakistan Upgrades Nuclear Arsenal'.
66. *The Hindu*, 9th July 2010.
67. *Ibid.*, 20th October 2011.
68. Happymon Jacob, 'A Precarious Indo-Pak Nuclear Balance', *Ibid.*, 26th January 2012.
69. *Ibid.*
70. *Kyodo News International*, 13th June 2013.
71. *Ibid.*

❑

4

Nuclear Power: Problems and Challenges

In the context of ever-growing nuclear power of India, the issue of its safety and waste management has become significant. Unlike other plants, nuclear plants must be carefully guarded against both attempted sabotage and possible theft of nuclear material. It is common knowledge that some of the pioneers who experimented with radioactivity including Marie Curie, suffered serious radiation ailments. Those engaged in making luminescent watch dials and early X-ray technicians suffered radiation induced sicknesses. Even in the early years of the nuclear weapons programmes in the United States, the Soviet Union and the United Kingdom, radioactive discharges, from military facilities contaminated the surrounding countryside.[1] Society at present does not perceive industrial risk as it used to in the early days of nuclear energy; it is now expected from nuclear plant operators that they will operate their plant with the highest safety standards, choosing to safest design. Nearly forty countries have nuclear weapons materials and not all of these are secure. With globalisation and the information revolution, the wherewithal to build weapons is relatively easy to access today. The number of nuclear weapon states may grow in the years to come, as the nuclear Non-Proliferation Treaty regime is seen to be inequitable, and powerful incentives for weaponisation continue to exist[2]. Despite efforts made to control the numbers of nuclear weapons, prevent their spread, prohibit their use and seek their elimination, little headway has been made to reduce the risk of nuclear annihilation. After the accidents at Three Mile Island in the US in 1979, and at Chernobyl in the former Soviet Union in 1986, the leaders of nuclear industry all over the world met in Moscow in 1989, whose objective was to spread the culture of safe operation of nuclear power plants through the sharing of operating experience in order to achieve improved nuclear safety all over the world. Likewise the accident of March 2011, in Fukushima (Japan) cast a negative impact on free use of nuclear energy and immediately followed a Summit in Seoul on March 26 and 27, the same year. Although nuclear security is primarily a national responsibility, but it must be supplemented through sustained and effective international cooperation.

Nuclear Power: Safety vs Waste Management

Like any large scale industrial activity, there have been numerous accidents and technical defects occured at Nuclear Power Plants and reprocessing facilities. In the circumstances, safety is taken very seriously by those working in nuclear power plants. The main safety concern is the emission of uncontrolled radiation into the environment which could cause harm to humans both at the reactor site and off-site. Since nuclear reactors contain a core of highly radioactive fuel, and around that core a complex cooling system which is also significantly contaminated, nuclear power plant operators need to invest considerable resources in keeping these structures intact, functioning, and isolated from the environment. In environment, humans are exposed to low-level radioactivity constantly from naturally occurring radioactive isotopes and cosmic rays from outer space. However, in large doses this radiation has many harmful effects. Therefore, it is necessary for Nuclear Power Plants to in-build many safety mechanism in order to keep the population safe. This includes the workers as well as humans living around the nuclear power plant. It is also necessary for independent parties to monitor nuclear power plants. This ensures that plants adhere to world safety standards and to make sure none of the waste plutonium is diverted for use in nuclear weapons. Sensitive nuclear technology such as uranium enrichment and spent nuclear fuel reprocessing are ostensibly employed to create fuel in power reactors, they may be easily adjusted or redirected to produce weapon grade fissile material. Moreover, power reactors themselves produce plutonium which may be used in bombs. In practice, there is no way to segregate nuclear technologies employed for peaceful purposes from technologies that may be employed in weapons–the former may be and have been, transformed into the latter. The International Atomic Energy Agency (IAEA) have developed programmes to detect such activity. Nuclear power plants in France, Sweden, Canada and Finland have shown that it is possible for the generation of electricity through nuclear power to be extremely safe.

Of the total nine nuclear-related accidents, a few such as Three Mile Island power plant, US (1970), Chernobyl Power Plant, Russia (1986) and Fukushima Daiichi Power Plant, Japan (2011), are considered as substantial with Chernobyl termed as horrific.[3] The history of nuclear power shows that design failure have played an important role in all severe accidents. This is true of all enquiries. The Kemeny Commission, set up by Jimmy Carter to analyse the Three Mile Island accident pointed out that the suppliers, Babcock and Wilcox, shared culpability. The disaster at the Chernobyl reactor, which was built by the Soviet predecessor of Rosatom, was caused by a combination of two grievous design features: a positive "void coefficient of reactivity," and "the lack of appropriate containment". And alike these this is true to recent accident at Fukushima, where the underlying problems with the Mark-1 design had been recognised many year earlier.[4] The first major accident in nuclear plant at Three Mile Island was due to meltdown problem in nuclear reactor design. A melt down is what would theoretically happen in certain nuclear power plant designs if control of the nuclear chain reaction were completely lost. If that were to happen, the inside of the nuclear power plant would melt, and there would be a radioactive to clean up. Some of these obsolete plants are still in use in the United States. Even though a meltdown is extremely unlikely, and they are explicitly designed to contain any radiation in the event of a meltdown, they should still be replaced with more recent designs at some point. In reasonably modern nuclear power plant designs this simply cannot happen. If control stops, or coolant is cut off, or any other drastic failure occurs, a modern nuclear power plant will simply shut itself off. Designs vary in how much effort it takes to restart them after such a drastic failure, but that's an economic issue, not a safety issue. In this regard the Union of Concerned Scientists have stated that reactor owners have never been economically responsible for the full costs and risks of their operations. Instead the public faces the prospect of severe losses in the event of any number of potential adverse scenarios, while private investors reap the rewards if nuclear plants are economically successful.[5] For all practical purposes, nuclear power's economic gains are privatised, while its risks are socialised.

On April 26, 1986, a reactor of Chernobyl exploded, setting off the world's worst nuclear catastrophe. Following the multiple explosions and fire that sent huge radioactive plumes into the atmosphere, workers covered the remains of the reactor with sand, lead and eventually entombed it with concrete to halt the release of radiation. The accident caused large scale releases of radioactive materials into the environment. Design deficiencies and operator errors caused the accident. During a recent panel discussion on Russian TV, Rafael Arutyunyan, First Deputy Director of the Russian Institute for Safe Development of Nuclear Power Industry said, 'Chernobyl was "a serious disaster accident", which became a catastrophe only when the Soviet Union adopted a law that promised social protection to all people living in radiation affected territories'.[6] Many researchers in Russia and other countries claim that the nuclear lobby has been deliberately suppressing the truth about radiation risks. Soon after its establishment in 1957, the IAEA signed agreements with the World Health Organisation (WHO), the Food and Agriculture Organisation (FAO) and other UN agencies which imposed constraints on independent studies of radiation and health. The agreements played an extremely negative role for the study of radiation effects in Chernobyl. According to Natalia Mansurova a radio-biologist, some information was withheld and selective methods were applied to exclude large number of radiation-affected people from being monitored for medium and long-term effects.[7] Recently, after the nuclear accident at Fukushima, Ban Ki-Moon, the UN Secretary General, visited the site of Chernobyl and said, 'As we are painfully learning once again, nuclear accidents respect no borders. They pose a direct threat to human health and the environment. They cause economic disruptions affecting everything from agricultural production to trade and global services'. He also added, 'It is time to face facts squarely. We owe it to our citizens to practice the highest standards of emergency preparedness and response, from the design of new facilities through construction and operation to their eventual decommissoning'.[8]

The nuclear plant accident at Fukushima in Japan on 11th March 2011 was the third worst after Three Mile Island in 1979, and Chernobyl in 1986. The Chernobyl involved one reactor, whereas at Fukushima they have three stricken reactors plus four storages of spent fuel, which is even more dangerous because it contains long-living elements-cesium, strontium and plutonium. Together they hold 25 times more radioactivity than Chernobyl and it has been leaking into the atmosphere, the ground and the sea for months and it will keep on seeping for a very long time. Japan after all is one of the world's most advanced industrial nations, an acknowledged leader in the technologies of the twentieth century with several decades of experience in handling nuclear matters in all its varied aspects. Japan is a world leader in the design of earthquake-resistant structures. The reactors themselves had withstood the ravages of earlier earthquakes and despite some incidents, nothing had happened, either at Fukushima or at other nuclear complexes in Japan. But despite the advanced level of Japanese technological capabilities, the reactors of Fukushima, it now emerges, have had a troubled history. From as far back as 1971, warnings have been sounded regarding the specific unsafe features of the General Electric Mark-1 boiling water reactors as this class of reactors is known, warnings that went unheeded.[9] However, the real shock has been the relative ease with which safety systems, procedures and protocols were rendered ineffective by the earthquake and the tsunami. In designing the system to withstand the severe but rare natural calamity, the potential for such an event to overwhelm all safety systems had clearly not been anticipated. Again after the Fukushima accident the role of IAEA was criticised and it appeared that the nuclear powers have no special role to play, at least in a manner visible in the public domain, in the event of a serious nuclear accident in a country that is a trusted signatory to the NPT. The precise mechanism for transparent and rapid exchange of scientific information and expertise in such a crisis is not clear. If no such adequate mechanism exists or is not functional, it is a sorry comment on the functioning of the IAEA. Issues of nuclear power and safety are no longer purely matters of national policy, alone. They are a matter of global public interest. We need international standards for construction, agreed guarantees of public safety, full transparency and information-sharing among nations.

The safety of any large scale industrial activity like nuclear is an on-going concern and must always be taken seriously. Unfortunately, the US nuclear industry did not given it the full attention it needed before the Three Mile Island accident. Nuclear plants in the Western World use a "Defence in Depth" concept which is a system with multiple safety components, each with back-up and design to accommodate human error. The components include:

(i) Control of radioactivity;
(ii) Maintenance of core cooling;
(iii) Maintenance of barriers that prevent the release of radiation, etc.

Control of radioactivity requires being able to control the neutron flux. In a nuclear reactor, when a neutron is captured by a fuel nucleus, the nucleus splits releasing radioactive particles. Hence, if we decrease the neutron flux, the radioactivity will get decreased. The most common way to reduce the neutron flux is include neutron absorbing control rods. These control rods can be partially inserted into the reactor core to reduce the reactions. The control rods are very important because the reaction could run out of control if fission events are extremely frequent. In modern nuclear power plants, the insertion of all the control rods into the reactor core occurs in a few seconds, thus halting the nuclear reaction as rapidly as possible. In addition, most reactors are designed to that beyond optimal level, as the temperature increases the efficiency of reactions decreases, hence fewer neutrons are able to cause fission and the reactor slows down automatically. For maintenance of core cooling in any nuclear reactor some sort of cooling is necessary. Generally nuclear reactors use water as a coolant. However, some reactors which cannot use water use sodium or sodium salts.

For safety point of view barriers are also erected that prevent the release of radiation in a nuclear plant between the radioactive core and the environment. For instance, at the Darling Nuclear Generation Station in Canada the reactors are enclosed in heavily reinforced concrete which is 1.8 m thick. Workers are shielded from radiation via interior concrete walls. A vacuum building is connected to the reactor buildings by a pressure relief duct. The vacuum building is a 71m high concrete structure and is kept at negative atmospheric pressure. This means that if any radiation were to leak from the reactor, it would be sucked into the vacuum building, and therefore, prevented from being released into the environment. In the context, design of the reactor also includes multiple back-up components, independent systems, monitoring of instrumentation and the prevention of a failure of one type of equipment affecting any other. In addition, Ban Ki-Moon, the UN Secretary-General, after his visit to Chernobyl, put forward a five-point strategy to improve nuclear safety for future.

- First, it is time for a top to bottom review of current safety standards both at the national and international levels.
- Second, we need to strengthen the work of the International Atomic Energy Agency on nuclear safety.
- Third, we must put a sharper focus on the new nexus between natural disasters and nuclear safety. Climate change means more incidents of freak and increasingly severe weather. With the number of nuclear facilities set to increase substantially over the coming decades, our vulnerability will grow.
- Fourth, we must undertake a new cost benefit analysis of nuclear energy, factoring in the costs of disaster preparedness and prevention as well as clean-up when things go wrong.
- Fifth and finally, we need to build a stronger connection between nuclear safety and nuclear security. At a time when terrorists seek nuclear materials, we can say with confidence that a nuclear plant that is safer for its community is also more secure for the world.[10]

Another challenge for nuclear power is dealing with the left over, highly radioactive and long lived nuclear waste. Nuclear power plants generate large quantities of highly radioactive material. This is due to the left over isotopes (atoms) from the splitting of the atom and the creation of heavier atoms, like plutonium, which the nuclear power plant does not utilise.

It is called nuclear waste. The generation of electricity in a nuclear power plant is made by splitting uranium atoms. The uranium used as fuel in a nuclear plant is formed into ceramic pellets about the size of the tip of our little finger. The uranium atoms in these pellets are bombarded by atomic particles, they split or fission to release particles of their own. These particles, called neutrons, strike other uranium atoms, splitting them. When the atoms split, they also release heat. This heat is known as nuclear energy and is responsible for creating electricity. Simultaneously, other reactions also take place in the nuclear reactor such as neutron capture. Neutron capture is a term used for the scenario where a neutron comes close to a nucleus and the nucleus captures it and becomes a different nucleus. In this case when uranium-238 captures a neutron it becomes uranium-239. After uranium-239 emits a beta particle or electron, it becomes neptunium-239. Then neptunium-239 also emits beta particle and becomes plutonium-239. The plutonium can also be used as nuclear fuel. In the meantime, certain changes take place in the ceramic fuel pellets during their time in the reactor of the nuclear power plant. During the life of the fuel, the radioactive particles collect within the fuel pellets. The fuel remains in the reactor until trapped fission fragments begin to reduce the efficiency of the chain reaction. The spent fuel also contains plutonium and uranium that was not used up. The fission products and the left over plutonium and uranium remain within the spent fuel when it is removed from the reactor are called high-level waste as they are extremely hot and very radioactive.

In fact, nuclear power is not a clean energy source. It produces both low and high-level radioactive waste that remains dangerous for several hundred thousand years. Generated throughout all parts of the fuel cycle, this waste poses a serious danger to human health and environment. Eventually, the nuclear waste will have to be stored indefinitely because of the long time it takes for some of the waste isotopes to decay to a safety level. The first stage in disposal involves extensive reprocessing to retrieve usable material and reduce the activity of the waste. Subsequently, find disposal, usually of solid material in strong metal canisters, involves burial of the material. The two currently favoured categories of sites for burial are deep 600 metres mined cavities in stable geological formations on land and in red clay some 50-100 metres below the seabed away from tectonic plate margins and where the currents at the bottom of the sea are weak.[11] In doing so, we must ensure that the radioactive waste does not move from its burial site or that it does not escape into the environment. If it does it could have dire consequences for future generations such as contamination of drinking water. To ensure that the radioactive waste is contained the current consensus is to use a multi-barrier system to store the waste. The geological disposal system consists of firstly surrounding the conditioned and packaged solid waste by several human made barriers then placing this at a depth of several hundred metres in a stable geological environment. The geological formation is the most important of the isolation barriers. The barriers act in concert to initially completely isolate the radioactive particles so that they can decay and then limit their release to the environment. The combination of man-made and natural geological barriers is called a multi-barrier system. The barriers surrounding the solid waste vary from country to country but most countries believe that barriers should be made of materials that occur naturally in the earth's crust.

However, currently no country has a complete system for storing high-level waste permanently but many have plans to do so in the next 10 years. There are a number of well-developed proposals from the USA, Sweden, Finland and France for the disposal of long-lived radioactive waste. In line several countries including the Japan, France, Britain, Russia and USA have removed the ban on recycling used fuel because 95 per cent of the potential energy is still contained in the used fuel after the first cycle. The spent nuclear fuel contains uranium and plutonium which are used as fuel in a nuclear reactor. It is possible to isolate much of the uranium and plutonium from the other fission products in spent nuclear fuel so that it can be recycled as fresh fuel to power the nuclear reactor. This is called reprocessing. After reprocessing the left over waste is largely liquid. The world nuclear industry appears to have reached a consensus to pursue Geologic disposal as final phase of nuclear waste management. Currently, waste from nuclear power plants is being held in temporary storage facilities until such time as long-term disposal is decided. Eventual final disposal of nuclear waste means that the radioactive isotopes will be buried in an appropriate disposal site for a very long time. Nevertheless every one of the proposal–disposal methods faces strong opposition from environmental groups. In addition, numerous unresolved problems remain with the geologic and hydrologic suitability of the proposed site, and serious questions have been raised about its ability to contain highly radioactive waste for the time required.

Nuclear Safety and Waste Management in India

Historically, nuclear policy-making in India was not transparent and involved only a handful of people in the government. The Department of Atomic Energy has exploited this arrangement. Unfortunately, the political leadership left the operational aspects of nuclear affairs entirely to DAE without creating any institutional mechanism for independent technical and policy advice on civilian as well as military aspects.[12] In the context till recent it was an absolute secret and perhaps guided by the statement of John Locke, a British liberal who wrote in 1695, that for 'day labourers and tradesmen, the spinsters and dairy maids.....hearing plain commands, is the sure and only course to bring them to obedience and practice'. The greatest part cannot know, and therefore they must believe.'[13] The Indian ruling classes have evidently taken these medieval ideas to heart. In India, all Indian nuclear plants are in the public sector and so are the agencies that exercise regulatory functions and promotional responsibilities. In this situation, conflict of interest between regulation and promotion is inevitable. Their separation and the creation of statutory body for regulation are essential to win public confidence. Over decades, the concept became obsolete but transition from absolute secrecy to engagement with the public without following a systematic procedure had clearly backfired. Today, the time has changed since the setting up of nuclear power plants in India. Before 2008, the entire Indian nuclear power sector was shrouded in complete secrecy. There would barely be any public discussion on nuclear power project or its impact. But this situation changed after India signed the 123-Agreement with the United States and obtained the required exemptions from the Nuclear Suppliers Group. The Indian civilian nuclear power programme opened its doors to the participation of foreign countries and companies. These developments thrust civilian nuclear power into the limelight and immediately created a requirement for the authorities to formally engage with local communities.

Gradually, but soon the situation on the issue of safety of nuclear plants in India received a further boost. According to a senior official of Atomic Energy Regulation Board there were three events all of which happened around the same time. First, the nuclear accident of Fukushima; second, a public awareness campaign commenced by the authorities, which included information about emergency measures, safety precautions etc. and three, high noise levels at the testing stage of the power plant produced by the release of steam. All three factors combined to create an atmosphere of panic among the people, who suddenly felt threatened by an installation that had been set up before their eyes but which now loomed over like an unknown phantom.[14] At this juncture, the French approach on the issue may be considered. More than 75 per cent of power in France is nuclear generated. France has generated positive public opinion on nuclear power to such an extent that different parts of the country actually compete to have nuclear power plant set up in their region. The entire process of engaging with the public has been institutionalised through law and the setting up of autonomous bodies for engaging with the public. The public engagement process in France commences much before operationalising the project and goes on throughout the life of the nuclear facility. Over a period of 13 to 15 months, the public is given as much information as possible about the project. Thereafter, a public debate seeking opinions and suggestions is undertaken. A socio-economic plan to accompany the project, which focusses on education and training, financing and long-terms planning for employment in consultation with the local community is also undertaken. All of this is supported by constant communication channels using the Internet, free-phone numbers, information centres, weekly mails, and regular press releases. Significantly, a local information commissioner is appointed, who is responsible for providing regular information to the public on any issue pertaining to the nuclear facility.[15] In Indian case, people have valid reasons to distrust the government and only a transparent approach can serve towards regaining this trust. In the light of the Fukushima accident, the lesson for India is not necessarily a roll-back on the nuclear energy option. It is that there is an imperative need to allow for the unimagined very low probability event with high impact potential in safety analyses.[16] Transparency in matters of nuclear safety is needed more than ever, in post-Fukushima.

Especially, after Fukushima accident public demonstration for halting ongoing construction of new plants and eliminating nuclear power altogether from energy portfolios also followed. Social demonstrations against the construction of any new nuclear power projects in India and bringing on stream of the nearly complete Kudankulam plant in Tamil Nadu are parts of this phenomenon. An Inter-governmental Agreement on Kudankulam project was signed on 20th November 1988 by the then Prime Minister Rajiv Gandhi and Soviet President Mikhail Gorbachev, for the construction of two reactors. The project remained in limbo for a decade due to the political and economic upheaval in Russia after the post-1991 Soviet break-up. Since the plant was conceived in the mid-1980s, an anti-nuclear group Peoples Movement Against Nuclear Energy was opposing the plant due to the environmental impact of nuclear power and its threat to the people and environment. It was 1988 when peaceful rallies against the plant started immediately after the project was mooted and the police responded with live ammunition. At the public hearing for the environmental impact assessment of the proposed units, the project met with overwhelming opposition; the government simply ignored this.[17] On the other hand, India and Tamil Nadu in particular, faces a severe shortfall of energy. With electricity demand touching 11,500 MW and generation remaining at 7,500 MW, the state is reeling under acute power shortage, prompting the government to resort to long hours of unscheduled power cuts. The Tamil Nadu Electricity Board (TNEB) has been forced to increase the quota during the power cuts in the state, leaving Chennai, most of the districts face outages lasting over eight hours. In addition, demand is rising by the day, but the TNEB is not in a position to purchase power.

As a result of another agreement, signed in 1997, with Russia–the Kudankulam Nuclear Power Plant (KKNPP) was revised and construction on the site began. But this time problem erupted on legal ground as well as due to change in original agreement. After the first agreement between 1989 and 1997 the Coastal Regulation Zone (CRZ), and Environment Impact

Assessment (EIA) Notifications were issued in 1991 and 1994, mandating compulsory clearances by environmental regulators before any new plant could be set up. The CRZ prohibited all industrial activity within 500 metres of the high-tide line. The only exception of this was industries and projects of the Department of Atomic Energy (DAE) directly requiring waterfront or foreshore facilities. The KKNPP today claims exemption from CRZ notification, although it was set up by the Nuclear Power Corporation of India (NPCIL), and is registered under the Companies Act as a commercial venture to engage in the business of power projects.[18] Besides, there were two significant changes to the project. The first was that contrary to the original proposal to ship out the Spent Nuclear Fuel (SNF) to Russia, the highly radioactive SNF from the nuclear power plant was to be stored, transported and reprocessed within India. The second change was equally, major: the freshwater requirement was now to be met by the construction of six desalination plants instead of sending piped water from Pechiparai dam. The environmental impact of the desalination plant on coastal ecology and marine life are serious concerns with implications for the livelihoods of the fishing community.[19] Despite protests a small port became operational in Kudankulam on 14th January 2004.

However, after the nuclear plant accident in Fukushima, Japan in March 2011; nations of the world including India became conscious regarding safety measures at their nuclear plants. As said rightly by the late Alvin Weinberg that 'a nuclear accident somewhere is a nuclear accident everywhere'.[20] In post-Fukushima period many countries initiated a reconsideration of the role of nuclear power in their current and future energy portfolios and checks of their safety features at operating plants. In April 2011, the Indian Prime Minister Manmohan Singh and the Russian President Dmitry Medvedev met at Sanya in China and decided that in the light of Fukushima nuclear power plant accident, additional features would be incorporated in the two Russian-origin nuclear plants under construction at Kudankulam in Tamil Nadu and the next two that would shortly come up at the same site. 'They both discussed the need for international efforts to re-examine nuclear safety, standards and to see what can be done internationally quite apart from international procedures which both of us have put into place, internal review which both have put into place as a result of what happened in Fukushima'.[21] Earlier immediately after the event India's top nuclear scientist and officials, Srikumar Banerjee, Chairman, Atomic Energy Commission, S.K. Jain, Chairman and Managing Director, Nuclear Power Corporation of India, and S.S. Bajaj, Chairman, Atomic Energy Regulatory Board, assured the nation that they would revisit all safety aspects of atomic plants in the country and analyse the nuclear crisis, arising in Japan after the tsunami as it had offered new lessons to fine tune existing emergency preparedness. Although the Fukushima incident is a rarest of sequence of combination of events, we will be doing a complete analysis of it as to what might have gone wrong and how. Design safety, safety analysis capacity are available as a back-up of operating plants which is unique to India. In spite of all these, with open mind we will be visiting the safety aspect and share them with public.

Among the scientists S.K. Jain said that they had taken the events in Japan seriously and safety audits of nuclear plants were of primary concern. Unlike regulatory practices in other countries, in India the regulatory board gave clearance for five years at a time and after that it was mandatory to conduct a safety assessment to seek relicensing. He added that all the nuclear plants in the country operated on a high-level of safety. In the Indian context, the issue of safety of the Tarapur nuclear power plant, which houses BWRs similar to Fukushima has been raised. He disclosed that at the Tarapur atomic power station two units are forty years old, they had undergone detailed safety audits in 2004 and requirements to upgrade the safety systems to current levels were incorporated. An NPCIL statement said Indian nuclear plants remained safe when two natural calamities struck India in the past decade. Despite a major earthquake in Bhuj on 26th January 2001, the Kakrapar Atomic Power Station near Surat, Gujarat, continued to operate safely. Similarly, during the December 2004 tsunami in Tamil Nadu the Madras Atomic Power Station was safely shut down without any radiological consequence. Besides, especially the Tarapur Atomic Power Station (TAPS) maintains a large inventory of water in huge reservoirs and has a much bigger suppression pool than those in Fukushima, which exploded in one of its units. Further improved and redundant back-up power as well as passive cooling have been incorporated at TAPS. As regards the other mainstay reactors of the Pressurised Heavy Water (PHWR) kind, the safety features are much superior to earlier generation Boiling Water Reactors (BWRs).[22] India also stressed the highest standard of safety and security when at the end of March 2011, a plenary session of the Nuclear Security Summit was held in Seoul. It was attended by 53 countries and five international organisations where Indian Prime Minister Manmohan Singh took the opportunity to underline India's responsible citizenship of a nuclear world and backed the modest expansion of the scope of international cooperation. 'Nuclear Security is primarily a national responsibility but there are benefits to be gained by supplementing responsible national actions through sustained and effective international cooperation, he added.[23] Also further in August 2011, the Indian Prime Minister denied any compromise on safety while addressing the Saha Institute of Nuclear Physics (SINP), Kolkata, 'We are in the process of expanding our civil nuclear energy programme. Even as we do so we have to ensure that the use of nuclear energy in India meets the highest safety standards. This is matter on which there can be no compromise.[24] In post-Fukushima period India needs to carry out a thorough-going review of the current status of nuclear safety, a review with independent scientific and technical expertise, drawn also from outside the ranks of the atomic energy establishment.

But particularly on Kudankulam nuclear power plant, the Central government's attempts to assure the public of the safety of the plant failed and the demonstrations continued. In line, in October 2011, thousands of protesters and villagers living around the Russian built Kudankulam nucler plant in the southern Tamil Nadu state blocked highways and staging hunger strikes, preventing further construction work, and demanding its closure as they fear of the disasters like the environmental impact of nuclear power, radioactive waste, nuclear accident similar to the radiation leak in March at Japan's Fukushima nuclear disaster. The protesters had stated several reasons for opposing the Kudankulam nuclear power plant project. According to S.P. Uday Kumar of the voluntary People Movement Against Nuclear Energy. 'the nuclear plant is unsafe' and 'the safety analysis report and site evaluation study have not been made public. No public hearing was held. It is an authoritarian project that has been imposed on the people. In response, apart from the assurance by the Prime Minister Manmohan Singh to Tamil Nadu Chief Minister J, Jayalalitha that all precautions would be taken at the Kudankulam nuclear plant to maintain the highest safety standards, the Central government constituted a 15-member Experts Group to interact with the local people in and around the Kudakulam plant. The group examined the dsign of the KKNPP and found 'all safety related structures, systems and components of the plant are located well above the maximum flooding that can cover the site from all possible causes including tsunami. The expert ruled out a repeat of Fukushima at Kudankulam. In November 2011 former President A.P.J. Abdul Kalam also visited the site and expressed satisfaction and happiness with the sophisticated safety features of the reactors and added further that there is no need for panic since it is only a boon to the future generation.[26] He said that structural and the mechanical safety system had made the reactors the safest in the nuclear industry across the globe.

Barring this, the issue of Kudankulam was dragged to legal battels. A writ petition challenging the fuel loading at the Kudankulam project was filed at the Madras High Court. The Madras High Court, while refusing to halt the project, had highlighted the many benefits it would bring to the local people. The High Court had also directed that serious measures suggested by Dr. A.P.J. Abdul Kalam for establishing schools, hospitals, roads, providing portable water facilities, internet, should be undertaken by the government for the benefit of the local communities. Although the Court observed that no further fresh hearing is necessary on different aspects of the project, however, going forward, the local community would have to be kept involved in developments pertaining to the power plant. The court had clearly expressed the opinion that giving *post facto* benefits to the local community after having taken all the substantial decisions without their engagement would invariably lead to protest. Involvement of teachers, doctors and local leaders who are trusted by their communities would boost the confidence of the people in the project, it added.[27] Further a Public Interest Litigation (PIL) was also filed in the Supreme Court of India jointly by Common Cause: the Centre for Public Interest Litigation; former bureaucrats, including T.S.R. Subramanian; the former Chief Election Commissioner,

N. Gopalaswami; and university professors seeking a safety reassessment of all nuclear facilities in the country, and a comprehensive long-term cost benefit analysis of the plants. Among other things the PIL sought a stay on all proposed nuclear plants until the safety and cost-benefit analysis was carried out. It quoted the March Fukushima nuclear disaster in Japan which had turned out far graver than originally feared. The reactors and overheated spent fuel pools had spewed out radioactivity that had now spread over hundreds of square kilometers. In a continuous discussion on the PIL, the Supreme Court made it clear that it would not go into the policy aspects relating to the safety of all nuclear plants in the country as it was the domain of Parliament.[28] It also referred to the nuclear safety Bill pending in the Parliament.

In another legal battle on the issue of the safety of nuclear plant and waste management, in a landmark judgement, the Supreme Court delivered in the first week of May 2013 said that there is no basis to the fear of the radioactive effects of the Kudankulam nuclear power plant. A Bench of justices K.S. Radhakrishnan and Dipak Misra, disposing of petitions challenging the commissioning of Kundankulam nuclear power plant clearly said, 'We are convinced that the KKNPP design incorporates advanced safety feature complying with the current standards of redundancy, reliability, independence and prevention of common cause failures in its safety systems. The design includes the provisions for withstanding external events like earthquakes, tsunami/storm, tidal waves, cyclones, shock waves, aircraft impact on main buildings and fire. It also said, apprehension, however, legitimate it may be, cannot override the justification of the project. Nobody on this earth can predict what would happen in future and to a larger extent we have to leave it to the destiny. But once justification test is satisfied the apprehension test is bound to fail.[28]. R.K. Sinha, Chairman of the Atomic Energy Commission welcomed the Supreme Court judgement. He called it a shot in the arm for the DAE, 'It is indeed a great relief for all of us in the DAE because it has given us the benefit of the decision of the Supreme Court and it will help us in enhancing the public confidence in nuclear power. The DAE will continue to step up its public outreach activities to ensure that the benefits of nuclear energy and the DAE's contribution in all areas relevant to national growth are brought to the attention of the public'.[29] He was hopeful that the verdict would remove the apprehension in the minds of a section of the public on nuclear energy.

Next to safety in nuclear plant is the problem of nuclear waste management which concerns the public mind in India. As far as nuclear waste is concerned, waste storage for disposal or recycling is done in corrosion-proof containers that can withstand long years of heat and moisture. Radioactive wastes are the result of the nuclear fission process. In this context, India has adopted the policy of 'closed fuel cycle'. Under it, the fuel after irradiation in a reactor is reprocessed to remove the plutonium and unburnt uranium. These two are fuel materials, which can be used in a fast breeder reactor. The high level, long-lived waste product is fixed or immobilised into a glass, which is then encapsulated in stainless containers of high integrity. This immobilised waste can initially be stored at the site of the reprocessing plant and eventually at a geological repository. France, which operates one of the largest commercial reprocessing plant has been successfully storing the immobilised waste in a safe manner.[30] India has built waste immobilisation plants as adjuncts to its reprocessing plants. While fast breeder reactors reduce the amount of waste that needs ultimate storage under surveillance, a further reduction is possible when using Accelerator Driver System (ADS). In it, the waste is bombarded with high energy neutrons to kill or burn radioactive elements. This is called transmutation. Transmutation is the way of handling actinides that have long half-lives. Besides ADS, it can also be done in faster spectrum reactors where neutrons of higher energy are used. This is the scientific solution to waste management.

In India, Sekhar Basu, the Director, Bhabha Atomic Research Centre (BARC), Mumbai, has worked extensively on several aspects of nuclear reprocessing and waste management. He has designed and built reprocessing plants, fuel storage facilities and nuclear waste treatment facilities at Trombay, Tarapur and Kalpakkam. In an interview to *The Hindu*, published at the end of October 2012, Basu said that since we generate power there will be some waste. And this waste is only two to three per cent of the total fuel we put into the reactor. Entire spent fuel is not waste; plutonium and uranium are recycled which contribute about 97-98 per cent of the spent fuel.

So, only the remaining two-three per cent of spent fuel is waste. If we compare nuclear power with coal, uranium requirement is about 30,000 times less. He mentioned another problem with nuclear power waste is that it will remain radioactive for a few hundreds of years and even more. But this waste can be divided into two parts–one where within 300 years, 99 per cent of the waste becomes non-radioactive and the rest is going to remain radioactive for longer time. Taking care of the waste that remains radioactive for about 300 years is not of much concern. Properly designed buildings and structures can stand for 300 years. It is kept in three to four layers of steel casing and ultimately stored in a concrete structures or buildings.[31] Basu also took the opportunity to quote India's policy which is to reprocess all the fuel that we put into a reactor. In addition, there are proposals to create a global nuclear fuel company under the IAEA which will collect nuclear waste from reactors across the globe, reprocess it and then redistribute to the fuel to those power plants. In response to a PIL, filed on the issue in the Supreme Court, the delivered judgement also cautioned the Union of India and NPCIL to find out a place for a permanent deep geological repository. The NPCIL and the Union of India are bound to look at the probabilities of potentially harmful events and consequences in future, the court observed. This recent nuclear accidents, public agitation and judicial guidance definitely accounted for the new safety measures and waste management programme of the Indian government. It is time for us to decide the future course of action on exploitation of nuclear energy in the safest way with waste management.

Nuclear Power and Health Hazards

Systematic studies on relative risks to human health from different sources of energy, including coal, oil, gas and wind and those from nuclear, hydel and solar sources show that risks with gas, and hydel and nuclear-based ones, are much lower than with coal, oil, wind and solar-based ones. From nuclear energy the most dangerous is the fact that running a nuclear reactor essentially releases radioactive material into the environment. Radiation is a energy travelling in the form of electro-magnetic waves or photons. It is also a stream of particles, especially alpha or beta-particles from a radioactive source or neutrons from a nuclear reactor. Radiation damages generally living organism as a result of exposure to energetic electrons, nucleons, fission, fragments, or high-energy electromagnetic radiation. In inanimate materials the damage may be caused by electronic excitation, ionisation, transmutation, or displacement of atoms. In organism, these mechanisms can cause changes to cells that alter their genetic structure, interfere with their division or kill them. In human, these changes can lead to radiation sickness, radiation burns or to long-term damage of several kinds, the most serious of which result in various forms of cancer.[32] This fact was proved in a study conducted by US government to assess the late effects of radiation among the atom survivors of Hiroshima and Nagasaki. These are the only two occasions when nuclear force was intentionally developed and deployed to kill human life. Thus, there is some correlation between radiation exposure and cancer risk, which must be acknowledged. However, the notable aspect is that, contrary to popular belief, the findings clearly state that the effect of such exposure is limited only to the exposed generation. To quote the report our studies have not found so far any inherited genetic effects from parental radiation exposure among the children to atom bomb survivors.[33] Over the years, the technology has been advancing and the human capability to contain nuclear disasters has definitely advanced. Compared to the Chernobyl disaster of 1986 showed how much progress we have achieved in nuclear emergency management over a period of about three decades. The Fukushima-Daiichi plant was almost five times big in terms of power generation and, more significantly, contained about nine times the nuclear fuel at the time of the accident. Yet, with better emergency management learnt over the years the maximum radiation was less than 0.4 per cent of that released during the Chernobyl disaster.[34]

However, there is no doubt in the fact that there is a large biological effects of radiation. Several types of radiation naturally occurring, terrestrial and internal radio-nuclides are present in the planet having very different responses from living and biological cells. Naturally occurring environmental sources of radiation include cosmic radiation which occurs when sub-atomic particles from outside the solar system interact with the Earth's atmosphere and produce a shower of gamma rays, neutrons and leptons. Terrestrial radiation includes naturally occurring radio-nuclides such as uranium, radium and thorium which are present in rocks, soil and water. While internal radio-nuclides includes most common potassium-40 which emits beta and gamma particles as it decays, and may be found as a fraction of the total amount of potassium in the body. The largest source of our dose from background radiation is from radon-220 and radon-222 gases, which are the airborne products of the decay of terrestrial uranium. In our daily life activities, we are exposed to ionising radiation both from natural and human-made sources. The passage of ionising radiation through the body may produce adverse biological effects. The effects of concern are primarily although not solely, due to damage to the genetic material inside the cell; the DNA or double helix' molecule that carries genetic information. The current scientific data suggests that there is no safe minimum, or threshold, for adverse radiation effects on the DNA of biological systems and that even small doses can produce consequences for the organism. The biological systems are composed of many individual tiny cells; each with its own DNA. If there is catastrophic damage to vital cell function by radiation energy absorption, the cell may cease to function and die.

Among the damages done to cells and DNA the most common and fierce is cancer induction. In this case, the DNA is damaged or altered but the alteration is not lethal to the cell. If the normal regulator genes which control the rate at which cells divide and die are rendered malfunctioned the cells may become immortal and multiply at an abnormal rate producing an out of control growth of a line of abnormal cells. This is a cancer. Most tissues can produce cancers with enough radiation damage but rapidly dividing tissue lines, such as blood forming haemopoietic gene which may produce lukemias, are particularly vulnerable. The risk for cancer production in the general population is estimated to be approximately 0.06 cases per million Micro-Sieverts of absorbed dose. Besides, it is also responsible for genetic damage to future generations. This can arise because mutations or changes in the pattern of bases in the DNA, can occur in the DNA that ends up in sperm or eggs and becomes a permanent feature of any resulting babies. Most often, radiation induced damage to such egg or sperm DNA is incompatible with the life of the foetus in utero but there is a finite chance of a live baby being born with defects. This is of particular concern because the damage to the genetic material can then be passed on to all future generations and become a permanent features of the gene-pool; damaging many individuals. Of course such mutations are also a natural part of life and the evolution of biological systems. The concern is that we do not want to increase the mutation rate above the natural background rate. The estimated risk of permanent damage to a second generation or grandchild individual is 0.02 cases per million Micro-Sievert of exposure. According to a study published in 2005 and conducted by the Health Protection Agency of Great Britain on the incidence of childhood cancer around the nuclear power plants, the team concluded there have been no increase in childhood cancers for children living less than 25 kilometres from a nuclear power plant. In contrast, the radiation burns are the sorts of effects seen immediately after the bombing of Hiroshima; but lesser effects can occur with smaller doses which in normal life does not produce detectable damage.

The theoretical description of nuclear power plant on human body does not appear much devastating as it is in practice right from the days of dropping the atomic bomb on Hiroshima and Nagasaki, Japan, in 1945 the humanity has faced the disaster. After this the Chernobyl nuclear plant accident of 1986, proved most fatal for human health and its after-effects are studied even today. The death toll from the Chernobyl explosion remained a hotly-debated issue between the International Atomic Energy Agency and the various writers, researchers. While recently in April 2011 Yukiya Amano, the Director General IAEA told in an international conference on Chernobyl accident that around fifty people engaged in the immediate emergency and recovery operations had died, many experts find this figure grossly understated. Green-peace has predicted that Chernobyl may ultimately cause some, 2,70,000 cancer cases, more than 90,000 of which could prove fatal. In a book published in 2007, Russian biologist Alexei Yablokov and two Ukrainian researchers concluded that some 9,85,000 people had already died, mainly of cancer, till 2004. In between the two is the official view of the UN watchdog which expected that death toll among those affected by high radiation doses at Chernobyl may reach 4,000 in the coming decades. But according to the official data from Ukraine's Health Ministry: 530,000 died from radiation in the former Soviet state between 1987 and 2004.[35] Dr. Yablokov also claimed in his book that his casualty estimates were based on over 5000 scientific papers and radiological surveys, whereas the IAEA and the WHO used only 350 sources for their conclusions. Thus, while the IAEA is of the opinion that the ecological situation around Chernobyl is improving independent researchers say it is in fact, getting worse.

Apart from health hazards caused due to accident in a nuclear plants, because of radiation and other related factors are also responsible for slow death of plant workers and bad health in surroundings. Under normal peacetime conditions, workers who handle X-ray machines or radioactive isotopes are exposed to very small doses of radiation. Afterwards, sometimes years afterwards, many of them are afflicted the most painful forms of dermatitis and cancer, and a large number died from the effects of the rays. Similar affects have been observed in individuals, who have ingested substantial amounts of radioactive substances. Not all of these are equally dangerous, and the body can tolerate quite large amounts of some radioactive-isotopes which are exerted rapidly.[36] On the other hand, elements such as radium, which lodge in bones, are extremely dangerous are known to induce malignant bone tumours and also cause leukaemia–a malignant disease of blood. After the disastrous start, several attempts have been made to define the maximum dose of X-rays which can be regarded as "safe", at least as far as one individual's life-time is concerned.[37] In India too, there have been a few independent epidemiological studies of the health of people living in the vicinity of nuclear facilities. One study compared the health status of the inhabitants of five villages within 10 kilometres of the Rajasthan atomic power station and four other villages more than 50-kilometres away. It observed statistically significant increases in several indices including the rates of congenital deformities, spontaneous abortions, still births and solid tumours in the villages closer to the reactor.[38] Although this survey does not reveal the precise cause of these differences, but the absence of any other plausible factor, indicated that it is the nuclear plant that is responsible in some way.

In the recent radioactive release–iodine and cesium after the Fukushima nuclear accident in Japan in March 2011, the big worries were expressed. According to Thomas B. Cochran, a senior scientist in the nuclear programme of the Natural Resources Defence Council, a private group in Washington,

'They imply some kind of core problem.' The active core of a nuclear reactor splits atoms in two to produce bursts of energy and, as a by-product, large masses of highly radioactive particles. The many safety mechanism of a nuclear plant focus mainly on keeping these so-called fission products out of the environment.[39] Of the two iodine-131 has a half-life of eight days and is quite dangerous to human health. It absorbed through contaminated food, especially milk and milk products, it will accumulate in the thyroid and cause cancer. Located near the base of the neck, the thyroid is a large endocrine gland that produces harmones that help control growth and metabolism. Likewise, over the long-term, the big threat to human health is cesium-137, which has a half-life of 30 years. At that rate of disintegration, John Emsley wrote in his book *'Nature's Building Blocks,* published in 2001', It takes over 200 years to reduce it to one per cent of its former level. 'It is cesium-137 that still contaminates much land in Ukraine around the Chernobyl reactor.'[40] Cesium-137 mixes easily with water and is chemically similar to Potassium. It get metabolised in the body and can enter through many foods including milk. After entering cesium gets widely distributed, its concentrations said to be higher in muscle tissues and lower in bones. Thus, the nuclear power is a proved health hazards for plant workers and nearby dwellers permanently not only but for the whole of humanity in case of nuclear explosion or of nuclear plant accident.

Nuclear Power in Perspective

Like the present day world, the focus of India on forms of energy is on the march to achieve 'energy swaraj' or self-reliance. All the resources that can promote energy generation have to be kindled because development demands electricity or other forms of energy. In a developing country like India large scale advance and improved production will be possible equally in village and city, if more electricity is available. Advanced industrialisation cannot be achieved without a robust agrarian base. Indeed, agriculture, industry and technology cannot be divisively developed and none of them can be accelerated without abundant electrification and popular cooperation in extensive, using their creative faculties. Electrification plus people's participation is socially sensitive, economically locomotive democracy in its egalitarian glory.[41] Without power everything from water supply to cooking and medical radiology will cease.

Fans, television sets, air-conditioners, telephones, computers, and similar facilities needed to make life bearable will become impossible to use. Even right to life guaranteed by the Constitution will stand negated by the state if power supply stops. The energy sector in India has a vast range from solar and tidal power to wind farms, biogas and other newly-researched and discovered sources.[42] Among all solar energy can abundantly replace hydro, coal, nuclear and other sources of electricity to heat water, cook food and for other purposes if duly stored. The dawn of energy resource revolution dates back to the age of primitive mans' discovery of fire for warmth, light and production.

As a result of growing pressure against the expanding use of fuels-coals, oil and natural gas, nuclear generated energy has been relied by many nations to meet the bourgeoning energy demands. The nuclear age began in 1919 at Cambridge University in UK with Rutherford's experiments on the structure of atom. Nuclear fission was first achieved in 1934 by Hahn and Stress Man. The slogan 'atoms for peace, raised the hopes of nuclear energy providing a panacea. Nuclear energy could provide limitless, inexpensive and much cleaner source. Many people had insulated nuclear energy as a sensible modern answer to the world's future energy requirements.[43] The nuclear fuel cycle begins with the mining, extraction, purification and other processing steps of uranium ore. Power is generated through fission from enriched uranium, releasing hundreds of highly radioactive in the process. Fission also procures heat, and this is what is used to create electricity. The reactors are so designed that they cannot explode as in an atom bomb. But nuclear reactors routinely release small amounts of radioactive gases, primarily xenon, krypton-85 and radioactive iodine into the air and flush small amounts of liquids contaminated with radioactive tritium and cesium into local water-ways.[44] In the overall picture, every year, human activities are adding about 30 billions of CO_2 into the atmosphere. The Inter-Governmental Panel on Climate Change (IPCC) estimates that 26 per cent of this emission is a direct consequence of electricity generation requirements. This is not really air pollution but it adds to the risk of climate change, which is exhibited in changing rain fall patterns, sea levels and temperatures, leading to food shortages, malnutrition, and disease alternation. The WHO estimates that about 1.3 million people lose their lives as result of urban outdoor air pollution alone, and about 140,000 are casualties to adaptation challenges of climate change.[45] Thus, the pollution caused by power generation activities, and the climate change associated with them, are directly or indirectly responsible for about 481,000 deaths every year.

In fact, India lacks abundant indigenous supplies of oil and gas but it is loaded with coal, and seventy per cent of the coal mines in India goes into producing electricity. India ranks fourth in the world in terms of coal reserves, and is the world's third largest coal producer behind the US and China. However, coals that are available in India are of poor quality and malpositioned. Moreover, with 35 per cent ash and low energy-content, India has already resorted to importing cheaper, high-quality coal, adding to congestion at its ports. Without 'clean-coal' technology, an increased use of coal would add to India's already significant problems with pollution.[46] Coal accounts for nearly half of India's that total energy use, a large part of it for electricity production. Most of the present day generators use 200-MW to 500-MW sub-critical boilers with a thermal efficiency of thirty-five per cent or less. Older units of 60-MW and 110/120-MW have lower efficiency. All new generators should use super-critical boilers in the size range of about 800-MW, which can achieve an efficiency of about forty per cent. While most of the coal now used in domestic, imports will be needed in the decades ahead for power stations located in the south and west of India for which port infrastructure should be built.[47] A further gain in efficiency is possible when the integrated coal gasification technology is available. In the context, some collaborative work with the US and other countries is planned, a prototype development in India jointly between National Thermal Power Corporation (NTPC) and Bharat Heavy Electrical Limited (BHEL) is warranted.

In comparison to coal, natural gas is lesser evil among fossil fuels with less than half of the carbon content and hence it is a viable option for a carbon-constrained world. Abundant and less whimsically distributed than crude oil or coal, its fungibility improved by liquefaction technology and less demanding of water than coal or nuclear power. The natural gas is a versatile fuel that finds use in a wide range of applications such as fuel for power generation, industrial processes and in automobiles and feedstock in fertilizers and petrochemicals, natural gas is also an ideal cooking fuel whether piped to houses or bottled as LPG in cylinders. In power generation, the efficiency factor could be as high as sixty per cent in a combined cycle as opposed to around thirty per cent in the most efficient coal-based power plant. Its efficiency could be even higher in combined heat and power applications when waste heat from the turbines is utilised in other industrial processes.[48] In developed countries natural gas accounts for almost a quarter of the energy basket, but in India the share of natural gas in its commercial energy quota has stagnated at less than ten per cent despite major new domestic discoveries in recent years. First discovered in Assam in the late 19th century, natural gas has became the mainstream fuel in India in the 1960s after major reserves were discovered in the Cambay Basin on the west coast. Acknowledging its value as a national resource, the government has prioritised its application in power and fertilizer plants. From 1997, India opened its acreages to international investors in exploration and production through a structured licensing process termed–New Exploration Licensing Policy (NELP) of which nine rounds have been completed recently. Of the 239 blocks awarded to investors so far 68 fields, of both oil and gas, are claimed to have been discovered.[49] With global crude prices spiralling and coal becoming increasingly unacceptable, gas may suddenly find itself attractive, viable and competitive. It could greatly contribute to enhancing India's quest for energy security provided we get our act together in time and play our cards right to drive hard bargains. Thus, oil and gas are the fastest growing segments of our energy basket and should maximise their availability to run our economy.

In addition, hydel and solar energy are essential for the development and bright future prospect of the country. People living in areas where large hydel potential exists need to be provided incentives as they may perceive that their energy wealth is going to enrich people living in other parts of the country. A similar approach is required to access the large hydel potential available in Bhutan and Nepal, beyonds the needs of the populations of these countries. Another energy option of great interest is solar energy. Considering its abundance in India the country must embark on a mission mode programme, comparable to atomic energy and space, to develop economically viable solar power systems. Department of New Energy Sources needs to be headed by a competent scientist or technologists and sponsor new Research and Development in solar energy, fuel cells, bio-fuel, hydrogen production and storage and so on. Solar water heaters and solar cookers need to be promoted through better designs and incentives.[50] Energy efficiency in a country like India will have to be achieved in industry, transport, domestic appliances and agriculture. Agricultural pumping is notoriously inefficient due to electricity being supplied free. Similarly, power losses in transmission and distribution can be reduced drastically through investment in transmission and distribution systems and better transformers.

The biggest pollutions on our planet are the result of the use of fossil fuels–gasoline, oil and coal but modern society is simply unthinkable without them. The governments of rich states instead turning to alternative energy sources like wind energy, sun energy and geo-thermal energy are still more focussed on decreasing the pollution caused by the use of fossil fuels rather than search for acceptable alternatives. Also alternative energy resources are only used in rich countries in order to decrease the pollution in their own lands. To make things even worse, rich countries, more often transfer their own dirty industries to poor countries that do not have the appropriate knowledge of the means to even think about ecology, and are pretty much dependent on these absolute technologies.[51] At the series of meetings of the Inter-Governmental Panel on Climate Change (IPCC) held earlier, a consensus emerged that man-made additions to the global atmospheric CO_2 were indeed responsible for warming and that all countries should adopt measures to reduce carbon emissions. The evidence of warming is based on the occurrence of the affects of unbearable hot years in succession, increased intensity of cyclonic storms and hurricanes, abnormal rainfall patterns, glaciers feeding the great rivers of the world receding, extensive melting of Arctic ice, appearance of flora and fauna of the warmer areas in the Arctic, and so on. In the context, the US in recent years has maintained that unless China and India committed to a CO_2 reduction programme, there would be no significant reduction in overall emissions. In 2004, the world's total emissions of CO_2 was 27 billion tonnes. Of this, the US accounted for 5.9 billion tonnes, China 4.7, Russia 1.7, Japan 1.3 and India 1.1 billion tonnes.[52]

All other countries were below the one billion level. If we calculate per capita annual emissions, the rough workout for US is 23.6 billion tonnes, followed by Japan 13, Russia 10, 4.7 China and only one billion tonnes for India. Keeping in view the gravity of the situation the G-8 summit concluded in 2007, and the member countries agreed to a vague emission reduction programme by 2050. But there was a difference of opinion among the present members and India's Prime Minister Manmohan Singh reiterated the importance of accelerated economic growth to eliminate poverty and deprivation and said India could not take on binding commitments when its per capita emissions were low. The Chinese National Development and Reform Commission has stated that the first and over-riding concern was economic and social development and poverty eradication.[53] In general the developing countries including India, China and Brazil are opposed to mandatory capping of emissions as that would hinder their development.

In the circumstances, a very important non-carbon energy power is nuclear power. Nuclear power holds the key to reducing global emissions of carbon dioxide (CO_2) and sulphur dioxide (SO_2). The seventeen per cent reduction in emissions due to reduced coal-fired generation being taken up by nuclear is equivalent to twelve per cent of UK emissions and eight per cent of emissions from the EU-25 countries. Assessing the role of nuclear power becomes very important when there is a growing awareness among the countries of the world on the need to exploit the nuclear power for meeting energy challenges. India's quest to rapidly develop this source has been hampered by a very limited resource base of uranium, that too of low grade, and technological isolation imposed by US non-proliferation policies. In a bid to raise the contribution of the nuclear power to energy generation, India planned to install another 25-30 nuclear reactors in coming years.[54] Without 'clean-coal' technology, an increased use of coal would add to India's already significant problems with pollution. While coal will continue to dominate as a fuel for India's electric power sector, the country's leaders are anxious to shift a clear means of generating electricity. In the context specifically, nuclear power makes no contribution to global warming through the emission of carbon dioxide. Nuclear power also produces no notable sulphur dioxides or particulates when nuclear power is produced, nothing is burned in a conventional sense. Heat is produced through nuclear fission not oxidation. Nuclear power does produce on spent fuels of roughly the same mass and volume as the fuel that the reactor takes in. These spent fuels are kept within the reactor's fuels assemblies, thus unlike fossil fuels, which emit stack gases to the ambient environment, solid wastes at nuclear power plants are contained throughout the generation process, no particulates or ash are emitted.[55]

Thus, nuclear energy is a safe source of energy. This does not mean that nuclear energy would replace coal, but to some extent it would reduce the burning of fossil fuel and low quality coal, thereby reducing environmental hazards. Moreover, in the long-run nuclear energy would be economical and environment-friendly than any other alternatives. The successful culmination of the civil nuclear deal would open the way for the exchange of advanced technology of the times that was restricted in the past due to US-India nuclear proliferation issue. The civil nuclear agreement is important for India because it helps to achieve its long-term nuclear technology thrust, reduction in coal transport congestion and emission reduction targets. Increased share of nuclear power in the Indian energy mix will help diminish the reliance on fossil fuels and reduce carbon emissions from India. In this matter, India is ultimately pinning its hopes on the eventual use of thorium as a source of energy, as it has abundant reserves of this substance.

References

1. M.R. Srinivasan, 'Is the Nuclear Power Option Safe for India', *The Hindu*, 9th October 2007.
2. N.S. Sisodia, 'Lessons from an Atomic Catastrophe', *Ibid.*, 6th August 2009.
3. Madhumita Dutta, 'Desirability of Nuclear Power is the Real Question', *Ibid.*, 27th September 2012.
4. M.V. Ramana and Suvrat Raju, 'Nuclear Safety Before Vendor Interests', *Ibid.*, 30th October 2012.
5. Koplow, Doug, 'Nuclear Power : Still Not Viable Without Subsidies', *Union of Concerned Scientists*, February 2011, p. 2.
6. Vladimir Radyuhain, 'Twenty-five Years After Chernobyl', *The Hindu*, 26th April, 2011.
7. *Ibid.*
8. Ban Ki-Moon, 'A Visit to Chernobyl', *Ibid.*, 28th April 2011.

9. T. Jayaraman, 'Nuclear Power After Fukushima', *Ibid.*, 21st March 2011.
10. Ban Ki-Moon, 'A Visit to Chernobyl'.
11. A.M. Goldstein, *A Dictionary of Physics (*Delhi : CBS Publishers and Distributors (1986), pp. 217-18.
12. T.N. Srinivasan, T.S. Gopi Rethinaraj and Surya Sethi, 'How Fukushima is Relevant to Kudankulam', *The Hindu*, 18th March 2012.
13. Suvrat Raju and M.V. Ramana, 'Where the Mind is Full of Fear', *Ibid.*, 19th September 2012.
14. Mohit Abraham, 'Why Kudankulam Dissolved into Fission and Acrimony', *Ibid.*, 25th September 2012.
15. *Ibid.*
16. *Ibid.*, (editorial), 21st March 2011.
17. Suvrat Raju and M.V. Ramana, 'Where the Mind is Full of Fear', *Ibid.*, 19th September 2012.
18. D. Nagasaila and V. Suresh, 'Kudankulam on Shaky Legal Ground', *Ibid.*, 5th September 2012.
19. *Ibid.*
20. As quoted in T. N. Srinivasan, T.S. Gopi Rethinaraj and Surya Sethi, 'How Fukushima is Relevant to Kudankulam'.
21. *The Hindu*, 14th April 2011.
22. 'Learning from Fukushima' (editorial), *Ibid.*, 21st March 2011.
23. *Ibid.*, 28th March 2011.
24. *Ibid.*, 22nd August 211.
25. *Ibid.*, 20th November 2011.
26. *Ibid.*, 7th November 2011.
27. Mohit Abraham, 'Why Kudankulam Dissolved into Fission and Acrimony'.
28. *The Hindu*, 6th December 2011.
29. *Ibid.*, 7th May 2013.
30. M.R. Srinivasan, 'Is the Nuclear Power Option Safe for India.'
31. *The Hindu*, 29th October 2012.
32. A.M. Goldstein, *A Dictionary of Physics*, p. 216.
33. As quoted in A.P.J. Abdul Kalam and Srijan Pal Singh, 'Nuclear Power is Our Gateway to a Prosperous Future', *The Hindu,* 6th November 2011.
34. *Ibid.*
35. 'Vladimir Radyuhin, 'Twenty-five Years After Chernobyl'.

36. J.M. Valentine, *Atomic Physics* (London: The English Universities Press, 1960), 181-82.
37. *Ibid.*
38. Suvrat Raju and M.V. Ramana, 'Where the Mind is Full of Fear'.
39. William J. Broad, 'Radioactive Releases in Japan Worrying', *Ibid.,* 14th March 2011.
40. *Ibid.*
41. V.R. Krishna Iyer, 'Kerala and Alternative Energy Resources', *Ibid.,* 25th August 2008.
42. *Ibid.*
43. Sanjoy Choudhury, 'Nuclear Energy and Its Effects on the Environment', *South Asia Politics,* Vol. 8, No.17, November 2009 (New Delhi : 2009), p. 26.
44. *Ibid.,* p. 27
45. A.P.J. Abdul Kalam and Srijan Pal Singh, 'Nuclear Power is Our Gateway to a Prosperous Future'.
46. Mark Bucknam, 'Power to the People of India: US Nuclear Cooperation With India', *Strategic Insights*, Vol. VI (1), January 2007.
47. M.R. Srinivasan, 'Climate Change and India's Options', *The Hindu,* 30th June 2007.
48. Sudha Mahalingam, 'An Alternative to Nuclear Power', *Ibid.,* 27th April 2011.
49. *Ibid.*
50. M.R. Srinivasan, 'Climate Change and India's Options'.
51. Tarun Bikash Sukai, 'Environment Awareness in Society', *South Asia Politics*, Vol. 9, Nos. 3rd and 4th July-August 2010 (New Delhi: 2010), p. 37.
52. M.R. Srinivasan, 'Climate Change and India's Options'.
53. *Ibid.*
54. T.V. Paul, 'The US-India Nuclear Accord : Implications for Non-Proliferation Regime', *International Journal*, Vol. LXII (4), Fall 2007 (Canada : 2007), pp. 858-59.
55. Sanjoy Choudhury, 'Nuclear Energy and its Effects on the Environment', p. 28.

5

Analysis of Indo-US Civil Nuclear Agreement

A major breakthrough came in the nuclear history of India on 18th July 2005, when the Indian Prime Minister Manmohan Singh and US President George William Bush, in a joint statement outlined the provisions and commitments of Indo-US civil nuclear cooperation which was further clarified on 2nd March 2006. It took more than three years in negotiations/discussions but finally in October 2008 a civil nuclear cooperation agreement was signed between the two countries, which, on the one hand, ended India's nuclear isolation since the days of its first nuclear explosion in May 1974, and gave a strong foothold to the US against China in the region. It was the result of India's recognition as a responsible nuclear power but US took keen interest in removing the other impediments in the way of nuclear deal. As a follow up action, India and the US made changes in its internal laws to accommodate the new deal. Apart from passing the Agreement from Legislatures of the respective country, the US enacted the Hyde Act and India established an understanding with the International Atomic Energy Agency (IAEA) on the issue of nuclear plant supervision and nuclear safeguards. The understanding between India and the US was furthered when the Nuclear Suppliers Group (NSG) waived restrictions on India's nuclear import. It opened India's option to buy enriched uranium, nuclear technology and other materials from different countries of the world in order to generate electricity and industrial development. As India entered the mainstream of nuclear world, several nuclear agreements were signed with countries of the world and powerful technologies are being poured to India to meet energy needs. In the context, to facilitate the nuclear supply and establish nuclear installation, India had passed in 2011 the Civil Nuclear Liability Bill to provide risk-related concessions to foreign investors. Criticisms apart, now the nuclear deal is a reality. Greater cooperation with the US will not only bring in big business, it will change the geo-political balance in Asia. India will have to be guarded not to do the US's bidding in the region and to retain an independent foreign policy. In essence, the nexus of energy, economic growth and global power status are now at the heart of India's foreign policy.

Antecedents of Indo-US Nuclear Relations

Even before the advent of India as an independent, sovereign country in the comity of nations, the world's balance of power went in favour of nuclear capability. For long in the post-war period the power politics appeared developing a bipolar pattern–the concentration of most of the world's power, military, industrial and otherwise in the two super powers and these two powers–USA and USSR in contrast with the multi-power world of the past, seemed to have emerged as the major determinants of international politics.[1] Of the two, the USA was first to become a decidedly nuclear power in mid-1940s and the release of nuclear energy has revolutionalised the concepts of national defence and strategy along with the art of planning the realisation of military goals. It has always been a consistent policy of the United States to protect its national interests with all possible means, however, immoral they may be and never allow a prospective and upcoming contender to proceed ahead so that it may challenge the might of the US. This is called "real politicking" and was very much eulogised and theorised by American scholars and policy-makers like Morgenthau, Kelsen and Henry Kissinger during past decades after IInd World War.[2] In the context, the question of the importance that South Asia acquires in the US interests and scheme of priorities remained a persisting debate and there is a difference of opinions. One school of thought accords a very low priority to South Asia since it is geographically distant and economically uninspiring from the US point of view. The other school regards the US involvement in South Asia is being strategically vital and therefore, deep and pervasive. However, over the years, the second opinion gained weightage and it was felt that as long as the United States had an adversary relationship with both China and the Soviet Union, the US would remain concerned with minimising their role in South Asia.[3] Accordingly, the US involvement in South Asia fluctuated, depending upon its intensity and style of competition with other great powers at the global level.

India, with its independence in August 1947, shared a lot of common ideals and institutions such as democracy, freedom of press, freedom of religion, respect for individual liberty, human rights, independance of judiciary, federalism etc. But the foreign policy of a country, far from being an independent variable, depends on number of factors, which especially include domestic concerns and institutions of that country. It is the domestic context in which a country's foreign policy arises. The domestic context pertains to those important aspects such as the geo-strategic location, historical, socio-cultural and politico-economic environment of the country which prescribes the parameters within which the foreign policy-makers of a country have to shape its foreign policy. This significance of the international milieu in the shaping of Indo-US relations notwithstanding, policy convergences or divergences between two democracies have often been explained mainly in the context of external environment. In the period of Cold War rapprochement, and difference between two countries took fair amount of time due to both internal and external compulsions. From the start, the United States is a super power whereas India is a middle power. And further, a superpower's domestic compulsions may not be directly related to its relation to any one regional power while a regional power's approach to international politics is invariably linked to the role of the global power in its internal and neighbourhood politics.[4] In the circumstances, it is quite natural that the US perceives its national interest in global context while India's immediate concern often hinges around preserving its internal autonomy. A super power could accommodate another super power, because the alternative would be equally devastating to both. But the relationship between a super power and a middle power is of different kinds. The former may not accommodate the latter while the latter cannot allow itself to be a satellite of the former.

This simple difference in situation is responsible for much of the tension afflicting their mutual relations.

On the issue of Indo-US relations there are some who believe that bilateral relations 'should be separated from the strategic and multilateral issues and such analysts argue that on some issues which do not directly affect their bilateral relations, the countries may afford to have disagreements, However, in practice, this is not feasible. First, because there is interaction and mutual influence between bilateral and multilateral issues. Second, there are some middle range issues which belong to both worlds. One such issue is the nuclear relationship between the United States and India. It directly affects the vital interests of India, if not those of United States. It is a part of the international debate on nuclear non-proliferation in which both the US and India are active participants, championing opposite points of view. On India's part, its commitments to the peaceful use of nuclear energy is firm, although, at times, it has been subjected to some strain. During the stewardship of Jawaharlal Nehru, India's commitment in this respect was unequivocal. No doubts were cast on his bona fides, during his lifetime. Only a Nehru could assure the world on behalf of any future government of India that this country would not go in for nuclear weapons. Even after the security environment had radically changed in 1962, there was no policy change in this regard and he considered nuclear weapons as a "symbol of evil". Only nine days before his death, Nehru is on record reiterating his commitment that India would "never" make a bomb. In addition to its commitment to the peaceful use of nuclear energy, India has maintained its right of independence in decision-making on nuclear issues. It has not allowed its sovereignty to be compromised by succumbing to external pressures or by accepting unequal treaties. As early as 1948, Vijyalaxmi Pandit, India's representative to the UN General Assembly told that while India was willing to give the International Atomic Development Authority all power necessary to ensure the peaceful use of nuclear energy, it strongly opposed the idea of giving it any authority which might restrict its sovereignty over the peaceful utilisation of atomic energy resources.

However, over the years, particularly in post-Nehru era, the pro-nuclear lobby became active which included Indian elites

K. Subhramanayam, the Director of the Institute of Defence Studies and Analysis, New Delhi, Sisir Gupta, a Professor of Diplomacy in Jawaharlal Nehru University, New Delhi and Subramanyam Swami, the Janata Dal M.P. and an economist. They emphasised that India's nuclear option would give it a lot of leverage *vis-a-vis* the three big powers. They argued that nuclear weapons are simply the "currency of power", and India will always be regarded as a second-rate developing country until it has its own nuclear arsenal. They cite the example of China which earned the respect of Americans after it went nuclear. In addition, some Indians strongly feel that India should have a nuclear deterrent against a nuclear China which is hostile to India and against Pakistan which is frantically trying to explode a nuclear device. Some of the hard-liners also believe that if India possessed nuclear weapons, the border dispute with China would be quickly settled through negotiation and nuclear "haves" would be subjected to strong pressure gradually to agree to vertical non-proliferation.

In just opposite is the US nuclear understanding which revolves round the policy of nuclear deterrence and non-proliferation. It is of the opinion that the US should possess a large number of powerful weapons which would be an effective deterrent against a first nuclear strike by any other nuclear power, especially the Soviet Union. As a result, Washington's commitment to nuclear non-proliferation has been half-hearted and partial. It favours only horizontal non-proliferation, without offering any commitment even to a gradual vertical non-proliferation. The nuclear policy of the US thus sharply clashes with that of India, whose commitment to nuclear non-proliferation is total and which advocates vertical as well as horizontal non-proliferation.[5] India feels that a non-proliferation agreement ignores the present proliferation and pre-occupies itself with the future proliferation which is naturally unrealistic, ineffective and therefore unacceptable.

But despite differences on nuclear issue, India and the United States of America had entered into an agreement of cooperation on 25th October 1963 to supply enriched uranium upto 1993 to the Tarapur Atomic Power Station. A contract incorporating the agreement was signed on 17th May 1966. The contract bound India not to obtain supplies of nuclear fuel from any other sources.[6] On the other, the US fuel supply to the

Tarapur nuclear reactor could never be consistent. It never honoured its treaty, commitments particularly after the nuclear explosion by India in May 1974. Before the event, Washington did not work hard even for horizontal non-proliferation. Its main concern was to defend its pre-eminence in the market of nuclear export *vis-a-vis* other nuclear powers, especially its own allies in Western Europe. Of course, some concern was expressed by public interest groups in the United States over the possible hazard to health and the pollution of the environment by the nuclear plants and the danger that the nuclear terrorists might pose to the security of the world. In general, the West sharply reacted to India's nuclear detonation. Both the American government and the press decried it on the ground that it would encourage further nuclear proliferation. They did not accept India's argument that it was a peaceful explosion. Earlier, Bangladesh's emergence as a free country in December 1971, followed by nuclear explosion in 1974 only effected a qualitative change in India's military potential but also torn into pieces the so-called balance between India and Pakistan and established New Delhi's, pre-eminence in the sub-continent. The US was angry because a strong India, worse still a nuclear India, was bad for the US and therefore had to be contained. Despite the statements and actions of the Government of India that it was not on the nuclear path, demands were made in the US for making a complete review of the nuclear relationship between the two countries.

Earlier, with the explosion of the first nuclear weapon in 1945, the chances of terrorists and additional nations going nuclear increased that caused anxiety all over the world. After a series of efforts made by the nations of the world in post-World War-II pahse for disarmament, the Soviet Union and United States of America took up fresh negotiations in the second half of July to initial Partial Test Ban Treaty (PTBT). It was signed by the USSR, the USA and the UK on 5th August 1963 and came onto force on 10th October 1963. About a 100 nations joined this treaty with France and China refusing it to sign. The treaty prohibited all nuclear weapon test explosions on the surface, in the atmosphere and underwater including territorial waters and high seas. It prohibited all tests for peaceful nuclear explosives (PNEs), at a place under the jurisdiction of a party to this treaty. The treaty stated that the underground tests were not prohibited. All states were invited to join the treaty which is of unlimited duration. In extraordinary event a state, which having signed the treaty, became a party to it, was given the right to withdraw.[7] Although being the first treaty in sphere of disarmament it did bring about a breakthrough in relation to the problem, yet it had only a limited value, for it failed to secure ban on all nuclear tests. At least it paved the way for further negotiations for more effective arms control measures. It was ratified by three original signatories, ninety-eight other members of the United Nations including India, and seven non-member states of the UN.

Signing of the PTBT in 1963 did not satisfy the nations of the world, the Big in particular. The international community realised that a wider proliferation of nuclear weapon would pose a threat to world security. This led to the development of many rules and institutions both national and international. Since the end of the Second World War, countless smaller wars have been fought. Hundreds of thousands of lives have been lost. In the situation assessment of nuclear proliferation continues to be very important and every country is interested in preventing the further spread of nuclear weapons. If many countries acquire nuclear weapons the threat to their neighbours would increase and sooner or later threaten the security of the new owners themselves. This would lessen the security for all.[8] The treaty of 1963 sought to solve the most urgent environmental problem. But the problem of qualitative and quantitative nuclear arms race and the danger of nuclear proliferation remained. The growing world-wide interest in nuclear power caused the danger of nuclear proliferation. Many countries including India were interested only in nuclear energy for peaceful purposes. But the problem was that the line between energy for peaceful purposes and nuclear arms manufacture was very thin. Therefore, public pressure was built for a ban on nuclear proliferation. As a step further in this regard, two separate though identical treaties were proposed by USA and USSR in the UN General Assembly which endorsed the proposal by a big majority on 12th June 1968. It was opened for signature on 1st July 1968. The treaty is known as Nuclear Non-Proliferation Treaty (NPT). It was immediately signed by UK, USA, USSR and over fifty other countries. Initially, it was for 25 years but in a conference held in 1995 to extend the treaty for a limited or unlimited period, it was extended for indefinite period.

The NPT entered into force on 5th March 1970 with the best hope: (i) That the nuclear weapon states not assist others to acquire weapons; (ii) That the non-nuclear weapon states agree not to acquire them, and (iii) That facilities in the latter states capable of producing fissionable materials that might be used in weapons be subject to surveillance by the International Atomic Energy Agency (IAEA) to assure that they were not being used.[9] At the same time, the treaty establishes a framework within which nations can cooperate to obtain the benefits of the peaceful atom under strict controls to prevent its misuse for nuclear explosive purposes. The treaty contained several Articles but Articles 1 and 2 comprise essential non-proliferation-undertakings. Article 1, places the nuclear weapon state under the obligation not to transfer to any recipient whatsoever nuclear weapon or other nuclear explosive devices or control over them, and not in any way to assist, encourage or induce any non-nuclear weapon state to manufacture or acquire such weapon or devices. Article 2 pledges the non-nuclear weapon states not to receive nuclear weapons or other nuclear explosive devices as well as not manufacture them or receive assistance in their manufacture.[10] The first part of the Article has not as yet given rise to formal complaints. But the second part of Article 1 has led to controversy. Nuclear material and technology destined for power programmes have been exported by Non-Proliferation Treaty parties to non-parties. There have been certain forms of nuclear cooperation which has led to the development of nuclear weapon capability in several countries. For instance, the willingness of China to sell nuclear commodities without strict control to Pakistan has contributed to its nuclear weapons capability. According to Article 2 of the non-proliferation treaty, every non-nuclear weapon party to the treaty have to conclude a safeguard agreement with the International Atomic Energy Agency whether or not it is actually engaged in nuclear activities.

On the provisions of NPT the United States is of the opinion that developing countries have the right to pursue the peaceful uses of nuclear energy. If a country chooses; as a party to the NPT, it is entitled to do so under safeguards. The NPT explicitly recognises signatories, "inalienable right" to use nuclear technology for peaceful purposes. That this inalienable right includes the right to enrich is clear from the NPT itself, its negotiating history and decades of state practice, with at least a dozen non-weapons state parties having developed safeguarded fuel cycle infrastructures potentially able to support weapons programme.[11] In fact, it has helped countries to benefit from the peaceful uses of nuclear energy like meeting their needs in power, medicine, health-care, science, industry and agriculture. The NPT calls upon all states particularly the nuclear weapons states, to pursue good faith negotiations to end the nuclear arms race.[12]

Unfortunately, the NPT is against nuclear have nots acquiring nuclear weapons. But it is silent about nuclear haves increasing the size of their arsenals. The NPT whose ostensible objective is world peace, seems to advocate a strange logic. Vertical proliferation helps peace while horizontal proliferation endangers it. The protagonists of the NPT argue that nuclear powers, due to their long experience in handling nuclear weapons, are "mature and" responsible while the "threshold" powers who lack this experience may be trigger-happy and irresponsible, precipitating a nuclear holocaust. The nuclear powers, in fact, have violated the letter and spirit of the NPT. They have during the last decades increased their nuclear strength many folds. Their record in helping the transfer of nuclear technology is very poor.[13] As long as the US and other nuclear weapon powers continue to rely on them for their security into the indefinite future, the rest of the countries will come under severe domestic pressure to acquire nuclear weapons to improve their political leverage. The restraint they have accepted under the NPT cannot be expected to last forever, especially when the weapon states have not kept their part of the bargain to denuclearise themselves over a period of time.[14] However, the nuclear weapon states had a lot of expectation from the NPT which would help immensely in halting the arms race.

The Non-Proliferation Treaty of 1968 was not signed by India as Indira Gandhi thought that it would be a major hurdle for the peaceful experiments. Jawaharlal Nehru's commitment to work and support nuclear disarmament and nuclear arms control was unequivocal. There was a coherence in the policy which he maintained that India would never make nuclear weapons; that it would work for the abolition of nuclear weapons; and that since it was difficult to achieve that objective, it would support measures that might inhibit or control the race for nuclear arms. In Nehru's nuclear policy there was no discrepancy in the principles and precepts. But after Nehru, the situations and circumstances have greatly changed. Accordingly, although his policies are still upheld in principle, there are changes in actual practice. As a result, when the question of implementing Nehru's policies in regard to nuclear arms control comes up, the changes in approach of the successive Government become apparent. These are changes forced upon the decision-makers by the changed environment. The situation deteriorated sharply with the Chinese detonation of their atomic device in October 1964. Reacting on the development Lal Bahadur Shastri, the then Prime Minister of India, held that 'it was natural that ..... people in India should think of having a similar bomb. They wanted to retaliate. It was human nature.[15] The incident not only changed the security environment but public opinion in the country was demanding change in India's nuclear policy. The Chinese nuclear test strengthened India's pro-disarmament commitment and made its political leaders for more conscious of the increasing disparities between nuclear haves and have nots. India raised the issue at the UN. Participating in the initial debates in the UN General Assembly on nuclear Non-Proliferation Treaty in November 1965, India's representative stressed the need to establish 'an acceptable balance of mutual responsibilities and obligations of the nuclear and non-nuclear powers.[16]. Thus, India's policy towards nuclear arms control was changed. Endorsement of Nehru's step-by-step approach was given up but only to a limited extent.

After explosion of nuclear device in 1964, and around the years 1965-68 there was tremendous pressure built up at home against the discriminatory provisions of the Non-Proliferation Treaty. Most of the members of the Indian Parliament were in favour of India not signing the proliferation treaty. Indira Gandhi, the then Prime Minister of India, remarked in the House during the discussion, 'Mankind today is at the cross-roads of nuclear peace and nuclear war. There can be no doubt that we should take the road to nuclear peace. But the first step in this direction is yet in sight. It is vitally important, therefore, for the nuclear weapon powers to undertake as soon as possible meaningful negotiations on a series of measures leading to nuclear disarmament...... This is a situation which cannot be viewed with equanimity by non-nuclear countries, especially as they are called upon to undertake not to manufacture or acquire nuclear weapons for their own defence'.[17] Everyone, whether for or against India's nuclear-weapons option, opposed the NPT. The anti-proliferation regime that the NPT sought to establish was anathema to the more articulate section of the Indian elite. However, the final decision not to subscribe to the NPT was taken in April-May 1967. C.S. Jha, the then Foreign Secretary of India, said that security consideration was an important factor in reaching that decision; for the decision was taken after the visit of the then Secretary to the Prime Minister L.K. Jha, to Moscow, Washington and London and C.S. Jha's visit to Geneva had confirmed in April, 1967 that credible guarantees against nuclear attack and nuclear blackmail were not available.[18] The Indian approach under Indira Gandhi sought only to redefine the concept of nuclear proliferation. It demanded control on the race for nuclear arms among the five nuclear-weapons power (vertical proliferation) and on the spread of nuclear weapons (horizontal proliferation) simultaneously. Even thereafter India continued to support measure which were designed to control the race for nuclear arms, like the comprehensive test ban, regional denuclearisation and even non-proliferation of nuclear weapons, if the Indian definition was accepted to the rest of the world.[19] For long, India's focus primarily revolved around the commitments towards general and complete nuclear disarmament as well as on the discriminatory nature of the Nuclear Non-Proliferation Treaty. Great Powers converted, as Subrahmanyam argued, the NPT into licensing unlimited nuclear proliferation to the five nuclear weapon powers with a total ban on acquisition of nuclear weapons by all other nations.[20] India argued that it was not willing to be a party to an inherently discriminatory treaty, which institutionalised nuclear apartheid.

Several provisions of the NPT were criticised by the non-nuclear weapon countries of Third World including India. The reasons why India has refused to sign the Treaty are many: Firstly, so far, nuclear weapon powers have not ceased the arms race and there were no sign, that they are going to do so in future. Secondly, the United States and Britain have not submitted as the non-proliferation treaty says that non-nuclear countries who will become members of the treaty will be favoured with regard to the supply of nuclear technology and material, but they have not yet been the exclusive beneficiaries of such aid and trade. Fourthly, Articles 1 and 2 of the treaty concerning transfers and safeguards are extremely unfair to non-nuclear weapons powers. The nuclear powers are free to transfer nuclear weapons and explosive devices and even to encourage each other to acquire and manufacture nuclear weapons. While this is not applicable to the non-nuclear weapons countries. They can only receive nuclear material and equipment under rules.[21] In another discriminatory provision of the treaty the benefit from nuclear explosion would be made available to treaty partners at a low cost. Needless to say that no such benefits have such been made available to non-nuclear countries. The promise of protection for non-nuclear countries is also valueless. Therefore, in its early phase the non-proliferation treaty fell short of all reasonable expectations as a disarmament measure.

Above all the Indian Government felt that America was trying to prevent India from becoming an autonomous nuclear power. Opposition members in India felt that America was trying to blackmail India. In fact both the super powers did not want a nuclear proliferation in South Asia. But at the same time, the United States had been conniving at Pakistan's bomb-making by waiving the Symington Amendment. When the Soviet Union warned General Zia not to go in for nuclear weapons programme, the United States issued a stern warning to Moscow to keep its hands off Pakistan. The danger of a nuclear war exists more amongst the smaller nations than amongst the super powers. The smaller nations can be provoked into using the nuclear weapons as the last alternative to national demise.[22] In the situation India's upcoming stature of becoming a major regional power and super power is not to the liking of the US. India's stand of not signing to NPT and of late Comprehensive Test Ban Treaty (CTBT) and successfully developing indigenous technology as regard nuclear reactors and nuclear fuel, thereby reducing its dependence upon them, adds to their discomfiture. When the first nuclear test was successfully carried out at Pokharan in 1974, and 1998, when five nuclear tests were conducted, India had proved the success of its indigenous nuclear technology giving it self-reliance as well as self-confidence despite sanctions imposed on India since 1974 through Nuclear Supplier's Group and other sanction methods.

Background of Indo-US Civil Nuclear Agreement 2005

Since its birth as an independent nation India has confronted with the steadily worsening regional and global security environment. Security is the primary concern of every state. The first task of foreign policy-makers of every country is to ensure its security which primarily means territorial integrity and sovereignty. The security of a country may be threatened in many ways and the fear of nuclear weapon is one of them. Earlier in August 1945, the world had witnessed the unprecedented destruction caused by the two bombs dropped at Hiroshima and Nagasaki. Therefore, India became the first country to officially ask for stoppage of nuclear tests. Jawaharlal Nehru, the first Prime Minister of India told the Parliament in April 1954, "Nuclear tests are a crime against humanity and a crime against survival of the human race. No country pleading the interests of its security has the right to perpetuate this nuclear holocaust. The nuclear explosions are "the most visible manifestation of the arms race".[23] India's general the estimation of the probability of war with the country concerned, and of the probability of that country using or threatening to use nuclear weapons in such a war, play important roles in the development of threat perception. In the Indian context, the only issues in this area on which there is consensus are that China and Pakistan are both possible future adversaries and that India is unlikely to fight a war with them.[24] India's strategic experts cite China rather than Pakistan for country's compulsion to maintain its nuclear option. Indeed ever since China went nuclear in 1964, there has been a demand in India that Delhi must have a nuclear deterrent against China. Gradually, India was compelled to take maximum care of its security by developing all the modern scientific tools needed for nuclear power.

Developing its nuclear capability India conducted a test at Pokharan in May 1974, but at the same time repeatedly insisted that India did not wish to make a bomb and it supported complete disarmament. At the point it also clarified that we would keep our option open. It meant that if ever India felt that her security was being threatened, it would not hesitate in exercising its nuclear option. Pakistan's response to the Indian explosion was a combination of frustrations and aspirations. It was dismayed and frustrated by the impressive scientific advancements demonstrated by India and consequently the then Pakistani Prime Minister expressed determination to quickly match the Indian accomplishment.[25] This explosion marked a watershed in Indo-American nuclear relations and in the non-proliferation policy of the United States. The United States reacted strongly. She voted against loans to India at the International Development Association while Japan and Britain cut bilateral aid. The shock waves also led to a virtual nuclear trade embargo against India and provided a major impetus to the United States to review its contractual fuel supply obligations under the 1963 Indo-US nuclear cooperation agreement. Understandably, the United States and the Western nuclear powers avoid a frontal resolving of India's status in the realm of nuclear weapon capability banking on the escapist and timid Indian official policy. In fact, this strategy fits in with the declared American objective of capping India's fissile material capability, followed by its elimination. For this purpose, a consistent line is in operation ever since India's nuclear scientists established a firm grip over plutonium weapon technology and developed it sizeably to bring India in the position of creating a nuclear stockpile, giving it deterrence status.[26] The short point is that India's post-1974 position on nuclear question has become unsustainable. No one regards India's objections to the NPT – absolutely valid and substantial as the real reason why it refuses to sign the treaty.[27] In the past, India faced the challenge of reconciling its quest for military and nuclear status with the need to persuade the international community of its peaceful intentions.[28] For decades, India's nuclear policy and discourse have been built on a curious mix of hard power and principle.

In post-1974 period, India has been coerced into de facto accession to the NPT, CTBT, FMCT, and all other international instruments designed to serve the pre-eminent position of nuclear powered peer group, led by America and ensuring perpetual bondage or slavery for India or any upcoming nation like India.[29] Especially, after the end of Cold War, and the US ascendance to the status of the sole superpower, it has been seeking to establish its right to stop the proliferation of nuclear weapons by the use of force, if other forms of discouragement failed. The publicity given to its counter proliferation initiative is intended to gradually mould international public opinion to accept that position. Considerable efforts are being made simultaneously to build up the intelligence and operational capabilities needed to take out proliferation targets with acceptable levels of collateral destruction.[30] In a way determined attempt was made to legitimise precisely such a division, firstly by making the discriminatory Non-Proliferation Treaty permanent through an amendment adopted in 1995. Then a similar discriminatory Comprehensive Test Ban Treaty (CTBT) was foisted without any link to the goal of nuclear disarmament, a link that India has consistently insisted upon. These moves would have permanently forestall India's option to acquire a fully-tested nuclear weapon arsenal, while those already in possession of nuclear weapons would enjoy an asymmetrical advantage in perpetuity. This would have severally undermined India's security making it vulnerable to nuclear threat and blackmail.[31] Perhaps due to these developments in sphere of nuclear diplomacy prior to India's second time explosion (1998) many political leaders demanded from time to time that India should not delay in acquiring nuclear weapons, as officially India neither closed its option nor exercised it. Brahma Chaalleney, a defence expert of the Centre for Policy Research, in a critical comment wrote, 'There could not be a better example of India's tendency not to take decisions, than its policy in regard to nuclear option. India had remained committed to its nuclear option for decades, but it had hated to exercise this option as a direct security asset. India had paid heavy price of its decision, for it had neither had the courage to give up the option, nor determined will to exercise it.'[32] It is in this background that an opinion was emerging in India that the country should give up its vague policy and exercise the nuclear opinion. Assuming office of Vajpayee Government in March 1998, proved an appropriate moment for exercising the nuclear option.

In accordance with the agenda of the new government installed in March 1998, India conducted three and two nuclear explosions on 11th and 13th May respectively. In the same month, India's nuclear account was evened by Pakistan when it exploded five nuclear devices on 28th May and it even went ahead of India when conducted one more device on 30th May 1998. The May 1998 nuclear tests by India and Pakistan and more so the bedlam that followed has deeply divided India's strategic community in its assessment of the military threats faced by the country, both in the short and long-term. In the short term it is clear in India-Pakistan context: One India's insurgencies have strong internal causes. Two, neither nuclear weapons nor the threat of a punishing conventional strike can dissuade Pakistan from providing insurgency and terrorist support below a certain threshold. Three, India can lower that threshold more effectively by enlisting international support than by threatening Pakistan militarily. Four, there is no way that Pakistan can win a conventional or nuclear war against India. Five, it is very unlikely that India can break Pakistan politically or economically by ratcheting up security spending. Six, using nuclear weapons to thump chests without developing the needed Command, Control, Communication, Computer, Intelligence, Information, Surveillance and Reconnaissance (C_4I_2SR) systems can increase the risk of irrational, suicidal war. Likewise, in Chinese context it may be: One, China is not going to create border problems for India in the short-to-medium term, given its strong current research for a responsible image. Two, China has been accelerating away from India economically for the last 20 years, and unless India does some quick catching up, the two countries would move to different leagues altogether. Three, it is very important for India to forestall future problems by arriving at a border settlement with China. Four, with the best efforts of India, it will take a very long time to get China to cease helping Pakistan. And lastly, it is futile to seek western support against China in the short-to-medium term.[33] As to the long-term, it would depend as much on how India develops its economic, social and military strengths. There are various other factors like a nation's political commitment and resolve as also its financial and technical capabilities that determine the nature and potential of its nuclear profile. But at the end, the exact nature of the nuclear assets as also their operational nuclear doctrine are shaped by a country's perceived security threats which in turn dictate a country's nuclear doctrine.[34] Any analysis of a nation's nuclear posture has to be understood in the context of its threat perceptions.

Following the nuclear tests of 1998, Prime Minister Atal Bihari Vajpayee stressed that the tests and India's future nuclear policy would "continue to reflect a commitment to the sensibilities and obligations of an ancient civilisation, a sense of responsibility and restraint.[35] India's nuclear tests were a means of establishing India's international status and prestige. In the wake of tests, India stressed its peaceful intentions, announced a voluntary moratorium on further testing, limited itself to a minimum credible deterrent, and later pledged a no-first-use policy. In practice, if not in theory, the international community has accepted India's nuclear ambivalence. The credibility of Indian claims to nuclear restraint and responsibility contributed without doubt. However, with new declarations of strength must come new reassurances. Public statements from the highest level that explicitly reiterate India's abiding policy of nuclear restraint would go some way towards allaying international fears. For instance, China reacting to the development held the view that India's tests were an enhancement rather than a negation of an essentially peaceable but unquestionably powerful Indian civilisational self. The clearest evidence for this is that India's gradual build-up of military and nuclear capabilities from the 1970s onwards have not resulted in new policies based on the use of force.[36] In addition, dominant thinking in international relations finds it hard to reconcile the two trends, and many have scratched their head in puzzlement over the incongruity of India's peaceful intentions and hard power hype, or the juxtaposition of "the land of Gandhi" and the bomb. Not surprisingly, the two positions were reconciled back in 1952 by G.S. Bajpai, a pioneer of the Indian Foreign Service, by claiming that the acquisition of material power need not eclipse India's moral pre-eminence, and that power was indeed essential for moral projection.

Justifying the decision to conduct the nuclear tests, Vajpayee said, "We live in a world where India is surrounded by nuclear weaponry. No responsible government can formulate a security policy for the country as abstract principles". Of all two countries China and USA who themselves were nuclear weapon states reacted very sharply. The United States was the first country to react with imposition of economic sanctions. On the other UK, France and Russia made it clear that they will not impose sanctions against India which may prove to be counter-productive. Even with the US at this juncture and thereafter India can mention its objectives one by one. Sanctions have of course to go. In this context, the first major technological deal which was also a bait for France and United States was for a massive programme of these countries' light water reactors for

India's nuclear power programme on financial terms similar to those entered into with Russia. Such a deal would break the technological Berlin Wall put up by the West on advanced technology coming to India. On the other hand, India has to take a close look at the constraint which the FMCT would impose on this country.[37] Since nuclear weapon deterrence capability is India's strategic need and India is not entering a matching race with the nuclear weapon big powers there should be no shying away from the prospect of a deadline on fissile material production. The nuclear explosions of May 1998 also raised the hopes of nuclear reconciliation and a breakthrough in relations between the two countries. Despite their disparate interests one is a super power and another a rising power of the Third World, the prevailing global political and economic scene opens up prospects of India-US rapport as never before.

Unlike the nuclear test of 1974, the 1998 explosions, far from widening the old cleavage between India and USA actually bridged it because from a long-term point of view, these tests were seen as creating new opportunities and opening of new windows. Owing to the past history of bitterness and motivated miasma of misunderstanding between USA and India and the projected danger to the USA from China in future, India can be an ideal partner to contain China.[38] Perhaps the US also considered the honest, consistent and long track record of our commitment for peaceful use of nuclear energy; requirement of nuclear deterrence for us as we have to deal with two hostile neighbours viz., China and Pakistan; discriminate application of NPT and CTBT; special provisions for Israel, China and Pakistan and unjust operation of International politics lacking ethics and morality and clear-cut enforceable rules; and other unjust provisions are the genuine demands by India which the US must accept and provide.[39] In the circumstances, a clear shift of policy/preference became imminent for India and the United States of America.

For India, according to Huntington, if it wants to refashion and redesign her foreign policy initiatives, there are three ways; either to join Russia or through its lot with Asian nations or align with America. If India opts for the first, it would become an isolated country to be marginalised in the end. If India goes for the second option, it would remain subservient to China. Only an alignment with USA can ensure India's economic prosperity and enhanced security.[40] Akin to what Huntington suggested is the view of scholar couple Llyod Rudolph and Susanne Hoeber Rudolph in an article, 'Why Bush Blinked; New Geopolitics Shape US Foreign Policy' they put up almost similar policy initiatives; (i) either to band wagon with USA who is an offshore balance in India; (ii) create a balance against US unilateralism; (iii) join with likeminded political actors to promote a multi-polar balance of power.[41] The scholar-cum-analysts strongly placed in favour of good India-US understanding which means for India to remain with the winning side, the most powerful country in the world, while balancing against the US super power status means to distinguish between USA and China and to find who is more dangerous and inimically disposed towards India. A careful and conscious consideration suggests that the first option/strategy as best because US power poses no danger to India whereas China definitely does.

The American policy perception of South Asia has also undergone a remarkable change over the years. In post-cold war period, after the collapse of the Soviet Union and in the context of changing strategic situation the US has gone into reshape its political, economic and strategic partnership with India and Pakistan acquiring nuclear weapons capability. USA has expressed deep concern over the nuclearisation of the region. So, it gave top priority to developing anti-proliferation strategies, enforce international barriers to proliferation and deter the acquisition of nuclear weapons by India and Pakistan. On the other hand, at the regional level, security perceptions of India and Pakistan have been different. While Pakistan considered India as a principal threat, India retained its nuclear options open as a deterrent against Pakistan. After nuclear tests by India and Pakistan in May 1998, USA has given top priority to normalisation of relations between India and Pakistan and to support the ongoing dialogue between the two countries on bilateral issues.[42] Another issue of concern to US in South Asia is growing terrorism. Especially after the 9/11 incident there is a visible paradigm shift in America's strategy towards South Asia. America is anxious about the chance of nuclear weapons getting into the hands of terrorist groups. In the context India's growing nuclear and technological capabilities compel US to follows a policy of constructive friendship with India particularly in nuclear fields. As a result, there has also been a shift in Chinese perception of the US. For a long the United States and India have both regarded China as a destabilising factor in nuclear equations in South Asia. The United States now appears to be looking China as a stabilising factor in South Asia. The implications of the new American move have to be adequately understood in India and Pakistan. Now for more than a decade the United States has begun to work with China for a common policy to bring about nuclear stability in South Asia, "Nuclear stability" rather than non-proliferation appears to be the revised target of America's new engagement with South Asia. Nuclear stability means that the United States has reconciled itself to the nuclear capability of India and Pakistan[43]. Its objective now is to persuade the two countries not to weaponise but to freeze their capabilities at the present state.

India's nuclear diplomacy has focussed on two aspects of the South Asian nuclear situation. First, it has sought to blame China and the United States, for abetting Pakistan's nuclear capability, China directly, United States indirectly, but no less effectively. Two, Indian diplomacy has stressed the imperative of holding on to the nuclear option in view of the actual and potential nuclear threats from Pakistan and China.[44] So far as India's future nuclear test is concerned international reaction will depend very much on the circumstances and context. If the test comes out of the blue without any visible provocation, the reactions will be harsh and punitive. If it is in response to testing by others, especially in the neighbourhood, criticism will be muted and offset by some understanding of strategic imperatives.[45] Pakistan nuclear policy is reactive to India while latter's policy is primarily autonomous. On various occasions, India has reiterated that it will not abandon its option until the five nuclear powers have agreed to untake total abolition of nuclear weapons gives the Indian option the stamp of permanency. As long as the option is alive, India is open to temptation or pressure to proceed to weaponisation and the world is tempted to speculate that India is already running a weapons programme. Particularly, China's involvement in South Asian nuclear issue gives India an opportunity for a relevant and productive initiative. The initiative should aim at a "no first strike" agreement between Pakistan, India and China. A tripartite, "no first strike" agreement will stabilise the South Asian nuclear situation.

Not only the policy of India and the US, but the Chinese policy too have undergone a change in South Asia from the early 1990s which was based on good neighbourliness and cooperation. But the growing economic and military might of China is as much worrisome to USA as it is to India and Japan. Despite an outward bonhomie between US and China, there is also a lurking suspicion of the latter. Publicly, USA denies that she is befriending India with an anti-China strategic objective, but in reality she is not oblivious of the consequences of an over-heated, over saturated China. The whole gamut of relations were narrated by Robert Blackwell, former US Ambassador to India, "India is properly attentive to the rise of Chinese power. Let me make clear that this will lead to joint India-US containment of PRC. Worrying that this could be self-fulfilling, no Indian politician of any consequence supports such a policy. But it does not mean that behind New Delhi's elevated rhetoric regarding relations between India and China, Indians understand that Asia is being fundamentally changed by the weight of PRC economic power and diplomatic skill."[46] If not openly but secretly all policy-makers concede that this is the only reason for US overdrive in mending her fences with India. They put it, "Nobody will publicly state so bluntly but there are a lot of policy works in the administration who see India as bulwark against China in the long-term."[47] Providing strategic stability is the main plan of the US foreign policy in South Asia, meaning "keeping open the opinion of using India to help counter-balance China whenever that prove necessary. The Bush Administration indicates that the subject of non-proliferation should not stand as the obstacle to the maintenance of the US-India relationship based on common interests. Now non-proliferation and arms control are no longer on the agenda of the Bush Administration.[48] On the other hand, India needs Washington active support to enhance its nuclear energy resources, be rid of the NPT regime constraints and find its way into nuclear suppliers group as a responsible nuclear weapon power.

The BJP-led NDA government in India carried the nuclear weapon tests at Pokharan in 1998 followed by Pakistan in the same month. As a result both countries were placed under international sanctions but the tests led to a profound revaluation of India in the US. After the explosion Jaswant Singh, India's Minister for External Affairs, declared that India, like Pakistan was a nuclear weapon state. He said, 'Reality can neither be deined nor wished away. This category of 'nuclear weapon state' is not .... a conferment. Nor is it a status for others to grant. It is rather an objective reality.' The United States of America and its allies saw in it a challenge to their hegemonic position. Realising that India was not going to bow before the P-5, the United States Government soon initiated a dialogue with India. Now, Washington embarked on its most concerted effort to officially understand and deal with India in the form of a dozen or more talks with US Deputy Secretary of State Strobe Talbott and Indian Foreign Minister Jaswant Singh. The Talbott – Jaswant talks, as they became known, provided the diplomatic groundwork for an American review of India that ended with President Bill Clinton making a triumphant visit to India.[49] By that time significant changes were noticed in the policies of major powers, China took important steps in the direction of improving bilateral ties with India. The US Administration also began to reorient its policy towards India. The Bush Administration installed in January 2001, took the Clinton eve and elevated India to an even closer partnership. Although the change of guard took place in India in May 2004 under the Premiership of Dr. Manmohan Singh assumed the reign of administration, no shift of policy was indicated. The talks held between the two governments and development of understanding on nuclear issue paved the way for signing the Indo-US Civil Nuclear Agreement on 18th July 2005. It was considered a major breakthrough in their relations and a shift of policy/interest on their part in a globalised world politics.

Aims and Objects of the Agreement

The historic agreement between Prime Minister Manmohan Singh and United States President Grorge William Bush concluded on 18th July 2005, declared their resolve to transform the relationship between their countries and establish a global partnership.[50] It was signed in the background of India's indigenous nuclear programme, 30 years record of responsible behaviour on non-proliferation matters and uniqueness as a country with democratic, accountable and transparent government. The United States Atomic Energy Act of 1954, in its Section 123, has provided for such cooperation as it was crucial for mobilising greater political and material support for achievement of US global and regional non-proliferation, objectives, specially with respect to dissuading, isolating and, if necessary, sanctioning and containing states that sponsored terrorism and terror groups that are seeking to acquire nuclear weapons capability or other weapons capable of mass destruction and the means to deliver such weapons.[51] The India-United States nuclear deal that was supposed to be a path-breaking agreement has run into stiff opposition in both countries where critics say that each has given too much for too little. For India, the deal was supposed to provide nuclear energy to make good the short fall, access to high technology, be an economic bonanza for the future and grant legitimacy as a major power. For the US, it was part of a larger game plan. The deal was a means to cap India's strategic programme, provide access to India's growing defence market, and become a strategic partner in US foreign policy initiatives globally.[52] The signed landmark agreement for "full civil nuclear cooperation" with the United States in exchange for a specific set of commitments, there were three sets of concerns that analysts on the Indian side raised. The first related to technology. Would the deal hamper India's indigenous three-stage plans in the civil nuclear field by increasing our import dependence and subjecting our reactors and research facilities to intrusive international inspections? The second set of concerns was linked to 'national security'. To the extent to which nuclear weapons-rightly or wrongly-have come to occupy a central position in the country's security calculus, would the deal weaken or cap the Indian nuclear weapons capability? Finally, there were political and strategic concerns.[53] Thus, there have been different interpretations of the deal in two capitals–New Delhi and Washington.

After a prolonged period of mistrust and uneasy relationship spanning six decades, the US decided to redefine and reconfigurate the old relationship and forge a new one. For long India's complaint against USA was that despite a commonality of democratic ideas between the two nations, USA maintained relational parity between India and Pakistan despite a great asymmetry between these two Asian neighbours. The intention of USA was to placate Pakistan, her ally by according her parity with India but far from creating a climate of cordiality, this policy only fuelled misgivings between India and USA and Indians perceived it as a tilt towards Pakistan.

This change in the stance of USA is vital to the reformulation of her policies towards the sub-continent and in particular as regards Pakistan, which has been, an old ally of USA and also, the only Muslim nuclear state.[54] This was a tectonic shift from the earlier US position which had ostracised India and treated her as a nuclear outcaste for her refusal to sign the NPT. This shift in US perception towards the nations of the sub-continent, caused largely by geo-political and economic/trade reasons.

In the context although some supporters believe that strategic partnership with USA will contribute to restrain China's influence, the main cause behind signing of the deal by India is shortage of electricity, one of the biggest impediments in way of fast growing Indian economy. Nuclear energy, which at present accounts for only about three per cent of India's total electricity generation is an attractive alternative to coal, expensive imported oil and natural gas.[55] Supports' view that nuclear energy will reduce India's dependence on coal and address the issue of global warming by reducing carbon emissions. However, to reduce carbon emissions, focus should be more on the transport and industrial sectors because no country, including France and Japan, that get 70 per cent and 40 per cent of their electricity, respectively, from nuclear power, has seen a reduction of carbon emissions since transport and industry comprise major sources of emissions. With the deal, there is a very optimistic estimate is about 13,600 MWe in the next ten years and a total of 68000 MWe between now and 2052. Even if there is no addition of LWRs, from our own PHWRs and FBRs, the total nuclear contribution to the Indian grid can be as high as about 207 GWe by the year 2052. That is only one-fourth of the nuclear power in the country would come from and use imported uranium. The total electricity production in India by the year 2052 to meet the GDP growth rate is 1344 GWe. So, the consequence of no nuclear deal is that the nuclear share to the total electricity production would be down to 15.4 per cent from a possible of 20 per cent or so.[56] The World Energy Council (WEC) has projected that if a global nuclear renaissance takes place, the total nuclear power in the world will increase to about 1120 GWe, by the year 2050, a three-fold increase from the current 400 GWe installed nuclear capacity. While a major part of the new nuclear power will be in Asia–China and India.[57] For the overall positive nuclear health of the country the immediate benefit is that it allows the import of natural uranium thereby easing the hand to mouth existence with respect to fuel for our "INDU" pressurized heavy water reactors. A second benefit will be the import of enriched uranium required to continue to run the Tarapur boiling water reactors beyond 2006. Then there is the added attraction of the import of light water reactors from aboard (Russia, France and the United States), which will substantially supplement our own indigenous nuclear power programme based on PHWRs and FBRs.

The Indian Prime Minister Manmohan Singh called the deal a 'giant step forward' while replying to the debate on the motion of confidence in the Lok Sabha in July 2008. He said that it is all about widening our development options, promoting energy security in a manner which will not hurt our precious environment and which will not contribute to pollution and global warming. India needs to grow at the rate of at least 10 per cent annum to get rid of chronic poverty, ignorance and disease which still afflict millions of our people. A basic requirement for achieving this order of growth is the availability of energy particularly electricity. We need increasing quantities of electricity to support our agriculture, industry and to give comfort to our house holders. The Prime Minister stressed the need to make full use of atomic energy which is a clean environment- friendly source of energy. Narrating the handicaps of India's nuclear programme he counted. First of all, we have inadequate production of uranium. Second, the quality of our uranium resources is not comparable to those of other producers. Third, after the Pokharan, nuclear test of 1974 and 1998 the outside world has imposed embargo on trade with India in nuclear materials, nuclear equipment and nuclear technology.[58] As a result our nuclear energy programme has suffered. The nuclear agreement that we wish to negotiate will end India's nuclear isolation, nuclear apartheid and enable us to take advantage of international trade in nuclear materials, technologies and equipment. It will open up nee opportunities for trade in dual use high technologies opening up new pathways to accelerate industrialization of our country.[59] Thus, it is all for economic prosperity and industrial health of the country. Even the text of document titled 'Implementation of the India-United States joint Statement of July 18, 2005: India's Separation Plan' reiterated that the nuclear establishment in

India not only build nuclear reactors but promoted the growth of a national industrial infrastructure.

It is widely said that the deal will create opportunity for Indian manufacturers to supply spares and components to global manufacturers of nuclear power plants besides creating new business opportunities for Indian power plant construction firms. The nuclear deal grants India a special concession at par with Japan and European countries by permitting India to reprocess spent nuclear fuel acquired from external sources.[60] After all the huffing and puffing, India has now been granted the special privilege of spending enormous amounts of hard earned money running into billion of dollars to purchase uranium and nuclear reactors which is expected to meet around six per cent of our total energy requirement, as per government's own estimate.[61] The meeting of NSG members at Vienna in September 2008, in a consensus resolution exempted India from its rule of prohibiting trade with non-members of the NPT. The waiver at Vienna says, 'In the event that one or more participating governments consider that circumstances have arisen which require consultations, will meet and then act in accordance with paragraph 16 of the guidelines'. Other minor changes include substitution of the phrase partnership with India by cooperation with India in the paragraph 3(a) reference to the intensification of dialogue between the NSG and New Delhi.[62] A bilateral agreement then went to US Congress for final approval, and was signed into law on 8th October 2008. Similar agreements apply with Russia and France. The ultimate objective is to put India on the same footing as China in respect to responsibilities and trade opportunities, though it has had to accept much tighter international controls than other nuclear-armed countries. However, in a latest development, the 46-nation NSG had adopted new guidelines in June 2011 for the export of sensitive nuclear technology including enrichment and reprocessing (ENR) equipment and technology that made the sale of these items conditional on the recipient state fulfilling a number of "objective" and "subjective" conditions. The first of these conditions, namely NPT membership and full-scope safeguards, were specifically designed to dilute the 2008 waiver.[63] For India, it is a setback and diplomatic effort is needed to recover lost ground and ensure that India is excluded from the purview of the new ENR restrictions imposed by the NSG.

At this juncture, India's expectation is that our international partners will fully honour their commitment in this regard.

India, while moving forward in signing the nuclear deal kept its strategy at the lowest. But in larger view, the new understanding reinforced strategic ties between the United States and India. If anything appears, India is developing strategies to address old and emerging security challenges. An integral part of this paradigm shift in the security ambitions of India was the Next Steps in Strategic Partnership (NSSP) initiative of 2004, which subsequently led to Joint Statements of July 2005 and March 2006 passed by the Government of India and the United States of America. An ambitious aftermath of these engagements is the formulation of the Indo-US Nuclear Deal in the form of '123 Agreement'.[64] However, the strategic side of India became more important in the backdrop of changes in US geopolitical strategy pursued by the Bush Administration. US belief that India can offset China's increasing influence has been an important factor. Supporters of the deal in India view this as an opportunity for India to emerge as a quasi legitimised nuclear weapons power. In their statement on 2nd March 2006, President George William Bush and Indian Prime Minister Manmohan Singh expressed satisfaction with the great progress the United Stated and India have made in advancing their strategic partnership to meet the global challenges of the 21st century. Reviewing the progress made in deepening the global partnership, they reiterated their commitment to freedom and democracy; a celebration of national diversity, human creativity and innovation; a quest to expand prosperity and economic opportunity worldwide; and a desire to increase mutual security against the common threats posed by intolerance, terrorism, and the spread of weapons of mass destruction.[65] Consistent with objective their area of cooperation included economic prosperity and trade, energy security and clean environment, innovation and the knowledge economy, global safety and security and deepening democracy and meeting international challenges.

Besides this, the deal enables India, a non-signatory to the NPT to have civil nuclear trade with US and rest of the world, which is in gross breach of United States fundamental principles and existing NSG norms. This can be viewed as a quasi-recognition of India as a legitimate nuclear power unlike

Israel, Pakistan or North Korea–the countries which have been deprived of the privilege due to their not being signatories to NPT. The virtual legitimisation of India's nuclear status can be seen as a severe blow to the prospects of nuclear non-proliferation and global nuclear disarmament.[66] But for India an important factor behind the signing the deal has been sources of electricity. It promised international support in terms of nuclear fuel, energy, equipments and technology which can be viewed as a solution to the problem. It has also paved the way for sufficient supply of uranium to fuel India's nuclear reactors. The whole issue, on the part of India, involved the independence of India's foreign policy with two issue at heart. First, any process of negotiation should seek to limit the levers of influence the US or any other country or group of countries can exercise over India. Second, to the extent to which the US offer of nuclear cooperation is motivated by unrealistic expectations on a wider set of issues, the Government of India needs decisively to clear the air so that there is no room for future misunderstanding.[67] When two countries are developing friendly relations over a wide area, it is a legitimate expectation to seek support in areas of concern to one party or the other.[68] However, it is unreasonable to expect India to be supportive of US policies across the board; where India's own interests are involved, convergence may not be possible.

The major shift that took place in US objectives in relation to India and the region South Asia was not without reason but in the background of India's explosion in 1998, the events of 9/11 which heightened US concerns about security against Jihadi terrorism and Islamic extremism and American isolation after an aggression against Iraq, which invited world-wide censure. In such a situation, USA needed an ally on the other side of globe. This could be only India, which shared with USA a commonality of shared perception on democracy, free trade and threat from Islamist Jehadis. Needless to say that apart from Japan and South Korea, India was the only nation that was aware of, if not apprehensive about, the growing economic clout of China and the diplomatic leverage, she has all over the world. Philip Zelikow, who was adviser of the Secretary of State, Condoleezza Rice, in 2004 and 2005 held, 'The US had wasted five years following the 1998 nuclear tests trying to contain the Indian atomic genie. But as the strategists of the Bush administration surveyed the post-Iraq war, they asked themselves whether this failure could somehow be turned into the pillar of a new approach. One, where India's obvious military strengths were recognised, including the reality of its nuclear weapons, and an attempt made to harness its abilities so that they could further US interests in the region.[69] The new policy initiative of US State Department concerning India read, 'its goal is to help India become a major world power in the 21st century 'and by way of clarification or amplification it was further added, 'we understand fully the implications, the military implications of that statement'.[70] At first, during the first four years of Bush administration it had sought to deepen military-to-military ties with the Indians with the stress on exercises, leading eventually to the sale of equipment.

In the context, the National Security Strategy document announced in 2002, also outlined new vision, a new focus on South Asia highlighting the geo-political significance of the changed US policy priorities towards India.[71] This is in keeping with US policy of remaining on top and yet creating a ring of regional super powers to encircle China. India, Japan and South Korea are the countries that share a common vision with US regarding China's growth. With this aim in view, US proposed to help India in creating a second green revolution by modernising agriculture, making her a manufacturing hub and strengthening her military sinews to become a regional superpower to act as a counter-weight to China. India's geographical propinquity with China and a long border between the two together with a vast, untapped economic market, bring India closer to USA.[72] In line, from the year 2002-2003 the talks in nuclear direction started between the two countries. First up, the High Technology Group, which has been set up in 2002, got a boost. Later that year, the Next Steps in Strategic Partnership took shape. By September 2004, India had agreed to sign the End Use Verification Agreement that considered commerce a key-bench mark of India's willingness to accommodate American concerns. Now policy-makers in US began to think that a nuclear deal could become the cornerstone of a grand strategic bargain with India. Gradually, the logic of a nuclear deal with India became so compelling that it appealed to the American establishment cutting across institutional, ideological, political and sectoral barriers.[73] As a step further was the Defence

Framework Agreement of June 2005 which foregrounded defence sales. It easily paved the way for the historic joint statement of 18th July 2005, which detailed the framework of nuclear deal between India and the United States.

The game of nuclear deal in US remained confidential and even non-proliferation specialists were kept on the periphery of the drafting process, although a journalist like Nicholas Burns knew enough of US policies to try and strive for some tactical icing on the strategic cake. The nuclear deal was premised on Indian nuclear weapons not being seen as a threat by Washington as far as the global balance of power is concerned. But this was so only as long as the Indian weapons programme did not become too ambitious. Burns and his colleagues sought to make the non-proliferation agenda an essential part of the nuclear deal even as the wider strategic partnership was designed to be the principal goal.[74] However, Nick Burns was not against the deal and in a statement he clearly enunciated of what the US expects from the deal. He said, 'The 123 Agreement brings India....back into the non-proliferation, mainstream in a way it was not before. And that is a tangible gain for India, as well as the US and rest of the world. He also spoke of the advantages that American companies will have in selling the "finest nuclear technology" to India. Simultaneously, he hoped for greater defence cooperation between India and the US leading to more exercises, training and defence sales. Both countries were already working together in South Asia on Bangladesh, Sri Lanka and Nepal in trying to form a better functioning relationship between India and Pakistan.[75] The India-US nuclear deal is part of an overall plan which includes the defence Framework Agreement, the Agriculture Deal and the Disaster Management Agreement. The idea is to engage India at all levels.

At the beginning of the year 2007 five former US secretaries of state–Henry Kissinger, James Baker, Waren Christopher, Madeleine Albright, and Colin Powell took part in a round table discussion entitled, 'Bipartisan Advice to the Next Administration' and during their conversation the relationship with India was also discussed. In this discussion. Kissinger responded, 'The relationship with India is one of the very positive things that is happening'. We can cooperate with them both on ideological grounds and on strategic grounds. 'It is one of the positive legacies that the new administration will inherit'.[76] Another famous scholar on the subject Karl F. Inderfurth, who also served as US assistant secretary of state for South Asian affairs from 1997-2001, is also of the view that strong India is important for balance of power purposes in Asia and for providing stability in the strategically important Indian Ocean littoral area. India is in a position to safeguard sea lanes that are used to transport more than half the world's oil and gas. The navies of the United States and India have begun to conduct joint exercises aimed against threats to maritime commerce.[77] Thus, after decades of being "estranged democracies", the United States and India have entered a new era that can best be described as "engaged democracies".

These apart, there are economy and energy related aspects which compelled the United States to sign the deal with India. As a matter of fact, the US Secretary of State Condoleezza Rice was already on record having stressed in *Washington Post* that, "Our agreement is good for American jobs, because it opens the doors to civilian nuclear trade. India plans to import eight nuclear reactors by 2012. If US companies win just two of these reactor contracts, it will mean thousands of new jobs for American workers".[78] The US Chamber of Commerce, the apex body of American business having a staggering three million members on its roll, floated a coalition for partnership with India, the canvass support for the deal. Apart from this, several American companies such as GE Energy Boeing Lockheed were pressurising Bush Administration to go ahead with the deal. The hardware manufacturers like Lockheed, Boeing and Martin, which earlier did business with India, could hope to sell their fighter jets here after the deal. Thus, the deal was also going to help the US economy and enhance employment prospects for American population. Moreover, the United States believed that a demographically and economically vibrant India could serve as a counter-weight to expanding China's influence.

With the announcement of Indo-US Civil Nuclear Agreement in July 2005, the United States explicitly recognised India's status as a full-fledged nuclear power, and committed itself to a partnership in the realm of civilian nuclear energy. However, in US too, the energy need is increasing at the rate of 1.8 per cent a year, which is low compared to the increasing demands in India and China. According to an estimate the additional demand for nuclear power in the US could be as high 400 to 500 GWe in the next fifty years. As per the Nuclear Energy Institute of the US, currently there is a substantial shortage of engineers of all types at nuclear power plants and this shortage will only increase as new plants are built. For one, there has been no new construction of nuclear reactors in the US since 1980. They have missed a whole generation of nuclear technologists. For another, interest of students in science and engineering has been on the decline in the West including the US. Nuclear engineering departments in many universities have been closed down and enrollment of nuclear engineering students have gone down by more than half in the last decade. The gap between the demand and supply of nuclear engineers in the US which was 350 during the fiscal year 1999-2000 has increased to more than 500 in the fiscal year 2002-2003 and should have grown further in the last years. Further, according to some experts, up to thirty per cent of the current nuclear engineering workforce could retire within the next five years. On 30th December 2005, for the first time in six years the Nuclear Regulatory Commission (NRC) certified the design of a new reactor-the 1000-MW Westinghouse advanced passive reactor. General Electric's simplified boiling water reactor is yet to get this certification and it will take many years for the construction of both these types to be licensed by the NRC. Now, the American nuclear companies are collaborating with foreign nuclear establishment to construct and produce energy in the US. One such joint venture has been constructed with the French Nuclear Company, AVERA recently which showed the lack of adequate trained nuclear scientists and engineers in the US.[79] In many fora, related to nuclear technology and nuclear knowledge management, many of the American scientists have said they look forward to a large input of human resource of competent nuclear scientists and technologists from foreign countries for the nuclear power industry of the United States of America.

Themes of the Agreement

Before 5th July 2005, when President George Bush and Prime Minister Manmohan Singh met at Washington and declared a joint statement on Indo-US civil nuclear cooperation, there was a long stalemate between the two because of US insistence that India sign the Nuclear Non-Proliferation Treaty

(NNPT), put her nuclear facilities under international inspection and cap her nuclear weaponisation programme. India successfully resisted this demand, which created a log jam between the two countries. Earlier in 1974 and in 1998 India, successfully conducted its nuclear tests keeping in view its regional security considerations. But on both these occasions, the West in general and the US in particular reacted sharply and threatened India to see the consequences. In 1974, US Administration subtly indicated their intolerance towards increasing nuclear potential of India by imposing sanctions as a reaction to India's first nuclear test. In 1998 also, in response to India's second nuclear test, United States permanently suspended fuel shipments to India. The US Atomic Act, 1954 restricts its trade with countries which are not parties to the NPT.[80] In the light of developments particularly, Indian explosion of 1974, the US in 1978, amended the Act of 1954 and the new Nuclear Non-proliferation Act which also prohibits the US nuclear cooperation with any country that has not accepted full scope safeguards under the International Atomic Energy Agency (IAEA). The understanding of July 2005 was preceded by discussions between the two Governments, particularly between President Bush and Prime Minister Manmohan Singh of the global energy scenario and the long-term implications of increasing pressure on hydro-carbon resources and rising oil prices. These developments led to the announcement in April of an Indo-US Energy Dialogue that encompassed the entire spectrum of energy options ranging from oil and gas to coal, alternative fuels and civilian nuclear energy. Through the initiation of a sustained dialogue to address energy security concerns, the two countries sought to promote stable, efficient, predictable and cost-effective solutions for India's growing requirements. At the same time, they also agreed on the need to develop and deploy cleaner, more efficient, affordable and diversified energy technologies to deal with the environmental implications of energy consumption.

In the joint declaration of 5th July, 2005, the US agreed that "as a responsible state with advanced nuclear technology, India should acquire the same benefit and advantages as other such states". Accordingly the American President understood to "seek agreement from Congress to adjust US laws and policies" and "work with friends and allies to international regimes to enable full civil nuclear energy cooperation and trade with India". In return, India said it would reciprocally agree that it would be ready to assume the same responsibilities and practices and acquire the same benefits and advantages as other leading countries with advanced nuclear technology, such as the United States".[81] In other words, behind this there was a simple proposition: in exchange for India assuming a number of costly "responsibilities and practices" in the nuclear field the US was saying that it would (i) no longer treat India as a non-nuclear weapons state in political or legal terms; and (ii) adjust its domestic statute and the guidelines of the Nuclear Suppliers Group (NSG) to allow nuclear commerce with New Delhi in line with the new reality. The two governments agreed on 18th July 2005 to undertake reciprocal commitments and responsibilities that would create a framework for the resumption of full cooperation. On its part, the United States undertook to :

(i) Seek agreement from the Congress to adjust US laws and policies to achieve full civil nuclear energy cooperation.

(ii) Work with friends and allies to adjust international regimes to enable full civil nuclear energy cooperation and trade with India, including but not limited to expeditions consideration of fuel supplies for safeguarded nuclear reactors at Tarapur.

(iii) In the meantime, encourage its partners to consider fuel supply to Tarapur expeditiously.

(iv) To consult with its partners to consider India's participation in ITER.

(v) To consult with other participants in the Generation-IV International Forum with a view towards India's inclusion.[82]

In response, India had conveyed its readiness to assume the same responsibilities and practices and acquire the same benefits and advantages as other leading countries with advanced nuclear technology, such as the United States. Accordingly, India for its part undertook the following commitments:

(i) Indentifying and separating civilian and military nuclear facilities and programmes in a phased manner.

(ii) Filing a declaration regarding its civilian facilities with the IAEA.

(iii) Taking a decision to place voluntarily its civilian facilities under IAEA safeguards, and

(iv) Signing and adhering to an Additional Protocol with respect to civilian nuclear facilities.[83]

The joint statement acknowledged that India's nuclear programme has both a military and civilian component. Both sides had agreed that the purpose was not to constrain India's strategic programme but to enable resumption of full civil nuclear energy cooperation in order to enhance global energy and environmental security. Such cooperation was predicated on the assumption that any international civil nuclear energy cooperation offered to India in the civilian sector should, firstly, not be diverted away from civilian purposes, and secondly, should not be transferred from India to third countries without safeguards.

As a step further and commitment of the US President made in joint statement to bring about required changes in US laws Henry J. Hyde United States–India Peaceful Atomic Energy Cooperation Act of 2006 (Hyde Act), was passed which modified the provisions of Section 123 of the Atomic Energy Act (1954) to permit US nuclear cooperation with India and exempt it from signing the NPT. It was signed into law by President Bush in December 2006, and mainly relates to fuel assurances, technology transfer and IAEA safeguards. Regarding fuel assurances it provides that civil nuclear assistance to India will not directly, or in any other way, assist India's nuclear weapon programme. In technology transfer, the Hyde Act makes Nuclear Suppliers Group's guideline binding on the 123 Agreement and mentions, "No item subject to the Agreement made be transferred to India if such transfer would violate or be inconsistent with transfer guidelines of the NSG."[84] Likewise, the new law is stringent on IAEA safeguards and laid emphasis on India's agreement with the IAEA "in perpetuity, in accordance with IAEA standards, principles and practices". Thus, under the terms of the July 2005 Agreement, the Bush administration was supposed to work with Congress to adjust US laws and policies to enable full civil nuclear energy cooperation and trade with India. However, it was a half-hearted

Act because the US agreed not to treat India as a non-nuclear weapon state (NNWS) anymore. It should have either included a waiver to Section 123(a) (4) in the Hyde Act, or amended the definition of nuclear weapon state in its domestic statute to remove the tight linkage with the NPT. But it did neither.

The Hyde Act is categorical on Indian testing and other nuclear-related matters. If India conducts a test the whole deal will collapse. It restricts US supplies of fuel to only that quantity needed for normal operating conditions of all our nuclear reactors. Hyde is against our building up any strategic reserve of fuel to ensure our reactors continue to operate stably even if the US terminates fuel supplies. But Hyde requires that even if we build up a reserve, the US government should ensure that the size of that reserve is not so large as to enable India to ride out any fuel supply cut off and civil nuclear sanctions that the US Congress would impose as soon as we undertake any nuclear explosive test. In addition, the Hyde Act also requires the US government to extract from the Indian government an "specific future date" after which we will not produce weapon grade plutonium even from our own unsafeguarded reactors. India is also required to follow US diplomatic and negotiating positions on the Fissile Material Cut-off Treaty (FMCT), although our position on the Treaty differs cardinally from the US position.[85] Not confirming itself to nuclear matters, the Act requires the Indian government to adopt a foreign policy across the board fully concordant with the US government. In the light of commitments made in July 2005, and by March 2006–Separation Plan the Hyde Act falls short. As early as July 2006, when the House and Senate versions of the Act were finalised, India in fact handed over a 12-page dossier to the US. At every stage India received assurances that the final law would be consistent with the White House's obligations. Now, after passing the Bill it is clear that it is inadequate and the US side is trying to reopen and reinterpret commitments with India.

Consistent with the joint statement of July 2005, and March 2006 under a separation plan India has agreed to abide by only IAEA safeguards that will be reflected in an India-specific Safeguard Agreement with IAEA. Much before signing the said agreement Indian Prime Minister Manmohan Singh made it clear that the separation plan is not only consistent with the imperatives of national security, but it also protects our vital research and development interests. "We have ensured that our three-stage nuclear programme will not be undermined or hindered by external interference. We will offer to place under safeguards only those facilities that can be identified as civilian without damaging our deterrence potential or restricting our research and development effort or in any way compromising our autonomy of developing our three-stage nuclear programme".[86] According to him, the separation plan will create a clearly defined civilian domain, where IAEA safeguards apply. On our part, we are committed not to divert any nuclear material intended for the civilian domain from designated civilian use or for export to third countries without safeguards. The July statement was not about our strategic programme. It was intended to be the means to expand our civilian nuclear energy capacities and thereby to help pave the way for faster economic progress. In the light of these out of the 14 indigenous reactors under the civilian nuclear programme eight more reactors will be brought under IAEA safeguards in addition to the six which are already under safeguards.[87] With these themes an India-specific agreement was negotiated between India and the IAEA providing for safeguards to guard against withdrawal of safeguarded nuclear material from civilian use at any time as well as providing for corrective measures that India may take to ensure uninterrupted operation of its civilian nuclear reactors in the event of disruption of foreign fuel supplies. There is a difference between civilian and military nuclear facility. Fission of uranium atoms in a reactor to produce heat to make steam is necessary to generate electricity. The important element called "critical mass" is the minimal amount of nuclear material necessary to sustain a chain reaction. As opposed to a nuclear explosion where the chain reaction occurs in a split of second and enormous amounts of energy are released, in a power reactor the chain reactions are initiated, controlled and sustained at a steady rate.[88] The ostensible difference in the nature of civilian and military facility is "in the way fuel is irradiated to produce plutonium of weapon grade quality. Fuel in power reactors is irradiated for longer periods to generate maximum heat through higher burn up for electricity production.[89] The world community and IAEA hailed the agreement. Nicholas Burns, Under Secretary of State, had hoped that if Congress and US approve the deal, India would embark on a massive expansion of its civilian nuclear sector.

It was only after the five rounds of meetings between India and the IAEA that the 23-page negotiated document which was made public as the Agreement. The said Agreement places India mid-way between nuclear weapon states and non-nuclear weapon states in terms of its rights and obligations. The most important part of the Agreement from the perspective of international law is the preambular assertion that 'an essential basis of India's concurrence to accept IAEA safeguard" is (i) the conclusion of international arrangements for the uninterrupted and continuous access to nuclear fuel, and (ii) support for an Indian effort to develop a strategic reserve of nuclear fuel. The same section of the preamble also notes that "India may take corrective measures to ensure uninterrupted operation of its civilian nuclear facilities in the event of disruption of foreign fuel supplies".[90] The preamble is an integral part of the agreement and cannot be separated from the operational section without the latter part losing its entire context. According to Article 52 (c) the agreement provides for India to report to the IAEA without delay "any disruption of operation of safeguarded facilities on account of material violation or breach of bilateral or multilateral arrangements of which India is a party." Likewise Articles 105 and 106 allow India to raise these violations directly with the IAEA Board.[91] The safeguards agreement represents an attempt to tie down the political commitments of July 2005 and March 2006 into a legal framework in which India has clearly defined rights.

As a follow up of the statement of 18th July 2005 on the Indo-US Civil Nuclear Cooperation-22 pages and 17 Articles document was made public in the year 2007. It crossed the first hurdle in November 2006, when the Bill was adopted by 85-12 margin by 100-member Republican-controlled Senate. Richard Lugar, Chairman of the Senate Foreign Relations Committee, who moved the legislation ranking Democrat Joseph Biden, described the deal as most important diplomatic strategic initiative undertaken by the President. "It is an opportunity to build a vital, strategic partnership with a nation that shares our democratic values and will exert increasing influence on the world stage. We should move forward now. He described India as an emerging world power with 'awesome responsibility and the strategic relations between the two nations gave the US an opportunity to make a gigantic difference to the world.[92]

However, it took years in finalising the agreement. In the last quarter of 2008, the Indo-US nuclear deal was approved by the US Congress and US President George Bush signed 123-legislation on India-US nuclear deal into the new law called 'US-India Nuclear Cooperation Approval and Non-proliferation Enhancement Act'. Signing of the deal by the President had paved the way for signing it between the two countries. It was passed by Congress on 1st October and the President gave his assent on 8th of the same month. In a brief statement on the occasion of signing Bush sought to allay Indian concerns about the United States derogating from its obligation under the 123 Agreement. These concerns arose because of the statement the President himself made in a letter to Congress last month that the fuel supply assurances contained within the 123 represented a "political" rather than a legally binding commitment.[93] The passed Act is also known as H.R. 7081, and as it emerged finally from the Senate, subjected the 123 Agreement to precisely this kind of "cosmetically less glaring" alteration by embedding riders about the fuel supply assurances being mere political commitments.

Soon after the Presidential approval, in a formal ceremony at the State Department in New York, it was signed by Pranab Mukherjee, India's External Affairs Minister and Condoleezza Rice, the US Secretary of State on 10th October 2008. In a statement prior to the actual signing of the Agreement Mukherjee noted that the Agreement was the "first step" to civil nuclear cooperation and trade between India and the United States. The Agreement was about civil nuclear cooperation and reflects a careful balance of rights and obligations. Its provisions are now legally binding on both sides once the Agreement enters into force. We look forward to working with US companies on the commercial steps that will follow to implement this landmark Agreement.[94] After signing he again, issued a statement and emphasised that India intends to implement this Agreement in good faith and in accordance with the principles of international law and I am confident that the US will also do the same. But no such assurance was given from the US side other than the State Department saying the Agreement provided the "legal framework" for nuclear cooperation. A preliminary reading of the agreement suggested that a serious effort was made by both India and the US to square a very difficult circle.

The Indo-US nuclear deal made for the cooperation in civil nuclear sphere between the two countries is subject to the internal laws of both countries. Article 2.1 of the 123-agreement states in the clearest possible terms. "Each Party shall implement this Agreement in accordance with its respective applicable treaties, national laws, regulations and licence requirements concerning the use of nuclear energy for peaceful purposes". This means that in the case of US the 123-agreement is subject to all the present internal laws of the country right from the US Atomic Energy Act 1954 to the Hyde Act 2006, all inclusive. Besides, it will be subject to amendments to these present laws and to any new law that may be enacted in the future. Articles 3.3 and 5.2 of this agreement also made it clear further. Article 3.3 states, "This agreement does not require the transfer of any information regarding matters outside the scope of this agreement or information that the Parties are not permitted under their respective treaties, national laws, or regulations to transfer". Similarly, Article 5.2 mentions that transfers of dual use item could be used in enrichment, reprocessing or heavy water production facilities will be subject to the Parties respective applicable laws, regulations and licence policies.

From the beginning, the role of US Congress, especially, the Senate has a vital and deciding constitutional power over the international treaties/agreements undertaken by the US government. Professor Michael J. Glennon explained the role of US Senate in Treaty ratification in a 1983 essay, in the *American Journal of International Law*, in which he wrote, 'It may amend its resolution of ratification by adding material, normally called a reservation, understanding, interpretation declaration or statement, or it may amend the resolution of ratification by inserting a condition that the text of the treaty be amended. Each form of alteration is equally binding on the President. International law, similarly, regards a reservation to a bilateral treaty as tantamount to a proposed amendment. The principal reason that the Senate sometimes prefers the 'reservation' mode to the 'amendment' mode is diplomatic: domestic political considerations in the non-reserving state may make it easier for its government to accept a treaty alteration that is cosmetically less glaring'.[95] So far as the position of 123-Agreement in the US is concerned, it is also a settled matter in

US law that documents intended to have mere moral or political weight, but not to be legally binding, are not international agreements. Since, the 123-Agreement is manifestly an international agreement, it follows that all of its provisions are equally binding in a legal sense. In the US constitution, this executive-legislative divide stems from the differing definitions of treaty and executive agreement. The US constitution and convention as well defines treaty as an agreement that is made with the advice and consent of the Senate or whose terms law has approved as the case may be. International agreements not submitted to the Senate are called executive agreements. While a treaty is a binding international agreement, an executive agreement applies to in domestic law only. Under the convention, however, both types of agreements are considered binding. Since the 123-Agreement requires a Congressional consent and is founded on US laws, it is a treaty under the US definition as well and will be bound by international law.[96] Thus from all accounts the stated US position on 123-Agreement implies that it would abide by the convention whose Article 18 says; Upon signing a treaty, a nation is obliged to refrain from acts which would defeat the object and purpose of the treaty.

In India too, executive cannot act independently of Parliament on nuclear deal. Justice V.R. Krishna Iyer and P.B. Sawant, former judge of the Supreme Court of India, and justice H. Suresh, former judge of the Bombay High Court, had issued a statement on the powers of the Executive with reference to the Indo-US nuclear deal. In the context the executive has no power to enter into any agreement, either with a foreign government or a foreign organisation, which is binding on the nation. The agreement will be binding only when it is ratified by Parliament. There is no provision in the Constitution which gives such authority to the Executive. They mention Article 73, and 253 and Entries 6, 13 and 14 in the Union List of the Constitution which refer to the powers of the Executive. Article 73, among other things, states, '........the executive power of the Union shall extend (i) to the matters with respect to which Parliament has powers to make laws, and (ii) to the exercise of such rights, authority and jurisdiction as are exercisable by the Government of India by virtue of any treaty or agreement'. This simply means that the matters on which Parliament has no powers to make laws are also matters on which the Union

Government cannot exercise its executive power. Also mentions Article 253, 'Notwithstanding anything in the foregoing provisions of this chapter, Parliament has power to make any law.....for implementing any treaty agreement or convention with any other country or countries or any decision made at any international conference association or other body.[97] The Union List Entry six makes 'Atomic energy and mineral resources necessary for its production', a subject matter of legislation of Parliament. Entries 13 and 14 are also in support of the legislature and provide a vast subject matters of legislation by Parliament.

Thus, under the various provisions of the Indian Constitution the present Indo-US Nuclear Deal cannot be implemented by the Union Government unless it is translated into a law enacted by Parliament. In addition, Parliament is entitled to review, scrutinise, and modify or cancel any and every act of the executive. There is no such thing as a 'prerogative power' of the executive, immune from Parliamentary scrutiny. The 123-Agreement cast a deep impact and influence in a very large measure, the economic, political, military, and foreign policies of our country apart from the energy sector. In short, whatever the executive does in exercise of its executive power or otherwise, it is accountable to Parliament. Indeed, in a Parliamentary democracy and particularly under our constitutional system, it is unthinkable that there is any sphere of activity of the executive in respect of which it is not accountable to Parliament.

Finally, a forty-year Indo-US Nuclear Deal in the form of 123-Agreement came into effect after signing by India's External Affairs Minister Pranab Mukherjee and US Secretary of State Condoleezza Rice on 10th October 2008. It completed the legal and formal formalities from both sides and became an integral part of international law. The 22-pages agreement contained 17 long Articles and covered a wide range of subjects relating to nuclear testing, safeguards, the US right to return material, reprocessing issue and termination of the Agreement, etc. However, the most important provision which compelled India to undertake a nuclear cooperation deal with the US was the supply of fuels material to India and end decades of its isolation in nuclear world. Under Section 123(a), (4) of the US Atomic Energy Act (1954), every nuclear with a non-nuclear weapons state must include a clause granting the US, the right to seek the return of nuclear materials and equipment exported pursuant to the agreement in the event of the recipient state exploding a nuclear device. Article 14 of the Agreement dealt in detail regarding the various provision and Article 14.4 unambiguously grants the US, 'the right to require the return......of any nuclear material equipment, non-nuclear material or components transferred under this agreement and any special fissionable material product through their use'. This includes nuclear fuel as well as any plutonium that is produced from the reprocessing of US origin spent fuel. Earlier, when formal negotiations on the text of the bilateral nuclear agreement started, the US made it clear the 'right of return' would have to be included. At this juncture, the Indian side had two options. It could either walk away or try to make the best of a bad situation by crafting balancing provisions. The Indian negotiators sought to enshrine the commitments, the US had made in July 2005 and March 2006, and protect the country from disruption that would inevitably result from any American attempt to take back nuclear fuel or vital reactor components following an Indian test. Needless to say, the US 123-agreement with China does not include such a clause, nor does its 123 with Euratom as far as cooperation with Britain and France are concerned. The only stipulation is that these countries will not detonate a nuclear device using US material.

Several provisions have been made in 123-Agreement to protect Indian interests in case the US seeks its right to return the fuel materials and technologies. In particular Article 5.6 on fuel supply assurance, Article 13 and 14 on the procedures, Article 10.2 on safeguards and Article 16.3 on duration showed that a solid web of protection has been woven by the interlocking nature of all rights and commitments contained in the agreement. Under protection Article 14.5 says that India and the US recognise that exercising the right of return would have profound implications for their relations. Prior to the removal of any items under the exercise of this right the agreement provides for several layers of insulation. First, the US is obliged to "undertake consultations" with India. These consultations are envisaged to be separate from the Article 14.2 consultation on termination. Secondly, such consultations shall give special consideration to the importance of uninterrupted operation of nuclear reactors in India. Thirdly, Article 14.6 says fair market value compensation must be agreed upon and paid to India prior to the removal of any items and an agreement must be reached with Delhi on "methods and arrangements" for the return. Fourthly, 14.7 says prior to any return India shall satisfy itself that full safety, radiological and physical protection measures have been ensured in accordance with its existing national regulations. Fifthly, bearing in mind the importance of uninterrupted operation of nuclear reactors, 14.8 stresses that the consultations between the parties shall address mutual commitments on continuity of fuel supplies contained in Article 5.6 of the agreement. This Article incorporates the fuel supply assurances spelt out in the 2nd March Indo-US agreement on the separation of Indian nuclear facilities. The same clause adds, 'It is not the purpose of the provisions of this Article regarding cessation of cooperation and right of return to derogate from the rights of India under Article 5.6. Sixthly, and finally India retains, the right, under Article 5.6 (c) to take "corrective measures" on safeguards front if there is disruption of fuel supplies pursuant to any US action.[98] Under Article 5.6 (c) India will use corrective measures to ensure uninterrupted operation of its civilian nuclear reactors in the event of disruption of foreign fuel supplies. The legal status of these corrective measures has been further enhanced by three additional clauses-14.8., 10.2 and 16.3 of the 123-Agreement. The 123-Agreement's clear link between the perpetuity of IAEA safeguards even on US supplied material, and the assured supply of fuel for the life-time of all of India's nuclear reactors provides a powerful deterrent to any US desire to seek the return of exported material or terminate the agreement. Even under a worst case scenario where the US ignores its obligation to ensure the continuous operation of Indian reactors, presumably citing the Hyde Act, India would be under no obligation to entertain an American request for the return of nuclear items.

The 123-Agreement will remain in force for forty years but Article 14.1 gives the US the right to terminate the agreement on one year's written notice. It should also provide the reasons for seeking this termination. Article 14.3 also allows for termination in the event of violation of the agreement by India. If termination is based on violation of an IAEA safeguards agreement, a "crucial factor" will be whether the IAEA Board of Governors had made a finding of non-compliance. Once the US serves the termination notice, Article 14.2 says that before the agreement is terminated, the US and India "shall consider the relevant circumstances and hold consultations based on the recognition that both are States with advanced nuclear technology, which have agreed to assume the same responsibilities and practices and acquire the same benefits and advantages as other leading countries with advanced technology. There is no time frame for these consultations but they cannot be open-ended: one year after notice is served, the agreement stands terminated. The US has signed the 123-Agreement with many countries but with different provisions. For instance Japan's 123-Agreement provides for compensation and says that before the US terminates cooperation or requires the return of its exported nuclear items, 'the parties shall consult for the purpose of taking corrective steps and shall carefully consider the economic effects of such actions, taking into account the need to make such other appropriate arrangements as may be required'. But in case of China's 123-Agreement no such return clause is required.

In course of discussions for the 123-Agreement between India and the United States the issue of Indian right for reprocessing the spent fuel remained at the top. For India, reprocessing is central to the integrity of the indigenous nuclear programme. 'We were the first country to have reprocessing capabilities in Asia since 1965. There is no danger of leakage contributing to weapons programme unlike breakout countries where a little bit of cooperation might make all the difference'. India remained apprehensive before signing the Indo-US nuclear deal in October 2008, because on four of this month US Secretary of State Condoleezza Rice reiterated her government's intention of pressing for a ban on enrichment and reprocessing (ENR) equipment and technology when the Nuclear Suppliers Group meets again and described cleverly the proposal to ban ENR sales to countries that are not signatories to the Nuclear Non-Proliferation Treaty as a "criteria-based approach that was not singling out India. The 123-Agreement signed between the countries in Article 6(iii) in the beginning states 'the Parties grant each other consent to reprocess or otherwise alter in form or content nuclear material transferred pursuant to this agreement'. Anil Kakodkar, the then Chairman of the Atomic

Energy Commission, in an interview given to English daily, *The Hindu*, in Mumbai on 6th August 2007, made the point very clear and said that there is no ambiguity about it. Now, the important point to recognise is that we need to establish arrangements and procedures with regard to safeguards, physical protection, storage and environment, and such other parameters. Parties will agree on arrangements and procedures, and consultation for this purpose will start in six months from the date of the request and it will be completed in one year.[99] In addition, the agreement has a non-hindrance clause, which says that there cannot be any hindrance or interference in India's unsafeguarded programme or programmes involving military nuclear facilities and so on. So there is an explicit statement in the agreement itself–a legal provision that we can carry on our programme unhindered, according to our policies. Similarly, we can carry on with the reactors which are supplied to us under this agreement. We can reprocess the fuel supplied under this agreement and we can re-use the plutonium, derived after reprocessing the spent fuel, in safeguarded national facilities.

However, there are two pre-conditions to operationalise the major concession of reprocessing spent fuel. One, for allowing us to reprocess, we must build, at our own cost, a national reprocessing plant, estimated to cost Rs. 10,000 crore. Furthermore, before we actually start building such a plant, we must provide all detailed drawings and other technical documentation, data, calculations and so on to the International Atomic Energy Agency to review and clear. Second, it is required to accept a whole range of arrangements and procedures stipulated by the US to run our own national plant. After that we have also to sign another agreement with the US government, under Section 131 of the US Atomic Energy Act, which must be approved by the Congress.

The much-debated agreement on modalities for reprocessing was finalised and signed in the year 2010. It was finalised at the end of March in which India was allowed to retrieve recyclable material found in spent fuel from US origin nuclear plants for further generating electricity. The US State Department and the Indian Department of Atomic Energy simultaneously announced that the reprocessing plants would operate under International Atomic Energy Agency (IAEA) procedures. Earlier, the US wanted the agreement to cover only one reprocessing facility, while India felt the 123-Agreement envisaged multiple facilities. In the end, the final text says the pact will apply to two facilities, with India allowed to make additions and modifications. According to Indian officials this clause will allow the country to augment it reprocessing capacity without going back to the negotiation if the need arises for more plants. The US State Department too hoped that the completion of these arrangements would facilitate participation by US firms in India's rapidly expanding civil nuclear energy sector.[100] Timothy Roemer, US Ambassador to India also said that these arrangements will help open the door for US firm in India's rapidly expanding energy sector, creating thousands of jobs for the citizens of both our countries. Four months later at the end of July 2010, India and the US signed accord on reprocessing spent fuel in pursuant to Article 6(iii) of the bilateral '123-Agreement' on civilian nuclear cooperation. It was signed at a State Department ceremony by Indian Ambassador Meera Shankar and US Under Secretary of State for Political Affairs William Burns. On the occasion, the State Department in a statement said that as per the agreement the reprocessing would be undertaken at a new, safeguarded national facility to be established by India, while its spokesman hinted at some of the key factors driving this agreement mentioned that the Civil Nuclear Cooperation Initiative had facilitated significant new commercial opportunities across nuclear energy market, including the designation of two nuclear reactor park sites for US technology in the States of Andhra Pradesh and Gujarat.[101] This is only the third pact signed by the US the earlier ones being with Japan and Euratom–a European consortium.

After signing the nuclear deal in October 2008, the two countries signed three pacts in July 2009 when US Secretary of State Hilary Clinton visited India and assured that US Administration would not block the transfer of enrichment and reprocessing technology to India which is a part of Indo-US Nuclear Deal. The pacts signed during her visit were related to Science and Technology, Space Cooperation and End User Monitoring Agreement (EUMA). Of them, the pact relating to End User Monitoring Agreement allows India to buy sensitive, high-tech military equipment and technology from US which government feels necessary for modernisation of its defence forces. The US has hailed the EUMA with New Delhi as a 'landmark event' and 'very significant agreement' as it brings India into the non-proliferation mainstream and is part of the fulfilment of the nuclear deal. But the pact EUMA evoked a strong reaction because it barred India from selling the materials to other countries and the agreement authorises Washington to monitor the use of US made military equipment sold to New Delhi.[102] The avowed aim of the agreement is to enhance the American national security and foreign policy objectives as EUMA explicitly restrict what India can do with the US origin defence equipments. Under its terms, India cannot modify the imported weapon system in any form. Also, to keep the importing state dependent on US, EUMA restricts India from getting US sold defence equipments serviced by any other country without prior American permission. The government owes an explanation to the Parliament and the country as to how and under what circumstances did it sign an agreement designed by the United States which meddles with India's strategic autonomy and its right of embettered deployment and use of weapons bought with hard cash.[103] Above all now the EUMA will serve as an umbrella arrangement covering all future defence deals.

Both the pacts-Indo-US nuclear deal and EUMA were signed by the US keeping in view its global/regional strategy at large as well as America's economic interests. The much-debated Indo-US nuclear deal as followed by End User Monitoring Agreement and the pacts came as a major boost to American arms companies like Lockheed, Martin Corporation, Boeing etc which were eyeing mega deals with India, one of the world's largest importers of conventional weapons.[104] These companies are going to earn a huge benefits out of the deal. To make the matter worse, intense lobbying started to exempt American nuclear suppliers of any liability in case of nuclear accident in reactors, they are planning to sell to India. Earlier in an important India promised the US in 2008 that it would sign the Convention on Supplementary Compensation (CSC) for nuclear damage. It was also a commitment that India made at the time of signing the landmark 2005 nuclear agreement with the United States. The CSC is an international covenant which provides a framework for channelling liability and providing speedy compensation in the event of a nuclear accident. After signing the CSC, Indian officials hoped that now there is nothing which stands in the way of American companies having commercial negotiations for the sale of their reactors. With India signing and the Barack Obama administration issuing the requisite 'Part 810' licensing certifications, the stage is now set for the Nuclear Power Corporation of India to begin full-fledged commercial negotiations with the General Electric and Westinghouse for supply of two 1000-MWe reactors.

In the circumstances, clearly under the pressure of American companies and the government as well India prepared a Civil Nuclear Liability Bill, 2010 (CNLB). In fact, the US companies did not want extended battles for liability and compensation as it happened after the Bhopal gas tragedy. The proposed law is supposed to be a key step operationalising the US-India Civil Nuclear Agreement. For long the US nuclear suppliers had been demanding legislation like this one and complete exemption from liability in case of a mishap.[105] Behind the Bill, the government's prime concern was to 'put in place a system that would restrict the sort of irresponsible behaviour seen in the Union Carbide case'.[106] Dr, Srikumar Banerjee, the then Chairman Atomic Energy Commission, in an interview to the English daily, *The Hindu*, on 2nd September 2010 in Chennai said, "the basic purpose behind the nuclear liability Bill is that in the very unlikely event of a nuclear incident, we do not want the victims to go for an extended process of litigation to claim compensation. The victims must get prompt and no-fault compensation. Prompt in terms of time, and no-fault meaning that you do not have to prove the fault of the operator or anyone to get the compensation."[107] To examine the whole issue and seek suggestions a panel was set-up by the Federation of Indian Chambers of Commerce and Industry (FICCI) after signing of nuclear deal that comprised representatives of the government and private power companies. The panel was headed by S.K. Jain, Chairman and Managing Director of the Nuclear Power Corporation of India Limited (NPCIL), a unit of the Department of Atomic Energy.

The Panel, in its report, suggested that it is imperative to indemnify industry and the participants from any damage arising from any circumstances beyond control through normal diligence that is expected at nuclear installations. It underlined that the liability should be solely attached to the operator because the nuclear accidents result in large scale damage involving a multitude of claimants and attributing and fixing fault to a party is a lengthy and technical process. The panel also sought an 'absolute waiver' to agencies responsible for handling and transportation of radioactive material from any liability. Accordingly, such non-operator liability shall stand transferred to the operator. Given the fact, at present the Indian Government operates all the nuclear plants in India. This would mean that all liability stands transferred to the government and that the government would have to pay damages to the victims if a mishap occurs in a nuclear power plant supplied to India by US or any other country.[108] The panel's report and draft of the Civil Nuclear Liability Bill created a furor and charged that it was being done to appease the foreign investors. Political criticisms apart, the judiciary of India, the Supreme Court, in particular, linked the damage to the protection of the Right to Life enshrined in Article 21 of the Constitution of India. Supreme Court by creative interpretation ruled that the expression 'life' does not connote merely physical existence but embraces the right to live with "human dignity and all that goes along with it, namely, the bare necessaries of life such as adequate nutrition, clothing and shelter over the head". Thereafter, it further expanded the concept of the right to live with human dignity to encompass within its ambit, the protection and preservation of environment, ecological balance, free from pollution of air and water.[109] Even the concept of liability was elaborated by the Supreme Court in 1996, in the case of Indian Council for Enviro-Legal Action. Justice Jeevan Reddy, speaking for the court pointed out that the rule of absolute liability is premised on the very nature of the activity carried on and "it is the enterprise carrying on the hazardous or inherently dangerous activity alone has the resource to discover and guard against hazards or dangers". The court further introduced the Polluter Pays Principle, which according to it requires that the financial costs of preventing or remedying damage caused by pollution should lie with the undertakings that cause the pollution. Under this principle, it is not the role of government to meet the costs involved in either prevention of such damage or in carrying out remedial action, because the effect of this would be to shift the financial burden of the pollution incident to the taxpayers. The responsibility for repairing the damage is that of the offending industry.[110] According to the Polluter Pays Principle that has been embedded in our jurisprudence, the liability and responsibility for compensating the victims of accident and remedying the environmental damage caused is that of the offending industry alone. No part of the liability can be limited nor passed on to the government.

The government's draft bill on civil nuclear liability faced opposition from the BJP, left parties and others mainly on the ground that government wanted undue favour for foreign investors at the cost of national interest. In August 2010, the government conceded major points regarding supplier's liability and the amended Section 17 (b) now reads. "If accident has resulted as a consequence of an act of supplier or his employee, which includes supply of equipment or material with patent or latent defects or sub-standard services the operator shall have a right of recourse, it means that operator can sue the supplier for recovery or any damage paid. There is no need for supplier to agree to this in contract or to have intentionally caused an accident, as earlier drafts proposed.[111] Section 6(2) clearly states that nuclear operators to be strictly liable for damages resulting from an accident but their liability is capped at Rs. 1,500 crore, unless a higher amount is notified by the government. In earlier draft, the cap was Rs. 500 crore. Beyond this cap, government assumes responsibility for damages. The Bill also specifies "maximum liability" of 300 million SDRs, approximately Rs. 2,100 crore. In section 1(3A), it was provided that only government or government company can benefit from the liability cap but the latter is defined as one where the Central government has not less than 51 per cent ownership. That paves the way for the liability burden of any private sector partner to be subsidised by the taxpayers. Other relevant provisions have also been made in Sections 18 (b), 16 (1), 35 and 46. While Section 18 (b) increases the time period of filing claims in case of personal injury from 10 to 20 years. Section 16 (1) mentions that claims for damages must be disposed of within three months of applications. Victims have been given the right to approach High Court and the Supreme Court for review of compensation amounts under Section 35, but with an ambiguous wording Government says that victims can file tort claims.[112] Thus, the whole Bill is between the victims and the operators. It creates a new legal authority called the Claims Commission or the Claims Commissioner. That authority will determine, depending on the scale of the event, how much compensation should be given.

Having converted the Bill into Act, the Government of India, in November 2011, notified the rules to implement nuclear liability law ahead of Prime Minister Manmohan Singh's meeting with United States President Barack Obama in Bali on the sidelines of the East Asia Summit. The notified rules give the nuclear plant operator the right to recourse for the period for which the supplier of equipment has taken liability for patent or latent defects or sub-standard services under a contract. A supplier includes a person who manufactures and supplies either directly or through an agent, a system, equipment or component or builds a structure on the basis of functional specification. In an hour long meeting with President Obama, Indian Prime Minister Manmohan Singh expressed India's readiness to address US concerns on nuclear liability.[113] To sum up all, it may be said that despite criticisms, the deal is now the reality. Within the limits of the terms of the agreement, India must make focussed efforts to minimise its losses and resist any undue pressure from the United States which might threaten its sovereignty, dignity and the interests of people of India. The government should enact laws which take due care of human concerns and public safety.

The Nuclear Deal: Evaluation and Overview

In recent past, the United States has been doing everything in its power to get India signed both the Comprehensive Test Ban Treaty (CTBT) and the Fissile Material Cut Off Treaty (FMCT), and thus make it entirely sub-servient to Washington.[114] Having these measures failed, since the 1990s, the US government made overtures to the Indian government for a military alliance. When the Bush administration came to power, it wanted India to be a part of its missile defence shield. After 9/11, the Indian and US navies and Special Forces have conducted a number of joint exercises in the Indian Ocean and in the hills of India's North-East. In the context of new developments, Christian Rocca said in 2002, 'Military to Military cooperation is now producing tangible progress towards the objective of strategic diplomatic and political cooperation as well as sound economic ties.[115] In going forward for the nuclear deal there are two clear US motives, articulated as explicitly as possible by various US sources: the commercial gain from nuclear commerce, and the more important one of containing India's nuclear weapons programme, both qualitatively and quantitatively. Bring the breeder reactor programme under international safeguards, pushing India to sign the FMCT and continuing embargoes on uranium enrichment and re-processing are all parts of this strategy.[116] The fundamental flaw lies in the fact that the US has provided unenforceable commitments in lieu of enforceable commitments from India. Under it, India has undertaken several obligations, including identifying and separating civilian and military nuclear facilities, declaring civilian facilities to IAEA and placing them under safeguards; continuing its nuclear testing moratorium; and working with USA for 'Fissile Material Cut-Off Treaty'. It has agreed to abide by MTCR and NSG guidelines, although it belongs to neither. Unlike India, the US accepts no similar obligations, like safeguarding more facilities or continuing its nuclear testing moratorium.[117] All this sufficiently indicates that deal treats India as a junior partner.

Basically, the Indo-US nuclear deal was founded on July 18, 2005 joint statement and March 2006 agreement between India and US. The July 2005 agreement gave the impression regarding fuel supply that when India placed some of its reactors under "voluntary safeguards" such safeguards were linked to nuclear fuel supplies being maintained. In March 2006 agreement on the issue, Washington insisted on the provision of "safeguards in perpetuity. To assuage Indian concerns, the US agreed that India could maintain adequate stockpiles of nuclear fuel to tide over any possible disruptions in supply. It also agreed to work with other nuclear suppliers to enable India to secure nuclear fuel so that its nuclear power stations could continue to operate.[118] But the overall conclusion drawn from the July statement was that it was poorly negotiated: First, while the US obligations contained in the statement are essentially those of intent, India's obligations are definitive and substantive like the commitment to continue the moratorium on testing as part of the deal. Second, the suggestion in the statement that the Indian obligations such as separation of civil and military nuclear facilities, placement of all civil nuclear facilities under IAEA safeguards, and signing of an Additional Protocol in respect of such facilities are identical to those undertaken by nuclear weapon states constitutes a factual inaccuracy. And third, the statement contains a dissonance between an effort in the Indian projection to try and pass off India as a nuclear weapon state and the US projection which does not lend itself to any such interpretation.[119] The July statement was sought to be justified on the grounds that the nuclear deal was the answer to India's energy problem; that it would help anchor India's stragegic ties with the US, that establish India's status as a nuclear weapon state; and that it would promote flow of high technology to India.

Further in 2006, the US in the name of adjusting its internal laws to pave the way for nuclear deal passed Hyde Act which is also called United State–India Peaceful Atomic Energy Co-operation Act of, 2006. There are several provisions in the Act that cause serious concern as they put in place a series of measures designed to neuter India's strategic capabilities, compromise its sovereignty and erode the independence of its foreign policy. The intent of the Hyde Act is to bring India into the NPT obligations without conferring on India an NPT weapon state status. In the debate on the Bill the legislators realised that without India in, US non-proliferation policies could not succeed. After India held out against the NPT for more than three decades and established an independent nuclear future in spite of great odds, it does appear that the US wishes to induct the country into the NPT, essentially as a non-weapon state, but with perhaps a weapons programme as a transient phase. In the statement of policy, the Hyde Act called for achieving a moratorium on the production of fissile material for explosive purposes by India, Pakistan, and the People's, Republic of China. It also goes on to say that the US shall "seek to halt the increase of nuclear weapon arsenals in South Asia and to promote their reduction on eventual elimination".[120] India's policy has always been that nuclear weapons should be eliminated as early as possible in all parts of the world. India has consistently opposed proposals for regional nuclear disarmament. By going ahead with nuclear cooperation with the US under the Act, India will lose all leverage to pursue the goal of universal nuclear disarmament and will be tied to elimination of nuclear weapons in South Asia.

In course of evaluation of the deal finally made in 2008, it was found that it failed to accomplish the promises and commitments mentioned in the joint statement of July 2005 and March 2006 agreement between the two countries. It left India indefensible on future nuclear testing and assurances on fuel supply issue along with reprocessing of spent fuel. Among the issues, the most important provision, which directly affects India's future nuclear programme/strategy is relating to its nuclear testing. As outlined in Article 14 of the 123-Agreement, should India detonate a nuclear explosive device, the United States has the right to cease all nuclear cooperation with India immediately, including the supply of fuel, as well as request the return of any items transferred from the US, including fresh fuel.[121] Especially, in the situation when India has to be wary of two countries, Pakistan and China, this provision of the deal is unacceptable as it hampers India's ability to conduct nuclear tests. India has border disputes with China while Pakistan's armed forces hate India, as do certain Islamic fundamentalist elements and Islamabad has waged four wars against India including the last at Kargil in which the Pakistan Army was even contemplating use of nuclear weapons against India. China may test its own improved design and Pakistan too may carry out a test for its own reasons. We are aware that the United States itself is working on the design of a 'Reliable Replacement Weapon (RRW) to modernise its nuclear arsenal and may indeed carry out a test in future, if it considers this necessary. Regarding testing the 123 states, "Parties agree to take into account whether circumstances that may lead to termination resulted from a Party's serious concern about a changed security environment or as a response to similar actions by other States which could impact national security".[122] Firstly, the US only agrees to take into account" our circumstances, not necessarily accept them. Secondly as soon as we test, all hell will break loose. Nobody will look at the elaborate convoluted wording in the 123. The US Congress will immediately demand the cancellation of the nuclear deal under Hyde.

Likewise India's position on fuel supply and reprocessing of spent fuel is very weak and several substantial powers have been given to the United States of America. On September 10, 2008 US President George Bush repudiated a key provision of the 123-Agreement when he declared the fuel supply assurances recorded in Article 5 (6) of the agreement were not legally binding. In its replies to the House Foreign Relations Committee (HFRC), the State Department also undermined the sanctity of the fuel supply assurances in six ways. First, it refuses to consider the assurances in March 2006, Bush-Manmohan joint statement to be of a binding legal character, calling them instead "important Presidential commitments" that the US will uphold only to the extent they are "consistent with US laws". Secondly, it arbitrarily restricts the meaning of "disruption of supply" in Article 5.6 of the 123-Agreement by saying this "is meant to refer to disruptions in supply to India that may result through no fault of its own" such as a trade war resulting in the cut-off supply; market disruptions in the global supply of fuel", etc. Reprocessing of spent fuel to separate plutonium is extremely important in the Indian context. The Indian nuclear fuel-cycle is crucially dependent on the use of Fast Breeder Reactors is the second stage and of thorium-based systems in the third stage. Separation of plutonium is essential for the eventual use of thorium as a nuclear fuel. India, therefore, expects that reprocessing will be an important activity of its nuclear energy programme. While the process designs will no doubt be an Indian activity, denial of access to certain equipment or materials required by India, even when these activities are under IAEA safeguards, would be most unreasonable.

The Indo-US nuclear deal and allied national laws as a result of the understanding invited a lot of criticisms–nationally, regionally and globally. In Indian context, the issue involves US suzerainty over India's national economy and foreign policy. American nuclear big business is keen to make India its mega-market using for the purpose of a willing and weak Prime Minister. George Bush's stubborn hegemonistic strategy promoting US big business investment has become India's national policy, facilitated by the Sonia-Manmohan commitment. This is virtually a reversal of the Nehru-Indira socialistic non-alignment stance and the principles of Panch Sheel. In the whole process, we remained a mere satellite and not a sovereign nation. We do not decide our import investment policies, the direction of Swadeshi agriculture and native industrial development.[123] The three great nuclear scientists – Dr. P.K. Iyengar, Dr, A. Gopalakrishanan and Dr. A.N. Prasad, have fiercely opposed US imports for reasons they have spelt out in a signed statement.[124] Among them P.K. Iyengar, a former chairperson of the Atomic Energy Commission, frankly stated, the so-called "benefits" of a US-India nuclear deal "are outweighed by costs in terms of the strains on our sovereignty". Delicately put, but so true. The US wants to control Indian scientific thinking. "The control on the thinking process is the worst thing that can happen to any country". [125] But that seems to be Bush strategic aim. Quoted in the Asian Age, A.N. Prasad, the former director of the Bhabha Atomic Research Centre had said 'India's three-stage nuclear programme, which is geared towards harnessing thorium, is a prized jewel that cannot be sacrificed at the alter of politics".[126] Given the reality of the agreement on the ground and the different priorities of both governments it has to be remembered in New Delhi that this is not a two-way deal: 'India is not selling something of critical interest to America in return for nuclear fuel or nuclear technology. India is a buyer. It is a one-way transaction.[127] This of course makes the situation an unequal one, one which is heavily contested both by the opposition, mainly BJP and Left parties.

Regionally, many including Indian scholar Praful Bidwai and Achin Vanaik are critical of the deal because of their concern for peace. Analysts view that the deal would intensify the instability of South Asian sub-continent. Over the past few years, the Indian and Pakistani governments have made strides toward easing the tensions between the two countries. People-to-people contacts have increased and the governments are in discussion over the many outstanding issues that divide the two states. One of the means to build confidence in the region was the creation of a natural gas pipeline from Iran through Pakistan into India. The "Peace Pipeline" would have tied the region together and raised the stakes for negotiations over belligerence. The Bush administration offered India's nuclear power in exchange for Iranian gas as part of its plan to isolate Iran. Apart from this, the nuclear deal does nothing to hamper the Indian nuclear weapons sector, whose growth would fuel an arms race with Islamabad and Beijing.[128] According to Bidwai, 'Contrary to the claim that waiver and more generally the US-India nuclear deal, will bring India into the global non-proliferation mainstream or promote nuclear restraint for India's part, it will allow India to expand its nuclear weapons arsenal and encourage a nuclear arms race in Asia, particularly in the volatile South Asian sub-continent, where Pakistan is India's significant rival. With the waiver under its belt, India can proceed to import Uranium fuel, and a range of other nuclear materials, equipments and technologies for its civil nuclear programme.[129] But it can divert uranium exclusively for weapons purposes. Achin Vanaik is also of the view that though India has placed 14 out of its 22 civilian nuclear reactors under IAEA's safeguards, which means that no nuclear material from them is allowed to be diverted to military purposes. India can still use the remaining eight reactors to produce as much plutonium as it likes for its weapons programme.[130] However, in US calculations a strong India is the world's best bet for peace and stability in South, South East and Central Asia, as also in the Persian Gulf. This volatile region, with some two billion inhabitants, needs a strong secular and democratic power from within the region, to ensure stability and to serve as a counterpose to transnational fundamentalism as also to China. Neither the US nor Israel can play this role, as they will end up stoking religious fundamentalism as has happened in Iraq, Afghanistan, Pakistan and Iran. Like the Americans, the Russians too have no cultural affinity or acceptability in most of these regions.[131] It is therefore, in the US interest not to curb the natural growth of India's military and soft power, so that it can play an increasing role in this region.

In addition, the nuclear deal with the US cast a dark shadow on India's relations with two controversial neighbours–China and Pakistan. There have been a hardening on the Border dispute in Arunachal Pradesh. China is a major player in the nuclear suppliers group and is worried how the deal would impact on them. China is further worried by the quadrilateral for democracy which includes India, the US, Australia and Japan and which it sees as anti-Chinese. The quadrilateral is due to hold naval exercises in the Bay of Bengal in the first week of September 2007 with Singapore. Nuclear submarines, aircraft carriers, destroyers and frigates will participate and it is coined the largest exercise since the end of the Cold War.[132] After signing the nuclear deal relations between India and Pakistan could be profoundly altered as India is seen as given preferential treatment despite Pakistan's cooperation with the US in the war on terror. In fact, Pakistan's first reaction was to warn the US of a potential arms race.[133] Strategic stability has been threatened as India will be able through the nuclear deal to develop larger amounts of fissile material for nuclear weapons. In one possibility among others, the deal will help Pakistan to seek a closer alliance with China to balance the new geo-political reality in South Asia.

No less than these, it is the charge of international community, although not explicit, that the deal has weakened the framework of international law. In one stroke, the deal has exhibited the Bush administration's disregard for the Kyoto protocols on climate change, for the International Criminal Court, for the Geneva Conventions, for the United Nations and so on. India refused to sign the non-Proliferation Treaty in 1968 because, it claimed, the NPT put into place a hierarchy between nuclear weapons states and non-nuclear weapons states. There is no demand for universal nuclear disarmament. Neither the US nor any other state is in legitimate possession of nuclear weapons. Now, the US government is playing King-maker, pretending that it is in a lawful position to welcome India into the nuclear weapons club. India's nuclear history is similar to that of Iran, but that Iran signed the NPT and yet the Bush administration with contempt for reason and international law, made a deal with one country and demonises another.[134] Even American scholars, Joseph Cirincione and Miriam Raj Kumar, considered the nuclear deal as reversing the US nuclear policy of non-proliferation measures adopted so far. They think the nuclear deal would be a trend-setter in extending similar exceptions to NPT to other states. They quoted the example of Pakistan approaching China for similar deal.[135] In May 2010, the deal between China and Pakistan to build two nuclear reactors in Pakistan came to be a reality which had drawn several criticism from non-proliferationists. Unlike them, the Indian scholars, Bidwai and Vinaik not merely supported non-proliferation but are also against destructive weapons and in favour of global nuclear disarmament. To quote Bidwai, 'Indian nuclear scientists campaigned against inclusion of fast breeder reactors under the supervision of IAEA and succeeded but at its core is a cynical agenda of legitimising the most destructive weapons known to humanity by sealing as a close Indo-US strategic partnership.'[136] Thus, upon closer evaluation, terms of the agreement show that the US has very cleverly hidden key clauses in it that places India in an unfavourable position.

In the aftermath of the successful conclusion of the US-India Civil Nuclear Cooperation Agreement, a number of concerns have been raised in India. The main concerns are that India's strategic programme including nuclear weapons testing would be compromised; that the Agreement would compromise

India's three-stage programme leading to the utilisation of thorium; and finally that it would impinge upon India's autonomy in the conduct of its foreign policy. But the fact is that in the light of constraints, this is the best and most practical agreement that could have been hammered out.[137] In the final negotiations, as the deal proves, Washington had conceded a lot of ground but of course, without India everything. Now, it would be entirely unpragmatic to even think of getting everything one wants from a bilateral agreement. Diplomacy is the art of bargaining, compromise and accommodation. A deal can never be struck if everyone were to look for the maximum payoffs. When the minimum positions of all the parties are met the deal is supposed to be struck.[138] One set of opposition in the Indian domestic scene is marred by the "curse of memory", specifically rooted in instintive anti-Americanism: a policy centered on opposing anything to do with America. The Left in India, despite its long history in Indian politics has never been so close to the corridors of power and at least in this case, its new found power seems to have affected the realisation of pragmatic deal. As for the BJP, this is a deal that it would have accepted with fanfare and "cries of victory" when in power.[139] However, serious and fruitful opposition had definitely helped in firming up the stand of the government in its negotiations with the American government.

Also a few in Western media opposed the deal. London-based economist devoted two cover stories to criticise the deal, called it a double speak on non-proliferation and appealed to the Congress to reject it. In the context. *The New York Times* argued that Bush administration publicly slighted Pakistan, an old ally of USA.[140] But the apprehensions are baseless as India has one of the cleanest export control records despite not being a part of the nuclear non-proliferation regime; and India would retain its exempt status only under compliance of non-proliferation norms which includes the prohibition of nuclear testing. In the circumstances, if India conducts a test, the reactions would certainly be determined by the situations. If it comes without any sort of provocation from anywhere, the international reactions would be harsh and immediate as it should be. On the other hand, if it comes as a result of certain and visible provocations, which threaten the security concerns, then the reactions would certainly be weighed under the conditions of strategic imperatives. In the context, India is not the first country to have the civil nuclear cooperation pact with a nuclear power state outside the NPT. In 1985, the Reagan administration reached a bilateral civilian nuclear power agreement with the People's Republic of China which was yet not an NPT signatory.

Today, countries that face no perceptible military threat feel the need to retain, grow and modernise their nuclear capabilities such as France and the United Kingdom. India, with two nuclear powers on its borders should have at least the same degree of freedom in pursuing its nuclear efforts. This will require enrichment and reprocessing facilities, and may require testing to prove and perfect weapons. The positive reponse about the nuclear deal from reputed scientists and clarification given by Atomic Energy Commission chairman are manifestations of an honest and credible pact which is unprecedented in the history of nuclear world. The criticisms of opposition parties – the Left and BJP, are mostly based on political reasons. For the rest, the deal is as good as clinched. There is no holistic disapproval of the deal by the rest of Indian intelligentsia, which is a proof of its having matured over the years. The deal is now the reality. Within the limits of the terms of the agreement, India must make focussed efforts to minimise its losses and resist any undue pressure from the United States which might threaten its sovereignty, dignity and the interests of people of India.

References

1. D.N. Mallik, *Post-war International Politics – A Quadripartite Survey* (Muzaffarpur : Veena Mandir Publishers, 1973), pp. 55-61.
2. Sudhanshu Tripathi, 'Indo-US Civil Nuclear Deal : Must Seek its Revision', *South Asia Politics,* Vol. 7, No. 6, October 2008 (New Delhi: 2008), p. 28.
3. Myron Weiner, 'Critical Choices for India and America', in Donald C. Hellmann (ed.), *Southern Asia : The Politics of Poverty and Peace* (Massachusetts : Lexington Books, 1976), p. 66.
4. Bibhuti Bhusan Biswas, 'Domestic Pressures in Foreign Policy : The Case of US-India Dialogue During the Clinton Administration', 68th Session, Part-II, *Proceedings of the Indian History Congress* (New Delhi : Indian History Congress, 2008), pp. 1196-97.
5. J.K. Baral, 'The US-India Nuclear Diplomacy', *Indian Journal of American Studies*, 1982, p. 131.

6. V.S.P. Kurup, 'America's Double Standards : Politics of Nuclear Fuel,' *The Times of India*, 25th April 1978.
7. V.N. Khanna, *Foreign Policy of India* (New Delhi : Vikas Publishing House, 2001), pp. 192-93.
8. Dr. Poonam Singh, *Indo-American Relations* (Delhi : Vista International Publishing House, 2006), p. 97.
9. George Rathjens, 'Rethinking Nuclear Proliferation', *The Washington Quarterly* (1995), pp. 181-82.
10. Tarun C. Bose, 'Wither NPT 1995 and Beyon', *Journal of International Relations* (1994), p. 21.
11. Flynt Leverett and Hillary Mann Leverett, 'Why the Failure in Almaty is a Big Deal', *The Hindu*, 6th May 2013.
12. Kenneth L. Adelman, 'Third Review Conference held for Non-Proliferation Treaty', US *Deparment of State Bulletin* (1985), p. 38.
13. J.K. Baral, 'The US-India Nuclear Diplomacy', p. 132.
14. M.R. Srinivasan, 'Nuclear Weapon-free World-a Mirage?' *The Hindu*, 16th June 2007.
15. M.J. Desai, 'India and Nuclear Weapons', *Disarmament and Arms Control*, Vol. 3, No. 2 (1965), p. 141.
16. Swaran Singh, 'China Factor in India's Nuclear Policy', *Journal of Peace Studies*, Vol. 5, No. 3, May-June 1998 (1998), pp. 23-38.
17. B. Rahamathulla, *Indo-American Politics 1970-78* (Delhi : Stanford University Press, 1980), p. 61.
18. C.S. Jha, 'The Non-proliferation Debate: Relevance of India's Stand', *The Times of India*, 22nd February 1978.
19. *The Hindustan Times*, 20th November 1977.
20. K. Subrahmanyam, 'Indian Nuclear Policy 1964-98 : A Personal Recollection', in Jasjit Singh (ed.) *Nuclear India* (New Delhi : Knowledge World, 1998), p. 28.
21. Dr. Poonam Singh, *Indo-American Relations*, pp. 102-3.
22. *Ibid.*, pp. 100-108.
23. V.N. Khanna, *Foreign Policy of India*, pp. 190-91.
24. Verghese Koithara, *Society, State and Security–*The *Indian Experience* (New Delhi : Sage Publications, 1999), pp. 259-60.
25. Pervaiz Iqbal Cheema, 'Security in South Asia : An Approach', in Shelton U. Kodikara (ed.), *External Compulsions of South Asian Politics* (New Delhi : Sage Publications, 1993), pp. 46-47.
26. O.P. Sabherwal, 'India's Nuclear Policy Under Siege, *One India One People*, August 1997 (Mumbai : 1997), p. 17.
27. Praful Bidwai, 'Nuclear Policy in a Mess-NWFZ, the Realistic Way Out,' *The Times of India*, 28th November 1991.

28. Kate Sullivan, 'Do Not Let Agni Vs Shock and Awe Endanger Asian Stability', *The Hindu* 23rd April 2012.
29. Sudhanshu Tripathi, 'Indo-US Civil Nuclear Deal : Must Seek Its Revision', *South Asia Politics,* Vol. 7, No. 6, October 2008 (New Delhi: 2008), pp. 29-30.
30. Verghese Koithara, *Society State and Security–The Indian Experience,* p. 261.
31. Shyam Saran, 'Weapon that has More Than Symbolic Value', *The Hindu,* 13th May 2013.
32. V.N. Khanna, *Foreign Policy of India,* pp. 200-01.
33. Verghese Koithara *Society, State and Security–The Indian Experience,* p. 264.
34. Swaran Singh, 'Evolution of Nuclear Posture', in G.P. Deshpande and Alka Acharya (eds.), *Fifty Years of India-China-Crossing a Bridge of Dream* (New Delhi : Tulika, 2002), p. 370.
35. *The Hindu,* 23rd April, 2012.
36. *Ibid.*
37. O.P. Sabherwal, 'Indo-US Nuclear Deal', *The Hindustan Times,* 10th November 1998.
38. Bhawani Singh and Vibhuti Singh Shekhawat, 'Swords Vs. Plough Shares : Indo-US Nuclear Deal : The Return of Spring', *The Indian Journal of Political Science,* Vol. LXVII, No. 4, October-December 2006 (Meerut : 2006) p. 908.
39. Sudhanshu Tripathi, 'Indo-US Civil Nuclear Deal : Must Seek Its Revision', p. 31.
40. Arun Shourie, *Will the Iron Fence Save a Tree Hallowed by Termite: Defence Imperatives Beyond the Military* (New Delhi : Rupa and Co., 2005), p. 213.
41. *The Times of India,* 14th March 2006.
42. Midatala Rani, 'Nuclear Issue in Indo-Pakistan Relations', in *Proceedings of the Indian History Congress* Part-II, 68th Session (Delhi : 2008), p. 1212.
43. Bhabani Sen Gupta, 'Towards Nuclear Stability', The *Hindustan Times,* 21st November 1997.
44. *Ibid.*
45. Ramesh Thak, 'Is India so Weak That It Must Fear Success', *The Hindu,* 4th September 2007.
46. Bhawani Singh and Vibhuti Singh Shekhawat, 'Swords Vs. Plough Shares : Indo-US Nuclear Deal: The Return of Spring', p. 910.
47. *India Today,* 6th March 2006 (New Delhi : 2006), p. 37.
48. Steven Hoffmann, 'Indo-US Strategic World View', in Ashok Kapur (ed.), *India and the United States in a Changing World* (New Delhi : 2002), pp. 236-37.

49. Stephen Philip Cohen, 'Indo-Pak Track-II Diplomacy: Building Peace or Wasting Time', in P.R. Kumaraswamy, *Security Beyond Survival* (New Delhi : Sage Publications, 2004), pp. 199-200.
50. M.R. Srinivasan, 'The Last Mile in the Nuclear Negotiations', *The Hindu*, 13th July 2007.
51. Alka Mudgal, 'From Civil Nuclear Deal to Civil Nuclear Liability Bill', *IJPS*, Vol. LXXI, No. 3, July, September 2010 (Meerut : 2010), pp. 826-27.
52. Vikram Sood, 'The Nuclear Deal : The Larger Picture', *The Hindu,* 5th September 2007.
53. Siddharth Vardarajan, 'Assessing the Nuclear Balance Sheet', *Ibid.,* 7th July 2006.
54. *India Today*, p. 40.
55. Annupurna Nautiyal, 'The Indo-US Nuclear Deal : What is There', *Strategic Insights*, Vol. VI (4) September 2008 (California : 2008), p. 2.
56. Placid Rodriguez, 'The Nuclear Deal : What If It Falls Through?' *The Hindu,* 28th February 2006.
57. *Ibid.*
58. *Ibid.,* 23rd July 2008.
59. *Ibid.*
60. Mark Bucknam, 'Power to the People of India: US Nuclear Cooperation with India', *Strategic Insights*, Vol. VI (1) January 2007 (California : 2007), p.3.
61. Sudhanshu Tripathi, 'Indo-US Civil Nuclear Deal: Must Seek Its Revision', p. 29.
62. Siddharth Vardarajan, 'Thirty Words that Saved the Day', *The Hindu*, 8th September 2008.
63. Siddharth Vardarajan, 'Challenges Ahead for India's Nuclear Diplomacy', *Ibid.,* 1st September 2011.
64. Monish Tourangbam, 'An Assessment of the 123-Agreement', "To be or Not to be", *South Asia Politics*, Vol. 6, No. 9, January 2008 (New Delhi : 2008), p. 32.
65. For detail see the text of the joint statement issued by Prime Minister Manmohan Singh and US President George W. Bush in New Delhi on 2nd March 2006, in *The Hindu*, 3rd March 2006.
66. Alka Mudgal, 'From Civil Nuclear Deal to Civil Nuclear Liability Bill', p. 825.
67. Siddharth Vardarajan, 'Taking Stock of the Indo-US Nuclear Deal', *The Hindu,* 17th August 2007.
68. M.R. Srinivasan, 'The Last Mile in the Nuclear Negotiations'.
69. Siddharth Vardarajan, 'The American Dilemma at the NSG', *Ibid.,* 28th August 2008.

70. Chidanand Rajghatta, 'The Inside Story of Bush Administration's Discovery of India', *The Times of India*, 26th February 2006.
71. *Ibid.*
72. Bhawani Singh and Vibhuti Singh Shekhawat, 'Swords Vs. Ploughshares : Indo-US Nuclear Deal; The Return of Spring', pp. 911-12.
73. Siddharth Vardarajan, 'The American Dilemma at the NSG'.
74. *Ibid.*
75. Vikram Sood, 'The Nuclear Deal : The Larger Picture'.
76. As qutoted in Karl F. Inderfurth, 'The US and India Expanding Engagement Agenda', *The Hindu*, 10th September 2008.
77. *Ibid.*
78. *India Today*, 3rd April 2006 (New Delhi : 2006), p. 38.
79. Placid Rodriguez, 'The Nuclear Deal : What If It Falls Through ?'
80. P.M. Kamath, 'Civilian Nuclear Deal : Turning Points in Indo-US Relations', *India quarterly*, Vol. LXII (3), July-September 2006 (New Delhi : 2006), p. 28.
81. Siddharth Vardarajan, '123 as Countdown to CTBT by the Backdoor', *The Hindu*, 17th May 2007.
82. From the text of the document titled 'Implementation of the India-United States Joint Statement of 18th July 2005: India's Separation Plan' tabled in the Parliament on 7th March 2007, in Ibid., 8th March 2006.
83. *Ibid.*
84. Michael Krepon and Alex Stolar, 'The 123-Agreement: From Bad to Worse', *Ibid.*, 25th August 2007.
85. Ashok Parthasarathi, 'Judge the Nuclear Deal on Facts, Not Convictions', *Ibid.*, 15th July 2008.
86. The suo moto statement of Prime Minister Manmohan Singh in the Parliament on 27th February 2006.
87. Monish Tourangbam, 'An Assessment of the 123-Agreement, "To be or Not to be", p. 33.
88. *India Today*, 6th March 2006.
89. *Ibid.*
90. Siddharth Vardarajan, 'Praising the India-Specific Safeguards Agreement', *The Hindu* 12th July 2008.
91. *Ibid.*
92. *Ibid.*, 18th November 2006.
93. Siddharth Vardarajan, 'Bush Signing Statement on 123 Leaves Flaws Intact', *Ibid.*, 10th October 2008.
94. *Ibid.*, 12th October 2008.

95. As quoted in Siddharth Vardarajan, 'Bush Signing Statement on 123 Leaves Flaws Intact'.

96. R. Ramachandran, '123 Agreement and the Internal Laws', Ibid., 19th September 2007.

97. *Ibid.,* 13th September 2007.

98. Suddharth Vardarajan, 'A Guide to the Provisions of the 123- Agreement', *Ibid.,* 4th August 2007.

99. *Ibid.,* 11th Aguast 2007.

100. *Ibid.,* 30th March 2010.

101. *Ibid.,* 1st August 2010.

102. Alka Mudgal, 'From Civilian Nuclear Deal to Civil Nuclear Liability Bill', p. 832.

103. Brahma Chellaney, 'Strategic and Technical Aspects of End Use Monitoring Agreement–End Use Monitoring Woes for India', *The Hindu,* 27th July 2009.

104. Brahma Chellaney, 'Factsheet on US-India Accord on End Use Monitoring Agreement', *India Abroad,* 31st July 2009.

105. Dinesh C. Sharma, 'Pressure for Soft Nuclear Liability Law,' *Mail Daily,* Vol. 2 (245), 19th July 2009, pp. 1 and 6.

106. *The Hindu*, 22nd August 2010.

107. *Ibid.,* 6th September 2010.

108. Annpurna Nautiyal, 'Indo-US Nuclear Deal : What is There ?' p. 7.

109. Soli J. Sorabjee, 'Capping Nuclear Liability is a Non-starter', *The Hindu*, 14th December 2009

110. *Ibid.*

111. *Ibid.,* 26th August 2010.

112. *Ibid.*

113. *Ibid.,* 19th November 2011.

114. M.V. Kamath, 'US Tactics of Pressuring India', *Organiser*, 25th November 2007 (New Delhi: 2007), p. 17

115. *The Hindu*, 3rd September 2007.

116. *Ibid.,* 7th August 2007.

117. Praful Bidwai, 'Indo-US Defence Accord: Sanctifying Atomic Apartheid', *Frontline*, Vol. 22, July 30-August 12, 2005.

118. Satish Chandra, 'Nuclear Deal: On the Brink of Disaster', *The Hindu,* 9th June 2007.

119. *Ibid.*

120. M.R. Srinivasan, 'India May Lose Control of its Nuclear Future', *Ibid.,* 14th December 2006.

121. Brahma Chellaney, 'Revelations Unravel Hype and Spin', *Ibid.,* 5th September 2008.

122. Ashok Parthasarathi, 'Judge the Nuclear Deal on Facts, Not Convictions'.

123. V.R. Krishna Iyer, 'A Betrayal of India's Constitutional Vision', *Ibid.*, 17th July 2008.

124. *Ibid.*

125. M.V. Kamath, 'US Tactics of Pressuring India'.

126. *Channel News Asia Online,* 'India and US Unveil Landmark Nuclear Deal', 3rd August 2007.

127. M.J. Akbar, 'A Good Deal Walks on Two Legs', *The Asian Age*, 5th August 2007.

128. *The Hindu*, 3rd September 2007.

129. Alka Mudgal, 'From Civilian Nuclear Deal to Civil Nuclear Liability Bill'.

130. Praful Bidwai, 'Nuclear Waiver: Blow to Non-proliferation', *Inter Press Service*, 8th September 2008.

131. *The Hindu,* 7th August 2007.

132. *The Asian Age*, 5th August 2007.

133. *The Financial Times*, 2nd August 2007.

134. *The Hindu,* 3rd September 2007.

135. Aziz Haniffa, 'The Nuclear Deal : Recognition Denied or Dangerous Model', *India Abroad* (New York, 29th July 2005.

136. Praful Bidwai, 'The Day After : Fallout of a Deeply Disturbing Deal', *Khaleej Times*, 11th March 2006.

137. M. Veerappa Moily, 'The Highest Feat of Diplomacy', *The Hindu,* 28th August 2007.

138. Monish Tourangbam, 'An Assessment of the 123 Agreement', "To be or Not to be", p. 34.

139. *Ibid.*

140. Bhawani Singh and Vibhuti Singh Shekhawat, 'Swords Vs Plough Shares' : Indo-US Nuclear Deal; The Return of Spring, p. 913.

❑

6

Current Status of Nuclear Politics in South Asia

South Asia is an area which has got more security challenges at present than any other part of the world. There are large numbers of historically existing inter and intra-State conflicts in this region and therefore there is a problem of working together towards a common aim in the South Asia region.[1] Although politics is essential for a country's overall development, but degeneration in the calibre and motivation of the leadership and political leaders in South Asia has caused negative impact on this region. Even in pre-1998 phase, India along with Pakistan occupied a threshold country's position in view of the international non-proliferation regime, possessing, or quickly capable of assembling one or more nuclear weapons, especially the nuclear weapons capability at the technical level was recognised when in the year (1998), India tested its nuclear device second time followed by the first test of nuclear device by Pakistan in the same month. Apart from this, it is the growth and modernisation of China's nuclear arsenal and its assistance with Pakistan's nuclear power programme, and reportedly with missile technology has remained a constant concern for India. In the region, the USA had, for some years pursued a variety of initiatives to persuade India and Pakistan to abandon their nuclear weapons programmes and to accept comprehensive international safeguards on all their nuclear activities. Following the 1998 tests and attack of 9/11, the challenges of nuclear proliferation and nuclear counter-terrorism have become a matter of global concern which required an alternative framework to help deal with the specific challenges of the region. In fact, nuclear proliferation in South Asia is in part a consequence of the security dilemma existing in the sub-continent. The South Asian nuclear security complex involves several security dilemmas, including Pakistan/India, India/China, and Russia/United States.[2] A further security dilemma is that of the United States and China, since it has an impact on attitudes in India and Pakistan, and helps shape their nuclear decisions. The recently concluded Indo-US civil agreement is also considered in the context which will help Pakistan to seek a closer alliance with China to balance a new geo-political reality in South Asia.

Nuclearisation of South Asia

The region was nuclearised in May 1974, when India exploded its nuclear devices. But again dangers were multiplied in May-June 1998 with nuclear explosions by India and Pakistan. After the tests, New Delhi and Islamabad had claimed to be member of world's nuclear club. In 1974, after its Pokharan explosion, if India had declared itself a nuclear weapon power, it would now have been in the same positions as China, an accepted member of the nuclear club, instead of an applicant being black-balled. At the time India wanted nuclear status as well as the right to exercise its "land of Gandhi and Buddha," syndrome. To that end, it went to convoluted lengths, denying that it had conducted a nuclear test and calling it a mere "peaceful nuclear blast". In the post-Pokharan II Phase, the United States imposed economic sanctions on both–New Delhi and Islamabad despite its reservations for Pakistan, President Bill Clinton, in a Rose Garden statement, called upon the South Asian rivals to "cool it and take a deep breath". He said, "Developing weapons of mass destruction is self-defeating wasteful and dangerous. It will make their people poorer and less cure". Its Secretary of State, Madeleine Albright had headed an urgent meeting of the Permanent Five Foreign Ministers, at Geneva, and set three goals. To defuse the escalating arms race by stopping nuclear testing, deployment and mating of missiles with nuclear warheads; to deal with the underlying conflict and discuss the status of Kashmir to shore up the international non-proliferation system. Outlining US agenda for the meeting

Clinton said that its goal was to forge a common strategy with five other nuclear powers to move India and Pakistan back from their nuclear arms race and to begin to build a more peaceful, stable region. He appreciated China for chairing the Geneva Conference and took it as an evidence how important role Beijing could play in meeting the challenges of the 21st century and the constructive Chinese leadership that would be essential to the long-term resolutions of issues involving South Asia. He pleaded in favour of US engagements with China which would serve America's interests, stability in Asia, preventing the spread of weapons of mass destruction, combating international crime and drug-trafficking, protecting the environment.

Despite Clinton's prodding, Beijing should reflect carefully on the wisdom of trying to mediate between India and Pakistan over Kashmir. Although, it is fashionable to view Kashmir as an Indo-Pak issue, China also is deeply involved in it. Way back in the 1960s, Pakistan ceded to China 2,600 square kilometers of Jammu and Kashmir territory in the name of border adjustment. Around 38,000 square kilometers of the State's territory in Aksai Chin is under China's occupation for about four decades. Just as India has to sort out the Kahmir issue with Pakistan, it has also similar agenda with China. Apart from being a staunch ally of Pakistan, even other circumstances rule Beijing out as a mediator. Several other issues relevant to a stable and long-term relationship would have to be addressed. There has never been greater need for transparency in their relations than now. China and India must engage themselves in exploring each other's geo-strategic perceptions. One result of China undertaking America's assignment in South Asia would be a considerable lessening of Beijing role in Asia Pacific affairs in the coming years.

In fact, in the post-test phase, the US was not as worried about India's capacities for restraint and responsibility regarding its nuclear weapons as about the effect of India's weaponisation in the Asian region, certain parts of which are of vital strategic and economic interest to the US. The apprehension was about the horizontal proliferation of nuclear weapons in the Asian region where a number of countries have the aspiration and could have the capacity for acquiring nuclear weapons. The US wants India to understand that American concerns about nuclear weaponisation are not Indo-centric. It has larger international strategic and security dimensions. The US refusal to legally acknowledge India as a nuclear weapons state is not an impractical exercise of flying in the face of the fact of India's established nuclear weapons capacity. It was an attempt at preventing the legitimisation of the nuclear weapons status of countries which have gone against international orientations and against horizontal proliferation carefully structured by the five nuclear weapons powers. Hence, the demand is frequently made that cap India and roll back its nuclear weaponisation programme, that India signs the Comprehensive Test Ban Treaty unconditionally, and that India agree to join the negotiations on the fissile material cut-off treaty without any reservation. And also that India's commitments to abide by the other international regimes related to missile control, stockpiles of nuclear material, and transfer of nuclear and missile technologies.[3] In September 1998, Bill Clinton, in course of his visit to Moscow, asked his Russian counterpart Boris Yeltsin to stop military cooperation with India saying that nuclear rivalry in South Asia could lead to a war in which the two super powers might get embroiled.

However, in a US think-tank study report conducted by an independent Task Force and co-sponsored by the Brookings Institution and the Council on Foreign Relations, held China responsible for the situations in South Asia. The report noted, "China bears some responsibility for the situation in South Asia, given its own nuclear and missile programme that concern India and the assistance it had provided over the years to Pakistan's nuclear and missile programme." It felt that China has an incentive to act responsibly since it would not really like to see India building up its nuclear arsenal. Realising the need of China in this regard it acknowledged that it would be difficult, if not impossible to stabilise the situation in South Asia without Beijing's constructive participation. India's relations with China have certainly suffered a setback after Pokharan II. During that last ten years relations between the two countries had improved although at a slow speed. These need to be put back on the track by both countries. Beijing also needs to realise that the rise of fundamentalists forces in Afghanistan and Pakistan–which had received arms and nuclear technology from China–could ensure problems for China also, particularly in provinces like Sinkiang, which has a sizeable Muslim population. There is also a need for resumption of dialogue between New Delhi and Beijing to sort out differences on many issues including nuclear one. Ties between Beijing and New Delhi turned sour after India cited a "Chinese Threat" for its nuclear test. Beijing adopted a tough stand on the South Asian nuclear tests which was expressed by China's top disarmament official, Sha Zukang, who also heads the arms control and disarmament department of the Chinese Foreign Ministry, that New Delhi was going about consulting other members of the P-5 and engaging in strategic dialogue while completely ignoring China. He said, 'The South Asian tests have severally interrupted the 'good momentum' of global non-proliferation efforts since the end of Cold War. Zukang also called for "concerted action" by major powers to halt the slide and favoured a robust international non-proliferation regime which is in the interest of all countries.

Beijing is dead against of making India an overt nuclear-power state. A key Chinese policy goal had always been to prevent the emergence of India–whose nuclear programme is older than China's-with a fullfledged nuclear deterrent. It was the same goal that prompted the Chinese in 1974 to denounce India's first Pokharan test but unlike that "peaceful nuclear explosion" the Shakti tests of 1998 involved sophisticated nuclear warheads deliverable atop the China–pertinent Agni-series missiles. From the recent past what China wants is a peer competitor in India. Chinese weapons of mass destruction aid to Islamabad was designed to lock India in a low-level deterrent relationship with Pakistan, with the flow of assistance calibrated to match every Indian advance and keep this country boxed in the sub-continent. Nearly, a quarter century of Indian nuclear pusillanimity had made the Leninist rulers in Beijing conclude that their containment was working with the Indians tied down sub-continentally and rendered too meek to break-out of the strategic straitjacket.

During the next few years a strain on Sino-US relations was expected on nuclear related issues. Despite the recent charges of spying by Beijing Madeleine Albright, the Secretary of State, laid emphasis that it was important for the US to engage with a country of 1.3 billion people that has a huge land mass, and that has an influence within its region. "We are better off talking with them, dealing with them. We have made some progress in terms of their cooperation on nuclear proliferation on rogue countries. While leading Congressional Republicans accused the administration of not taking the theft of nuclear technology by China seriously enough and also of keeping Congress in the dark with regard to the full extent of the damage done to American security. China too viewed the US with suspicion as Zhou Gang, Beijing's Ambassador in India, said, "The US continues to believe that China is the last evil empire because it is still a communist country". According to William Cohen, Defence Secretary, the core of the US defence strategy and military posture in Asia is "America's commitment to protecting and promoting our interests by remaining forward deployed in the region. While the ring is aimed mainly at China's military might, the US also has an elaborate strategy to weaken the Communist regime from within the country. As the Communist regime has consciously opted for economic liberalisation in order to develop the country expeditiously, there is hope in the US administration that a higher standard of living would pave the way for widening the base for democratic aspirations, leading eventually to the replacement of Communism by democracy.[4] An indication of the view was given on 11th June 1998, when Clinton, on the eve of his visit to China, said, "Over time, I believe, China's leaders must accept freedom's progress because China can only reach its full potential if its people are free. In the information age, the wealth of any nation including China's, lies in its people, in their capacity to create, to communicate, to innovate. The Chinese people must have the freedom to speak, to publish, to associate, to worship without fear of resprisals," and added "only then will China reach its full potential for growth and greatness.[5] Beijing too was anxious over the US military designs in Asia. The strengthening of the US-Japan security cooperation, US plans to deploy theatre missile defence system in Asia and attempts to incorporate Taiwan into it, and supply of sophisticated weapons to Taipei had strengthened anti-US feelings among some of Beijing's foreign policy planners. The Chinese outburst against the alliance showed that Beijing was increasingly becoming suspicious of Washington's game plan, especially in Asia.

However, be it the Indo-Pak war of 1965, 1971 or 1999 at Kargil, Big Brothers had been the ultimate arbiter of peace in South Asia. In 1965, Pakistan looked for US support in the United Nations Security Council for the resolution calling for an end to hostilities as the Pakistani effort was rapidly grinding to a halt for lack of ammunition and supplies. In 1971, US Secretary of State Henry Kissinger told Pakistani leaders facing war with India that seeking US help at that juncture was tantamount to the US being asked to be in on the crash landing when it was not in on the take off. Thus, the US helped Pakistan by preventing India from attack. And the recent fighting in Kargil had again involved the US active diplomacy as Pakistan's Prime Minister Nawaz Sharif sought and got the help of American President on July 4th, 1999. Pakistan's decision to withdraw from Kargil was resulted in a military coup in the country with the rule of General Prevez Musharraf. But it is not unusual for the US administration and Congress to speak in different voices on a variety of issues. Particularly with regard to South Asia, the US Congress, by and large, had expressed itself in favour of developing a strategic partnership with India and urging a tough line towards the military regime in Pakistan, while the Clinton administration echoed the need for a swift return to democracy in Islamabad and at the same time, pointed to the folly of "Walking away from Pakistan". Perhaps, the Pentagon seemed unable to prevent its mind-set being tinged by the legacy of its past close relations with the Pakistani armed forces, particularly during the heady days when Islamabad was the willing conduit for massive arms transfers to the Mujahideen battling the Soviets in Afghanistan.

Strategies of cooperation and coercion are at the heart of international relations theory. Especially, in a relationship between a great power and smaller power outside the framework of alliances and collective security, it is a thorny task to build and sustain close cooperation as is evidenced in case of Indo-US relations. This type of relationship is crucial for the smaller power to fashion a diplomatic strategy with a clear set of goals and realistic expectations to advance its interests in a relationship between unequals. Reasons for seeking closer ties with the United States were many. It is expected to remain the world's pre-eminent power in the foreseeable future. America's importance to India has been accentuated by the continuing decline of Russia, the rise of an increasingly powerful and assertive China still inimical to Indian interests, the erosion of Japan's economic superpower status, and the emergence of an imbalance of power in Aisa. Even as most other powers seek a multi-polar world, unipolarity is getting stronger, with the US riding a major economic boom at home and dominating global information. As a superpower, the US role and actions in Southern Asia in the past impacted adversely on India's interests and in the years ahead, is expected to be the most active outside power in this region. The United States is in a position to help improve or worsen Indian security. It is thus important that Indian diplomacy should focus not on tactical, short-term gains but on building a stable, enduring relationship in which there is no significant conflict of interest between the two countries. This demands a foreign policy rooted not so much in a US-friendly approach but in realism, long-term vision and specific aims.

Global Powers' Motivation in South Asia

Today humankind must decide whether the road it would follow in the years to come would be that of creation or destruction. Would it be a road of peaceful co-existence of a sensible dialogue between countries with different political systems, and of scientific and technological progress ensuring the well-being of peoples, or that of an unrestricted nuclear arms race fraught with the risk of nuclear conflict and the destruction of life on earth? The emergence of atomic and, later of thermo-nuclear weapons of huge destructive power made it clear to mankind that a new World War would cause incredible devastation. From then on peace among nations has become an objective/necessary condition for mankind's survival. However, mankind did not remain indifferent to its fate and began a dogged struggle against thermo-nuclear war and for durable, universal, just and democratic peace. The outcome of this struggle is yet to be decided. Retreating under the pressure of the peace forces, the enemies of peace and detente cling to their battle lines and launch counter-offensives. But if the reasons fail to hold in check, it would bring untold sufferings to all nations.

From theoretical view point, two American strategic specialists, Lewis A. Dunn and Herman Kahan have listed as many as fourteen reasons or pressures encouraging a country to go nuclear. They have classified these reasons under several heads, such as, security, status or influence, bureaucratic and domestic factors. They have also identified eight types of events as 'trigger' activating consideration on the pressures or reasons for a country going nuclear. These are: (a) involvement in foreign crisis; (b) reduction in alliance credibility; (c) nuclearisation of other countries; (d) weakening or breakdown of international constraints; (e) domestic crisis; and (f) changed perception and utility of nuclear weapons. Another analyst S.M. Meyer, notes three basic types of incentives. First, incentives of international political prestige and image-building. These can affect the country's appearance and posture. Second, incentives to advance national military and security objectives, to minimise external threats to the country and to strengthen its relative power position and strength. Third, incentives to support and promote domestic policies and to prevail in domestic political struggles. In other words, four sets of arguments are frequently advanced by threshold states aiming to retain the nuclear options – military, security, political prestige and influence, economic gains and domestic pressures and compulsions.

In the South Asian context, non-proliferation is not merely a nuclear question. The larger forces and interests at work both within the region and outside have to be understood. Regional security cannot be considered in isolation from global or extra-regional conditions. The efforts have to be on two parallel lines. At the global level, the states in the region have to participate in the process to bring about a truly legitimate and non-discriminatory non-proliferation regime. At the regional level, efforts to build bridges of understanding among the countries in the region through confidence-building measures has to be sustained. Hence, in South Asia, proliferation can best be achieved through a proper mix of global and regional approaches. Particularly, because of the awesome destructive potential of nuclear weapons their actual use is unthinkable. Even in low-level nuclear combat with millions of fatalities there would be no winner, apart from the doubtful survivability of crude weapons. It is more so in the case of close South-Asian neighbours like India and Pakistan.

In case of both India and Pakistan national security concern has been the principal factor in the process of nuclearisation. Hostilities between the two countries have been there since partition in 1947. The key territorial issue of Kashmir has its root in the colonial history of the sub-continent and involved India, Pakistan and China. India's nuclear calculations are centered on China which has an expanding nuclear arsenal. While, in contrast, Islamabad's nuclear programme is driven mainly by its threat perception and security concern with respect to India. Pakistan sees its potential nuclear forces as a deterrent to India's conventional military advantages and strategic ambitions. However, India, whose military build-up was spurred by its humiliating defeat in the 1962 war with China, viewed its nuclear programme as the vital component of a strategic plan to deter against a more powerful China. The nuclear chain in the world has been rightly observed by John J. Schulz who says, "The rationale presented by leading government officials in New Delhi and Islamabad to justify the current state of their weapons programme is analoguous to the Ocean food chain –big fish eats little fish which has just eaten the littlest fish. China created its nuclear deterrent with fears of Moscow and Washington in mind. China is feared by India and India is feared by Pakistan. All three countries justify their present nuclear policies as a solution to security problems–a fully declared arsenal in China, a nuclear weapons option in India and now in Pakistan 'an ability to assemble as the equalising deterrent".[6]

Next to security, nationalism is the propelling force of Indian and Pakistani nuclear programme. This is evident from the national consensus in each country on nuclear policy. Both countries enjoy overwhelming domestic support to their nuclear programme. Nationalism has played a key role in shaping Indian politics since Independence. Nehru championed self-reliance as part of India's "neutralism" and New Delhi's drive for indigenous science, technology and nuclear capability reflects that self-reliance. The Pakistani nuclear programme has also emerged as the leading symbol of Pakistani nationalism and pride. According to a retired Pakistani Army General, it enjoys bipartisan and popular support and is above political controversy. Pakistan's national interest demands that her nuclear capability to be taken to its logical conclusion.[7] As Islamabad emerged as a technological leader of the Muslim World, its nuclear programme is a visible symbol of Islamic technological sophistication and power.

The desire to seek international respect and prestige is also an important incentive for nuclearisation in India and Pakistan. As one of the world's oldest and most populous civilisation, New Delhi saw the acquisition of a nuclear weapon capability as the key to winning greater power status. The Indian public opinion was pro-nuclear, without being particularly perturbed by the cost involved. There was strong feeling among an articulate section of Indian strategic analysts that without nuclear weapons India cannot be counted as major world power and cannot influence decisions for arms control and disarmament, nor can India stabilise its status as the dominant regional power in South Asia. Pakistan, though possessed the first Islamic bomb, is motivated by ethno-nationalism and the desire for regional respect and prestige from the "Muslim crescent" and Central Asia.

Apart from these, several factors make the pressure of nuclear weapon capabilities on the sub-continent more dangerous than the Super Power nuclear rivalry that preceded it. Too many of the specific conditions in the region, including an asymmetrical balance of power, bitter personal remembrance, wars within living memory border and religious disputes and unstable and highly emotional domestic constituencies point to the need for special and perhaps urgent efforts to prevent New Delhi and Islamabad from taking those last small steps to fully mount the proverbial nuclear tiger. Some current conditions in the region also bear striking similarities to several of the more destabilising elements of the Cold War relationship, which further explained why many experts worry over the prospect of two nuclear armed South Asian neighbours with so many simmering unresolved disputes.

The risk of nuclear conflict in South Asia is no doubt significant but the things have been blown out of proportion by the US Government. The US non-proliferation policy from its very beginning has been to restrict not only the development of nuclear weapon technology but also the spread of civilian nuclear technology as such, to maintain its nuclear monopoly and to prevent the monolithic from attaining nuclear weapon capability. The philosophy of American non-proliferation policy may be found in the words of President Truman. On August 9, 1945, after the bombing on Nagasaki he said: 'The atomic bomb is too dangerous to be let loose in a lawless world. We must constitute ourselves trustees of this new force to prevent its misuse and to turn it into the channel of service to mankind. It is an awful responsibility which has come to us. We thank God that it has come to us instead of our enemies and we pray that He may guide us to use it in His way and for His purpose. America's nuclear policy revolves round deterrence and non-proliferation. The former requires that the US should possess a large number of powerful nuclear weapons which would be an effective deterrent against a first nuclear strike by any other nuclear power. As a result, Washington's commitment to nuclear non-proliferation has been half-hearted and partial. It favours only horizontal non-proliferation, without offering any commitment even to a gradual vertical non-proliferation. In this way, the nuclear policy of the US sharply clashes with that of India, whose commitment to nuclear non-proliferation is total, and which advocates vertical as well as horizontal non-proliferation. India feels that a non-proliferation agreement which ignores the present proliferation and, preoccupies itself with the future proliferation is naturally unrealistic, ineffective, and therefore, unacceptable. India's option is a protest against the attempt of a few nuclear powers to decide the fate of all other nations technologically and militarily.

In South Asia, one of the cardinal principles of the US foreign policy during past few decades has been to deter the acquisition of nuclear weapons by India and Pakistan and it has made non-proliferation a central issue in bilateral relations with them. Since 1974, when India exploded its first nuclear device, successive US administrations have pushed for restraint by both countries, utilising a range of policy tools including diplomatic pressure, the withholding of cooperation, embargoes on the export of nuclear technology and the leverage of US assistance and arms sales. In fact, the US has sought to oppose proliferation in South Asia through all available means at its disposal. Its goal has been to inhibit the development or acquisition of such system as well as to prevent their use or threatened use. The US fear of a nuclear exchange in South Asia is, in fact, outcome of nuclear theology of the Western strategists which clearly state that nuclear weapons in the hands of non-nuclear and developing nations has greater possibility of their use. Joseph Nye of Harvard University once put it, "Paradoxically under any circumstances the introduction of a single bomb in some non-nuclear state may be more likely to lead to nuclear use than the addition of a thousand more warheads to the US and Soviet stockpiles". However, Noel Gayler, a retired US Admiral, who was involved in the testing of nuclear arms, called on the United States to assume the non-first use pledge and said, "The more you know about them, the less you like them, and the more you are convinced that they have no sensible military use....... They always boomerang on the user". From 1960, atomic wars were sporadic in the history of man. The developing science and technology have paved way for the growth of the Atomic power.

The answers to the question why does the US take interest in Indo-Pak non-proliferation, are many? India-Pakistan proliferation dynamics directly impinge on the US-Middle East concerns and interests which have normally been deemed vital due to their connection with access to Persian Gulf oil. Consequently, the proliferation of nuclear weapons in South Asia would have profound implications for US national security interest. Stephen P. Cohen, a renowned American expert on South Asia, held the view that the US non-proliferation interests fall into or touch upon three different areas. Firstly, there are purely nuclear related concerns that include slowing down or controlling regional military nuclear programmes by stemming or stopping the flow of nuclear materials and technology to India and Pakistan, ensuring that they do not aid other states with their nuclear military programmes, seeing to it that the South Asian example of creeping proliferation is not emulated or admired elsewhere. Secondly, to contain Russian and Chinese influence in South Asia. Finally, there are a number of regional American interests at stake. American policy since 1947, favoured the emergence of a stable and cooperative South Asia Regional System-based upon Indian and Pakistani cooperation so that all regional states might better solve their pressing economic and development problems.

However, the US non-proliferation policy in the sub-continent has been discriminatory. It has not only adopted a permissive approach towards Pakistan's nuclear programme but has favoured the emergence of a nuclear Pakistan and denied that Pakistan's nuclear programme has gone ahead under the overall patronage of the United States. Even many Americans agree that the US government did not take the desired steps to halt Pakistan's nuclear weapons programme in time, in spite of adequate information in that regard. On the other hand, the legislative measures that would have been taken were postponed several times through narrow interpretations of the legal provisions. Unlike Pakistan, India's nuclear programme has little US influence. It has never remained the US military ally or strategic partner or has it ever entered into security agreement with America. Partially in response to India's nuclear detonation, the Congress passed the Nuclear Non-Proliferation Act of 1978. Invoking this act, Carter administration had to suspend altogether the supply of nuclear fuel for Tarapur Atomic Power Station after the expiry of three years grace period in 1981. By doing so Washington attempted to use its leverage with respect to those fuel supply to compel Delhi to accept full scope safeguards. India has also been pressed to participate in multilateral conference on non-proliferation and regional security in South Asia which would have the main agenda of pressurising India and Pakistan to cap their nuclear programme. A recent US report on Progress Towards Regional Non-Proliferation in South Asia said, 'The US seeks to combat nuclear, chemical and biological weapons and ballistic missile proliferation in South Asia and to prelude either a nuclear or missile arms race. Our objective is first to cap then reduce and finally eliminate the possession of weapons of mass destruction and their means of delivery.

The main reason behind the US soft-line towards Pakistan's nuclear programme was its pressing need during the Afghan crisis. Till 1974, the year in which India exploded a nuclear device at Pokharan, Washington did not work hard even for horizontal non-proliferation. Its main concern was to defend its pre-eminence in the market of nuclear export *vis-a-vis* other nuclear powers, especially its own allies in Western Europe. The Pokharan explosion effected a qualitative change in India's military potential. Bangladesh's emergence as a free country in 1971 had torn into pieces the so-called balance between India and Pakistan and established former's pre-eminence in the sub-continent. Both the American government and the press decried it on the ground that it would encourage further nuclear proliferation. The US became angry because India's nuclear capability reinforced its determination to be an independent centre of power and dealt a severe blow to the "sub-continental balance" which it had been nourishing so long. Further, a strong India with proven friendship with the Soviet Union would be a hindrance of America's Indian Ocean strategy centered round Diego Garcia. A strong India, worse still a nuclear India, was bad for the US and therefore had to be contained. However, the post-Pokharan statements and the actions of the Government of India did not give any indication that it was on the nuclear path.

Gandhian Morarji Desai, who became the Prime Minister of India in March 1977, made a distinction between a nuclear explosion for military purposes (which he would not permit) and a nuclear explosion for developmental purposes (which he would not mind). Clarifying India's stand, Atal Bihari Vajpayee, the then Minister for External Affairs, stated that New Delhi supported the ideal of non-proliferation but wanted a halt to both vertical and horizontal proliferation. During his visit to the US, he met President Carter who told him that the United States, had decided to cut off its aid to Pakistan to stop it from developing nuclear weapons. This was quite obviously an attempt to sidetrack the main issue and to display US objectivity by equating India with Pakistan.[8] Vajpayee replied it when speaking on the Maryland University Campus and elaborated upon the rationale of Indian policy. He said that if Pakistan wanted to develop nuclear energy for peaceful purposes, it should not embark upon a programme to acquire weapon-grade uranium. He ruled out President Zia-ul-Haq's suggestion that India and Pakistan should make a joint declaration about putting their nuclear installations under international safeguards as "the question was a wide one and not solely between the two countries."[9] But in the meantime, India's electronic industry, missile construction, guidance technology and nuclear research were all in the uprising, which could be channelled into weapon-making, if the chips were down. In January 1980, when Indira Gandhi became the Prime Minister, she all but said this much and accelerated the nuclear programme in every field.

In December 1979, Soviet troops crossed into Afghanistan and installed a leader of Moscow's choice in place of Hafizullah Amin. It was the first time that Soviet troops had been committed outside the Warsaw Pact area, and it involved them in a country which for over a century had been recognised as a buffer state between the Russian realm and the powers of South Asia. In Washington's eyes, Pakistan overnight became a "front line" state, sharing a thirteen hundred mile frontier with a country, the Soviet Union now sought to control.[10] The geo-strategic situation in the region had already been dramatically disrupted by the revolution in Iran, which ejected the Shah and brought in a band of religious Zealots, who quickly dismantled the Shah's proud army and state structure. Instead of being buffered by the mountains, deserts and ravines of Afghanistan – which for so long had separated Russia from the sub-continent, Islamabad could only watch helplessly. The shadow of Soviet Power hung over the entire area, as never before. Within months of the invasion, Pakistan was inundated by a flood of refugees. And Soviet aircraft periodically violated Pakistani air space.

The day after invasion, President Carter telephoned President Zia and offered his help. The US had greatly improved Pakistan's military capability in the mid-1950s and perhaps it might be helpful again. Carter's subsequent sweeping commitment in his State of the Union Message to defend the Gulf seemed to presage an end to America's apparent disinterest in the affairs of South Asia. Washington might be prepared to lift its virtual quarantine, first implemented because of Bhutto's nuclear programme, and subsequently intensified because of Zia government's dubious human rights record. It was also under the psychological pressure to demonstrate as much to themselves as to the rest of the world that it was not a flabby and helpless giant.[11] The professionals in Pakistan's Foreign Ministry, however, were less enthusiastic than the military. They were aware of the profound doubts in Washington about once again getting involved in South Asia. Understandably, then Zia rejected the American offer and pursued a policy of engaging in verbal boldness at the UN and among his Islamic breathren, while exercising caution on the frontier. Several analysts including Stephen Cohen who had studied the sub-continent's security problems, and Brigadier (Retd) Abdur Rahman, editor of the then Karachi-based monthly magazine, *Defence Journal*, were of the opinion that the American strategic interest in Pakistan is indirect; it is concerned less about Soviet influence in Pakistan than Soviet influence in the Persian Gulf and the Arabian Sea. The Brigadier pointed out that this interest would wax or wane with changes in Washington's perception of Moscow's designs in the region. Hence, should either the Russian withdraw from Afghanistan or the two Super Powers agree to a detente in Europe or there be a change of heart between Washington and New Delhi, the American interest in Pakistan would decline.

Jimmy Carter was followed by Ronald Reagan. The latter administration's fascination for Pakistan, in spite of its anti-democratic credentials, was apparently determined by its intense concern to contain Russian thrust into South West Asia and the

Gulf region. Fukuyama had also presented several arguments in favour of Pakistan by expressing the fear that Soviet occupation of Afghanistan would lead to the Soviet domination over the entire Gulf region. Apart from these, J.A. Coon, US Deputy Secretary of State for Near East and South Asian Affairs, in a testimony before a House Sub-committee, had pleaded for an effort to help Pakistan resist Soviet pressures and to become stronger and more self-confident. It all prompted the Reagan administration to resume aid to Pakistan on a large scale. In the process, it had to lift the Symington Amendment which stood in the way of American aid to countries like Pakistan which were trying to acquire nuclear capability. The showering of praise and aid upon Pakistan by the United States was too bitter to be digested by India which feared that the ultimate victim of a military revitalised Pakistan would be India itself. In the circumstances, when Washington declared its decision to supply sophisticated and powerful F-16 warplanes to Pakistan, it posed a serious threat to the delicate military balance prevailing in South Asia. Indians expressed concern that the US was trying to inject a "New Cold War" into the Indian sub-continent. If global strategy was the justification for the rearming of Pakistan by both America and China, we should be pardoned if we were forced to take certain immediate steps to safeguard our own border and frontiers. We could not think that the US was going to take back the arms from Pakistan nor they could do it even if they want to. An alert India should anticipate increased border trouble and mischief.[12]

Of late, the United States has realised that complete nuclear disarmament in South Asia may no longer be a feasible policy objective and that the technical knowledge of nuclear weapon production cannot be reversed. The only workable solution can be the lowering of the nuclear weaponary to the level of 'minimum deterrence' or what Mikhail Gorbachev has termed as 'reasonable sufficiency' or 'defensive defence' of lowering the parity for the strategic stability. The facts on file Dictionary of Military Science described the Cold War concept of deterrence as "The prevention of an action by creating a fear of its consequences." Hence deterrence, which shuts out the "Kamikaze" mentality did not comprise merely the possession of nuclear weapons but it would deter aggression and coercive diplomacy. And in the remote contingency where deterrence fails, having the political will and capacity to retaliate with nuclear weapons after absorbing the first strike. It is the certainty of the unacceptable damage of this second strike which could deter the first use of nuclear weapons. Deterrence operates best between two countries when the window of vulnerability between them is the least or non-existent and there is full transparency in capabilities. Keeping these all in consideration, now the US has set its sights on arms control and near term concrete tension reduction measures, including nuclear and non-nuclear confidence and security building measures to avoid a nuclear war in the region.

Presently, Pakistan seems to be suffering from a sense of inferiority complex *vis-a-vis* India in the nuclear as well as other fields. The sooner it gets over this complex the better it would be for Pakistan and Indo-Pak relations. However, geo-politics in the area is primarily responsible for Pakistan being tolerated by Western countries. In 1971, Pakistan played as the mediator between USA and China which led to Dr. Kissinger's visit, followed by President Nixon's historic visit in 1972 and meeting with Chairman Mao in Beijing. Over the years, Pakistan was basking in the goodwill and support from both China and USA. When Brezhnev committed the supreme folly of marching the Russian Army into Afghanistan in the winter of 1979, USA went for it with the single-minded purpose of teaching Russia the lesson of its life. For ten years beginning from 1979, Pakistan became the most important ally of USA in this part of the world and the weapons for Afghan *Mujahideens* were passed on through Pakistan. This also enabled Pakistan to receive substantive military aid as well as quite acceptance of its indulgence in nuclear technology extended by China. The prevailing global geo-political ambience is neither unipolarity, bi-polarity or multi-polarity but unashamed opportunism in the pursuit of national interest. Domestic political compulsions for the ruling elite as recommended by special "customers and dominant interest groups would increasingly shape foreign policy options thereby eroding the inviolability of the once sacred 'long term national interest' which is now subservient to the primacy of market forces. Consequently, the perennial grapple for nation-states between the principled pursuit of core values and ethical norms on the one hand and the nurturing of tangible power interest on the other, would become less tortured as a new permissiveness that defies profit permeats international relations in the post-Cold War world.[13]

In the changed atmosphere, it appears that the earlier US policy of limiting Chinese engagement without endorsement is a posture of the past. China is Washington's newest strategic partner and the new flavour is broad-based engagement in political/economic/military spheres and vigorous endorsement of Beijing as the second pillar of stability in the post-Cold War world. Whether it is the likely devaluation of the Yuan and the concomitant impact on the Asian economy or the Chinese role in proliferation of weapons of mass destruction, the US now acknowledges that it has no option but to cohabit. The inherent contradiction of the US embracing an authoritarian regime when it is ostensibly wedded to the spread of democracy is one more example of inconvenient reality and principles being relegated to the sidelines. In fact, the US strategy in South Asia is directed at carving out a sphere of influence for American power.

Nuclear Dilemma and Diplomacy in South Asia

Pokharan-II had catapulted India into a situation radically different from the past. It had now become urgently necessary to abandon the mind-set of yesterday in bilateral and multilateral negotiations relating to political and security concerns. India's new self-image would need to be based on a positive and unified national perspective, of a democratic and responsible power capable of acting in a rational manner to develop the reciprocal control systems necessitated by its nuclear deterrent. In the changed circumstances, there was no place for knee-jerk reactions as we stand on the threshold of a new international reality based on our overt nuclear status. Before any serious talk of far-reaching global arms control, we have to ensure acceptance of "minimum nuclear deterrence" for India. However, we should not forget that the tests were only the first step to counter, rising, regional and extra-regional threats to Indian security from weapons of mass destruction. Still, New Delhi faces three major challenges in achieving its deterrence goals. First, the country's small reserves of weapon-grade plutonium and limited financial resources dictate that it can only have puny nuclear forces. The pre-determined diminutive size of the Indian nuclear arsenal imposes high reliability and security standards on New Delhi. Without the luxury of allowing numbers to compensate for equality, India would have to rigorously meet the technical imperatives of its deterrent. Unlike Pakistan and Israel which can draw on China and the United

States respectively for continued nuclear warhead design assistance, India is the only non-NPT nuclear state without an external benefactor.[14]

Secondly, India has to build a credible minimal deterrent in a global environment, openly hostile to further overt weaponisation, particularly by a new nuclear weapons state. Each new action, such as, an Agni-II test or the commencement of serial production of warheads would draw adverse international reaction. Thus, it is vital that the follow-up steps to erect an appropriate deterrent are taken quietly and without the official braggadocio so characteristic of every Indian advance, however small. Classified projects in other democracies are kept under tight wraps, but in India inside information has been leaked out on the nuclear propulsion project and various missiles. Transparency is important in terms of strategic posture, not strategic projects. The US for example released little information on its 1998 missile tests, testing and deployment of the new earth-penetrating B61-II nuclear warhead and top classified advanced vortex satellite that blew up atop a failed Titan 4-A rocket.

Thirdly, India is still at some distance from acquiring the technical superiority to terminate a Chinese nuclear threat and needs plug this vulnerability on a war-footing. A deterrent against Pakistan was never the central mission of Indian nuclear strategy. There is not a single political or military reason for India to build a deterrent against Pakistan. An Indian deterrent makes strategic sense only in the context of China. Without being able to stand up to China, New Delhi would never be able to persuade Beijing to halt its containment of India or its covert nuclear and missile transfers to Pakistan. India can live with nuclear disparity with China, in the same way Beijing had done with the USA. But India cannot live with a nuclear capacity that does not provide basic cover against China. Because of a very late start, India would lag far behind China in the foreseeable future. Even if Beijing were to dramatically halt its ongoing nuclear expansion and India were to build nuclear weapons at the maximum rate possible with its present plutonium production capacity. New Delhi would still not be able to match China's nuclear might even in a quarter century from now. The nuclear test ban treaty and the proposed Fissile Material Cut-off Treaty (FMCT) would ensure that.[15]. The central challenge for India is that, unlike deterrence relationships elsewhere in the world, it has to adequately deter two hand-in-glove nuclear adversaries, China and Pakistan.

New Delhi, by conducting five nuclear explosions on 11th and 13th May 1998, had blown a hole into the global disarmament agenda. Its reason for doing so was explained by Atal Bihari Vajpayee himself – not so much to the Indian people as to US President Bill Clinton in his May 11 letter. The arguments in favour of Pokharan II – that it was a bold act showing that India had stood up and become an equal of at least China saw the situation in terms of the US-Soviet Union face-off, ignoring local conditions. However, this mechanical transplantation of the Cold War scene to the Indian sub-continent overlooked was that Pakistan *vis-a-vis* India was not what the Soviet Union was to the US. There is no ideological quarrel between India and Pakistan over whether Capitalism or Communism should dominate the world. Instead, there is what may be called a blood fuel between close relatives over property rights – a very common cause of family fights – compounded by religious difference and India's role in dismembering Pakistan which the latter could neither forget nor forgive. These factors make the situation in the sub-continent far more complex than the US-Soviet Union tussle. The strategic experts in India had hailed New Delhi's acquisition of this "new currency of power". But the currency has proved to be something like the precious 'Kohinoor' which is not quite legal tender. What is usually far more effective in day-to-day life are plastic cards in wallets and ordinary cash in the bank. In military terms, India might have been able to hit back with much greater vigour and perhaps even take recourse to what is known as "hot pursuit" to eliminate the terrorist camps in Pakistan, if it had been an ordinary military power and not a nuclear one – at least not an overt one.[16] In this situation, Pakistan would have dared to launch its latest misadventure because it would have been aware of India's greater strength. But having become a nuclear power itself, Pakistan knows that India's options are limited since it always has to bear in mind that it cannot provoke Islamabad too much.

After the Indian explosions, the 15-month-old Nawaz Sharif Government faced with its most difficult situation amid mounting domestic pressure to go nuclear on the one hand and, global pressure and economic compulsions to exercise restraint, on the other. As a nuclear tit-for-tat Pakistan had conducted five nuclear explosions on 28th May 1998 and went ahead of India by exploding one more on 30th May (within 48 hours). With India and Pakistan having completed their nuclear tests for the present, the emerging picture needed to be analysed carefully. There was a view that with mutual deterrence established, Pakistan and India would settle down to hold talks and sort out the various problems. Mirza Aslam Beg, former Chief of the Pakistan Army has said, much before the tests, that minimal nuclear and missile deterrence should be kept intact as they were the cheapest options for peace and had helped maintain peace between India and Pakistan. Dr. Abdul Qadir Khan, the Pakistani nuclear scientist, had also said on May 31 that he believed that the tests were a peace guarantor and would improve relations between India and Pakistan. But the overall picture emerging from Pakistan was not so simple or clear: the frequent fulminations of Pakistan Foreign Minister Gohar Ayub Khan hardly inspire confidence. He said that Pakistan was getting ready to equip Ghauri missiles with nuclear warheads and that further nuclear tests could not be ruled out. He also dismissed India's offer of no first strike treaty on the plea that the strike time for missiles either way was a matter of minutes and that the question of first strike or second strike was meaningless as it would be difficult to find out who struck first.

Above all, India and Pakistan were justified in conducting nuclear weapon tests only as a gesture of protest against the inequity and irrationality of the nuclear weapons limitation and test-ban treaties sought to be imposed upon them and other nations by the nuclear big powers, and not becuse of the demands of their national security perceptions. They cannot, however, escape the charge that by increasing the probability of another nuclear assault on life and civilization on earth, their nuclear armament exercises contribute to the cumulative humiliation of the victims of the Hiroshima and Nagasaki carnage: whose only redemption lies in the possibility that what happened to them would never happen to any group of human beings again. And there was more bad news for those in India and Pakistan, who would heed the voice of conscience and refrain from denying the possibility of redemption to victims of unthinkable evils.

The five plus one nuclear tests by Islamabad in reply to the earlier tests by New Delhi signalled the beginning of a nuclear arms race in the Indian sub-continent. The issue is not of creating a strategic symmetry but of doing one better than your adversary in developing weapons of mass destruction. The Pakistani tests had come at a time when the national consensus on the Indian nuclear tests of May 11th and 13th was finally coming unstuck. The unquestioning enthusiasm, which seemed all set to engulf the nation in the immediate aftermath of the nuclear tests, appeared to be tappering off. In short, the self-congratulatory euphoria of mid-May had given way to utter dismay with the sudden realisation that the country is being pushed along the slippery slope of a nuclear arms race. There was no clear public support for such adventurism. It was considered economically unviable and its security rationale remained unclear. The "Scientific achievement" had been replaced by fear and apprehension of war in the public after the Pakistani tests. On top of this would be the cost of deployment – of creating the command, control, communications and intelligence structures. The expenditure involved could be as high as half-to-one per cent of the Gross Domestic Products or 25 to 40 per cent of the defence budget. The financial implications of creating and deploying even a minimum nuclear deterrent were enormous. On the other hand, at present Pakistan may or may not see its nuclear bomb as an "Islamic" bomb but there was no guarantee that there would be no possible clandestine proliferation of nuclear technology or even the sale of weapons by it at a future date. It is becoming increasingly clear that India and Pakistan's actions might have destabilised not only bilateral security equations but also the balance of power to the west and east of the Indian sub-continent.

As the time passes, the erosion of support for nuclearism is taking place. Many are discovering that a nuclear weapon is not just a larger bomb, but a weapon that is fundamentally anti-life and nihilistic. It kills not only one's enemies, but also total strangers and innocents, and even one's near ones. Some favourites of the bomb have nervously started saying that it would never be used, that it is only a symbolic weapon that acts as a deterrent or as a technical achievement meant to boost the self-confidence of the Indians. While, many have come to feel that given the ventality and moral decadence of the ruling classes in the two countries, if political miscalculation does not someday kill us all, bureaucratic or technical ineptitude would almost certainly do so. The Pakistani bomb may be even less indigenous than the Indian bomb, but that was hardly a consolidation for the Indians. A borrowed or stolen bomb is as effective as a home-made one. Indeed, the deterrence theory has worked better for Pakistan than for India. After nuclearisation, India may not have acquired parity with the West or China, but Pakistan has done so with India. Strangely neither side knew how advanced the other was. What was known, however, was that India had enormous conventional superiority and, therefore, Pakistan could not afford to provoke it beyond a point. But the moment Pakistan acquired nuclear parity, it realised that it could step up its campaign in Kashmir, for India could no longer attack it, as it did in 1965, when we nearly took Lahore, or in 1971. In the circumstances, if past mistakes are to be avoided, India should not allow its rhetoric to outstrip its capacity or its claims to overtake the reality. India has to put its head down and work with determination and humility on its tasks. Nuclear weapons, however, demand hard decisions. Deterrence requires not only the technical capacity but an unmistakable national will to severely punish a potential aggressor. A match is also must in New Delhi's economic capacity and security needs. The way Pakistan had sunk economically after conducting its tests, should serve as a lesson to India to accord the highest priority to putting its economic house in order. The basic reality is that India has been a soft state and hence it should be cognisant of the danger that nuclear weapons in the hands of a soft state can invite greater insecurity.

In the post-Pokhran-II Phase, it was felt that the government could have done more to educate public opinion about the objectives of acquiring nuclear weapons status and about the manner in which we would define our position in the international community and create stable equations with other important powers of the world. Prime Minister Vajpayee began to define India's nuclear doctrine in Parliament, at the Non-aligned summit in Durban and at the UN General Assembly in New York. The concepts articulated by him are; First, that India's nuclear weapons capacity is only for defensive and not for offensive purposes. Secondly, India shall not be the first to use nuclear weapons against any state (no-first-use doctrine). Third,

India would not use nuclear weapons against any non-nuclear state. Fourth, India's objective is to create and sustain a minimum credible nuclear weapons capacity. Lastly, he made it clear that India would decide on the procedures and mechanics of deployment of nuclear weapons keeping in mind security concerns and the strategic environment at given points of time with a sense of restraint.

A retaliatory action from Pakistan was imminent. Several newspapers including *The Times of India,* through its editorial came out with the view that nuclear explosions by Islamabad was in India's favour. "It is in India's interest that the Pakistani bomb comes out into the open and both countries clearly acknowledge the existence of mutual deterrence between them. During the Cold War, such a recognition of mutual deterrence and the consequent acceptance of the futility of initiating a war led to detente and arms control talks between the two superpowers. Such a recognition will also emphasise the futility of attempting to alter a long established status quo – as in Kashmir. The Pakistani test along with the Indian tests will convert two out of three hitherto undeclared nuclear weapon powers into declared weapons powers. In the field of economic sanctions, imposed on New Delhi after the explosion it would be beneficial. The collapse of Pakistan is not something the US policy-makers can contemplate with equanimity. Therefore, before long, the US will have to modify its laws and arrange to rescue Pakistan". It also added that sooner or later, the US, Japan and West Europe would realise that they cannot allow China to grow in power and a power vacuum to develop to the South of China. A nuclear India and a nuclear Pakistan independently or together would be able to ensure that an Asian balance of power emerges along with Russia and Japan and China is integrated smoothly into the international system. Nuclear fundamentalism of the nuclear weapon powers blinds them to realities of international politics.[17] Even before the explosions, on 22nd May 1998, Nawaz Sharif hinted that pressure was building on him to go-ahead for a nuclear test in reply to India's underground implosions at Pokharan.

On May 21, 1998, New Delhi announced that it had put a moratorium on further nuclear tests and offered to formalise it into an obligation through negotiations with key world powers. At a press conference Brijesh Mishra, Principal Secretary to the

Prime Minister said that India had conducted the nuclear tests for its defence. In reply to a question, he expressed India's willingness to have very good relations with both its neighbours (China and Pakistan) with a desire to engage in a dialogue to resolve outstanding issues. Referring to Pakistan, in particular, he made it clear that India was keen on a dialogue with Islamabad and was awaiting its response on the eight-point proposal made by I.K. Gujral to Nawaz Sharif during the India-Pakistan-Bangladesh economic summit in Dhaka in January 1998. India had tried to restore normalcy in relations with Pakistan and Atal Bihari Vajpayee the Indian Prime Minister, declared in Lok Sabha on 27th May 1998, that New Delhi was ready to discuss a no first-use agreement with Pakistan and other countries bilaterally or in a collective forum. In a statement, he disclosed that India would remain committed to the basic tenets of its foreign policy–a conviction that global elimination of nuclear weapons would enhance its security as well as that of the rest of the world.

Pakistan exploded its nuclear devices on 28th and 30th May and announced moratorium on nuclear tests in the second week of June 1998. It also made a formal offer for resumption of talks with India and proposed to sign a no-nuclear test agreement with New Delhi. In a message conveyed to the Indian High Commissioner Satish Chandra by Pakistan foreign secretary Shamshad Ahmed, it was said that the resumption of dialogue would be open on the basis of the agreement reached between the two countries on June 23rd, 1997 when both sides identified outstanding issues. Stating that the proposed no-nuclear test agreement was an important confidence-building measure, the statement hoped that India would reciprocate and contribute towards creating a conducive regional environment by taking further effective steps to overcome the security crisis and promote durable peace and stability in South Asia. But on the other hand, in an important decision Pakistan had banned the sale of Indian goods or renting out of Indian video cassettes in the cantonment areas of Lahore. In a military dispatched letter entitled "Economic Reforms" to all departmental and general stores in cantonment areas it stopped sale of Indian goods with immediate effect and other imported items from August 1st, 1998.[18]

Despite the fact that both India and Pakistan had obtained nuclear capability and exploded nuclear devices, big powers in general and the US in particular flatly refused to amend the Nuclear Non-Proliferation Treaty (NPT) that would include the said two as nuclear states. Madeleine Albright, the US Secretary of State had welcomed New Delhi's attitude on the Fissile Material Cut-off Treaty (FMCT) but added from Washington, "If we were to allow India and Pakistan to test their way to nuclear status under that agreement, we would create an incentive for others to follow their misguided example. The US Secretary of State also answered the other questions and said, "Some say nuclear Non-Proliferation is doomed and the sooner we accept that, the better off we will be. I say that is dangerously nonsense. To abandon (efforts to halt the spread of nuclear weapons) because they have been dealt a setback would be a felony against the future. The greatness of a nation is measured not by how much they can destroy but how much they can build."[19] Further, in the context of nuclear explosions, Washington rather doubted the advancement of their technology. After analysing seismic data recorded around the world in the wake of the May underground nuclear tests by India and Pakistan, scientists believed that both had exaggerated the size of their weapons as quoted in the *Newsweek*, a periodical published from New York.

Continuous but very slow progress witnessed in Indo-Pak relations in the post-Pokharan-II phase. The two Prime Ministers, met in Colombo at the SAARC summit but they failed to make a headway and even on the modalities of the talks, the two sides were poles apart. India favoured a sustained and composite dialogue process to settle all outstanding issues, while, Islamabad, in order to have the strobe-light on Kashmir, linking the festering dispute with the nuclear question that had come to bother the politically powerful P-5 and the economically advanced G-8 groupings. However, Atal Bihari Vajpayee made out a strong case for India and Pakistan. In reply to the Lok Sabha debate on foreign policy on 4th August 1998, setting aside contentious issues and turning their attention to areas where they could make a definite dent on bilateral relations, he expressed the view that intractable matters should be put on the "deep freeze". In its place, efforts should be pooled to give a push to bilateral trade and greater people-to-people contact.[20] Further, in September the two Prime Ministers had an occasion to exchange their views when they gathered to attend the sessions of UN General Assembly. The moment marked positive developments in Indo-Pak relations as admitted by Vajpayee that a significant outcome of the visit was the resumption of dialogue with Pakistan. "It is because of this that neither Pakistani attempt of raising Kashmir at the UN had been successful nor had it been able to link Kashmir with the nuclear tests". Indian view in this regard has always been clear that any proposal on nuclear issue should not be linked with the Kashmir problem. As a follow up of the decision taken during the visit, the foreign secretaries of India and Pakistan discussed regional security affairs, fully conscious of the implications of the nuclear weaponisation of both the countries. The Indian side carried eleven suggestions for confidence-building and ensuring security. Pakistan responded with three. The Indian suggestion regarding signing of the 'No First Use' of nuclear weapons and the extension of the agreement of 1991 to cover population centres and economic locations were rejected by Pakistan. Pakistan suggested instead modalities for strategic restraint and stabilisation and a No-War or Non-Aggression Pact. But both sides have agreed to discuss concrete proposals for maintaining strategic restraint and stabilisation in the next round, and to explore possibilities of incremental arrangements to prevent a nuclear conflict through accidental or unauthorised use of nuclear weapons.[21]

Status of Proliferation and Security After 1998

In recent years, the nuclear-related risks have increased mainly because of three factors: the growth and spread of nuclear weapons, the expansion of civilian nuclear programmes and the increase in extremist political groups waging campaigns of terror. In South Asia, the potential for nuclear terrorism is considered a matter of special concern for several reasons; one is the rapidly expanding nuclear programmes in India and Pakistan involving massive investments in the construction and operation of civilian nuclear power plants, research reactor, laboratories and reprocessing and enrichment facilities. Another reason is the growing stockpiles of nuclear fissionable materials, possibly of actual weapons, in each country; protecting them requires special technologies, safety systems and security checks and surveillance. A third reason is that both neighbours continue to be wracked by high levels of terrorist activities that pose major political challenges to their national leaders. A fourth reason is the growing sophistication of terrorist methods of operation and attack and the increasing availability of portable weapon systems.[22]

All these factors taken together are responsible for proliferation of nuclear weapons in the region which directly threat stability and peace prospect of South Asia. Its simple by-product is security dilemma that still exists in the region. In addition, the security dilemma in the South Asian sub-continent operates as a chain reaction that includes regional and extra-regional powers with competing interests. For countries like India and China, it is important to note that while the goals of non-proliferation are extremely crucial, perceived national interests are a greater factor in shaping the eventual policy direction.[23] In the aftermath of the fall of USSR, the uncontrolled spread of nuclear materials became a matter of concern. The scale and sophistication of the 9/11 attacks achieved to translate this concern into a concrete threat awareness. It requires stability which assumes a state of balance between two adversaries even though there may not be parity between them.[24] Recent developments pertaining to nuclear proliferation are likely to have far-reaching consequences both, regionally and in terms of the global non-proliferation regime.

The world, at large, witnessed the devastating power of atomic bomb when it was dropped on Nagasaki and Hiroshima on 6th and 9th August 1945 respectively. From there onwards the world public opinion in general and great power having the atomic bomb/capability, in particular wanted a specific ban on its proliferation. A treaty on the issue called Nuclear Non-Proliferation Treaty (NNPT) came into being in 1970, although India voiced against the nuclear weapons right from 1954, and it gave a call for an end to all nuclear testing. For long India's focus primarily revolved around the commitments towards general and complete nuclear disarmament as well as on the discriminatory nature of the NPT. Great powers converted as Subrahmanyam argued, the NPT into licensing unlimited nuclear proliferation to the Five Nuclear Weapon Powers with a total ban on acquisition of nuclear weapons by all other nations.[25] India argued that it was not willing to be a party to an inherently discriminatory treaty, which institutionalised nuclear apartheid. This contrasted with the position of Israel and Pakistan, which refused to join the NPT due to national security considerations. But the similarity in their stands ends with the fact that all the three countries termed it discriminatory.[26] This led to their being largely excluded from trade in nuclear plant or materials except for safety-related devices for a few safeguarded facilities. Throughout the period since the inception of the NPT, the thrust of American and Western policy in South Asia was to prevent nuclear proliferation by extending the 1970 treaty and then in 1996 by initiating the Comprehensive Test Ban Treaty (CTBT). This produced a number of unofficial dialogues, many of them funded by American and European government agencies and foundations.[27] Earlier at the historic 1995 NPT, Review and Extension Conference, which extended the Treaty indefinitely, NPT parties-including all members of Nuclear Suppliers' Group (NSG)–made a political commitment to refrain from nuclear cooperation with states lacking "full scope" safeguards.[28] Till recent eight specific ratifications are missing for the CTBT to enter into force: the US, China, Iran, India, Pakistan, Egypt, Israel and North Korea and the treaty is yet to become a global law.[29] The CTBT's zero-testing norm is the expression of a zero-tolerance stance against nuclear testing and proliferation as well.

On account of its discriminatory nature Nuclear Non-Proliferation Treaty was opposed by India and, as a result, it is excluded as a Nuclear Weapon State. India's weapons material initially came from the Canadian-designed 40 MWt CIRUS "research" reactor which started up in 1960, and the 100 MWt Dhurva indigenous unit in operation since 1985, using local uranium. CIRUS was supplied with heavy water from the USA and it was probably after the 1962 war with China and surely latter's nuclear explosion in October 1964, that it was employed largely to make weapons-grade plutonium. Development of nuclear weapons apparently began in earliest in 1967. According to Article III of the 1956 India-Canada Agreement the Government will ensure that the reactor and any products resulting from its use will be employed for peaceful uses only. Likewise Clause nine of the India-US Heavy Water Agreement noted that the heavy water sold here under shall be for use only in India by the Government in connection with research into and the use atomic energy for peaceful purposes. India violated these provisions of the Agreements with Canada and the US and exploded its nuclear devices in May 1974, using plutonium from CIRUS. It demonstrated that nuclear technology transferred to non-nuclear-weapon states for peaceful purposes could be misused. After twenty-four years, India again exploded its nuclear devices in May 1998.

Any government which takes power in Pakistan would have three choices: to expand, continue or cut back Pakistan's nuclear activities. Initially, Pakistan is believed to have working on reprocessing facilities in Chashma and Rawalpindi's PINSTECH and "New Labs" complex. The Chashma plant, the largest, is designed to have a 100-tonne reprocessing capacity and to be capable of producing 100 to 200 kilograms of plutonium in a year when completed. The "New Labs" are able to extract ten to twenty kilograms of plutonium. Pakistan also has two small heavy-water production plants at Multan and Karachi and a fuel fabrication facility at Chashma-Kudian.[30] From the beginning Pakistan had claimed that the Kahuta facility is intended to manufacture only Low Enriched Uranium (LEU) for its civilian nuclear programme. On the issue analysts questioned because Pakistan's sole operating power reactor did not need LEU nor the country realistically expected to construct a LEU-fuelled reactor despite its plan to build five of them. At the same, Pakistan declined to permit verification of its assurances to Washington that it will not enrich uranium above the five per cent level.[31] At the time most experts believed that Pakistan has succeeded in manufacturing High Enriched Uranium, and it was difficult to estimate how much of this weapons material it has already produced. In addition to this Pakistan and China signed the Border Agreement in 1963 that laid the foundation stone of Sino-Pak Axis, which had grown stronger since then. The Chinese stood with Pakistan in the Indo-Pak War in 1965 and 1971 and helped in a long way in helping Pakistan to build its nuclear capability and missile programme.[32] China's support for Pakistan has enabled that country to play a role in South Asia, South West and Central Asia, larger than its population, economy or domestic technological capacity allowed it to play.[33] At the close of eighties the world became confirmed that Pakistan possesses nuclear bomb. The People's Republic of China is in lead role in making Pakistan a powerful nuclear power in the region. In response to India's second explosion. Islamabad detonated its nuclear device in May 1998, and evened its nuclear account with India.

Before the nuclear explosions of May 1998 by India and Pakistan, the US had, for some years pursued a variety of initiatives to persuade India and Pakistan to abandon their nuclear weapons programmes and to accept comprehensive international safeguards on all their nuclear activities. To this end, Clinton administration proposed a conference of nine states, comprising the five established nuclear-weapon states, along with Japan, Germany, India and Pakistan. This and previous similar proposals were rejected by India, which countered with demands that other potential weapon states, such as Iran and North Korea, should be invited, and that regional limitations would only be acceptable if they were accepted by China. Because, the USA had not accepted the participation of Iran and North Korea hence such initiatives lapsed. One recent approach centred on the concept of containment, designed to 'cap' the production of fissile material for weapons purposes, which would hopefully be followed by "roll back". To this end, India and the USA jointly sponsored a UN General Assembly resolution in 1993 calling for negotiations for a cut-off convention, the Fissile Material Cut-off Treaty (FMCT).

However, despite the widespread international support for a FMCT, formal negotiations on cut-off have yet to begin. Apart from international efforts bilateral confidence-building measures between India and Pakistan to reduce the prospects of confrontation have been limited. In 1990, each side ratified a treaty not to attack the other's nuclear installations, and at the end of 1991, they provided one another with a list showing the location of all their nuclear plants, even though the respective lists were regarded as not being wholly accurate. Early in 1994, India proposed a bilateral agreement for a 'no first use' of nuclear weapons and an extension of the 'no attack' treaty to cover civilian and industrial targets as well as nuclear installations. For long both countries engaged in a conventional arms race including sophisticated technology and equipment capable of delivering nuclear weapon. In 1994, India reversed a four-year trend of reduced allocations for defence, and despite its much smaller economy, Pakistan pushed its own expenditures yet higher. By the time both lost their patrons: India, the former USSR; and Pakistan, the USA.

Following the 1998 tests the question of nuclear proliferation had reopened. The test were unambiguously military including one claimed to be of a sophisticated thermo-nuclear device. Their declared purpose was "to help the design of nuclear weapons of different yields and different delivery systems. Until May 1998, the region was satisfied with "existential deterrence", which kept both countries, nuclear capability in ambiguity and in a non-weaponised state. The 1998 demonstration of capability by Pakistan was carried out in something of a crisis situation. There was intense international pressure on Pakistan, including threatened punishments (sticks) and possible inducements (carrots), if it refrained from testing. Pakistan chose to suffer the sticks because it considered that a lack of response would erode the credibility of deterrence, which required not just demonstration of the "capability" but also demonstration of the "will" to respond.[34] Since 1998, the nuclear bomb has been a symbol of India's power and prestige, but the nuclear domain has always stood as a site within which India's unique moral judgement could be applied and exihibited. Dominant thinking in international relations finds it hard to reconcile the two trends, and many have scratched their heads in puzzlement over the incongruity of India's peaceful intentions and hard power hype, or the juxtaposition of "the land of Gandhi" and the bomb.[35] By explosions, in one stroke, the dam broke sweeping away the premise of virtually all of the Western, European, and Japanese-sponsored dialogues. This premise was that South Asians could be dissuaded, via dialogue, from exercising the nuclear option, or if they did possess nuclear weapons, from testing and declaring that they were nuclear weapons states.[36] This not only broke the existing test ban moratorium, for all practical purposes it buried the CTBT.

However, in practice, if not in theory the international community has accepted India's nuclear ambivalence. Following the tests, although both countries were placed under international sanctions, but tests led to a profound revaluation of India in the US. The Talbott-Jaswant talks, as they became known, provided the diplomatic groundwork for an American review of India that ended with President Bill Clinton making a triumphant visit to India. Further the Bush Administration took the Clinton cue and elevated India to an even closer partnership.[37] The credibility of Indian claims to nuclear restraint and responsibility contributed without doubt to the exceptional civil nuclear trading rights India received, outside the bounds of the Nuclear Non-Proliferation Treaty through the India-US civil nuclear agreement. Perhaps Washington has accepted India's threat perception from China, who is also on US radar. Analysts in New Delhi have long pointed to Chinese military modernisation as a clear-threat to India. This modernisation includes missile deployment, such as the current deployment of the DF-21 and DF-3 missiles in Qinghai and Yunnan provinces.[38] Furthermore, there is some suspicion among Indian analysts that though Beijing's stated policy is that of minimum deterrence, the stationing of missiles such as DF-3 and DF-21 reflects a posture of nuclear coercion, and under some conditions, does not preclude a first strike against its neighbours.[39] It is also possible that since 1998, Beijing may have deployed nuclear weapons on the Tibetan plateau in response to a perceived Indian conventional military advantage and the nuclear tests.[40] Even during Kargil, the world had saw that Pakistan acted with impunity providing the highest provocation to a self-respecting nation and yet India did not cross the line of control which Pakistan had isolated to cut off the supply routes to its forces.[41] In contrast to Pakistan, India had shown itself to be a responsible nuclear weapon state.

Of the two proliferations–vertical and horizontal, the latter is said to be on the strategic agenda of Pakistan. While the first is related to modernisation of nuclear arsenals by the nuclear power states, the second meant spread of nuclear-related base materials, technology and technological knowledge to aspiring nuclear weapon states and to non-state actors such as terrorist groups. If the nuclear arsenals of countries increase in size and in average weapon yield in the future, then multiple attacks on cities would become more likely in future war scenarios. This would further increase the risk of firestorms in cities suffering nuclear attack, which would increase the probability of toxic and radioactive debris reaching adjacent countries. It would also pose greater risk of regional climate disturbances arising from nuclear war.[42] The use of weapons of mass destruction is the very worst way for nations to solve international disputes. Moreover, most forms of nuclear weapons use are likely to be illegal under international law[43] and damage to non-combatant countries in war breaches international law.[44] In the context, the history of the A.Q. Khan network and its assistance to states such as North Korea and Iran deserves special mention. And what is more, Pakistan's ambitious nuclear agenda is now drawing a not-so-unwilling Sri Lanka into the brewing nuclear whirlwind in South Asia. Evidently, 'Pakistan is all set to begin consultations with Sri Lanka to help set up a nuclear power plant in Trincomallee's Sampur[45]. A hurt and frustrated Sri Lanka, so rendered by the outcome of the recently concluded United Nations Human Rights Commission (UNHRC) session, in all probability is very enthusiastic about the proposed venture, not so much because of the economic benefits it will bring about as it is because of the opportunity this new partnership presents to avenge the isolation, she suffered at the hands of India at said session. Added to this impending disaster is the more immediate issue of deviating state capital away from poverty alleviation. Ejaz Ghani, in his article 'The Poor half-billion: What is holding back lagging regions in South Asia?", aptly calls the region a "depressing paradox" where luxury and absolute poverty co-exist, mocking the astounding growth South Asia has achieved in the last few decades. Ghani presents an account of the two dimensions of Asia in existence, labelling one "Asia shinning" and the other "Asia suffering". The latter, he explains, "is doing no better than many Sub-Saharan African countries."[46] It is therefore, imperative for all South Asian states to appreciate that compromising regional solidarity will amount to compromising the interests of individual states.

Although the issue of nuclear proliferation remained at alert regionally and globally, the nuclear test by North Korea in October 2006, put renewed focus on the dangers of nuclear proliferation. Following the test New Delhi swiftly condemned the test and indirectly highlighted Islamabad's contribution to Pyongyang's nuclear test.[47] On the other hand, Islamabad refuted any suggestion that the activities of the A.Q. Khan network had contributed to the said test and stated that North Korea's nuclear programme is based on plutonium while Pakistan relies on uranium.[48] In this manner, for the time being, both India and Pakistan tried to ensure that proliferation in South Asia was not equated with proliferation in North-east Asia. To a certain extent, the Bush administration obliged the subcontinental nuclear powers, as senior officials dismissed any parallels between North Korea's path to nuclear weapons to those of India and Pakistan.[49] In the context while Pakistan denied any links to the test, it did not help Islamabad's case when Japanese sources stated that days before Pyongyang's test, several Pakistani nuclear technicians arrived in North Korea through China.[50] This augmented the suspicions that Pakistani agencies may have had some role in the test, perhaps through data sharing before or after explosion.

The A.Q. Khan's network which provided nuclear assistance to North Korea and Iran has represented the most serious proliferation problem in recent years. Since Khan's public confession in February 2004, the Musharraf regime has consistently asserted that this network was the work of a rogue scientist and that the Pakistani government and its military leaders were not involved in these activities. Analysts and officials in Pakistan as well as in the United States have expressed skepticism over Khan's confession and the implicit professed innocence of the Pakistani political and military establishment.[51] A highly publicised report released in April 2007 by the London-based International Institute for Strategic Studies, also stated that individuals and entities involved in the network could still be dormant and can conceivably be reactivated in the future.[52] Moreover, A.Q. Khan claimed in a signed statement that successive army chiefs in the 1990s, Generals Mirza Aslam Beg and Jehangir Karamat, had authorised the sales of nuclear technology.[53] While this could be taken as Khan's attempts to remove the burden of guilt, it is true that the military was closely associated with the nuclear and missile programmes. In fact, in 1990, General Beg warned US government officials that Pakistan would be forced to provide nuclear technology to Tehran if Washington did not offer support to Pakistan.[54] Other circumstantial evidence, such as visits by the Pakistani military leadership to North Korea throughout the nineties, suggests that there was a barter deal between Pyongyang and Islamabad.[55] Additionally, in August 2005, General Musharraf conceded that Khan had transferred centrifuge machines to North Korea through which uranium hexafluoride can be enriched for eventual processing into civilian reactors fuel or for military purposes.[56] Shipping out such large centrifuge machines without the military's knowledge would have been impossible. For a country to acquire a nuclear delivery system, the decision-making process incorporates several factors, as well as the opinions of numerous government agencies to ensure compatibility among the various systems.

The issue of the Pakistani military-scientific establishment's involvement or endorsement in the Khan's network activities is crucial due to its implications for contemporary proliferation routes and processes. If these elements within and outside Pakistan and their methods and routes remain undiscovered, it has two broad consequences for proliferation in South Asia. First, it allows Islamabad to potentially procure missile and nuclear technology in the future, in an attempt to catch-up with India. In this regard, a Pakistani national, Mohammed Aslam, working at the Tabani Corporation's Moscow office, was named by the Russian government in 2006 as having attempted to acquire dual-use technology and other materials for Pakistan's nuclear and missile development programmes.[57] Given Islamabad's need to construct a secure deterrent against India, especially long-range missiles that can reach southern and eastern India, it is possible that the said case is an instance of continuing efforts to exploit non-state networks to procure prohibited equipment. As one analyst noted aptly 'due to Pakistan's apparent inability to acquire nuclear weapons components legally, it is encouraged to look towards illegal sources.[58] Second, the continued existence of the kind of middlemen that the network generated increases the possibility of nuclear technology leakage out of Pakistan in the event of a coup or widespread instability from radical groups. According to some experts, the Iranian government has made use of these networks for its nuclear and missile programmes.[59] The previously mentioned IISS report also states, 'Tehran controls a clandestine nuclear materials network comparable to the one seen by Khan and in the past has procured technology from some of the same suppliers used by Khan.[60] And the elements of the network are still active.

The nuclear proliferation by Pakistan directly or indirectly did not stop here and there are links between the Middle East and South Asia. Even today Islamabad has nuclear connection to the Middle East through possible collaboration with Saudi Arabia. In past Saudi Arabia remained a significant factor in the development of Pakistan's nuclear power. News reports as well as US government officials analyses have claimed that Riyadh provided considerable financing for Pakistan's nuclear and missile programme in previous decades.[61] As reported apart from developing nuclear power for itself, it is working as a pool for other countries of the region. This is in line with the announcement in November 2006 by six Arab States–Saudi Arabia, Morocco, Egypt, Algeria, Tunisia and the United Arab Emirates that they would develop civilian nuclear programmes.[62] In addition German news reports stated in early 2006 that Pakistani Scientists assisted Saudi efforts to develop a nuclear programme and that this was done under the guide of pilgrimages to Saudi Arabia between 2003 and 2005.[63] Several high-ranking Saudi royals as well as government officials are among the few non-Pakistanis who have toured Islamabad's nuclear facilities. These include defence minister Prince Sultan who visited the Kahuta uranium enrichment facility in 1999 and a son of the current Saudi ruler, King Abdullah, who attended the test of the nuclear-capable 950-mile range Ghauri missile in 1999.[64] A 2003 news report quoted an anonymous Pakistan official, who claimed that Riyadh and Islamabad had concluded a secret agreement under which Pakistan would receive subsidised oil in exchange for transferring nuclear technology.[65] Even if there is no immediate possibility of such a transfer, Saudi Arabia could pursue this with Pakistan in the future to hedge against nuclear developments in the Middle East. In case of Saudi Arabia, it fulfils Pakistan's strategic purpose. Saudi Arabia could provide a base for stationing Pakistani nuclear devices[66] that would be safe from the reach of Indian missiles and give Islamabad a semblance of second-strike capability.

However, in order to demonstrate to the international community that it is a responsible nuclear power, Islamabad has decided to set-up a "Strategic Export Control Division" in its foreign ministry that will ostensibly prevent prohibited WMD-related technology from being exported.[67] But this does not necessarily address the problem of possible involvement of government entities and officials that have remained under the radar even after the network was discovered. As we all are aware that nuclear acquisition dynamics is mainly based on fissile material production and therefore, the renewed discussion on FMCT in 2006 focussed attention on the attitudes of India and Pakistan in which most participants put forward the argument that capping the production of fissile material in South Asia would be an important step toward nuclear stability in the sub-continent. The Government of India, in its way too, has attempted to ensure that they are in compliance with the latest international regulations against Tehran's nuclear programme. In course of discussions on the Indo-US civil nuclear deal, especially in the US Congress, concerns have been expressed over India's ties to Iran at a time when the IAEA and western powers led by the United States are working toward controlling Tehran's uranium enrichment programme. In response to US influence/pressure while, in February 2007, Pakistan froze assets of several individuals and other entities connected to Tehran's nuclear and missle projects in accordance with UN Security Council resolution 1937.[68] New Delhi voted against Iran at the IAEA in September 2005 and February 2006. In February 2007, New Delhi also banned exports of equipment and technologies to Iran that could be used in nuclear and missile development projects.[69] Although in strategic considerations the US signed a civil nuclear cooperation deal with India, politically and in theory, it continued to be tough on nuclear proliferation and in a proactive step, the US Congress under the Democratic leadership passed the Nuclear Black Market Counter Terrorism Act, in January 2007 which authorises the administration to implement "punitive actions" against states condoning or cooperating with entities actively engaged in nuclear proliferation.[70] Direct and indirect proliferation of nuclear materials is one of the reasons, why Washington has refused to offer a nuclear cooperation agreement to Pakistan.

From the view point of nuclear proliferation even the Indo-US civil nuclear deal has not scored much point in its stock. During the discussion and conclusion of the agreement a debate has arisen over its impact on the global non-proliferation regime. This agreement will allow India to acquire nuclear technology and materials from the United States and other suppliers. A basic feature of this agreement is that by acquiring uranium from foreign sources and by placing a set of nuclear facilities on the military list, India can increase its fissile material production for weaponisation purposes. According to a different line of interpretation India rather than increasing nuclear warhead production, it would use the expansion of its uranium supplies and enrichment capability to fuel its nuclear submarine project[71], a key element of India's desire to achieve a secure second strike capability under its credible minimum deterrence doctrine. Of the two separate lines of criticism of the deal, the first focusses on the non-proliferation objective, and the second on India's strategic needs. The first perspective is that the agreement will weaken the global non-proliferation regime by condoning India's nuclear weapon programme. It is argued that by introducing India-specific changes to global as well as domestic US non-proliferation laws, it will be more difficult to prevent nuclear transfers involving other countries such as China-Pakistan and Russia-Iran.[72] In sum, nuclear issues in South Asia cannot be examined in isolation from developments elsewhere. Historically, close political ties have existed between the South Asian sub-continent and the Middle East and therefore, regional rivalries and bilateral relations play an important role in shaping decisions that impact broader nuclear issues, including horizontal proliferation. It is clear that proliferation dynamics in the sub-continent are affected by numerous factors centred around security issues, regional and global power politics and domestic considerations.

Nuclear proliferation to the sub-continent, according to Rajesh Basrur, has led to South Asia's Cold War, ideationally rooted in collective memory and materially underpinned by the dynamics of power politics in the region.[73] The diametrically opposed interests of India and Pakistan mean that the two countries will pursue their strategies individually. Analyses of South Asian nuclearism take two polar positions in explicating the effects of nuclear weapons in the sub-continent. The first argues that their advent has made for a more stable South Asia, circumscribing armed conflicts and terminating major wars by the logic of deterrence. The second claims that nuclear proliferation has destabilised India-Pakistan relations, in particular, and South Asian security in general, by encouraging aggressive Pakistani military postures and massive conventional build ups on either side of the Line of Control (LoC).

In the South Asian context, we are faced with a unique situation. Both the adversaries locked in hostilities are nuclear armed. Any actual use of the weapon is likely to be suicidal. On the face of it, this equation should provide a credible deterrent to war. However, this has not happened. The stability, which many strategists thought would descend on the sub-continent with the acquisition of nuclear weapons, has continued to be elusive. In overall situation, it is said that the ability of the threat of use of nuclear weapon has removed the actual use of nuclear weapons to achieve certain specified objectives in a conflict.[74] So far nuclear weapons have been used only once and that too against a non-nuclear weapon state. When the US bombed Hiroshima and Nagasaki, it could do so because it faced no threat of equal retaliation.

Presently, providing strategic stability is the main plan of the US foreign policy in South Asia, meaning "Keeping open the opinion of using India to help counter-balance China, whenever that prove necessary. Stability, viewed in this context certainly involves preventing any war between India and Pakistan and generally controlling reducing the level of political violence in South Asia."[75] The Bush Administration indication that the subject of non-proliferation should not stand as the obstacle to the maintenance of the US-India relationship based on common interests. Now non-proliferation and arms control are no longer on the agenda of the Bush Administration.[76] On the other hand, nuclearisation has not fundamentally made India secure, and given its proclivity to project itself as a developing country, the test have not enhanced its international standing either. Even though China is in a similar situation, it still manages to be treated as a great power. This situation is largely a reflection of China's willingness to assert its position and face the consequences. India's democratic tradition, however, makes its task more difficult as contending view points have to be taken into consideration. In the sense, the process of finding a common national position is all the more difficult for India than it is for China.[77] At best, nuclearisation has provided India a temporary strategic depth *vis-a-vis* the global constellation of powers. It is entirely up to India to exploit this window of opportunity, to rearrange its priorities in order to enhance its economic progress, bring about greater social cohesion and political stability.[78] India's quest is for great power status and not just for survival. It wants to play a pre-eminent role in global politics.

Broadly speaking, the concept of security includes the practices involved in the physical custody of weapons and sensitive nuclear materials that will prevent theft or sabotage, and control procedures that will prevent unauthorised tampering with, access to, and use of nuclear weapons. Normally, it is defined in two contexts–strategic and technical. The strategic concept also refers to ensuring safety and survivability of nuclear weapons under all conditions - peace, on alert in crisis, and war.

Safety implies measures to prevent nuclear weapons from being involved in accidents and to permit them to perform as intended. While survivability refers to force deployment, mobility, dispersal, and hardened silos for weapons and command centres that will make nuclear weapons invulnerable. In the technical sense, stability implies comprehensively configuring the command, control, communication, and intelligence systems that guarantee a retaliatory second-strike capability, which the adversary must perceive as credible.[79] However, in any case for optimal deterrence crisis stability must be assured. By implication wars and dangerous military practices must be eschewed and command configurations made robust to meet high security requirements, provide communication redundancy, and obviate hair-trigger deployments that entail the risk involved in delegating authority to military field commanders. In the context of nuclear stability, each and every question must be answered in full with no room for an incorrect answer. Requirements of stability and the elaborate arrangements as applied during Cold War day stand valid today as Quinlan has written, 'Requirements do not, however, decrease proportionally with size; it is not to be supposed that a small nuclear force does not need sophisticated control–indeed, small size may entail potential vulnerability that heightens demands'.[80] In other words, there is a Zero tolerance for mistakes in nuclear management and the fact that command systems are still evolving in South Asia poses great risk.

For stable nuclear deterrence, three criteria must hold. The first pertains to the credibility of nuclear weapons system and the resolve of a country to use them, and the perception the adversary holds about these issues. Second, neither side must believe it can destroy its opponent's nuclear capability in a preventive or pre-emptive attack. The third criterion is fulfilled when nuclear forces meet the above two stability conditions under all circumstances. In general, South Asia currently meets the first criteria of stable deterrence, as both sides sufficiently understand the capabilities of the other. The second condition is linked with the decision-making system in each country and the perception that adversaries have of that system. For the present, the second criteria remains shaky and uncertain in South Asia. An outside analyst might conclude that in practical terms neither Pakistan nor India could successfully execute a pre-emptive attack. But the lack of trust on both sides in the process through which decisions are made in the other State means that this criterion of stability remains unrealised.[81] The third condition is also problematic under the conditions of South Asia. Till date in managing their nuclear arsenals, both India and Pakistan have demonstrated nuclear discipline during peacetime, as well as during the crises of recent years. The balance of power relationship is a dynamic one that needs continuous adjustment in the relationship to ensure equilibrium.

Prospect and Paths to Peace

At large, proliferation dynamics in South Asia are driven by a need to establish some measure of relative parity against their principal adversaries–India against China and Pakistan against India. Such competing security agendas ensure that nuclear modernisation, through production of fissile material and development of more effective delivery systems will continue for the time being. In a war-striven region, like that of South Asia, a desire for peace must demonstrate a change in priorities, reflected through increasing intercourse among institutions public interest groups and people of neighbouring countries through cultural exchange, communication and economic linkages.[82] Prior to the test, the BJP-led NDA government in India carried forward the generosity of the 'Gujral Doctrine' but in post-Pokharan concerns were raised at the government's genuine approach to her neighbourhood policy in South Asia. Yashwant Sinha, External Affairs Minister of the NDA government clarified India's moves by stating, 'In a world where weapons of mass destruction are still to be eliminated, nuclear weapons sadly remain the ultimate guarantor of a nation's security .... After the tests of 1998, the first thing India did was to declare a 'No First Use' (NFU) policy and a unilateral ban on testing. India has repeatedly reiterated its commitment to a complete and universal elimination of nuclear weapons. Despite attempts to politically isolate and economically weaken India, its response was to engage the leading nations of the world in patient dialogue. Cognisance must be taken of the fact that India is a mature nuclear power which takes the responsibility of possessing this awesome capability very seriously.[83] In post-1998, the spirit and euphoria of Lahore process disappeared soon and doctrinal and conceptual clarity on nuclear strategy became fundamental to the existence of stable deterrence. Although the strategic elites in both countries have pondered over their nuclear doctrines ad nauseam, they seem to have overlooked the ways in which credible cooperation may occur in order to achieve feasible nuclear risk reduction measures and nuclear stability.

In contrast to India's nuclear doctrine and overall policy towards neighbours, Pakistan's ambiguous nuclear doctrine has plunged India into a deep dilemma on how to respond to the proxy war that it believes Pakistan has unleashed upon it. Pakistan has apparently kept its nuclear doctrine ambiguous to continue to perplex Indian strategists. It has dismissed the credibility of India's declared NFU doctrine and but has not elucidated the conditions under which it would be prompted to use its nuclear weapons. Apart from outlining some painfully general conditions of potential nuclear use, Pakistan has deliberately kept its 'threshold levels' or the 'red lines' unclear, contending that this is its only possible option to prevent an Indian attack.[84] This ambiguity in the India-Pakistan conflict-dyad has led to deterrence instability in the region, rather than deterrence stability. In a conflict-dyad, theoretically speaking, when both parties clarify their nuclear postures, be relative stability. However, when both maintain doctrinal ambiguity there is likely to be increased stability; paradoxically, under such conditions deterrence has the maximum advantage.[85] On the other hand, when one party maintains doctrinal clarity and the other maintains doctrinal ambiguity there is likely to be instability rather than stability. This happens because the party that chooses to keep its doctrine ambiguous is also assumed to keep its various options open-flexible responses' including the tactical use of nuclear weapons. This generates a dilemma for its opponents, which is denied the option of similar flexible responses due to its pre-declared postures and resultant concerns about public opinion. In the circumstances, 'Cold Start' is the undeclared policy of Indian military which is assumed to be a response to this dilemma. Indian strategists believe that India were to use its 'Cold Start' doctrine, it would have a flexible response option that may counter the open-ended Pakistani nuclear strategy. South Asian countries often had different security paradigms and the fact that national security often becomes part of electoral dynamics further complicates the issue. Security policy is moulded by the interests of the ruling elite, thereby making an emergence of a collective security system rather difficult. The different strategies have adversely affected bilateral relations among the other countries of the South Asian region.

Consequently, the region now faces four political and strategic challenges. Two political challenges must be met to assure stability within the context of enduring India-Pakistan rivalry. The first challenge is how to break the current gridlock in bilateral relations. The second challenge is how to maintain a credible minimum deterrence force without engaging in an economically debilitating arms race. This challenge is greater for Pakistan than for India, but failure to address it will have negative implications for both countries. In their march into 21st century, India and Pakistan have essentially two paths from which to choose. The first is a confrontational path-based on cognitive biases. This path will involve an unconstrained arms race, dangerous military practices, and possibly the open deployment of nuclear forces in a "hair-trigger" alert status, resulting in increased security requirements. The second path is that of mutual accommodation and development of a cooperative security framework. This second path would imply a major political attitudinal change in both countries toward resolving outstanding political disputes, eschewing an arms race by building restraint regimes, and creating an environment that improves the socio-economic welfare of their citizens.

In line the first strategic challenge is how to create a security balance in the asymmetrical environment of South Asia. The second security challenge is how to configure the nuclear command system to assure safety (preventing accidents), security (maintaining authorised physical custody, preventing unauthorised tampering, access, and use) and survivability (mobility, dispersal and hardening silos and command centres) under the harsh conditions of South Asia.[86] In regard to the strategic challenges, unlike the Cold War, in terms of hardware, the technical stability of South Asian nuclear forces is currently lower than their Cold War counterparts. But peace-time experience will allow the command system to gradually mature. Safe management for nuclear weapons will also improve over time. However, the conditions of instability in South Asia have to do more with the software–the attitudes and policy choices than with hardware. In fact, India is the determining power as its "minimum deterrent" limits are measured against "unspecified enemies", implying both China and Pakistan. But Pakistan is much more affected by Indian decisions than China, as the potential threat to Pakistan is real. The challenge is for Pakistan to make prudent choices by assuring balance, but not parity. Given current dynamics, Pakistani choices, not Indian restraint, will be the crucial factor in determining whether the region avoids the trap of an arms race. In the situation, Pakistan must maintain its nuclear and conventional capabilities at a level that will make an adventure costly for India. Both India and Pakistan are expected to rely more on personnel and less on technology in their nuclear management systems. This emphasis will make the system prone to environmental and psychological challenges and human errors.[87] In both societies, religious extremism is on the rise, and propaganda and campaigning is on the rampage. Therefore, reliance on human beings, who are affected by emotions and patriotism, will increase the requirements of personnel reliability programmes. A middle course balancing reliance on personnel and technology will be more feasible because weapons are limited in numbers and are located within Indian and Pakistani territory.

In South Asia there is the existence of doctrinal ambiguities, security dilemma and deep mistrust of each other–combined with the lack of a clear civilian control of nuclear weapons in Pakistan means nothing short of a recipe for disaster for the people of both countries. Under normal circumstances, history suggests that achieving stability between nuclear antagonists requires years of confidence-building and willingness on both sides to make the concessions necessary for relations to mature into detente. In the region South Asia, political attitudes toward conflict resolution, domestic and regional compulsions, and conditions generating nuclear tensions continue to foster instability. Earlier, the demise of the Cold War made the strategic balance between the world's two nuclear superpowers irrelevant. But similar concerns about stability then became applicable to other regions, especially South Asia. In the region the challenges will be far greater because the environment and conditions are not the same. On the one hand, there are the geo-physical and strategic asymmetries between India and Pakistan that present challenges different from those faced during the Cold War. On the other hand, in both countries several aspects of the environment are identical and inimical to nuclear stability, including harsh climatic conditions, poor communications infrastructure, frequent power breakdowns, and a disturbed domestic climate with communal/ethnic violence. Thus, to maintain stability a cooperative security framework by negotiation is needed in present context.

Though there have been significant confidence-building measures between India and Pakistan, including an agreement on reducing nuclear risk as well as re-establishment of transport links, they have not yet brought about any significant progress on basic-security disputes, such as Kashmir and terrorist violence. Similarly, Sino-Indian negotiations on resolving the border question, while reiterating the need for a long-term solution, have not made any headway. In general, concerns of negative shifts in the future balance of power persuade the protagonists to adopt a more cautious policy. Thus, the driving forces for nuclear modernisation remain in place. At the same time, the threat of horizontal proliferation has not abated due to various interest groups in the region. In the prevailing situation, any cooperation agreements or treaties that are signed without the bedrock foundation of mutual understanding will certainly not prove viable. This proposition has already proven true in South Asia where numerous attempts at establishing communications and "hot lines" between India and Pakistan have fallen into disuse when the crises came. A key to the region's future lies in creating a foundation and framework for peace and security, which could function as a support base, especially during crises. Immediately after the 1998 nuclear tests, India and Pakistan conceded that since overt nuclearisation had occurred, the use of force and war were no longer feasible instruments of national policy. There remains an urgent need for a durable peace and security framework.

At this juncture, the region South Asia can take lessons from the experiences of Europe and the Middle East. In Europe earlier the Conventional Forces in Europe (CFE) agreement was reached and in the Middle East the Arms Control and Regional Security (ACRS) structure was followed. With these experiences along with its own recent experience the region should produce the contours of a structure for a future regional peace process. The first lesson derived from the above is that a peace process will collapse if progress toward the resolution of the underlying conflict is stalled. And second, a healthy conflict resolution process would lay the basis for military restraint and confidence- building measures, which in turn reduces the role played by military forces. Third, a process of conflict resolution between two countries is better than one involving multiple actors. Lastly, the facilitation provides room for less friction and dilutes biases and agendas. The United States in particular and the international community in general have major stakes in preventing a nuclear conflagration in South Asia. Outside actors can play a major role in assuring stability in the region. The United States is now in a unique position to have leverage on both countries. The US can seek asurance independently from each country that it will desist from dangerous military practices that could trigger a crisis and ensure that command systems are effectively working in peace-time under recessed and non-mated conditions.

Crisis Management can also be a useful strategy to avoid conflict in the absence of a dialogue and process to resolve issues. Indo-Pakistani crises must be avoided or, if this is not possible, contained. Aside from taking diplomatic measures, the United States can help provide crisis stability by strengthening technical stability measures in both countries. The US can help leadership in both countries by throwing light on the "blind spots" that currently exist. It might consider establishing a cooperative arrangement with India and Pakistan and assist them by providing timely information that could alleviate their concerns, especially in crisis situation. The US is also capable to involve Russia and China so as to placate any concerns of India and Pakistan regarding objectivity. However, the possibility of US intervention might be a dangerous paradigm emerge in the region-reliance on US intervention to ensure stability. Worse, there is a potential danger that US policy-makers may begin to believe that South Asian crises can always be managed with US diplomatic assistance, and therefore, they may leave the two protagonists in their current status quo, to sort it out between themselves, until the next crisis. Therefore, in the long run, India and Pakistan must themselves accord a high priority to achieving a bilateral agreement on aerospace developments for surveillance and satellite monitoring. Such a confidence-building measure will be critical to the nuclear future of both India and Pakistan.

The nuclear stability-instability paradox is alive and well in the sub-continent. Nuclear stabilisation will likely rest on a unique mixture of transparency and survivability for nuclear capabilities, as well as creative monitoring arrangements that provide reassurance without increased vulnerability. It would be a mistake to assume that the current environment will be the environment of the future. Like the first nuclear age, the Cold War, there are likely to be ebbs and flows in competition, with different problems and shocks developing over time, interspaced with periods of relative calm. India has mainly responded to Pakistan's nuclear build-up not with one of its own, but with strategy innovation, improved intelligence, missile, and a nuclear triad. The appearance of strategic innovation in South Asia is important, therefore, in a way that goes beyond the particulars of any one innovation. 'Cold Start' policy of India provides fascinating insight into the dynamic interactions that shows how both countries have shifted from conventional war-fighting to escalation strategies. This is not a matter of a conscious choice by either country, rather it is an emergent property of the interacting nuclear systems in South Asia. While escalation strategies have always existed in South Asia, they are now front and centre. This marks a fundamental change from the conventional attrition strategies of previous wars. Thus, in the current situation, enhancing Indian and Pakistani capabilities to ensure stability and peace and providing incentives to reduce the risk of a nuclear war is a goal that necessitates reconsideration of previous accepted principles and practices. The fact that there is still much to be uncovered adds to our curiosity.

References

1. Gurnam Chand, 'Growing Chinese Influence in South Asia and India's Security Concern', *South Asia Politics*, Vol. 10, No.1, May 2011 (New Delhi: 2011), p. 41.
2. Tariq Rauf, 'Learning to Live with the Bomb in South Asia: Accommodation not Confrontation', *Center for Non-proliferation Studies*, 30th December, 1998.
3. J.N. Dixit, 'Better Than Before', *The Hindustan Times*, 6th August 1998.
4. *Ibid.*, 1st March 1999.
5. *Ibid.*

6. Dr. Aftab Alam, 'Nuclearisation in South Asia: Incentives and Motivations', *Third Concept*, Vol. II, No.127, September 1997 (New Delhi: 1997), pp. 10-11.
7. *Ibid.*
8. *The Times of India* (New Delhi), 29th April 1979.
9. *Ibid;* 30th April 1979.
10. Thomas P. Thornton, 'Between the Stools: US Policy Towards Pakistan during Carter Administration', *Asian Survey*, Vol. 22, No.10, October 1982 (New Delhi: 1982), p. 969.
11. Girilal Jain, 'US Arms for Pakistan', *The Times of India*, 6th January 1980.
12. *Ibid.*, 9th February 1980.
13. *Ibid.*, 23rd June 1998.
14. Brahma Chellaney, 'India's Trial By Atom', *The Hindustan Times*, 4th November 1998.
15. *Ibid.*
16. Amulya Ganguli, 'India's Nuclear Insecurity', *Ibid.*, 9th June 1999.
17. *The Times of India* (editorial), 18th May 1998.
18. *Ibid.*, 12th June 1998.
19. *Ibid.*
20. *The Hindustan Times*, 6th August 1998.
21. J.N. Dixit, 'Signs of Progress', Ibid., 28th October 1998.
22. Paul Leventhal and Brahma Chellaney, 'Nuclear Terrorism: Threat, Perception and Response in South Asia', *Institute for Defence Studies and Analyses*, 10th October 1988 (New Delhi: 1988), pp. 1-2.
23. James R. Holmes, 'When Interests Collide', *The Bulletin of Atomic Scientists*, Vol. 63, No. 3, May-June 2007, pp. 21-23.
24. Rajesh Basrur, 'India's Evolving Nuclear Deterrence: The December 13 Crisis', as quoted in Feroz Hassan Khan, 'Challenges to Nuclear Stability in South Asia', *The Non-proliferation Review*, Spring 2003, p. 62.
25. K. Subrahmanyam, 'Indian Nuclear Policy - 1964-98: A Personal Recollection', in Jasjit Singh (ed.), *Nuclear India* (New Delhi: Knowledge World, 1998), p. 28.
26. Sandeep Dixit, 'Rajiv Gandhi Plan: A Valuable Solution', *The Hindu*, 9th August 2010.
27. Stephen Philip Cohen, 'Indo-Pak Track II Diplomacy: Building Peace or Wasting Time?', in P.R. Kumaraswamy (ed.), *Security Beyond Survival* (New Delhi: Sage Publications, 2004), p. 198.
28. William C. Potter and Jayantha Dhanapala, 'The Perils of Non-Proliferation Amnesia', *The Hindu*, 1st September 2007.

29. Jayantha Dhanapala, 'Defusing the Nuclear Powder Keg', Ibid., 4th April 2012.
30. Leonard S. Spector, *Going Nuclear* (Cambridge: Ballinger Publishing Company, 1987), pp. 121-22.
31. Paul Leventhal, *Testimony to House Foreign Affairs Committee,* 22nd October 1987, as quoted in Paul Leventhal and Brahma Chellaney, 'Nuclear Terrorism–Threat, Perception and Response in South Asia', pp. 9-10.
32. S.S. Bindra, 'Chinese Strategy in South Asia', *The Indian Journal of Political Science,* Vol. LXX, No. 4, October-December 2009 (Meerut: 2009), p. 1171.
33. *Ibid.*
34. Feroz Hassan Khan, 'Challenges to Nuclear Stability in South Asia', p. 63.
35. *The Hindu,* 23rd April 2012.
36. Stephen Philip Cohen, 'Indo-Pak Track-II Diplomacy: Building Peace or Wasting Time?', pp. 198-99.
37. *Ibid.,* p. 199.
38. 'Promoting Strategic and Missile Stability in Southern Asia', *IPCS Special Report* 17, April 2006 (New Delhi: 2006), p. 12.
39. Gurmeet Kanwal, 'China's War Concepts', *Air Power Journal,* Vol. 3, No. 3, July-September 2006, pp. 68-69.
40. Ming Zhang, *China's Changing Nuclear Posture: Reactions to the South Asian Nuclear Tests* (Washington: Carnegie Endowment for International Peace, 1999), p. 45.
41. Savita Datt, 'Threat of Nuclear Weapons: *The Hindustan Times,* 17th August 1999.
42. Moore M., 'World Court Says Mostly no to Nuclear Weapons', *Bulletin of the Atomic Scientists,* 1996, pp. 39-42.
43. Grief N., 'The World Court Project on Nuclear Weapons and International Law (Massachusetts: Aletheia Press, 1992), as quoted in Nicholas Wilson, 'Regional Nuclear War in South Asia: Effects on Surrounding Countries', *Medicine and Global Survival,* Vol. 6, No. 1, August 1999, pp. 26-27.
44. *Ibid.*
45. S. Shukla, 'Pakistan's Help to Sri Lanka for Nuclear Plant Alarms India', 12th December 2012, also available on http://indiatoday.intoday.in.
46. Ghani, E., 'The Poor Half Billion—What is Holding Back Lagging Regions in South Asia', also available on http://blogs.worldbank.org.
47. In March 2003, the Bush Administration sanctioned the Khan Research Laboratories in Pakistan for missile technology dealings with North Korea, See Martin de Lavernee, 'The Non-Traditional Nuclear Threat in South Asia: Managing the Focus'.

48. *The New York Times,* 17th October 2006.
49. *The Hindustan Times,* 11th October 2006.
50. *BBC, Monitoring Asia Pacific,* 27th October 2006.
51. Seymour Hersh, 'The Deal', *The New Yorker,* 8th March 2004.
52. *Reuters,* 8th May 2007.
53. David Armstrong, 'Khan Man?', *The New Republic,* 9th November 2004.
54. 'Pakistan Threatened to Give Nukes to Iran, ex-officials Say', *USA Today,* 27th February 2004.
55. John Lancaster and Kamran Khan, 'Musharraf Named in Nuclear Probe', *Washington Post,* 3rd February 2004.
56. Salman Masood and David Rohde, 'Musharraf's Disclosures a Factor in North Korea Talks', *International Herald Tribune,* 26th August 2005.
57. Translation of Russian Government White Paper on Proliferation Policy, *Centre for Non-Proliferation Studies,* August 2006.
58. Paul Anderson, 'Is Pakistan's Nuclear Programme Dying?', *BBC News,* 3rd March 2004.
59. Kenley Butler, Sammy Salama and Leonard S. Spector, 'Where is the Justice Bulletin of Atomic Scientists', November-December 2006, p. 29.
60. Elaine Shannon, 'A New Nuke Black Market for Iran', *The Times,* 9th May 2007.
61. Amir Mir, 'Where Terror and the Bomb Could Meet', *Asia Times,* 7th July 2005.
62. Richard Beeston, 'Six Arab States Join Rush to Go Nuclear', *The Times,* 4th November 2006.
63. 'Saudi Arabia Working on a Secret Nuclear Programme with Pakistan Help-Report', *Forbes Magazine,* 8th March 2006.
64. Arnaud de Borchgrave, 'Islamabad Trades Weapons Technology For Oil', *The Washington Times,* 22nd October 2003.
65. *Ibid.*
66. Stephen Blank, 'Saudi Arabia's Nuclear Gambit', *Asia Times,* 7th November 2003.
67. 'Non-proliferation Move' (editorial), *The Nation* (Islamabad), 2nd May 2007.
68. *Open Source Center,* 16th February 2007.
69. *The Indian Express,* 22nd February 2007.
70. *The Hindu,* 28th January 2007.
71. Scott Woods, 'Analysis of the US-India Nuclear Deal', *Defence and Security Analysis,* Vol. 22 No. 3, September 2006, pp. 325-28.

72. Gary Milhollin, 'The US-India Nuclear Pact: Bad for Security', *Current History,* November 2006, p. 371.
73. R.M. Basrur, *South Asia's Cold War: Nuclear Weapons and Conflict in Comparative Perspective* (New York: Routledge, 2008).
74. Savita Datt, 'Threat of Nuclear Weapons'.
75. S.S. Bindra, 'Chinese Strategy in South Asia', p. 1175.
76. G. Balachandran, 'Indo-US Relations: Perception and Reality', *Strategic Analysis,* Vol. XXIX, No. 2, April-June 2005.
77. P.R. Kumaraswamy, 'National Security: A Critique', in P.R. Kumaraswamy (ed.), *Security Beyond Survival,* pp. 29-30.
78. *Ibid.*
79. Jessica Stern and Gregory Koblentz, 'Preventing Unauthorised Access to and Use of Nuclear Materials and Weapons: Lessons from the United States and Former Soviet Union', *Stanford University Conference on Preventing Nuclear War in South Asia,* 4th August 2001 (Bangkok: 2001).
80. Michael Quinlan, 'How Robust is India-Pakistan Deterrence?' *Survival* (Winter: 2000-01), p. 148.
81. Feroz Hassan Khan, 'Challenges to Nuclear Stability in South Asia', p. 63.
82. Pratip Chattopadhyay, 'India's South Asian Neighbourhood', *The Indian Journal of Political Science,* Vol. LXXI, No. 4 October-December 2010 (Meerut: 2010), p. 1262.
83. Inaugural Address by Yashwant Sinha, Minister for External Affairs, at the Seminar on South Asian Cooperation, organised by the *South Asian Centre for Policy Studies,* Dhaka, 10th January 2003 (Dhaka, 2003), as quoted in *Ibid.*, pp. 1253-54.
84. Happymon Jacob, 'A Precarious Indo-Pak Nuclear Balance'.
85. *Ibid.*
86. Feroz Hassan Khan, 'Challenges to Nuclear Stability in South Asia', p. 68.
87. *Ibid.*, p. 69.

❑

SELECT BIBLIOGRAPHY

Documents

Annual Report, Department of Atomic Energy, Bombay 1987-88.

Annual Report to Congress: Military Power of the People's Republic of China, Office of the Secretary of Defence, 2007.

Blackett, P.M.S., *Scientific Problem of Defence in Relation to the Indian Armed Forces: A Report to the Honourable Defence Minister*, Government of India, New Delhi, 1948.

Constituent Assembly Debates 1947-1949.

David Albright and Tom Zamora, '*India's and Pakistan's Nuclear Weapons*', Bulletin of the Atomic Scientists, June 1989.

Government of India, Ministry of Information and Broadcasting, Jawaharlal Nehru's Speeches 1953-57 (Delhi, Publication Division, 1958).

International Atomic Energy Agency, Nuclear Power Status Around the Word Bulletin, 1998.

Indian Nuclear Doctrine, National Security Advisory Board, August 1999 (New Delhi, 1999).

India-Russia Agreement Regarding Establishing Power Reactor at Kudankulam, Tamil Nadu, 1988.

India-France Civil Nuclear Agreement, 30th September 2008.

India-Mongolia Civil Nuclear Agreement, 15th June 2009.

India-Namibia Agreement on Civil Nuclear Energy, 2009.

India-Argentina Agreement on Civil Nuclear Cooperation, 14th October 2009.

India-Canada Civil Nuclear Cooperation Agreement, 28th June 2010 (Toronto, 2010).

India-Kazakhstan, Inter-governmental Agreement for Cooperation in Peaceful Uses of Atomic Energy, 16th April 2011.

Kenneth L. Adelman, '*Third Review Conference held for Non-Proliferation Treaty*,' US, Department of State Bulletin (1985).

Pakistan-China Agreement on Nuclear Cooperation, 1986.

Pakistani President Pervez Musharraf's Address at the Woodrow Wilson International Centre for Scholars, 12th February 2002, (Washington: 2002).

Pakistani Foreign Minister Abdul Sattar's Address to the Carnegic International Non-Proliferation Conference, 15th June 2001, (Washington, 2001).

Parliamentary Records, Rajya Sabha, Statement by Minister of State for Science and Technology, 12th May 1988 (New Delhi, 1988).

Paul Leventhal, *Testimony to House Foreign Affairs Committee*, 22nd October 1987.

Report of the Comptroller and Auditor General of India, Union Government, Scientific Departments, No. 6 and 7 of 1988.

Report of the Ministry of External Affairs, 1956-1959 (Government of India Publication, New Delhi).

Resolution, Ministry of External Affairs (New Delhi, 1970).

Suhrawardy, H.S., *Statement on Foreign Relations and Defence* (Government of Pakistan, Karachi, 1957).

Text of Announcement of Indo-US Civil Nuclear Cooperation, July 2005.

Text of Indo-US Civil Nuclear Agreement, October 2008.

Text of India's Nuclear Doctrine, 2003.

United States Department of State, Patterns of Global Terrorism: 1987, Department of State Publication, August 1988.

US Government, Department of State, 'Security Decision-making in Pakistan', Report Prepared for the Office of External Research, Department of State, September 1980.

World Armament and Disarmaments SIPRI, Year Book (Oxford 1974-2000).

Books

Ahmed, Akbar S., *Pakistan Society: Islam Ethnicity and Leadership in South Asia* (Oxford University Press, New Delhi, 1988).

Adi H. Doctor, *Essays on India's Foreign Policy* (National Publishing House, New Delhi, 1977).

Allen, Douglas (ed.) *Religion and Political Conflict in South Asia* (Oxford University Press, New Delhi, 1993).

Appadorai, A. (ed.), *Selected Documents on India's Foreign Policy and Relations 1947-1972* (Oxford University Press, New York, 1982).

Ashley J. Tellis, *Stability in South Asia* (Santa Monica, CA: RAND, 1997).

Ashton Carter, John D. Steinbruner and Charles A. Zraket (eds), *Managing Nuclear Operations* (The Brookings Institution, Washington, 1987).

Ayub Khan, Mohammed, *Friends Not Masters: A Political Biography* (Oxford University Press, London, 1967).

Azar, Edward E., and Chung In Moon (eds.), *National Security in the Third World: The Management of Internal and External Threats* (Edward Elgar Publishing, Aldershot, 1988).

Baldwin, David A., *Foreign Aid and American Foreign Policy* (Praeger, New York, 1966).

Barry R. Posen, *Inadvertent Escalation: Conventional War and Nuclear Risks* (Cornell University Press New York, 1991).

Basrur, R.M., *South Asia's Cold War: Nuclear Weapons and Conflict in Perspective* (Routledge, New York, 2008).

Bhambhari C.P., *Foreign Policy of India* (Sterling, New Delhi, 1987).

Bhansali, S.R. (ed.), *Peace and Disarmament* (Faculty of Law, University of Jodhpur, Jodhpur, 1987).

Bhutto, Zulfikar Ali, *If I am Assassinated* (Vikas Publishing House, New Delhi, 1979).

Bose, Sugata and Jalal, Ayesha, *Modern South Asia-History, Culture Political Economy* (Oxford University Press, New Delhi, 2004).

Bruce Blair, *The Logic of Accidental Nuclear War* (The Brookings Institution, Washington, 1993).

Carranza, M.E., *South Asian Security and International Nuclear Order: Creating a Robust Indo-Pakistani Nuclear Arms Control Regime* (Ashgate, 2009).

Chakravarty, P.C., *India's China Policy,* (Indian University Press, Bloomington, 1962).

Chari, P.R., Cheema, P.I., and Cohen, S.P., *Perception, Politics and Security in South Asia: The Compound Crisis of 1990* (Routledge Curzon, London, 1990).

Chellaney, Brahma, *Nuclear Proliferation: The US-India Conflict* (Orient Longman, New Delhi, 1993).

Cirincione, J., *Bomb Scare: The History and Future of Nuclear Weapons* (Columbia University Press, New York, 2007).

Cohen, S.P., *India: Emerging Power* (Brookings Institution Press, Washington, 2001).

________, *Moving Forward in South Asia,* Policy Brief No. 81 (The Brookings Institution, Washington, 2001).

Cohen, S.P. and Dasgupta, S., *Arming Without Aiming: India's Military Modernisation* (Brookings Institution Press, Washington, 2010).

Cork, *Radioactivity and Nuclear Physics,* 3rd edition (Nostrand, D. Van, 1957).

Cressey, George B., *Asia's Lands and Peoples* (McGraw-Hill, New York, 1951).

Curtiss, *Introduction to Neutron Physics* (Nostrand, D. Van, 1959).

Davis, Kingsely, *The Population of India and Pakistan* (Princeton University Press, Princeton, 1951).

Dixit, J.N., *India-Pakistan in War and Peace* (Routledge, London, 2002).

Doorn, Jacques Van, *Armed Forces and Security* (Mouton, The Hague, 1968).

Emeka Ohajunwa, *India-US Security Relations 1947-1990* (Chanakya Publications, Delhi, 1992).

Esposito, John L. (ed.), *Islam in Asia: Religion Politics and Society* (Oxford University Press, Oxford, 1987).

Falik, Richard A., *Global Approach to National Policy* (Harvard University Press, Cambridge, 1975).

Gandhi, Rajiv, *Statements on Foreign Policy: November 1984 - April 1985* (Ministry of External Affairs, New Delhi, 1985).

George Perkorich, *India's Nuclear Bomb: The Impact on Global Proliferation* (University of California Press, Berkeley, 1999).

Gupta, R.C., *US Policy Towards India and Pakistan* (B.R. Publications, Delhi, 1977).

Haq, Iqramul, *Pakistan: From Hash to Heroin* (Anoor Publisher, Lahore, 1991).

Holsti, K.J., *International Politics: A Framework for Analysis* (Printice-Hall, Englewood, 1967).

Israni, Kimat and Haku Israni, *India: A Superpower* (Lancer International, New Delhi, 1989).

Jackson, Robert, *South Asian Crisis: India, Pakistan, Bangladesh* (Chatto and Windus, London, 1975).

Jalal, Ayesha, *Democracy and Authoritarianism in South Asia: A Comparative and Political Perspective* (Cambridge University Press, Cambridge, 1995).

Kapur, Ashok, *India's Nuclear Options: Atomic Diplomacy and Decision Making* (Praeger, New York, 1976).

Kapur, Harish, *India's Foreign Policy 1947-1992-Shadow and Substance* (Sage Publications, New Delhi, 1994).

Karnad, B., *India's Nuclear Policy* (Praeger Security International, London, 2008).

Kavic, Lorne, J., *India's Quest for Security: Defence Policies 1947-1965* (University of California Press, Berkeley, 1967).

Kodikara, Shelton U. (ed.), *External Compulsions of South Asian Politics* (Sage Publications, New Delhi, 1993).

Kukreja, Veena, *Contemporary Pakistan-Political Process, Conflict and Crises* (Sage Publications, New Delhi, 2003).

__________, *Military Intervention in Politics: A Case Study of Pakistan* (NBO, New Delhi, 1985).

Kumaraswamy, P.R., *Security Beyond Survival* (Sage Publications, New Delhi, 2004).

Kumar, Satish, *The New Pakistan* (Vikas Publishing House, New Delhi, 1978).

Laura Fermi, *All About Atomic Energy* (W.H. Allen, London, 1962).

Laxmi, Y., *Trends in India's Defence Expenditure* (ABC, New Delhi, 1988).

Madan, Gopal, *India as a World Power: Aspects of Foreign Policy* (Sagar Publications, New Delhi, 1974).

Mallik, Dev Narayan, *Post-War International Politics : A Quadripartite Survey* (Veena Mandir Publishers, Muzaffarpur, 1973).

Meyer, S.M., *Dynamics of Nuclear Proliferation* (University of Chicago Press, Chicago, 1984).

Michael Krepon and Chris Gagne eds., *The Stability-Instability Paradox: Nuclear Weapons and Brinkmanship in South Asia* (Washington, 2001).

Ming Zhag, *China's Changing Nuclear Posture: Reactions to the South Asian Nuclear Tests* (Carnegie Endowment for International Peace, 1999).

Mishra, Pramod K., *South Asia in International Politics* (Udh Publishers, Delhi, 1984).

Morten H. Halperin, *Limited War in the Nuclear Age* (John Wiley and Sons, New York, 1963).

Moore, R.J., *Tradition and Politics in South Asia* (Vikas Publishing House, New Delhi, 1979).

Nagar, K.S., Gautam Sharma (eds.), *India's Security and Super Power Threat* (Reliance Publishing House, New Delhi, 1990).

Naik, J.A., *Pak Bomb and Rajiv's India* (National Publishing House, New Delhi, 1986).

Nayak, Pandav (ed.), *Pakistan: Society and Politics* (South Asia Publishers, New Delhi, 1984).

Nehru, Jawaharlal, *Glimpses of World History* (L. Drummond, New York, 1949).

Ohlson, T., and M. Brozska, *Arms Transfer to the Third World, 1971-1985* (Oxford University Press, Oxford, 1986).

Palmer, Norman D., *South Asia and United States Policy* (Houghton Mifflin, Boston, 1966).

Pannikar, K.M., *The Problems of Indian Defence* (Asia Publishing House, 1960).

Paul, T.V., *The Tradition of Non-Use of Nuclear Weapons* (Stanford University Press, Stanford, 2009).

Perkovich, G., *India's Nuclear Bomb: The Impact on Global Proliferation* (University of California Press, Berkeley, 2002).

Pye, Lucian W., *Asian Power and Politics: The Cultural Dimensions of Authority* (Harward University, Cambridge, 1985).

Quinlan, M., *Thinking About Nuclear Weapons: Principles, Problems, Prospects* (Oxford University Press, Oxford, 2009).

Raj. Chengappa, *Weapons for Peace: The Secret Story of India's Quest to be a Nuclear Power* (Harper Collins Publisher, New Delhi, 2000).

Rasgotra M. Chopra, V.D. and Mishra K.P. (eds.), *India's Foreign Policy in the 1990s* (Patriot Publishers, New Delhi, 1990).

Roy, J.K., *Security in the Missile Age* (Allied Publishers, Delhi, 1967).

Rutherford, Chadwick and Ellis, *Radiation from Radioactive Substance* (Cambridge University Press, 1930).

Sagan, S.D. and Waltz, K.N., *The Spread of Nuclear Weapons: A Debate Renewed* (W.W. Norton, New York, 2003).

The Limits of Safety: Organisations, Accidents and Nuclear Weapons (Princeton University Press Princeton, 1993).

Semate and White, *Atomic Age Physics* (Rinehart, 1959).

Shankland, *Atomic and Nuclear Physics*, 2nd edition (Macmillan, 1960).

Singh, Jasjit (ed.), *Kargil 1999: Pakistan's Fourth War for Kashmir* (Knowledge World, New Delhi, 1999).

Singh, Mahavir (ed.), *International Terrorism and Religious Extremism-Challenges to Central and South Asia* (Anamica Publishers, New Delhi, 2004).

Singh, Rajkumar, *Less Tasty Indo-Nepal Political Relations 1947-1997* (Novelty and Co., Patna, 1998).

________, *India-South Asia Minus Congress Regimes* (Novelty and Co., Patna, 2000).

________, *Indo-Pak Nuclear Tension 1974-1998* (Samiksha Prakashan, New Delhi, 2001).

________, *India's Foreign Policy-The First Study in Continuity and Change* (Samiksha Prakashan, New Delhi, 2001).

________, *Past, Present and Future of Kashmir* (Gyan Publishing House, New Delhi, 2008).

________, *India and Pakistan-Social, Political and Military Perspectives* (Regal Publications, New Delhi, 2009).

________, *Global Dimensions of Indo-Nepal Political Relations-Post-Independence* (Gyan Publishing House, New Delhi, 2009).

________, *Relations of NDA and UPA with Neighbours* (Gyan Publishing House, New Delhi, 2010).

________, *Contemporary India with Controversial Neighbours* (Gyan Publishing House, New Delhi, 2011).

________, *Ethnic Politics and LTTE in Sri Lanka* (Kalpaz Publications, New Delhi, 2012).

________, *Myth and Reality of Terrorism in South Asia* (Kalpaz Publications, New Delhi, 2013).

Singh Rajkumar, *Be Update and Face to Face with Indian Republic* (Kalpaz Publications, New Delhi, 2014).

Smith, Chris, *The Diffusion of Small Arms and Light Weapons in Pakistan and Northern India* (Brossey's, London, 1993).

Spear, Percival, *India, Pakistan and the West* (Oxford University Press, London, 1958).

Subrahmanyam, K., *Security in a Changing World* (B.R. Publishing Company, Delhi, 1990).

Tahir-Kheli, Shirin, *The United States and Pakistan: The Evolution of an Influence Relationship* (Praeger Studies, New York, 1982).

Talbott, S., *Engaging India, Diplomacy, Democracy, and the Bomb* (Brookings Institution Press, Washington, 2004).

Tannenwald, N., *The Nuclear Taboo: The United States and the Non-Use of Nuclear Weapons Since 1945* (Cambridge University Press, Cambridge, 2007).

Taseer, Salman, *Bhutto: A Political Biography* (Vikas Publishing House, New Delhi, 1980).

Tellis, A.J., *India's Emerging Nuclear Posture: Between Recessed Deterrent and Ready Arsenal* (Santa Monica, CA: RAND, 2001).

Tellis, A.J., Fair C.C. and Medby, J.J., *Limited Conflicts Under the Nuclear Umbrella: Indian and Pakistani Lessons from the Kargil Crisis* (Santa Monica, C.A. RAND, 2001).

Thomas, Raju, G.C., *Indian Security Policy* (Princeton University Press, Princeton, 1986).

Tolansky, *Introduction to Atomic Physics,* 4th edition (Longman, Green, 1956).

Valentine, J.M., *Atomic Physics* (The English Universities Press, London, 1960).

Varma, S.P. and Misra, K.P. (ed.), *Foreign Policies in South Asia* (Orient Longman, New Delhi, 1969).

Verghese, Koithara, *Society State and Security–The Indian Experience* (Sage Publications, New Delhi, 1999).

Victor, Cecil, *India: The Security Dilemma* (Patriot Publishers, New Delhi, 1990).

Vital, David, *The Survival of Small States: Studies in Small Power/Great Power Conflict* (Oxford University Press, London, 1971).

Waseem, Mohammad, *Politics and State in Pakistan* (National Institute of Historical and Cultural Research, Islamabad, 1994).

Weiner, Myron, *Political Change in South Asia* (Farma K.L. Calcutta, 1968).

Zaidi, Akbar S. (ed.), *Regional Tribalance and Regional Questions in Pakistan* (Vanguard Books, Lahore, 1992).

Zinkin, Taya, *Challenges in India* (Walker, New York, 1967).

Ziring, Lawrence, ed., *The Sub-continent in World Politics* (New York, 1975).

Articles in Books, Periodicals and Newspapers

Abdul A.P.J. Kalam and Srijan Pal Singh, 'Nuclear Power is Our Gateway to a Prosperous Future' *The Hindu,* 6 November 2011.

Abraham, Mohit, 'Why Kudankulam Dissolved into Fission and Acrimony' in Ibid., 25th September 2012.

Acharya, Sukanta, 'Security Dilemmas in Asia', *International Studies,* Vol. 44, No1 (2007), pp. 57-60.

Adelman, L. Kenneth, 'Third Review Conference Held for Non-proliferation Treaty', *US, Department of State Bulletin* (1985), p. 85.

Akbar, M.J., 'A Good Deal Walks on Two Legs', *The Asian Age,* 5 August 2007.

Akhtar, Shameen, 'US Nuclear Policy and South Asia', *The Dawn,* 31st March 2006.

Albright David and Tom Zamora, 'India's and Pakistan's Nuclear Weapons', *Bulletin of the Atomic Scientists,* June 1989, p. 25.

Alam, Dr. Aftab, 'Nuclearisation in South Asia–Incentives and Motivations', *Third Concept,* Vol. II, No.127, September 1997 (New Delhi), pp.16-18.

Alam, Dr. Aftab, 'Pakistan's Nuclear Development and Capability', *Third Concept,* April-May 1998 (New Delhi), pp.16-17.

Aroor, Shiv, 'Beijing Test a Reminder, But India Not Interested', *The Indian Express,* 20th January 2007.

Aroor, Shiv and Amitav Ranjan, 'Armed Forces Wait as Showpiece Missiles are Unguided, Way off Mark', in Ibid., 12th November 2006.

Armstrong David, 'Khan Man', *The New Republic*, 9th November 2004.

Balachandran, G., 'Indo-US Relations: Perception and Reality', *Strategic Analysis*, Vol. XXIX, No.2, April-June 2005.

Baral, J.K., 'The US-India Nuclear Diplomacy', *Indian Journal of American Studies,* 1982, p. 131.

Baruah, Amit, 'India for Keeping Future Test Out of 123 Agreement', *The Hindu*, 23rd March 2007.

Bedi, Rahul, 'India's Nuclear-Powered Submarine Project Moves Ahead', *The Tribune*, 19th May 2007.

Bergh, Van den, Godfried Van Benthem, 'Nuclear Revolution into Its Second Phase in Gjelstad Jorm and Olav Njolstad (eds.), *Nuclear Rivalry and International Order* (London, 1996), pp. 86-87.

Beeston, Richard, 'Six Arab States Join Rush to Go Nuclear', *The Times*, 4th November 2006.

Bidwai, Praful, 'Nuclear Policy in a Mess-NWFZ The Realistic Way Out; *The Times of India*, 28th November 1991.

_________, 'Indo-US Defence Accord: Sanctifying Atomic Apartheid', *Frontline,* Vol. 22, July 30-August 12, 2005.

_________, 'The Day After: Fallout of a Deeply Disturbing Deal', *Khaleej Times*, 11th March 2006.

_________, 'Nuclear Waiver: Blow to Non-proliferation', *Inter Press Service,* 8th September 2008.

Bindra, S.S., 'Chinese Strategy in South Asia', *The Indian Journal of Political Science*, Vol. LXX, No. 4, October-December 2009 (Meerut, 2009), p. 1171.

Biswas, Bibhuti Bhushan, 'Domestic Pressures in Foreign Policy: The Case of US-India Dialogue During the Clinton Administration', 68th Session, Part II, *Proceedings of the Indian History Congress* (Indian History Congress, New Delhi, 2008), pp.1196-97.

Blank, Stephen, 'Saudi Arabia's Nuclear Gambit', *Asia Times,* 7th November 2003.

Bose, Tarun C., 'Whither NPT? 1995 and Beyond', *Journal of International Relations'* (1994) p. 21.

Broad, William J., 'Radioactive Releases in Japan Worrying', *The Hindu*, 14th March 2011.

Bucknam, Mark, 'Power to the People of India: US Nuclear Cooperation with India', *Strategic Insights*, Vol. VI(1), January 2007.

Chand, Gurnam, 'Growing Chinese Influence in South Asia and India's Security Concern', *South Asia Politics,* Vol. 10, No. 1, May 2011 (New Delhi), p. 41.

Chandra, Satish, 'Nuclear Deal: On the Brink of Disaster', *The Hindu,* 9th June 2007.

Chattopadhyay, Pratip, 'India's South Asian Neighbourhood', *The Indian Journal of Political Science,* Vol. LXXI, No. 4, October-December 2010 (Meerut), p. 1262.

Chellaney, Brahma, 'The Challenges of Arms Control in South Asia', *Survival*, Vol. XXXV, No. 3 (1993), p. 122.

________, 'India's Trial By Atom', *The Hindustan Times*, 4th November 1998.

________, 'Atoms for Might', in Ibid., 18th October 2000.

________, 'Fission for Trouble', in Ibid., 28th May 2007.

________, 'Revelations Unravel Hype and Spin', *The Hindu*, 5 September 2008.

________, 'Strategic and Technical Aspects of End Use Monitoring Agreement–End Use Monitoring Woes for India', in Ibid., 27th July 2009.

________, 'Factsheet on US-India Accord on End Use Monitoring Agreement', *India Abroad,* 31st July 2009.

Cheema, Iqbal Pervaiz, 'Security in South Asia: An Approach', in Shelton U. Kodikara (ed.), *External Compulsions of South Asian Politics* (Sage Publications, New Delhi, 1993), pp. 46-47.

Cheema, Iqbal Zafar, 'The Role of Nuclear Weapons in Pakistan's Defence Strategy', *Islamabad Policy Research Institute Journal* (Islamabad), Summer 2004.

Choudhury, Sanjoy, 'Nuclear Energy and Its Effects on the Environment', *South Asia Politics,* Vol. 8, No. 7, November 2009 (New Delhi), p. 26.

Cohen, Stephen Philip, 'Indo-Pak Track II Diplomacy: Building Peace or Wasting Time?' in P.R. Kumaraswamy, *Security Beyond Survival* (Sage Publications, New Delhi, 2004), pp. 199-200.

Dan, Smith, 'Uselessness and the Role of Nuclear Weapons: An Exercise in Pseudo-Problems and Disconnection', in Gjelstadjorn and Olav Njolstad (eds.) *Nuclear Rivalry and International Order* (London, 1996), pp. 86-87.

David, Albright and Tom Zamora, 'India, Pakistan's Nuclear Weapons: All the Pieces in Place', *Bulletin of the Atomic Scientists.*

Datt, Savita, 'Threat of Nuclear Weapons', *The Hindustan Times,* 17 August 1999.

Desai, M.J. 'India and Nuclear Weapons', *Disarmament and Arms Control,* Vol. 3, No. 2 (1965), p. 141.

Dhanapala, Jayantha, 'Difusing the Nuclear Power Keg', *The Hindu,* 4th April 2012.

Diwan, Vivek M., 'Perspectives on India-China Relations', *Third Concept,* Vol. 24, No. 288, February 2011 (New Delhi), p. 9.

Dixit, J.N., 'Better Than Before', *The Hindustan Times*, 6th August 1998.

________, 'Signs of Progress', in Ibid., 28th October 1998.

Dixit, Sandeep, 'Rajiv Gandhi Plan: A Valuable Solution', *The Hindu,* 9th August 2010.

Donnelly Thomas and Metissa Wisner 'A Global Partnership Between the US and India', *Asian Outlook,* August-September 2005.

Doug, Koplow, 'Nuclear Power: Still Not Viable Without Subsidies', *Union of Concerned Scientists*, February 2011, p. 2.

Dutta, Madhumita, 'Desirability of Nuclear Power is the Real Question', *The Hindu*, 27th September 2012.

Evan, Greth and Yoriko Kawaguchi, 'Nuclear Disarmament: Building the Momentum' in Ibid., 29th September 2009.

Fakung, Xui, 'Hedging Strategy Won't do Relationship Good', *China Daily*, 21st November 2005.

Gandhi, Gopalkrishna, 'The Lessons of July 16th, 1945' *The Hindu*, 16th July 2011.

Ganguli, Amulya, 'India's Nuclear Insecurity', *The Hindustan Tims,* 9th June 1999.

Garver, John W., 'The Security Dilemma in Sino-Indian Relations', *India Review*, Vol. 1, No. 4, October 2002, pp. 3-4.

Gopalakrishnan, A., 'A Nuclear Regulator Without Teeth', *The Hindu*, 16th September 2011.

Grief, N., 'The World Court Project on Nuclear Weapons and International Law, *Medicine and Global Survival*, Vol. 6th, No. 1, August 1999.

Gupta, Bhabani Sen, 'Towards Nuclear Stability', *The Hindustan Times*, 21st November 1997.

Gupta, Shishir, 'Down to Brasstacks', *India Today*, 28th May 2001.

Hali, S.M., 'Second Strike Capability', *The Nation* (Pakistan), 15th August 2006.

Haniffa, Aziz, 'The Nuclear Deal: Recognition Denied or Dangerous Model', *India Abroad* (New York), 29th July 2005.

Haq, Ihtashamul, 'Move for Indigenous N. Fuel Capability', *The Dawn*, 21st February 2007.

Hersh, Seymour, 'Watching the Warheads: The Risks to Pakistan's Nuclear Arsenal', *The New Yorker*, 5th November 2001.

_________, 'The Deal', in Ibid., 8th March 2004.

Hickman, Leo, 'Fukushima Slows Down But Does not Halt The Nuclear March', *The Hindu*, 28th December 2011.

Hoodboy, Pervez, 'Pakistan and the Deep Cut Regime', in Harold A. Feiveson (ed.), *The Nuclear Turning Point: A Blueprint for Deep Cuts and Dealcrating of Nuclear Weapons* (Brookings Institution, Washington, 1999) p. 227.

Inderfurth, Karl F., 'The US and India Expanding Engagement Agenda', *The Hindu*, 10th September 2008.

Iyer, Krishna V.R., 'A Betrayal of India's Constitutional Vision', in Ibid., 17th July 2008.

_________, 'Kerala and Alternative Energy Resources', in Ibid., 25th August 2008.

Jacob, Happymon, 'A Precarious Indo-Pak Nuclear Balance', in Ibid., 26th January 2012.

Jacob, K.S., 'Old Configuration, New Context', in Ibid., 11th April 2011.

Jain, Girilal, 'US Arms for Pakistan', *The Times of India*, 6th January 1980.

Jayaraman, T., 'Nuclear Power After Fukushima', *The Hindu,* 21st March 2011.

Jha, C.S., 'The Non-Proliferation Debate: Relevance of India's Stand', *The Times of India,* 22nd February 1978.

Johnson, Jo and Mure Dickie, 'China and India in 'Race to the Moon', *The Financial Times*, 30th May 2007.

Kakodkar, Anil, 'Reversing the Logic of the Nuclear Deal', *The Hindu,* 4th July 2011.

Kamath, M.V., 'US Tactics Pressuring India', *Organiser*, 25th November 2007 (New Delhi), p. 17.

Kamath, P.M., 'Civilian Nuclear Deal: Turning Points in Indo-US Relations', *India Quarterly,* Vol. LXII (3), July-September 2006 (New Delhi), p. 28.

Kanwal, Gurmeet, China's War Concepts', *Air Power Journal*, Vol. 3, No. 3, July-September 2006, pp. 68-69.

Kapur, S.P., 'India and Pakistan's Unstable Peace: Why Nuclear South Asia is Not Like Cold War Europe', *International Security*, 30 (2) (2005), pp. 127-52.

Khan, Firoz Hassan, 'Challenges to Nuclear Stability in South Asia', *The Non-Proliferation Review,* Spring 2003, p. 60.

Khan, Shahid-ur-Rehman, 'Pakistan Nuclear Reprocessing Plant May Yield Weapons-Grade Plutonium', *Kyodo World Service*, 7th May 2007.

Ki-moon, Ban, 'A Visit to Chernobyl', *The Hindu,* 28th April 2011.

Krepon, Michael, 'Nuclear Risk Reduction in South Asia in P.R. Kumaraswamy (ed.), *Security Beyond Survival* (Sage Publications, New Delhi, 2004), p. 231.

_________, 'Getting Ahead of the Sum of All Fears', *The Hindu*, 21st February 2013.

Kurup, V.S.P., 'America's Double Standards: Politics of Nuclear Fuel' *The Times of India,* 25th April 1978.

Ladwing III, W.C. 'A Cold Start for Hot Wars' The Indian Army's New Limited War Doctrine: *International Security*, 32 (3) (2007), pp. 158-90.

Lancaster, John and Kamran Khan, Musharraf Named in Nuclear Probe', *Washington Post*, 3rd February 2004.

Leventhal, Paul and Brahma Chellaney, 'Nuclear Terrorism: Threat, Perception and Response in South Asia', *Institute for Defence Studies and Analyses*, 10th October 1988 (New Delhi), pp. 1-2.

Leverett, Flynt and Hillary Mann Leverett, 'Why the Failure in Almaty is a Big Deal', *The Hindu,* 6th May 2013.

Mackay, David, 'The Future is Green, the Future is Nuclear', *Times Online,* 4th October 2009.

Mahalingam, Sudha, 'An Alternative to Nuclear Power', *The Hindu,* 27th April 2011.

Malik, Mohan J., 'China and the Nuclear Non-Proliferation Regime', *Contemporary Southeast Asia*, Vol. 22, No. 3, December 2000, pp. 445-78.

Malik, Mohan, 'China Responds to the US-India Nuclear Deal', *China Brief*, Vol. 6, No. 7, 29th March 2006.

Masood, Salman and David Rohde, 'Musharraf's Disclosures a Factor in North Korea Talks', *International Herald Tribune*, 26th August 2005.

McCurry, Justin, 'Japan's Thirty-Year Plan to be Nuclear Free', *The Hindu*, 15th September 2012.

Menon, N.C., 'Return of the Tilt', *The Hindustan Times,* 8th June 1998.

Milhollin, Gary, 'The US-India Nuclear Pact: Bad for Security', *Current History,* November 2006, p. 371.

Mir, Amir, 'Where Terror and the Bomb Could Meet', *Asia Times*, 7th July 2005.

Mohan, Raja C., 'Musharraf to Press China for Second Reactors', *The Indian Express,* 12th June 2006.

Moily, Veerappa M., 'The Highest Feet of Diplomacy', *The Hindu*, 28th August 2007.

Moore, M., 'World Court Says Mostly No to Nuclear Weapons', *Bulletin of Atomic Scientists*, 1996, pp. 39-42.

Mudgal, Alka, 'From Civil Nuclear Deal to Civil Nuclear Liability Bill', *Indian Journal of Political Science*, Vol. LXXI, No.3, July-September 2010 (Meerut), pp. 826-27.

Nagasaila, D. and V. Suresh, 'Kudankulam on Shaky Legal Ground', *The Hindu*, 5th November 2012.

Namboodiri, P.K.S., 'Perceptions and Policies of India and Pakistan', in K. Subrahmanyam (ed.), *India and the Nuclear Challenge* (Lancer International, New Delhi, 1985), p. 133.

Nautiyal, Annupurna, 'The Indo-US Nuclear Deal: What is There', *Strategic Insights,* Vol. VI (4), September 2004 (California), p. 2.

Nehru, Jawaharlal, 'Atomic Energy for Peace and Progress of Mankind', in Balwant A. Desai (ed.), *Atoms for Peace* (Radiant Publishers, Delhi, 1975), p. 8.

Nelson, Dean, 'Pakistan Upgrades Nuclear Arsenal', *The Sunday Times*, 30th July 2006.

Pandit, Rajat, India-made Brahmos to Hit Global Arms Market', *The Times of India*, 3rd January 2007.

Parthasarathi, Ashok, 'Judge the Nuclear Deal on Facts, Not Convictions', *The Hindu*, 15th July 2008.

Parthasarathy, G., 'India-US Nuclear Deal-The Politics of Proliferation', *Business Line*, 25th January 2007.

Paul, T.V., 'The US-India Nuclear Accord: Implications for Non-Proliferation Regime', *International Journal*, Vol. LXII (4), Fall 2007 (Canada), pp. 858-59.

Potter, William C. and Jayantha Dhanapala, 'The Perils of Non-Proliferation Amnesia', *The Hindu*, 1st September 2007.

Prakash, Arun, 'India's Deterrent Capabilities', *South Asia Politics*, Vol. 8, No. 11, March 2010 (New Delhi), pp. 3-4.

Quinlan, Michael, 'How Robust is India-Pakistan Deterrence?', *Survival*, Winter 2000-01, p.148.

Radyuhin, Vladimir, 'Twenty-five Years After Chernobyl', *The Hindu*, 26th April 2011.

Rajaraman, 'The Fizzle Doesn't Really Matter', in Ibid., 16th September 2009.

Raju, Suvrat and M.V. Ramana 'Where the Mind is Full of Fear', in Ibid., 19th September 2012.

_________, 'Why Kudankulam is Untenable', in Ibid., 12th November 2011.

Ramachandaran, Shastri, 'Test of Liberalism–Trapped Between Bomb and Bombast', *The Times of India* (Patna), 21st May 1998.

Ramachandran, R., '123-Agreement and the Internal Laws', *The Hindu*, 19th September 2007.

Ramana, M.V., and Sudvrat Raju, 'Nuclear Safety Before Vendor Interests', in Ibid., 30th October 2012.

Ramana, M.V., 'Deeper into the Morass-Ten Years After Pokharan' in Ibid., 11th May 2008.

Ramesh, Randeep and Julian Borger, 'Pakistan Launches Huge Nuclear Arms Drive', *The Guardian*, 25th July 2006.

Rani, Midatala, 'Nuclear Issue in Indo-Pakistan Relations', in *Proceedings of the Indian History Congress*, Part II, 68th Session (Delhi 2008), p. 1212.

Rathjens, George, 'Rethinking Nuclear Proliferation', *The Washington Quarterly* (1995), pp. 181-82.

Rauf, Tariq, Learning to Live With Bomb in South Asia: Accommodation not Confrontation', *Centre for Non-Proliferation Studies,* 30th December 1998.

Rodriguez, Placid, 'The Nuclear Deal: What If It Falls Through?', *The Hindu*, 28th February 2006.

Sabherwal, O.P., 'India's Nuclear Policy Under Siege', *One India One People*, August 1997 (Mumbai), pp. 16-17.

________, 'Indo-US Nuclear Deal', *The Hindustan Times*, 10th November 1998.

Salik, Ahmad Naeem, 'Pakistan and the Future of Non-Proliferation', *International Peace Research Institute Journal*, Vol. VI, No.1, Winter 2006, pp. 21-45.

Saran, Shyam, 'Weapon That has More Than Symbolic Value', *The Hindu*, 4th May 2013.

Seth, S.P., 'The Indo-Pak Nuclear Duet and the US', *Asian Survey*, Vol. XXIII, No. 7, (1988), p. 711.

Shannon, Elaine, 'A New Nuke Black Market for Iran', *Time,* 9th May 2007.

Sharma, Dhirendra, 'Do Nations Need Nuclear Weapons? *The Hindu*, 9th August 2010.

Sharma, Dinesh C., 'Pressure for Soft Nuclear Liability Law', *Mail Daily*, Vol. 2 (245), 19th July 2009, pp. 1 and 6.

Shukla, S., 'Pakistan's Help to Sri Lanka for Nuclear Plant Alarms India', 12th December 2012.

Siddharthan, Rahul, 'The Real Questions from Kudankulam', *The Hindu*, 14th September 2012.

Singh, Bhawani and Vibhuti Singh Shekhawat, 'Swords Vs. Ploughshares: Indo-US Nuclear Deal', The Return of Spring', *The Indian Journal of Political Science*, Vol. LXVII, No. 4, October-December 2006 (Meerut), p. 908.

Singh, Dr. Rajkumar, 'Nuclear Deterrence: More Real Than Myth', *Third Concept*, Vol. 19, No. 217, Mareh 2005 (New Delhi), p. 17.

Singh, Swaran, 'China Factor in India's Nuclear Policy', *Journal of Peace Studies*, Vol. 5, No. 3, May-June 1998, pp. 23-38.

_________, 'Evolution of Nuclear Posture', in G.P. Deshpande and Alka Acharya (eds.), *Fifty-year of India-China-Crossing a Bridge of Dream* (Tulika, New Delhi, 2002), p. 370.

Sisodia, N.S., 'Lessons from an Atomic Catastrophe', *The Hindu,* 6th August 2009.

Sood, Vikram, 'The Nuclear Deal: The Larger Picture', in Ibid., 5th September 2007.

Sorabjee, Soli J., 'Capping Nuclear Liability is a Non-Starter in Ibid., 14th December 2009.

Srinivasan, M.R., 'India May Lose Control of Its Nuclear Future', in Ibid., 14th December 2006.

_________, 'Nuclear Weapon Free World - a Mirage?', in Ibid., 16th June 2007.

_________, 'Climate Change and India's Options', in Ibid., 30th June 2007.

_________, 'The Last Mile in Nuclear Negotiations', in Ibid., 13th July 2007.

_________, 'Is the Nuclear Power Option Safe for India', in Ibid., 9 October 2007.

Srinivasan, T.N., T.S. Gopi, Rethinaraj and Surya Sethi, 'How Fukushima is Relevant to Kudankulam', in Ibid., 18th March 2012.

Stern, Jessica and Gregory, Koblentz, 'Preventing Unauthorised Access to and Use of Nuclear Materials and Weapons: Lessons from the United States and Former Soviet Union' *Stanford University Conference on Preventing Nuclear War in South Asia*, 4th August 2001 (Bangkok).

Subrahmanyam, K., 'Indian Nuclear Policy-1964-1998: A Personal Recollection', in Jasjit Singh (ed.), *Nuclear India* (Knowledge World, New Delhi, 1998), p. 28.

________, 'A Credible Deterrent-Logic of Nuclear Doctrine', *The Times of India*, 4th October 1999.

Subramanian, R.R., 'The Nuclear Factor in South Asian Strategy', *Strategic Analysis*, Vol. VIII, No. 9 (1984) p. 829.

Subramanian, Nirupama, 'Pakistan Presses US for Civil Nuclear Energy Pact', *The Hindu*, 26th October 2006.

________, 'Pakistan and China: Great Expectations', in Ibid, 23rd November 2006.

Sukai, Tarun Bikash, 'Environment Awareness in Society', *South Asia Politics,* Vol. 9, Nos. 3 and 4, July-August 2010 (New Delhi), p. 37.

Sullivan, Kate, 'Do Not Let Agni V's Shock and Awe Endanger Asian Stability', *The Hindu* 23rd April 2012.

Swami, Praveen, 'Pakistan's Hot Nuclear Greenhouse', in Ibid. 5th November 2012.

Thakur, Ramesh, 'Is India So Weak That It Must Fear Success', in Ibid., 4th September 2007.

Thornton, Thomas P., 'Between the Stools, US Policy Towards Pakistan during Carter Administration', *Asian Survey*, Vol. 22, No. 10, October 1982 (New Delhi), p. 969.

Tourangfam, Monish, 'An Assessment of the '123-Agreement "To be or Not to be", *South Asia Politics*, Vol. 6, No. 9, January 2008 (New Delhi), p. 32.

Tripathi, Sudhanshu, 'Indo-US Nuclear Deal: Must Seek Its Revision', in Ibid., Vol. 7, No. 6, October 2008 (New Delhi), p. 28.

Vanaik, Achin, 'The Idea That Bombed', *The Hindustan Times*, 23rd February 2000.

Vardarajan, Siddharth, 'Assessing the Nuclear Balance Sheet', *The Hindu*, 7th July 2006.

________, '123 as Countdown to CTBT by the Backdoor', in Ibid., 17th May 2007.

________, 'Taking Stock of the Indo-US Nuclear Deal', in Ibid., 17th August 2007.

________, 'Passing the India-Specific Safeguards Agreement', in Ibid., 12th July 2008.

________, 'Eleventh Hour for the Nuclear Suppliers' Group', in Ibid., 9th August 2008.

________, 'The American Dilemma at the NSG', in Ibid., 28th August 2008.

________, 'Thirty Words that Saved the Day', in Ibid., 8th September 2008.

________, 'Bush Signing Statement on 123 Leaves Flaws Intact', in Ibid., 10th October 2008.

________, 'Rush in Now, Repent Later', in Ibid., 25th April 2011.

________, 'Challenges Ahead for India's Nuclear Diplomacy', in Ibid., 1st September 2011.

Warwick, Joby, 'Pakistan Expanding Nuclear Programme', *The Washington Post*, 24th July 2006.

Weiner, Myron, 'Critical Choices for India and America', in Donald C. Hellmann (ed.), *Southern Asia: The Politics of Poverty and Peace* (Lexington Books, Massachusetts, 1976), p. 66.

Woods, Scott, 'Analysis of the US-India Nuclear Deal', *Defence and Security Analysis,* Vol. 22, No. 3, September 2006, pp. 325-28.

Newspapers

Asia Times

The Asian Age

The Dawn (Karachi)

The Financial Times (London)

The Guardian

The Hindu (Madras)

The Hindustan Times (New Delhi)

The Indian Express (Delhi)

The International Herald Tribune

The Khaleej Times

The Kyodo World Service

The Kyodo News International

The National Herald (New Delhi)

The Nation (Islamabad)

Navhind Times

The New York Times (New York)

The New Yorker

The New Republic

The Open Source Center

The Opinion (Weekly)

The Pakistan Times (Lahore)

The Patriot (New Delhi)

The Statesman (Delhi)

The Sunday Standard (New Delhi)

The Sunday Times

The Times (London)

The Times of India (New Delhi)

The Tribune (Chandigarh)

The Tribune (Chandigarh)

The USA Today

The Washington Post (Washington)

Periodicals

American Political Science Review (New York)

Asian Affairs

Asian Outlook

Asian Survey (New Delhi)

BBC Monitoring Asia Pacific

Bulletin of Atomic Scientists

China Brief (Jamestown)

Current History

Defence Security Analysis

Disarmament and Arms Control

Eastern Economists (Bombay)

Economic and Political Weekly (Bombay)

Forbes Magazine

Foreign Affairs (New York)

Foreign Policy Report (New Delhi)

Frontline (Chennai)

Indian Journal of American Studies

Indian Abroad (New York)

India Quarterly (New Delhi)

International Security

International Peace Research Institute Journal

India Today (New Delhi)

International Studies (New Delhi)

Journal of Peace Studies

The Non-Proliferation Review

Pacific Affairs (New York)

Political Science Quarterly (New York)

Strategic Analysis

Strategic Insights (California)

South Asia Politics (New Delhi)

Third Concept (New Delhi)

Washington Quarterly (Washington)

World Today (London).

❐

INDEX